The Great Siege of Malta

The Great Siege of Malta

MARCUS BULL

ALLEN LANE
an imprint of
PENGUIN BOOKS

ALLEN LANE

UK | USA | Canada | Ireland | Australia
India | New Zealand | South Africa

Penguin Books is part of the Penguin Random House group of companies whose addresses can be found at global.penguinrandomhouse.com.

Penguin Random House UK,
One Embassy Gardens, 8 Viaduct Gardens, London SW11 7BW

penguin.co.uk

First published in Great Britain by Allen Lane 2025

001

Copyright © Marcus Bull, 2025

The moral right of the author has been asserted

Penguin Random House values and supports copyright. Copyright fuels creativity, encourages diverse voices, promotes freedom of expression and supports a vibrant culture. Thank you for purchasing an authorized edition of this book and for respecting intellectual property laws by not reproducing, scanning or distributing any part of it by any means without permission. You are supporting authors and enabling Penguin Random House to continue to publish books for everyone. No part of this book may be used or reproduced in any manner for the purpose of training artificial intelligence technologies or systems. In accordance with Article 4(3) of the DSM Directive 2019/790, Penguin Random House expressly reserves this work from the text and data mining exception.

Set in 12/14.75pt Dante MT Std
Typeset by Jouve (UK), Milton Keynes
Printed and bound in Great Britain by Clays Ltd, Elcograf S.p.A.

The authorized representative in the EEA is Penguin Random House Ireland, Morrison Chambers, 32 Nassau Street, Dublin D02 YH68

A CIP catalogue record for this book is available from the British Library

ISBN: 978–0–241–52365–0

Penguin Random House is committed to a sustainable future for our business, our readers and our planet. This book is made from Forest Stewardship Council® certified paper.

Contents

List of Illustrations	vii
List of Maps	xi
Acknowledgements	xiii
Introduction: Sieges and What They Mean	1
1. Violence, Vanity and Vocation: The Knights of Malta	21
2. The Rewards of Relative Efficiency: The Ottomans	44
3. The Cruel Sea	67
4. 1551: The Precursor of the Great Siege	92
5. The Great Siege Begins	113
6. The Guns of July and August	143
7. Relief	172
8. Meanwhile . . .	192
9. And in the End	222
List of Abbreviations	243
Bibliography	245
References	265
Index	311

List of Illustrations

1. Anon., Pierre de Bourdeille, *c.* 1580 (reproduced by courtesy of the Bibliothèque Nationale de France, Paris).
2. Matteo Perez d'Aleccio, wall paintings of the Great Siege, *c.* 1578, Grand Master's Palace, Valletta (reproduced by courtesy of Daniel Cilia and Heritage Malta).
3. An extract from the *Libri Conciliorum*, records of the decisions of the Order of St John's governing body, dated 18 July 1566 (National Library of Malta, Valletta, AOM 91, fol. 169v).
4. John James Sandilands's graffito poem in the St Angelo *guva* (reproduced by courtesy of Daniel Cilia and Heritage Malta).
5. A wheeled vehicle among the graffiti in the St Angelo *guva* (reproduced by courtesy of Daniel Cilia and Heritage Malta).
6. The Siege of Rhodes (1522) in the *Süleymanname*, 1555 (Topkapı Palace Museum, Istanbul: Universal History Archive / UIG / Bridgeman Images).
7. Nakkaş Osman, Süleyman I in the *Semailname*, 1579 (Topkapı Palace Museum, Istanbul: Photo © Tom Graves Archive / Bridgeman Images).
8. Melchior Lorichs, Panorama of Istanbul, 1559 or possibly slightly later (reproduced by courtesy of Universitaire Bibliotheken, Leiden).
9. A Janissary in Nicolas de Nicolay, *Discours et histoire veritable des navigations, pérégrinations et voyages faicts en la Turquie*, 1568 and subsequent editions [pagination varies by edition] (reproduced by courtesy of the National Library of Malta, Valletta).

List of Illustrations

10 Süleyman and Barbarossa in the *Süleymanname*, 1555 (Topkapı Palace Museum, Istanbul: Sonia Halliday Photographs / Bridgeman Images).

11 Matrakçi Nasuh, The overwintering of the Ottoman fleet in Toulon, 1543–4 (Topkapı Palace Museum, Istanbul: Universal History Archive / UIG / Bridgeman Images).

12 Jooris van der Straeten (attrib.), Philip II of Spain, *c.* 1565 (© Colección BBVA and David Mecha Rodríguez).

13 Matteo Perez d'Aleccio, wall paintings of the Great Siege, *c.* 1578, Grand Master's Palace, Valletta (reproduced by courtesy of Daniel Cilia and Heritage Malta).

14 Matteo Perez d'Aleccio, wall paintings of the Great Siege, *c.* 1578, Grand Master's Palace, Valletta (reproduced by courtesy of Daniel Cilia and Heritage Malta).

15 Matteo Perez d'Aleccio, wall paintings of the Great Siege, *c.* 1578, Grand Master's Palace, Valletta (reproduced by courtesy of Daniel Cilia and Heritage Malta).

16 Matteo Perez d'Aleccio, wall paintings of the Great Siege, *c.* 1578, Grand Master's Palace, Valletta (reproduced by courtesy of Daniel Cilia and Heritage Malta).

17 Title page of the first edition of Francesco Balbi da Correggio's *La verdadera relación*, 1567 (reproduced by courtesy of the National Library of Malta, Valletta).

18 Giovanni Bandini, Portrait bust of Grand Master Jean de La Valette, *c.* 1566 (reproduced by courtesy of the Museum of the Order of St John, Clerkenwell).

19 Ottoman vessels in the Gulf of Aden, sixteenth century (Private collection: Photo © Tom Graves Archive / Bridgeman Images).

20 Theodor de Bry, engraving of Fort Caroline in Jacques Le Moyne de Morgues' *Brevis narratio eorum quae in Florida Americae provincia Gallis acciderunt*, 1591 (Service Historique de la Marine, Vincennes, France / Bridgeman Images).

List of Illustrations

21 The Great Siege in the Galleria delle Carte Geografiche in the Vatican, *c.* 1581 (© Governatorato dello Stato della Città del Vaticano, Direzione dei Musei e dei Beni Culturali).

22 Giuseppe Caloriti, View of Valletta and the Three Cities, early eighteenth century (reproduced by courtesy of Mużew Nazzjonali tal-Arti and Heritage Malta).

23 The memorial to Daphne Caruana Galizia at the base of the Great Siege Monument in Valletta (photo by author, December 2022).

List of Maps

1 The Mediterranean Sea
2 The Maltese Islands
3 The Siege of Birgu and Senglea, 1565
4 The Northern Indian Ocean
5 Florida and Cuba

Acknowledgements

My warmest thanks go, first, to my friend Theresa Vella, who, when we were on a family holiday in Malta in 2011, gave us what amounted to a private tour of Matteo Perez d'Aleccio's extraordinary wall paintings of the Great Siege in the Grand Master's Palace in Valletta. There is a clear 'flashbulb' quality to my memory of that visit: it was the moment when a medievalist who was beginning to nudge tentatively into the sixteenth century suddenly saw the direction that his future interests would take.

I am very fortunate that my research has enabled me to visit several excellent archives and libraries. Of all these, I would single out for particular mention three that have an especially close connection to the subject matter of this book. First, my thanks go to Abigail Cornick and the staff of the Museum of the Order of St John in Clerkenwell. Second, I enjoyed a very productive week at the Hill Museum and Manuscript Library; my thanks to Julie Dietman and her colleagues for their assistance. And third, I owe an enormous debt of gratitude to the staff of the National Library of Malta, led by the inestimable Maroma Camilleri. What a simply wonderful place the NLM is! One can only hope that the Maltese state continues to appreciate and protect the world-heritage treasure that it has in the very heart of its capital.

There are two further debts in particular that I must acknowledge: Gabriel Moss did a wonderful job of creating the maps; and Daniel Cilia was extraordinarily generous and gracious in making available images from his unparalleled collection of photographs of Malta's heritage sites. With respect to those images, my thanks also go to Joseph Farrugia and Heritage Malta.

It is an invidious task listing those friends and colleagues who have helped me in their different ways; one is bound to omit many

Acknowledgements

deserving of thanks. So, at the risk of appearing a shade minimal, I would like to thank the following for their support and encouragement at various junctures: Richard Barber, Jeremy Black, Graham Hill, Jasper Ludington, William Purkis, Amy Remensnyder, Alec String and Eren Tasar. To Simon Winder and his staff at Penguin Random House, thank you for your patience, skill and good grace.

Everything I have ever written inevitably bears the traces of the enormous influence of my former supervisor and mentor, Jonathan Riley-Smith. In the years up to his death in 2016, Jonathan enthusiastically and wholeheartedly supported me in what might otherwise have seemed a rather curious academic 'turn' to the early modern period and the Mediterranean. It feels as if I am honouring a debt by coming full circle. Jonathan's postgraduate students generally gravitated to one of two discrete subject areas, crusading or the Military Orders. (Jonathan himself, of course, was a leading expert in both fields.) I was a crusader (of sorts). But here we are – a book that, if not *about* one of the main Military Orders, tells the story of one of the most momentous events in its history.

Last but by no means least, my wife Tania and daughter Sasha are to all intents and purposes the co-begetters of this book. Any expression of my appreciation and love seems insufficient.

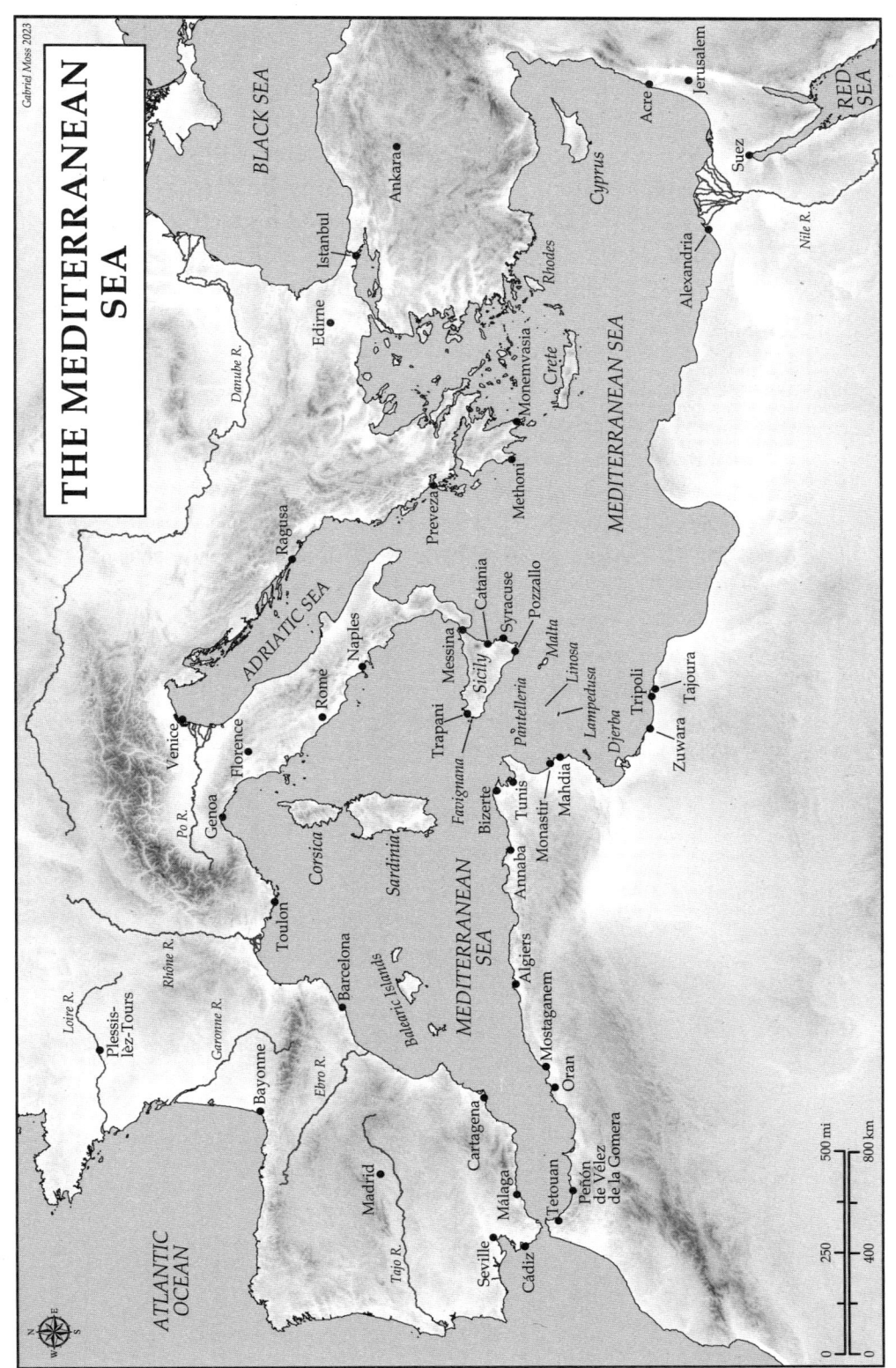

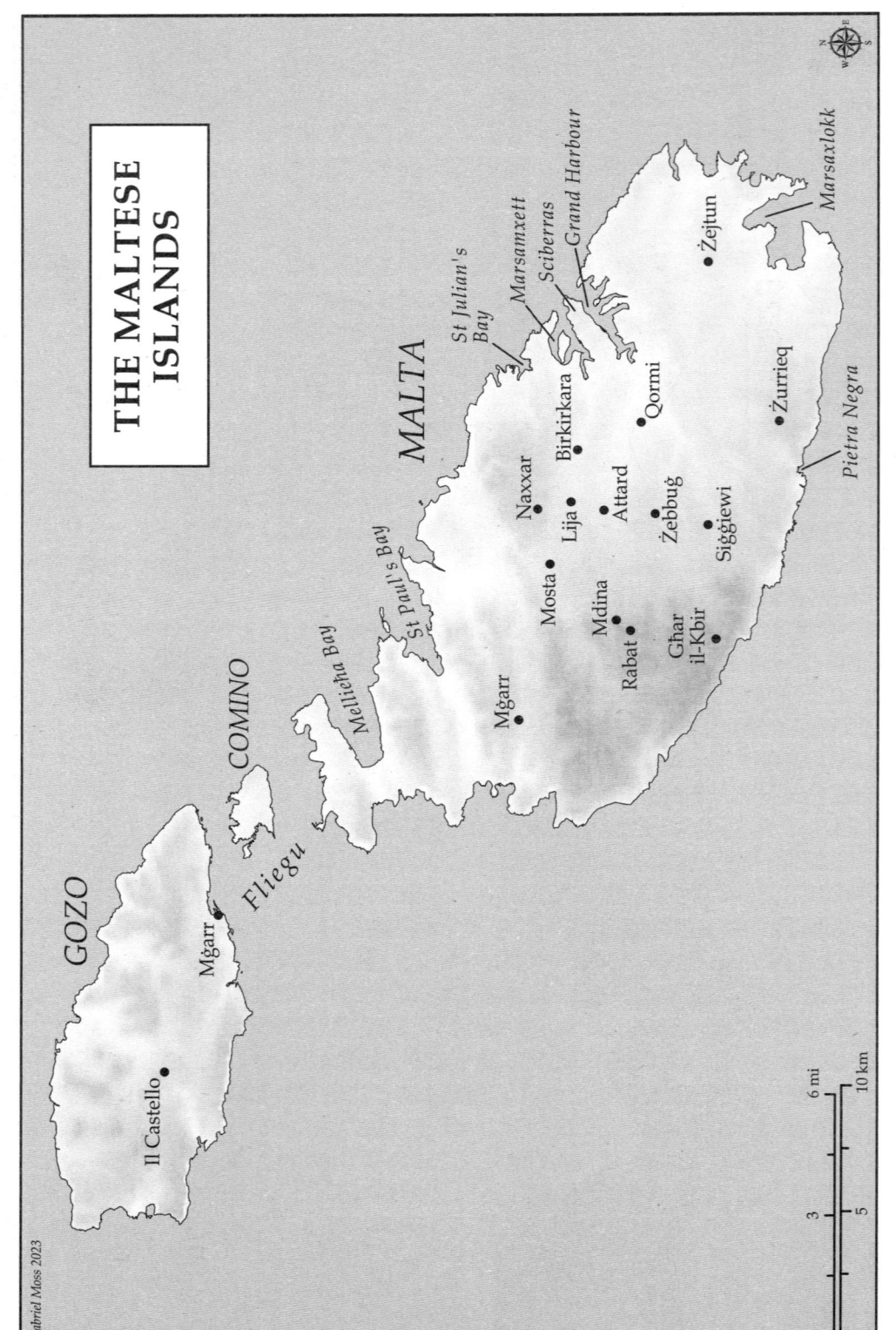

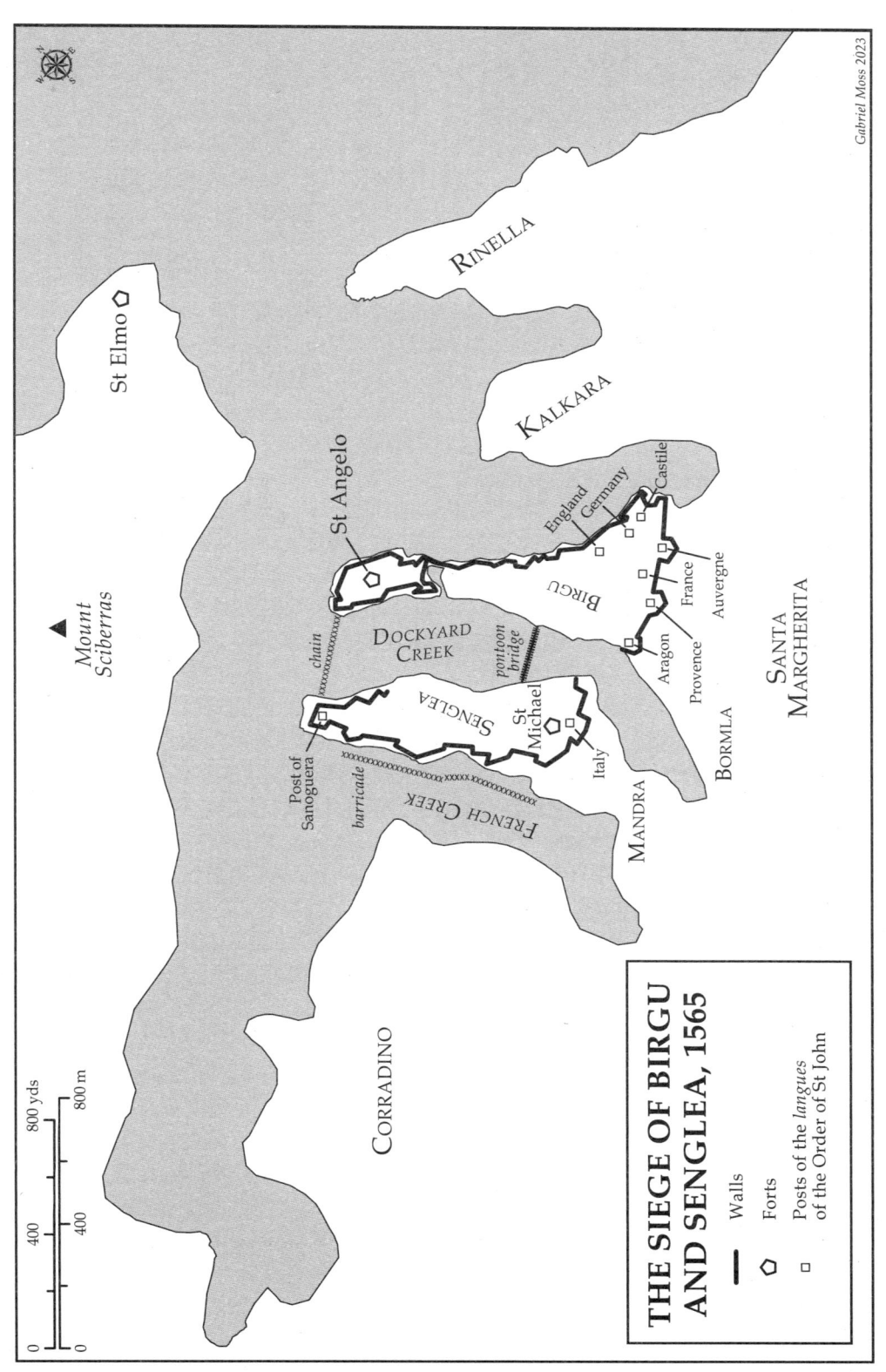

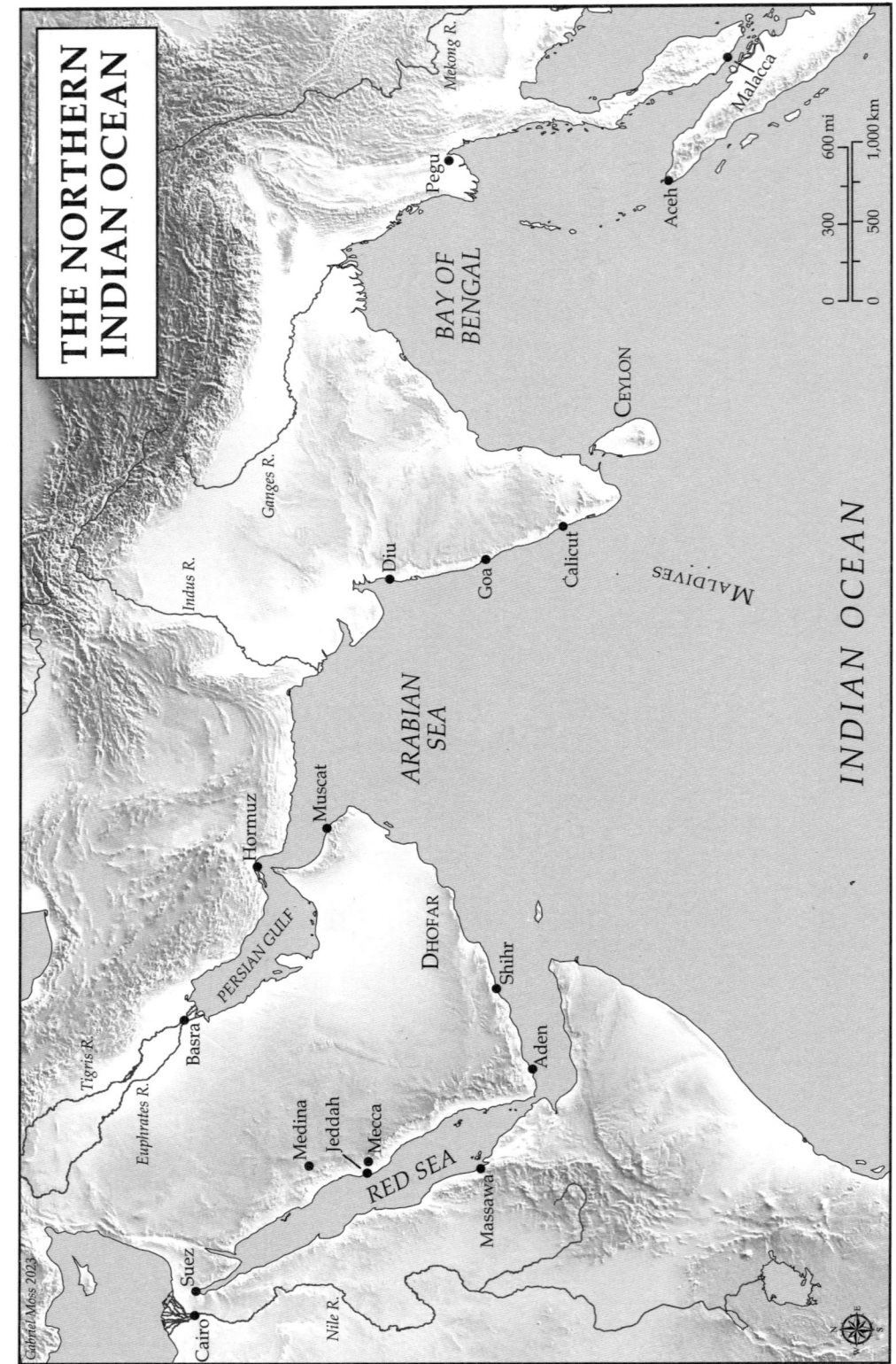

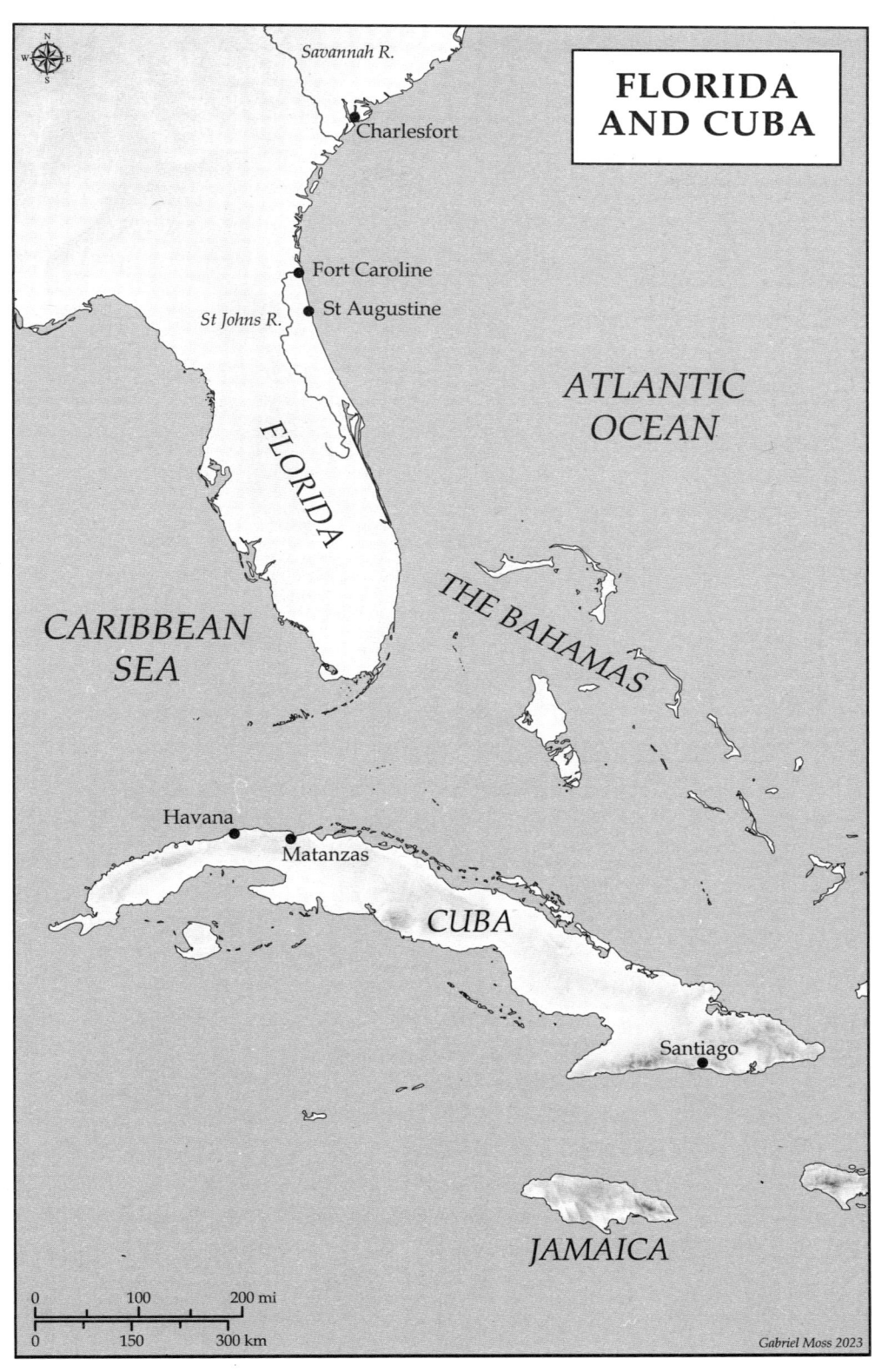

Introduction: Sieges and What They Mean

By November 1565 the French royal court had been on the road for nearly two exhausting years. In January 1564 the teenage King Charles IX and his mother and power behind the throne, Catherine de' Medici, surrounded by an enormous and constantly shifting entourage of officials, diplomats, courtiers, petitioners, merchants and servants, had embarked on a long clockwise tour of France.[1] One observer, the Florentine ambassador Giovanni Maria Petrucci, believed that the whole roadshow needed 15,000 horses to be able to move from place to place. There may have been, at some points in the itinerary, about the same number of people attached to the royal party; there would seldom have been fewer than 5,000.[2] The tour had first set out east towards the French borderlands with the Holy Roman Empire. From there it had moved south down the Saône–Rhône corridor to Provence and the Mediterranean, then west to Toulouse and Bordeaux. The most south-westerly point on the itinerary was Bayonne, where the king and his mother had conducted a summit meeting with representatives of the king of Spain. The court then worked its way up the western part of the kingdom to the lower Loire valley. It was by following the course of the Loire upstream, with some zigzagging to the north, that the royal party arrived at Plessis-lèz-Tours, just to the west of the city of Tours, on the evening of Tuesday 20 November. This would be its base for the next eleven days.[3]

The great circuit was a reaction to grave crisis. In 1562 France had plunged into a bitter civil war fuelled by religious rivalry between the supporters of the traditional Catholic faith and those – about 10 per cent of the population at the height of the popularity of the reformed religion in France in the early 1560s – who espoused Protestantism, particularly in its new and uncompromising Calvinist form.⁴ Religious differences unleashed a degree of ferocity and hatred that took moderate observers by surprise. The tone was set in what is traditionally considered the opening moment of the war, on 1 March 1562, when a group of Protestants who had assembled to worship in a barn near Wassy, in Champagne, was massacred by the followers of François, duc de Guise. The attackers were either passing by and spontaneously took exception to what they saw and heard or had already planned to make an example of heretics in the staunchly Catholic Guises' backyard.⁵ As Catherine de' Medici and the royal chancellor, Michel de l'Hôpital, realized, however, more had been at stake in the civil war than religious antagonism. There was a perception that there had been political weakness at the royal centre, probably since the death of Catherine's husband, Henri II, from injuries sustained in a jousting accident in 1559 and certainly since the death in December 1560 of his eldest son, François II, who had been succeeded by his young brother Charles. The fact that Charles had formally entered into his majority at the fairly young age of thirteen is an indication of the anxiety at the centre to prop up the royal regime by all means possible. There was also an understanding that one of the underlying causes of the civil war had been a loosening of the royal government's control of France's regions, a trend exacerbated by the emergence of rival, overmighty aristocratic families and their networks of clients and supporters. The tour was therefore more than the normal itineration of an early modern royal court writ large. The stakes were very high. This was an attempt to reunify the kingdom by presenting it to Charles, and him to it, in a long series of royal entries, civic displays and other elaborate rituals in which the king would project the reality of the royal presence to his people and, equally importantly, experience that same sense of control affirmed and reflected back on him by his welcoming subjects.

We know, as those at the time did not, that the healing effects of the grand tour would prove short-lived. Civil war would break out again in 1567, to be followed by a series of conflicts, now collectively known as the French Wars of Religion, that stretched into the 1590s

Introduction: Sieges and What They Mean

or, some scholars argue, beyond. But by the time that Charles and Catherine reached Plessis, there must have been an emerging sense of a job well done. There was still a long way to go: after Tours the court would travel further up the Loire to Blois and then turn south-east into the centre of the country, making an extended stay in Moulins in the Bourbonnais and reaching as far south as Clermont-Ferrand in the Auvergne before swinging north to arrive back in Paris on 1 May 1566, 829 days after the great journey had begun. But although the end was not quite yet in sight, at Plessis the Valois monarchy was re-emerging into its heartland and reconnecting with its sources of power. In Tours the cult of St Martin, the fourth-century bishop of the city, had been an important element of French royal ideology for many centuries. Beyond Tours the itinerary would go on to take the royal party to various Valois châteaux, including Chenonceaux, which Catherine de' Medici had vengefully appropriated from Henri II's former mistress Diane de Poitiers, as well as Amboise and Blois. The château of Plessis itself, not as famous today because most of it was destroyed in the French Revolution, played its part in the architectural staging of royal magnificence that characterized the middle Loire region. At Plessis the Valois were home. It was a fitting location, therefore, for the court to be entertained, at some point during its stay, by an uplifting story of bravery and resilience against the odds.

The story that was told was of the unsuccessful assault on Malta earlier that year by the army and navy of the Ottoman sultan, Süleyman I; and the narrator was Antoine de Flotte de La Roche, a Knight of the Order of St John, which had led the defence against the Ottoman forces. La Roche was one of a number of envoys who had been sent by the head of the order, the Grand Master Jean de La Valette, to the courts of Catholic Europe to announce the great victory and, more importantly, pave the way for requests for urgently needed subventions: Malta's defences were ruinous, the order's funds were exhausted, and there was every reason to suppose that the Ottomans would return the following year to finish the job.[6] The epic quality of La Roche's story would have been lent additional force for his listeners by the knowledge that the events it narrated were very recent: on the day that the Turkish fleet had appeared off Malta, 18 May, Charles IX's entourage had been staying at Mont-de-Marsan in Gascony; and on the day nearly four months later when the Turkish fleet had sailed away, 12 September, the royal roadshow had been working its way between Saint-Jean-d'Angély and La Rochelle.[7] Events in Malta had, moreover, already been brought home to the French court *in medias res* in a diplomatically fraught moment when an ambassador sent by the sultan, with whom the French were formally allied, presented himself just as the summit meeting with the Spanish, the principal supporters of the Knights of St John, was in full swing.[8] As the Turkish preparations in early 1565 were getting under way, the Valois monarchy had even sought, and received, reassurances from the Sublime Porte, the Ottoman government, that the armada would not harm French interests.[9]

By November, however, Malta's survival was assured, at least for the present, and the French court could afford to settle into La Roche's performance while telling itself that it had been on the right side of history all along. La Roche himself was not an unalloyed figure. In some of the early accounts of the assault on Malta, particularly that by the eyewitness Francesco Balbi da Correggio, he appears as a slightly pusillanimous staff officer who ought to have shown greater resolve at a crucial moment. When La Valette and his high command had to decide whether to persist in the costly defence of a weak fort, St Elmo, that was bound to fall sooner rather than later, but which was buying the Knights precious time, La Roche had acquitted himself poorly: during a visit to the fort's beleaguered garrison he had given the impression of being timorous and irresolute. That said, he was La Valette's former squire and one of the Grand Master's most trusted lieutenants; in anticipation of the Ottoman attack he had been given the vital job of supervising the supply of ammunition for the order's artillery.[10] Most importantly of all, for the purposes of holding forth at Plessis, La Roche was impeccably aristocratic; and he was French.

Introduction: Sieges and What They Mean

Our principal source for La Roche's performance, and the reaction that it provoked in his audience, is an account by Pierre de Bourdeille, *abbé* or *seigneur* of Brantôme in Périgord, who was almost certainly an eyewitness. A consideration of Brantôme and his writings helps us to understand the significance of this moment and the reasons why it made a powerful impression on him and others. Brantôme (c.1540–1614) is chiefly remembered today as a memoirist, but this is misleading, at least in part.[11] He is known to have written an account of his life in the full, autobiographical sense, but this has not survived. Instead, the title 'memoirs' was attached to his surviving body of work, some decades after his death, by his first publisher in order to cash in on a genre that was very much in vogue at that time. Brantôme's writings comprise an assemblage of what he termed *discours*, or essays. One is a treatise on duels and duelling, in which he was passionately interested. Another, for which he is now best known and which is conventionally entitled *Les dames galantes*, concerns the marital and sexual experiences of high-status women. It is replete with sometimes coy and allusive, sometimes racy and crude, sometimes disturbingly violent and cold anecdotes that draw, *inter alia*, upon Brantôme's reminiscences of his own sexual exploits. Most of his oeuvre, however, consists of biographies of famous figures, almost all of them his contemporaries or those of his parents' generation. Some are women, including Catherine de' Medici and her daughter Marguerite de Valois, *la reine Margot*, whose own memoirs are addressed to him.[12] One was Mary, Queen of Scots, whom Brantôme accompanied back to Scotland from France in 1561, after the death of her husband, François II, and whose memory he later venerated. Most of his subjects are, however, male, predominantly military men who embodied the aristocratic and martial qualities that the author valued particularly highly.

Brantôme's first publisher was not entirely off the mark, for the various *discours* resemble personal memoirs in the limited but important sense that the author does appear in his stories at many points, sometimes in asides and sometimes as a minor character in the action, functioning in effect as an extra in other people's life stories. It is from such autobiographical fragments, big and small, that most of what we know about Brantôme's life can be reconstructed. One of the more substantial fragments is an account of the circumstances that brought La Roche to the royal court, the reaction that his presentation elicited, and the conversation that it prompted. Unsurprisingly, this passage is embedded in Brantôme's biography of Jean de La Valette, and is cued by the author's insistence that the Grand Master's comportment during the assault on Malta served as the perfect illustration of his inestimable qualities as a 'great captain', the epitome of valour, and a proud Frenchman to boot.[13] We are told that La Roche caught up with the court at Plessis, where he was very warmly received and, before an attentive and enthusiastic audience comprising Charles IX, Catherine de' Medici (whom Brantôme describes as especially captivated), various officers of state and other courtiers, he was pressed to tell the story of the attack on Malta 'all the way through', after which he took questions, 'to the delight and admiration' of the king and his mother.[14]

Brantôme does not ventriloquize La Roche's report by inserting a narrative of the siege at this point. Instead, he moves immediately to a discussion of the wider significance of La Roche's story. Michel de l'Hôpital, he says, observed that the Grand Masters of the Order of St John when it had faced three major sieges at the hands of the Turks – on Rhodes in 1480 and 1522, and now Malta – had all been French, whereupon Catherine de' Medici turned to her young son and asked him to take particular note of the honour that this fact did both him and his kingdom. Once it had been established that all three sieges could be safely viewed through a French lens, the conversation turned to which could be considered the greatest. The constable, Anne de Montmorency, got things rolling with an argument in favour of the latter siege of Rhodes, in part because the Grand Master at that time, Philippe de Villiers de L'Isle-Adam, had been his kinsman. Brantôme was by no means a sophisticated writer. But his evocation of this whole exchange, in particular the questions prompted by Montmorency's intervention, is perhaps the

Introduction: Sieges and What They Mean

most carefully crafted sequence in his whole corpus, which runs to about 4,000 pages in its most recent complete edition.[15] Gradually the scene at Plessis recedes, like a fade in a film, and Brantôme's own narratorial voice takes over as he explores the various criteria by which the relative significance of a siege might best be judged. Several pages later, just as the reader is expecting one of the author's signature switches to an entirely different subject, the scene fades back in and we are returned to the court at Plessis, just as Montmorency is conceding that La Roche has persuaded him that the most recent siege was indeed the greatest of the three.

What, in Brantôme's estimation and, if he is to be believed, that of the great and good of the Valois court, made the siege of 1565 stand out? In the first place, he implies that it was a very good story that bore favourable comparison with other good stories. It is interesting that Brantôme makes a point of mentioning the best-known account of the siege of 1522, Jacques le Bâtard de Bourbon's *La grande et merueilleuse et trescruelle oppugnation de la noble cite de Rhodes*, as if to acknowledge that this event had received a suitably epic treatment. And, of course, the whole thrust of Brantôme's careful attention to the *mise-en-scène* at Plessis is not that the Valois court was thrilled at the outcome of the siege of Malta, news of which would already have reached it, but at the manner of its telling. More explicitly, Brantôme picks out various points of comparison and contrast between 1522 and 1565, 1480 having been quickly relegated to third place. One criterion was scale, though this had a qualitative as well as quantitative dimension: yes, the Ottomans had deployed more men at Rhodes, but many of these were non-combatants, whereas at Malta they had brought a greater number of trained and battle-hardened fighters. Military technology had moved on: in the intervening period the elite of the Ottoman forces, the Janissaries, had become expert sharpshooters with the arquebus, the matchlock long gun. Malta was, moreover, much smaller than Rhodes, allowing the enemy to concentrate its men and resources. The size of the Ottoman artillery trains was about the same at the two sieges, but that brought to Malta delivered more destructive firepower.

Whereas Rhodes enjoyed strong defences built up and perfected over the two centuries and more that the Knights of St John had ruled the island, Malta's defences were poorer and their construction rushed (a comparison not without some merit). Brantôme is prepared to concede that King Philip II of Spain had sent invaluable assistance to Malta, the implication being that this made a near-hopeless position just about defensible. In contrast Philip's father, the emperor Charles V, and Pope Leo X (named in error: Brantôme means Hadrian VI) had myopically abandoned Rhodes to its fate in order to concentrate on driving François I of France from Milan – a nicely tart dig. The Ottoman assault on Malta had taken everyone by surprise – not true, though there was criticism of hurried and insufficient preparation – whereas the defenders of Rhodes had enjoyed plenty of warning. Brantôme distils all these criteria into one essence when he ponders the extent to which each siege was *furieux*, a word which defies easy translation but which seems to bundle together 'intense', 'high-stakes', 'bloody' and 'epic in scale'.

One can see Brantôme's enthusiasm for the story of the siege of Malta working on two levels. In the first place there was his own personal fascination, which came to shade into a fantasy of actual participation. One of the reasons why the scene at Plessis stuck with Brantôme so powerfully was that it helped to explain how he would come to join a party of about 1,000 French aristocrats, adventurers and mercenaries which set out for Malta in the following spring. This would seem to have been a more significant undertaking than the rather jaunty references to it in Brantôme's text might suggest; the commander of Philip II's forces in Malta in 1566, Fernando Francesco d'Avalos, marquess of Pescara, certainly took it seriously.[16] For our present purposes, what is particularly striking is the frequency with which Brantôme refers to the expedition throughout his writings. The enterprise of 1566 crops up again and again, usually as a dating co-ordinate or by way of contextual background, and in some cases in relation to events that are tangential or unconnected to the expedition itself.[17] His usual term for expressing the expedition's purpose is *secours*, relief, which makes some sense

Introduction: Sieges and What They Mean

given that it was not until around June, by which time the French party had arrived in Malta, that the threat of a renewed Ottoman assault seemed to be receding. On occasion, however, Brantôme strays into wishful thinking with phrases such as 'When we were going to the siege of Malta', as if this had been an ongoing process that had folded over into the following year.[18]

The clear sense of longing, of wanting to be part of something important, was no doubt wrapped up in Brantôme's mind with a sense of disappointment over an opportunity lost. One of the most poignant, and deeply autobiographical, passages in his writings relates how his visit to Malta inspired in him an ambition to become a Knight of St John, only for him to be dissuaded by his friend Filippo di Piero Strozzi:

> When I was in Malta I would have resolved to take the cross [join the order] there and then, if it hadn't been for Strozzi, who was my best friend, and who changed my mind and stopped me from doing it, badgering me with this argument and that one until I accepted what he said. He made me understand that, just for the sake of a cross, I shouldn't forsake the good fortune that awaited me in France, whether courtesy of the king, or thanks to the lady – beautiful, fair and rich – whose eager and welcome servant I was at that time and whom I might have a chance of marrying. In light of all these arguments, I allowed myself to go along with what my friend was suggesting, and I returned to France.[19]

Brantôme did not receive any conspicuous preferment from the Valois. He did not get his lady. He never married, in fact. His relationship with Strozzi eventually cooled somewhat. And as this passage goes on to claim, he did not come by any good fortune other than a certain name recognition in high society. As Brantôme reflected on a life that he believed had been characterized by frustrations and disappointments, his enduring aspiration to be included in the story of the siege of Malta speaks to the power of wanting to feel a part of big history, an impulse to enjoy the status and consolations that it conferred and the sense of self-worth and inclusion that it imparted. Something about an epic siege would seem to have satisfied this desire.

On a second level, Brantôme's remarks speak to some of the ways in which sieges affirm not only individual strivings, but also collective identities and ideologies. One of the most interesting moments in Brantôme's re-creation of the scene at Plessis is Michel de l'Hôpital's deft move in immediately banishing the elephant in the room, which was France's diplomatic semi-detachment during the siege and its recent history of alliance with the Ottoman empire. This he did by making the story of the siege of Malta, in some reassuring way, all about French greatness. In claiming the siege for France, the chancellor could have made a forceful practical argument: that the single most important source of recruits for the Order of St John among the countries of Catholic Europe, and the location of the greatest concentration of its landed estates, was France. But by focusing instead on the nationality of the Grand Masters at the time of the three sieges, Michel de l'Hôpital was cleverly grounding the ensuing discussion in ideas of elite power, individual valour and strength, aristocratic masculinity, and membership of a distinct noble caste, or 'race' as this was sometimes termed. As we have seen, Montmorency instinctively picked up on this last by claiming the siege of 1522 as a source of his family's dynastic prestige.[20] Such an emphasis on elite values made perfect sense in the rarefied atmosphere of the Valois court. More generally, however, the chancellor's clever pivot attests to the great power that sieges can hold over groups' imaginations: if the French crown and nobility could stretch a point in November 1565 in order to make the siege of Malta about them, then there must be something particularly compelling and powerful about sieges in general.

Sieges have a long history as sites of meaning and value, especially in the western literary tradition. Two of that tradition's foundational texts place sieges front and centre. In the Old Testament Book of Joshua 6:1–27 the city of Jericho is tightly besieged by the people

Introduction: Sieges and What They Mean

of Israel: 'none went out, and none came in'. When the Ark of the Covenant is processed around the city to the sound of seven trumpets, the walls collapse, the Israelites pour in, and the city is wholly destroyed. Its wealth is stripped to be taken to the Temple and its population is put to death, with the sole exception of the family of Rahab the harlot, who has aided Joshua's spies. Tight encirclement, uncompromising antagonism, and the threat or actuality of ruthless massacre, looting and destruction: these are some of the most powerful associations that the word 'siege' carries in popular understanding. In Homer's *Iliad*, in contrast, the treatment of the siege of Troy is more balanced. Hector and some of the other Trojans are dignified characters and are described sympathetically. Achilles' slaying of Hector – the *mise en abyme* of the entire ten-year conflict – is represented as an appropriate vindication of his vengeful ire, but the grief and loss that the Trojans feel, which Achilles himself is made to acknowledge, are handled in a nuanced manner. This is not a world of black and white. Nonetheless it is the Greeks on the outside who are the principal focus of Homer's narrative.

The accounts in these two texts of their respective sieges are unusual in siding, wholly in one case, principally in the other, with those on the outside trying to get in. In contrast most historical and literary treatments of sieges sympathize with those on the inside trying to keep the aggressors out, and in doing so see the defenders' predicament through their eyes. This is nicely illustrated by the trajectory of the story of the siege of Troy after Homer. Contrary to a widespread misconception, the details of the fall of Troy, complete with Wooden Horse, do not appear in the *Iliad*, the climax of which is the duel between Achilles and Hector that takes place some time before Troy is captured; nor are they mentioned in anything other than brief and scattered passages in the *Odyssey*. A substantially fuller, and culturally influential, account of the conclusion of the siege appears in Book II of Virgil's much later *Aeneid*, which narrates how Aeneas, a member of the Trojan ruling elite, escapes the city as it falls, thereby setting in motion the sequence of events that will culminate in his foundation of the city of Rome. Virgil, like his younger contemporary the historian Livy, was fashioning a myth of origins at a time when Rome was shaking off the memories of bitter civil war and seeking to reconstitute itself and its sense of the past under Augustus, its first, and very image-conscious, emperor. The notion that Rome owed its origins to someone tainted by failure would have been preposterous. But no shame attached to Aeneas for having been on the losing side at Troy: if anything, his ability to survive defeat enhanced his heroic status and ennobled his sense of mission.

The rhetorical power of this repurposing of the siege of Troy so as to see it from the inside looking out is further demonstrated by the way in which authors in the Middle Ages, writing myths of origins for the peoples of their own day, took their cue from Virgil and plugged their stories into the Trojan past. For example, perhaps the greatest purveyor of enduring myths to the British historical consciousness – he is partly responsible for the fame of King Arthur – was Geoffrey of Monmouth. His *History of the Kings of Britain*, written in the 1130s, tells the story of how Aeneas's great-grandson, Brutus, set himself up as 'the leader of those who survived the fall of Troy'. After several adventures, Brutus reached Britain, which took its name from him, and established a kingdom there. A new kingdom needed a new capital city, and this was duly founded on the future site of London, its name *Troia Nova*, 'New Troy'.[21] Again, no shame or even a hint of equivocation attached to Brutus' dynastic connection to the story of Aeneas. Why wouldn't the descendants of the survivors of the siege of Troy have a right to rule over Britain? And why wouldn't they name their new city after their ancestral home?

We have a strong cultural preference for sieges told from the inside out. This extends to noble defeats after a period of steadfast defiance in the face of great odds, especially when the defeated are subsequently avenged and their cause vindicated. The Alamo is a case in point. That said, the single most common paradigm of a siege that is regarded as worthy to take its place in a nation's or other group's collective memory is of an assault pluckily survived, albeit after a great deal of suffering and several close shaves. Sieges told in this vein are often celebrations of shared purpose on the part of the defenders, sometimes to the extent that hierarchies of class, caste or gender are believed to dissolve, for a time at any rate, as everyone pulls together. Sieges of this type reaffirm senses of belonging and of place. They are lightning rods for cherished values, or at least the values of those whose view of the world is built into the dominant narratives that emerge during and after the event. If a culture attaches particular value to stoical self-control and physical toughness, these are the qualities that win the day. If there is a belief in a God who punishes the faithful for their sins but offers them a chance of redemption, a siege survived will be interpreted as a site of trial, atonement and purgation. Sieges in this sort of idiom clarify and simplify the world. They grant ideals and ideologies a cleaner edge and a topical resonance. In December 1870, during the Prussian siege of Paris, Gaston Paris (1839–1903), the future doyen of the academic study of medieval French literature, drew large audiences to a series of lectures on 'La *Chanson de Roland* et la nationalité française' in the Collège de France even as enemy shells were falling onto the city. The premise of his addresses was that the *Song of Roland*, which had attracted renewed interest since the discovery in the 1830s, in Oxford, of what is now accepted as its oldest manuscript incarnation, was the foundational text of French as a literary language. By extension, therefore, it amounted to the birth certificate of French greatness. France was now undergoing a cruel and catastrophic test, but its profound sense of national unity, as first evidenced in the pages of the *Roland*, would, Paris insisted, prevail. By further extension, only the French could be considered the true heirs of their heroic Frankish forebears, not their German foes, even though they too could in theory lay claim to some share of the Frankish past.[22]

The word 'siege' is difficult to define precisely, both as a term of art for military historians and in vernacular usage.[23] What we might think of as sieges shade into other forms of positional warfare, that is, combat structured by permanent and more or less securely fortified lines, such as the trenches of the First World War. Sieges are typically stages in the larger sweep of military campaigns that extend beyond them in space and time, not stand-alone episodes. Verdun in 1916 and Stalingrad in 1942–3 were complex conflicts that sucked in hundreds of thousands of combatants across large areas, but in French and Russian popular historical memory they tend to be configured as variants of the siege type, the dogged defence of vital positions. The Jericho-esque image of a walled city completely surrounded and cut off by an attacking force informs the prevailing sense of 'siege-ness' in popular understanding, and would seem to be the basis of metaphors such as 'siege mentality' or 'feeling under siege'. Surprisingly few events that we think of as sieges conform to this pure type, however. A good example is another siege of Paris, that of 1590, in which the French king, Henri IV, tried, and failed, to regain control of his capital, which was held against him by the forces of the Catholic League. Although Henri was able to give the defenders a constant reminder that they were indeed under attack by mounting his artillery on the heights of Montmartre overlooking the city, the walls of Paris were too long and his forces too few to make a traditional encirclement feasible. Instead Henri set up a blockade at strategic choke-points along the supply routes that fed the city. The effect on the population of Paris was devastating: although a matter of debate among historians, it is likely that those who died of starvation or disease brought on by malnutrition numbered many thousands.[24] A fervently pro-League account of the siege draws freely on the language of martyrdom and of noble suffering in a just and holy cause. Once again we see how, once a collective experience of some sort is understood as a siege, the opportunity is presented to supercharge its ideological loading.[25]

It is therefore noteworthy that, from the point of view of the defenders of Malta and those who identified with them, the word 'siege' – in Latin *obsidio*, Spanish *asedio*, Italian *assedio* and French (in its most frequent sixteenth-century rendering) *siége* – became attached to the events between May and September 1565 even as they were unfolding, and thereafter became the standard point of

Introduction: Sieges and What They Mean

reference. This was by no means inevitable. In a series of notarial documents beginning very soon after the siege, for example, in which Maltese peasants petition for relief from payment of dues because their farms and livelihoods had been severely damaged, the operative term is *la armata turchesca*. This shorthand is found elsewhere, including in the language of some of the Order of St John's own documents. The word 'armada' in sixteenth-century usage was not limited to a fleet, but used of any substantial amphibious force. Had things evolved differently, we might now speak of the 'Turkish Armada' of 1565 in the same way that the term 'Spanish Armada' is applied not only to the forces that Philip II sent against England in 1588 but also to the whole sequence of events that unfolded during the campaign of that year. Nonetheless 'siege' of Malta it is.

The Ottoman assault on Malta was an occupation – a partial and not always effectively conducted occupation – of the largest island in the Maltese archipelago in the central Mediterranean. Those fighting back against the occupiers enjoyed intermittent and shifting control over portions of the open countryside. But the core of their resistance was their possession of four fortified sites, control of which by the respective sides by the end of the campaign season – the meteorological window in which fighting on land or at sea was practicable – around mid September would represent the 'final score'. Loss of all four sites would lead to the near-total and almost certainly irreversible obliteration of the Order of St John, and profound changes in their political, religious and cultural environment for the inhabitants of the Maltese islands. If the attackers succeeded in taking three positions, their ultimate victory would be beyond reasonable doubt. The significance of a tie would depend on which two fortresses had fallen to the attackers, but the advantage would very clearly lie with them. In the event, and as we shall see, one of the positions fell to the Ottomans, two more just about survived sustained and heavy assault, while the fourth was not under immediate threat most of the time, though its strategic significance for the eventual outcome of the Malta campaign was to prove enormous. The result of all this was that when a large but by no means insuperable relief force landed on Malta in early September, the Ottomans were unsuccessful in their attempts to defeat it but had probably already concluded that they did not have sufficient control on the ground, nor the remaining human resources and supplies, to take their chances by extending the campaign into the winter months – always a high-risk strategy given the huge logistical challenges of premodern warfare, especially amphibious operations. The Ottomans therefore withdrew, probably in better shape than their triumphant opponents liked to believe. At the time it was fully expected that the Ottomans would resume their offensive against Malta in 1566. They did not return, however, and as the dust settled and the Knights began to regroup, the siege came to be seen as a stand-alone epic event, a turning point of some sort.

To the extent that the campaign of 1565 conforms to a truism of siege warfare, that for those on the inside winning comes down to not losing, the term 'Great Siege' is not a misnomer. This *was* a form of siege. What is more, if one had visited Malta between about two weeks after the arrival of the Ottoman fleet and about a week before its departure, one would have formed the powerful impression that this was a conflict characterized at the sharp end by all the apparatus of sixteenth-century siege warfare: cannon, trenches and mass assaults on fortified positions. Most of those who died as a direct result of violent action during the campaign did so in circumstances typical of siege warfare: in scrambling hand-to-hand combat for control of a contested perimeter, burned by incendiary weapons, struck by artillery rounds, crushed by falling masonry, or picked off by small-arms fire. For those on the ground, this was indeed a siege. In fact it was two sieges in one. First there was a siege-as-noble-failure of the Alamo type centred on the fortress of St Elmo. In due course this opening phase of the campaign would be elevated to the status of Counter-Reformation Europe's Thermopylae, a selfless sacrifice on the part of the defenders against formidable odds that blunted the aggressor's edge and bought precious time. The second siege, a series of assaults on the parallel peninsulas of Birgu and Senglea in Malta's Grand Harbour, conforms to the skin-of-the-teeth model. The story of the Great Siege thus conjoins two powerful paradigms, and this no doubt contributes to its enduring interest.

All of this is to say that we need to be alert to an instinctive inclination towards an inside-out perspective as against outside-in when thinking about the Great Siege and what it meant to all those caught up in it in various ways. This is made all the more challenging by the unevenness of the evidence at our disposal, in part a consequence of the Ottoman regime's record-keeping practices and the loss of some of its archives for this period, and in part because of the two sides' contrasting reactions to the outcome of the siege. For the Ottomans Malta was a blip, a serious but unusual and by no means irreversible setback that obviously did not invite the sort of commemoration that their many successful military campaigns occasioned. In the short term it was something to shake off by throwing resources at restoring the *status quo ante*, a typical Ottoman response to reverses. It was also something to learn from: witness the Ottomans' success in their next large-scale amphibious assault on a Christian island, Cyprus, in 1570–71, despite their being slowed down by another epic siege, that of Famagusta. In stark contrast, for Christian Europe, especially Catholic, Romance-speaking Europe, the siege was an occasion for celebration. For this reason, as well as the Order of St John's habits of careful record-keeping and the greater growth of print in the Christian world, we now have significantly more evidence from the perspective of the defenders of Malta and those who supported them. This imbalance is observable, first, in the extant archival record, in the form of letters, official pronouncements and administrative documents. On the Ottoman side, such materials do enable us to understand something of the organizational effort put into mobilizing the land and sea forces, though the intensity and scale of such preparations relative to other campaigns is not always clear. We are also able to catch a few, albeit tantalizingly fleeting, glimpses of the Ottoman regime's strategic planning and war aims, as we shall see. A remarkable record of the rewards handed out to those who distinguished themselves on

Malta allows us to introduce a human element to the experience of at least a few of those on the outside of the siege looking in. For all these fascinating glimpses, however, it is inevitably the case that the surviving records generated on the Christian side are much more numerous and more variegated.

The imbalance is still more pronounced when we turn to contemporary historical works and other narrative accounts of the events of May–September 1565. There are some compensations: the observations of some later Ottoman writers suggest that they had access to official campaign reports and other documents now lost to us.[26] But for most of the rich texture of the siege in terms of what the French call *histoire événementielle*, the finely grained quality of human action in its specific moment, we must rely on Christian accounts. The Great Siege was the stimulus for the publication of a host of narratives, beginning with short newsletters produced by enterprising printers even as the siege was happening, typically reproducing or paraphrasing letters that had been smuggled out of Malta, then eyewitness accounts in letter form, and finally stand-alone books.[27] As one would expect, these sources give pride of place to the story of the siege from the inside out; when they do open up their perspective, it is generally to recount the efforts that were made elsewhere to organize military assistance for the besieged. Of the book-length treatments, that written by Balbi, which in fact appeared in two editions, published in Spain in 1567 and 1568 respectively, is the best known and most frequently cited. It is the fullest account by an eyewitness who was present at the siege from beginning to end. Balbi is sometimes dismissed as a rather unsophisticated writer who was not privy to the important decisions that guided the defenders' actions and consequently struggled to understand what was happening in the round. But we should be wary of falling for the common literary cliché of the straightforward soldier memoirist whose no-frills honesty makes up in accuracy what his text lacks in authorial craft and perspective; Balbi was a more astute and reflective observer than such a categorization would imply. Another, rather underrated, account of the siege, printed in 1567, was written by Antonfrancesco Cirni, a senior Corsican cleric and experienced writer who travelled to Malta with the relief force in September 1565 and for a year thereafter travelled between Sicily and Malta collecting material for his narrative. His is an informed and intelligent version of events.[28]

Also of value is the narrative by Pierre Gentil de Vendôme, who was secretary to the Knights' representative at the papal curia in Rome; this placed him right at the centre of the most important information hub in Europe during and immediately after the siege. Although his account, which he published in both Italian and French, is not as detailed as those by Balbi and Cirni, it was the first book-length treatment to be written, before the end of 1565; it thus gets us that bit closer to contemporaries' initial reactions to the outcome of the siege.[29] To judge by the number of authors who appropriated, adapted or translated Vendôme, his was one of the most widely circulated versions of events. These three writers appear more than any others in the following pages, though they are complemented by the works of a significant number of other writers. Mention should especially be made of Giacomo Bosio, whose monumental history of the Order of St John was written in the years either side of 1600. Significantly, the siege occupies more space than any other event in the Knights' history. Bosio was an assiduous researcher, combing carefully through the order's records as well as earlier narratives of the siege. His is an impressive work of historical reconstruction. But it is also a highly ideological artefact in which the story of the siege is pressed into service as a celebration of the Knights' historical mission and of the merits of hierarchy and discipline, written in response to a period of severe turmoil in the order in the 1580s. Bosio is a mine of wonderful information, but his slant, evident, for example, in his very favourable treatment of Jean de La Valette, always needs to be borne in mind.[30]

When we read these narrative sources in particular, we need to be careful not to essentialize their image of the two opposing sides in the siege as monolithic entities acting and reacting in stock ways. Internal variety is easier to detect on the Christian side: the Order of St John was in effect a working alliance between aristocratic networks from different countries, and often political antagonisms in Europe could translate into tensions within the order's ranks. The two relief forces that were sent to Malta were multi-national. And we should not forget the Maltese themselves, for the most part a shadowy presence on the margins of the written evidence but very important in actuality. The Ottoman evidence is more difficult to parse for evidence of internal divisions, but on the basis of western diplomats' observations about the personalities at the highest level of the Sublime Porte in the years either side of the siege, we may surmise that there was a range of views in 1565, more or less hawkish, on the merits of the Malta campaign itself and its place in the Ottoman empire's larger strategic priorities. It is also important to remember that the Ottoman world was ethnically and linguistically diverse.[31] Western observers tended to label the Other by means of sweeping references to the 'Turks' or even an immanent 'Turk' in the singular, but this masked a far more complex reality. As we have noted, sieges simplify and clarify. They impose and legitimize clear binary distinctions: us–them, good–bad, in–out, right–wrong, possessor–interloper. But both sides – or more accurately, all sides – in 1565 resist such easy categorization. They were multifaceted, 'messy' entities, and their very messiness contributes to an understanding of why the Great Siege took place and why it turned out as it did. It is to the principal antagonists in this remarkable struggle, therefore, that we now turn.

I.

Violence, Vanity and Vocation: The Knights of Malta

The organization that, as we shall see, supplied the officer class that led the defence of Malta in 1565 still exists to this day. Now a small order of the Catholic Church dedicated to charitable projects, it goes by the formal title of the Sovereign Military Hospitaller Order of St John of Jerusalem, of Rhodes and of Malta. It has been known by many titles and shorthands over the course of its long history, including the Order of St John, the Hospital, the Knights of Rhodes, and the Knights of Malta. Around the time of the Great Siege it sometimes referred to itself, and was described by outsiders, as simply 'the Religion'. In this book, the terms of reference used of it vary in the interests of avoiding verbal monotony, or to register a particular facet of its operations or a phase in its development. But it is important to bear in mind that we are dealing with a single entity characterized by remarkable continuity, sometimes in defiance of daunting obstacles. When Brantôme was in Malta in 1566 and dreaming of joining the order, before Filippo di Piero Strozzi poured cold water on his ambitions, this organization had already enjoyed an unbroken institutional existence for about 500 years, and had been constituted in a form that Brantôme would have recognized for approximately 430.

The order had originated in the 1060s with the foundation by a group of merchants from Amalfi in southern Italy of a monastery, dedicated to the Virgin Mary, in the Christian quarter of Jerusalem close to the church of the Holy Sepulchre; this community would become known as St Mary of the Latins. The principal purpose of the foundation, and of a daughter house for nuns, St Mary

Magdalene, was to provide assistance to pilgrims who had travelled from western Europe to the Holy City. The Muslim authorities that ruled Palestine broadly tolerated the Christian visitors: Jerusalem was a holy site in Islam as well, of course, and the idea of pilgrimage was familiar from the institution of the *hajj* to Mecca. In addition, Christian pilgrims could also be made to pay entry fees and other burdensome dues, a practice that attracted unfavourable comment in western Europe.[1]

No doubt as a result of the pressure of pilgrim numbers, and the disruptions that this caused to the cloistered lives of the monks and nuns, a separate institution, dedicated to St John the Baptist and probably staffed by lay brothers, was in due course detached from the mother house. The terms in which this was described in closely contemporary sources do not permit us to differentiate clearly between a hospice or hostel on the one hand, and a hospital in something approaching the modern sense on the other. This would in any event have been a distinction without a difference. Unlike many pilgrimage shrines in western Europe which promoted themselves as thaumaturgic, which is to say places of healing, Jerusalem was not on the whole a destination for those seeking cures. If anything, many pilgrims travelled out in the hope or expectation of dying there. Most of those who set out in reasonable health, moreover, would most likely have arrived severely weakened by the rigours of the journey. By the time that the army of the First Crusade arrived outside Jerusalem in June 1099, the hospital had for several years been under the leadership of a certain Gerard, who is now revered, most probably correctly, as the effective founder of the Order of St John. Gerard survived the siege of Jerusalem and the crusaders' violent storming of the city on 15 July, and was therefore well placed to provide invaluable institutional continuity as the hospital adapted to Latin Christian control of parts of Syria and Palestine in the wake of the crusade, and to the substantial increase in pilgrim traffic from western Europe that resulted.[2]

The hospital became an important element of the emergent western Christian establishment in Jerusalem, a status confirmed by the grant in 1113 of its first papal bull, *Pie postulatio voluntatis*, which inaugurated what would be an enduring and important relationship with the papacy. A large complex was constructed in Jerusalem (it has now mostly disappeared) which one observer claimed, perhaps with some exaggeration, could house 1,000 patients in normal circumstances and twice that number in emergencies. There was a dedicated obstetric ward, with cots provided for newborns. Muslim and Jewish patients were sometimes admitted; it would seem that provision was made for their dietary requirements. It is a truism that western medicine at this time was less sophisticated than that practised in the east; and while this contrast is easily overdrawn, there is evidence to suggest that the regimen followed in the hospital was receptive to Muslim and Jewish medical knowledge. Additionally, it is probable that the order was influenced by the expertise being developed in Salerno, which is, significantly, close to Amalfi, and which in the later eleventh and twelfth centuries was becoming the principal centre of medical learning in western Europe. A signature element of the Salernitan approach to patient care was an emphasis on comfort, which one sees echoed in the hospital's attention to patients' well-being in matters of bedding, clothing and diet.[3]

In its concern for the welfare of pilgrims and others in need, the hospital was part of a creative burst of expressions of the religious life in western Christianity between the late eleventh and early thirteenth centuries. Some of the new institutions that emerged reasserted traditional monastic ideals of withdrawal and enclosure. But others sought to undertake pastoral responsibilities or to minister to the faithful in various ways. The Order of St John or 'Hospitallers', as we may now call them, fell into this latter category of active engagement with the world. This is important to keep in mind because it is the base-line explanation for how and why the Hospital came to assume a second, and on the face of it paradoxically incompatible, identity: that of a military order. The exact chronology of the militarization of the Order of St John is much debated, but the broad outlines are fairly clear. An openness to adopting some form of military function would seem to have emerged in the 1120s and to have become more entrenched over the following two decades, as suggested by the order's willingness, first in 1136 and then in the early 1140s, to assume responsibility for important castles in exposed frontier regions of the Latin East, the regions of Syria and Palestine ruled by western Europeans in the wake of the First Crusade. In theory a religious institution taking possession of a castle would have been able to contract its day-to-day operations out to vassals and mercenaries. But it is likely that already at this stage there were members of the order, brother-knights, who were specialists in military affairs.

By the third quarter of the twelfth century, if not before, the brother-knights were becoming the dominant element in the order's leadership. The Order of the Temple, which had been created in the 1120s as a dedicated military institution, may have exerted a gravitational pull on the Hospital's sense of mission and self-identity. From this point onwards the male membership of the Hospital – there were also sisters of the order – was tripartite: brother-knights, priests, and sergeants or servants, who performed subordinate military duties and other ancillary roles. The expansion of the order's responsibilities made good sense. The military pressure on the Latin East was enormous and its human resources were stretched very thin, whereas the Hospital was becoming ever richer thanks to donations of lands and incomes by benefactors in western Europe. Surely it made sense to use these resources not just for the healing of the sick but also for the defence of the Latin settlements. The militarization of the order, then, which had in no way been pre-programmed into its earliest incarnation, became, once entertained as a possibility, a central strand of its operations and self-image within the space of about a generation.[4]

The brother-knights are sometimes rather luridly described as 'warrior monks' or the 'monks of war'. This is inaccurate in the technical but important sense that the inspiration for the Hospital's vocation and its early regulations drew more on a text known as the Rule of St Augustine, which was geared towards religious orders that operated out in the world, than on the Rule of St Benedict, the standard blueprint for life in a monastery in the western Christian tradition. The brethren of the order took vows of poverty, chastity and obedience, as did monks and nuns, but not of stability, the promise to remain one's whole life in one place.[5] By the time of the siege the brother-knights had been the dominant element in the order for several centuries, both in terms of numbers and in the structures of governance. Although they were professed religious – they were bound by their vows to membership of the order for life and could not marry – they remained laymen in the sense that they were not ordained. The Hospital as a whole thus bucked the trend in the medieval period for male religious orders to become increasingly clericalized. A heavy burden was consequently placed on the priestly wing of the Hospital, fewer in number than the knights, to perform the necessary clerical duties such as hearing confessions and celebrating mass in the order's main churches. Recruitment of high-calibre clerics into the order was always a challenge; the brightest and the best would usually be able to secure more attractive and prestigious positions elsewhere.

Jerusalem fell to the forces of Saladin in 1187, after which the Hospitallers relocated their central convent, or headquarters, to the principal Palestinian city that remained in Latin Christian hands, Acre (modern Akko in northern Israel). When Acre itself was taken by the Mamluks in 1291, and the remnants of Latin control in Palestine and Syria were extinguished, the order was forced to move again, first to Cyprus as one element of the Frankish refugee community that gathered there, and then to Rhodes, which it conquered from its Greek rulers between 1306 and 1310.[6] By the thirteenth century, and possibly earlier, the order had developed some expertise in operating a flotilla of ships, which it needed to transport personnel, supplies and money from its properties in western Europe. It was a fairly small step, therefore, once on Cyprus, to expand its naval presence by acquiring galleys, the optimal vessels for aggressive military operations in Mediterranean waters. The relocation to Rhodes made this metamorphosis from a land-based military operation into a naval – or more accurately, amphibious – force a permanent reality. Although at the time of the order's move to Rhodes there was a Latin Christian presence in various parts of the eastern Mediterranean – in the kingdom of Cyprus, on islands governed by the Italian mercantile cities of Venice and Genoa, and in parts of Greece – the Hospital was ideally placed and ideologically primed to fashion itself as the principal legatee of the tradition of militant western Christianity in the region.

Rhodes is positioned tight up against the mainland of southwestern Anatolia, which is less than twenty kilometres away; and, as if a further provocation were needed to remind the local Muslim rulers of the order's nagging presence in their own backyard, in the early fifteenth century the Knights (as we may now label them, with a capital 'K') began the construction of the powerful castle of Bodrum on the mainland coast facing Kos. The period of the order's presence on Rhodes coincided more or less exactly with the Ottomans' rise from an emergent force in the confused politics of the Anatolian interior to imperial hegemony. It was against an increasingly unified and powerful near neighbour, therefore, that the order came to wage a *Kleinkrieg*, or 'small war', of raiding and the interception of shipping, in effect self-sanctioned piracy. The order survived several Ottoman assaults and, as those at Plessis-lèz-Tours well knew, a major siege in 1480. What doomed the Knights' already precarious position was the Ottoman conquest of Egypt in 1516–17, for now Rhodes threatened a shipping route between Alexandria and Istanbul that was vital to the Ottomans' strategic interests. On 1 January 1523, after a long and exceptionally hard-fought siege, and thanks to the notably generous terms offered by the young Süleyman I, the Knights, together with a significant number of Rhodiots, marched out of Rhodes city and sailed away, first to Crete and from there into an uncertain future.[7]

So began a fraught seven years of wandering from place to place in Italy and Provence.[8] Various European rulers were approached for help, including François I of France and Henry VIII of England. In practical terms, however, it was clear that any workable solution to the order's predicament would have to be found in the Mediterranean. This placed the onus squarely on the emperor, Charles V, who through his mother, Joanna, the daughter of the Catholic Monarchs, Isabella of Castile and Ferdinand of Aragon, had inherited not only their Spanish dominions but also a complex of territories across the western Mediterranean which included the kingdoms of Naples and Sicily, Sardinia and a series of fortified outposts, or *presidios*, on the north African coast. The Maltese archipelago had for several centuries functioned as a political outlier of whatever regime was in power in Sicily, and it was therefore in his capacity as ruler of that kingdom that Charles offered Malta to the Knights in 1527. After some back and forth, the Knights came to appreciate that they had no choice but to accept; and so it was that they took possession of the Maltese islands in August 1530.[9]

Part of the arrangement with Charles was that the Knights should also assume responsibility for the defence of Tripoli, in modern-day Libya, the most easterly and vulnerable of the Spanish *presidios*; this, rather than the political future of the Maltese islands, was most probably Charles's immediate priority at the time. An old-fashioned but persistent vision of the order's acquisition of Malta would have it that this was a case of a busy ruler with far-flung interests and much bigger fish to fry parking the remnants of a weak and curiously anachronistic organization out of the way. The apparently trivial nature of the *quid pro quo* that Charles stipulated in return, the annual gift of a falcon, is, in this view, proof that he was simply using a minor and peripheral portion of his dominions in order to solve a problem that was very low down his list of priorities, and at very little cost to himself. A more realistic interpretation of the relationship forged in 1530 is that, on the contrary, Charles was enthusiastic about the opportunity that the order's travails presented, in that it confirmed him in an emerging desire to pursue a more forward policy in the central and western Mediterranean, as subsequently revealed by his conquest of Tunis in 1535, a victory that was heavily exploited in aid of Charles's imperial self-fashioning, and the equally ambitious and grandiose expedition against Algiers in 1541, which ended in disaster.[10] The falcon, as a bird associated with the aristocratic pursuit of hunting and with notions of nobility, should, moreover, not be seen as an empty token, but as an appreciative nod to the value that the Knights resolutely attached to their high social status, even in their straitened circumstances. The fact that the order's records show that this annual obligation was assiduously respected is noteworthy.

Hugely disruptive as the order's odyssey must have been, the fact that only seven and a half years separated the departure from Rhodes and the arrival in Malta is significant, for it ensured that memories of Rhodes were sufficiently fresh to be carried over into the Maltese settlement. But what was it that Rhodes represented and how might it inform a renewed sense of purpose within the order? Did 'Rhodes' mean entrenching oneself in a maximally exposed position on the very margins of the religious frontier, in which case Tripoli should be the Knights' priority? Or did 'Rhodes' mean a relatively secure island-state, within a contested frontier zone, to be sure, and deriving its sense of identity from that fact, but not so liminal as to be relentlessly vulnerable on a day-to-day basis: in other words a blueprint for Malta?[11] For two decades after 1530 the order wrestled with the question of which paradigm should be decisive. In the later 1540s it decided on a phased relocation of the convent from Malta to Tripoli; Jean de La Valette, governor of Tripoli between 1546 and 1549 and future Grand Master of the order, was a staunch supporter of this policy. In the event, delays in carrying the plan forward meant that the problem was effectively taken out of the Knights' hands by the fall of Tripoli in August 1551 to an Ottoman armada.[12] As we shall see, this setback persuaded the order to invest more in Malta, literally and figuratively; work soon began on a programme of new fortifications which, because of cost constraints, were far from impressive but which in 1565 just about did enough to determine the outcome of the siege. As Michel de l'Hôpital's deft reaction to La Roche's presentation at Plessis suggests, the siege represented a further way of mobilizing the memory of Rhodes: as the site of epic resistance against a superior and inexorable Ottoman foe. It seemed fitting, therefore, a kind of ring narrative reaching a satisfactory closure, that La Valette was a living link between the two sieges, having fought on Rhodes in 1522 when he was in his later twenties.

Enfeebled as the order was as it began to establish itself in the Maltese islands, it nonetheless retained various sources of strength. One was its dogged retention of the hospitaller ideal as a demonstration of its institutional continuity. It is striking how assiduously the Knights ensured that a hospital was established wherever they fetched up during their years of wandering exile: at one point the hospital was set up on board one of their ships, at another under canvas on a beach in the Bay of Naples.[13] In this context it is worth noting that, over the course of its long history, the Order of St John did not by and large produce many star names in the spiritual or intellectual life of the Catholic Church, nor many who rose to the very top of the ecclesiastical hierarchy. The former Hospitaller Pope Clement VII (1523–34) was one of the exceptions. This was not a deficiency specific to the Knights, but a tendency among all those religious orders that performed practical, 'hands-on' roles in the world, as against those that were able to carve out the time and space for its members to pursue penitential asceticism, a charismatic preaching ministry, spiritual reflection, deep book-learning, or some combination of these. That being said, the order was unusual in pursuing two very different expressions of the religious life, an ambitious combination which struck contemporaries as interesting and laudable in itself. After all, an important reason why the Hospital had avoided the fate of the Templars when they were suppressed in 1307–12 was that it could appeal to its hospitaller tradition as an enduring source of legitimacy.

It would be wrong to dismiss the order's hospitaller activity as little more than tokenistic display, although there was always a tendency to draw attention to the work of the infirmary, the Sacra Infermeria, so as to cast the Knights in the best possible light. On Malta the hospital absorbed about 5–10 per cent of the order's annual income, which may not seem very much until one bears in mind the enormous, and constantly rising, costs of building, maintaining and garrisoning fortifications, and of operating even a small flotilla of galleys and support vessels. The cost margin represented by the hospital would have been very vulnerable had it not been non-negotiable. The order's attentiveness to the creation of a Maltese hospital, first in Birgu and, in due course, in an impressive complex modelled on that on Rhodes in Valletta, is particularly noteworthy because, unlike the convent's previous locations in the Holy Land and eastern Mediterranean, Malta was not a significant pilgrimage destination for outsiders, nor an important staging post for pilgrims en route elsewhere. Although there would have been some transient and seasonal population in the port area of Grand Harbour, which struck contemporaries as a quite cosmopolitan community, the main group served by the hospital – the members of the order had their own infirmary – would have been the Maltese themselves.

A second source of strength was the order's ability to draw on widespread resources in the form of landed estates spread across many parts of western Europe, property portfolios which in many instances had, as their core, lands, rights and incomes donated to the Knights by aristocratic benefactors in the first flush of popular enthusiasm for the order and its activities in the Latin East in the twelfth and earlier thirteenth centuries. Although the rate at which pious donors supported the order, as against other more fashionable expressions of the religious life, tailed off thereafter, the Knights received an unexpected boost to their assets when it was agreed that the Templars' properties (other than in Spain) should be transferred to them when the Temple was suppressed.[14] In the event, only some of the Temple's resources found their way to the Hospital, but they were nonetheless welcome just as the order was confronting the challenge of developing its new base on Rhodes. The Hospitaller property at Cressing Temple in Essex, famous for its surviving medieval barns, is, as its name reveals, one example of a Templar estate that did find its way to the Hospital. The order's properties were grouped into units called commanderies or preceptories, which were themselves organized into about twenty large regional blocs, or priories.[15] Although at least the wealthier commanderies could function as local religious centres and even make some modest provision for the sick or poor, they were essentially units of estate management. The commanderies, through the priories, were expected to send remittances, or responsions, to the central convent; by the sixteenth century this was generally fixed at a third of their incomes. In practice this target was not always met, but conversely the order could, and often did, make supernumerary demands: it is noteworthy that several such additional levies were decreed in the years leading up to the Great Siege, as the Knights did whatever they could afford to bolster Malta's weak defences. The responsions and levies were the order's economic lifeline. During his stay in Malta, Brantôme was told the story of the capture by corsairs off Naples of a galley bringing 20,000 *scudi*, a substantial sum, from France, the subtext of the anecdote being that any interruption of the movement of precious resources along the Knights' vulnerable supply routes would be met with great alarm.[16]

It was not just corsairs and storms in the Mediterranean that threatened the order's well-being. Its assets were vulnerable to political and religious disruptions in Europe. The effects of the Reformation and its hostility to religious orders were especially serious, as one would expect: the impacts were uneven but significant in Germany, in line with the patchwork quality of the spread of reform ideas in that area; but they proved wholly destructive in England because of the efficient central organization driving the Dissolution and the crown's appropriation of various orders' assets. Such was the devastation wrought on the Hospital in England, even after a period of modest revival during the brief reign of the Catholic Mary Tudor (1553–8), that by the time of the Great Siege there was, famously, only one English Knight in Malta, Oliver Starkey.[17] Scotland struggled on for a time as a source of recruitment and income. But just one year before the siege, in February 1564, the most senior surviving Knight in Scotland, Sir James Sandilands of Calder, effectively signed off on the extinction of the order there by surrendering all its Scottish properties to Mary, Queen of Scots, who then granted some of them back to him as a secular, hereditary barony centred on what had been the order's most important Scottish possession, Torphichen, west of Edinburgh. Sandilands clearly understood the way the wind was blowing in his homeland: last recorded among his fellow Knights in Malta in 1557, by 1560 he had cultivated ties to the Protestant Lords of the Congregation and in about 1563 even got married to a noblewoman.[18] The stop-start progress of the Reformation in northern Europe meant that the order was by degrees thrown back onto a southern, Romance-speaking core, which had in any event always been the area where most of its assets were located and from where the majority of its members were recruited. Its existence and form of religious life were reassuringly endorsed by the Catholic Church's formal response to the Protestant challenge, the Council of Trent (1545–63); and the order, somewhat reduced but more compact, could thenceforth make a virtue of presenting itself as the sword-arm of a newly reinvigorated and militant Counter-Reformation Catholicism.[19]

A final source of strength was the class or more accurately caste cohesion of the Knights, whose domination of the order meant that its ethical tone was grounded in the values associated with aristocratic status, hierarchy and notions of noble virtue. In practice the order was a coalition of the various inflections of nobility to be found in different parts of western Europe, reflexes, for example, of the degree to which the dominant social elite in a given area was an urban patriciate, as was often the case in Italy, or derived its wealth from the exploitation of rural estates.[20] The extent to which members of a national or regional elite gravitated towards the court of a ruler and built courtly behaviours and attitudes into their self-fashioning was another important variable. The order's military ethos served, however, as a powerful common denominator. Those wishing to join the order did not have to demonstrate a particular aptitude for navigation, seamanship or the skills specific to amphibious warfare, despite the centrality of the order's galley fleet to its military operations.[21] Although a working knowledge of matters of navigation and the waters of the Mediterranean would have been something that many Knights would have sought to acquire, in practice only a minority would have ever needed to develop a specialism as mariners. On the other hand, all new Knights were expected to bring to their vocation the traditional elite male accomplishments of horsemanship and a facility in handling swords and other bladed weapons. The Knights were not in the business of training their future *confrères* from scratch. Consequently, although boys and youths were sometimes admitted and served as pages and squires in anticipation of their joining the order fully in due course, the optimal age for the reception of new brethren was their later teens, by which time they would have spent their childhood and adolescence developing a proficiency in the aristocratic military arts and would already have been dubbed as knights.

In its early centuries, the order would seem to have mostly attracted the sons of families on the lower rungs of the aristocracy. By the sixteenth century, however, the median status of those entering the order had risen, in the process stimulating a mood of self-conscious exclusivity or, in plainer terms, an intense and assiduously cultivated snobbery. A clear indication of the order's elitism was the fact that a postulant seeking admission into the order, in addition to establishing that the standard impediments did not apply – that he was sound in body and mind, was not of ill repute, was not married, was not a member of another order, was not illegitimate, and was not in debt – needed to demonstrate that he was of noble descent. The order's sensitivity to matters of lineage can be traced back to the thirteenth and fourteenth centuries but was much more in evidence in the early modern period. If we look ahead to the seventeenth century, we find many surviving examples of beautiful documents presented by postulants which illustrated, with finely drawn coats of arms, their descent from their eight impeccably noble great-grandparents. We are not quite at this stage in the sixteenth century, though by the time of the siege the essentials of the system were already in place. Originally, the requirement as to proof of nobility had only applied to the paternal line, but under Grand Master Juan de Homedes (1536–53) this was formally doubled up to include the mother's side, which had only intermittently been considered up till then. This was confirmed in 1555 by the order's General Chapter, its supreme legislative body, which also insisted on purity of blood, an adaptation of the contemporary Spanish preoccupation with *limpieza de sangre*, the notion that someone should have no Muslim or Jewish ancestry. The sheer amount of time, painstaking effort and resources that the order was willing to expend in taking statements from witnesses and hunting down whatever written evidence of a postulant's noble pedigree might be available is compelling proof of the enormous importance that it attached to the policing of its social exclusivity.[22]

There was always an unresolved tension within the Knights' view of themselves, as well as in the perception of them by others. Were they the epitome, or at least one meritorious distillation, of the ideals of noble virtue, military masculinity and social prestige to which all aristocratic men in Europe should aspire?[23] Or were those elements of their vocation and way of life which set them apart from the normal run of the lay aristocracy what made them worthy of attention, affording them a visibility and cachet out of proportion to their numbers (which were usually about 1,200, not counting the priests and sergeants)? A good case has been made for supposing that characters representing the military orders play a respected but only marginal role in medieval works of literature that explored and celebrated the ideals of courtliness and chivalry.[24] On the other hand, there is evidence that, as the Hospital became more socially exclusive in the early modern period, the idea developed of a two-way ideological exchange between the Knights and the broader aristocratic culture from which they were recruited. This is demonstrated very clearly by the *Ricordi overo ammaestramenti* ('Recollections or Teachings') of a senior Italian Knight, Sabba da Castiglione (*c.*1480–1554). Sabba was a cousin of Baldassare Castiglione, whose hugely influential conduct book, *The Book of the Courtier*, was a source of inspiration for his own work.[25] Sabba, however, opened up his frame of reference beyond Baldassare's tight focus on life in and around a court in order to establish a programme of Christian ethics, infused with fashionable humanist values and classical models, that was applicable to male members of Europe's social elite.

The *Ricordi* was a notable success, going through twenty-six editions between 1546 and 1633. Sabba's work is framed as advice tendered to his great-nephew Bartolomeo, who had recently joined the order. Although much of the work comprised prescriptions that were, in the main, pertinent to Bartolomeo's future as a Hospitaller, it also contained a number of discursive essays on themes of general application to the Christian life. There is even a section on marriage and the qualities to be sought in a wife.[26] The model to which Bartolomeo should aspire, then, was Janus-faced, looking inwards into the particular demands that the Religion made of its members, and outwards into an ambitious ethical programme suitable for elite laymen in general. The image of the optimal Knight that emerges from the text is of someone who is quite held-in, self-disciplined, sober, and cautious in choosing his friends, but socially adaptable, trustworthy, respectful of hierarchies, mindful of his reputation, culturally accomplished and physically active. He should steer a middle course between greed and prodigality; he should keep himself clean and tidy, but shun the vain frippery of perfumes, jewels and fine clothing; and he should stay away from festivities, shows and other vulgar entertainments.[27] He should, of course, be knowledgeable in matters of war, including, it might be noted, siege craft and fortifications.[28] And he should be scrupulously chaste as well as attentive to the honour of women, especially that of poor women, given that their reputation is their only asset when it comes to making good marriages.[29]

Sabba's prescriptions were cited approvingly by later writers, including Giacomo Bosio in his *Corona del cavaliere Gierosolimitano* ('The Crown of the Knight of Jerusalem', 1588), and duly informed subsequent how-to manuals and works of advice for young Knights.[30] They thus became embedded in the image of itself that the order liked to cultivate and to present to the world. As Sabba noted, however, when commenting on life in ancient Rome but with clear reference to his own day, 'virtue was always a rare thing in the world'.[31] It is perhaps unsurprising, therefore, that a very different picture of the Knights emerges when we turn from Sabba's idealized image to the routinely sordid and vicious realities of life in the Maltese convent, as revealed by the order's records, in particular memoranda of the actions taken against malefactors by the Council, the order's executive and judicial board chaired by the Grand Master. We have to exercise caution, of course: most Knights were not found guilty of serious infractions of the order's Rule and statutes, and are in fact far more likely to appear in the surviving records as litigants in what we would term civil cases, often in suits brought against one another. A few names, moreover, obviously the notorious bad eggs, crop up in the criminal record time and again. On the other hand, it would be wrong to suppose that criminality was limited to a few hard-core miscreants. Anne Brogini has carefully tabulated the number and type of recorded offences in the decades after the order's arrival in Malta.[32] Some offences were crimes against property, particularly theft, or against the order's ethical code – blasphemy and disobedience. About half of the recorded cases, on the other hand, involved crimes against the person.

On the basis of Brogini's figures for the 1550s and 1560s, and given that the complement of Knights resident in Malta in normal conditions, when additional numbers had not been summoned in anticipation of particularly grave military threats, was around 300–400, it would seem that in any given year in those decades between 5 and 10 per cent of the Knights were involved, as a perpetrator, victim or both, in violent acts that were sufficiently serious and consequential to attract the attention of the authorities. That estimate nudges up somewhat when one bears in mind that several cases involved more than two principals, and could sometimes amount to large brawls or acts of organized collective violence. It is noteworthy that Brogini's figures go up in the 1570s and 1580s, before declining thereafter, as if to suggest, in ways that are difficult to specify, that the order was working through the traumatic effects

Violence, Vanity and Vocation: The Knights of Malta

of the siege, not least the death of about 300 members and the incapacitation of many more. Without overdramatizing day-to-day conditions in the convent, therefore, we can say that there were blurred boundaries between, on the one hand, the ideals of laudable and ennobling violence that were wired into the order's vocation and self-image, and which it believed it played out in its military operations, and on the other the various impulses and self-justifications that fed into numerous acts of private violence, be they hot-headed, soberly vengeful, or simply the expressions of a cold and vicious hauteur.

Part of the problem was demographic. The order's career structure required that young Knights should live in Malta in order to perform three 'caravans', each a period of several months' service on the galleys. This entitled the Knight to promotion to supervision of a commandery. Some Knights would have bided their time in Malta, weighing up their options and waiting for a preferred posting, but the net effect was to siphon mid-career, 'middle-management' brethren away from the central convent to the order's dispersed European properties. Some, a minority, would carve out careers in the hierarchy in Malta, and would in due course come to dominate the old guard ruling over mostly young men. Part, too, of the problem was domestic. In theory Knights resident in the convent were expected to live in the auberges, the dormitories of their respective langues, or national groupings; but in practice more and more were relocating to private dwellings, thereby gaining greater freedom from official supervision and routine peer pressure. In 1562, for example, a Scottish Knight, John James Sandilands (not to be confused with the James Sandilands whom we have already encountered), was granted permission by the Grand Master to sell a house that he owned in Birgu, quite possibly to pay off gambling debts.[33] A consequence of greater domestic autonomy was that Knights could more easily enter into a variety of sexual relationships ranging from one-off exchanges with prostitutes to long-term partnerships. Of all the vows taken by incoming Knights, that of chastity was the least scrupulously observed and the least policed, the order generally turning a blind eye to heterosexual liaisons which were conducted discreetly and with some nod to decorum.[34]

There was, as a result, a substantial community of courtesans and prostitutes in the Grand Harbour area. Their number, and the variety of places from which they came, struck Nicolas de Nicolay, a French visitor to Malta in 1551: the print that he chose to accompany his published description of the island is of a Maltese prostitute. The English traveller George Sandys, who visited Malta in 1611, was similarly taken by the number of prostitutes, most of whom he took to be Greek: as he wryly noted, they would sit in their doorways playing instruments and 'with the art of their eyes inveagle these continent by vow, but contrary in practice, as if chastity were onely violated by mariage'.[35] It was only when the domestic arrangements that Knights formed with female companions broke down, or they acted violently towards or over women, that this world within a world surfaces in the order's records. Sometimes the evidence is very laconic. In 1547, we are told, two French Knights named Gerard de la Tour and Claude Asuard wounded a man from Piacenza called Coghelena 'on account of a woman'.[36] Sometimes there is a little more circumstantial detail to work with, though the underlying human dynamics remain elusive. That violence against women came easily to several Knights is, however, abundantly clear.[37] In 1549 Giacomo Melleghini burst into a married woman's house and raped her, while his servant struck a second woman in the face with a stone; he may be the person of that name who around the same time was charged with exposing himself in public.[38] The following year Francesco Gesualdo was imprisoned for two years and ordered to pay twenty-five *scudi* as compensation to a woman named Agnese whom he had raped.[39] In 1552 an English Knight with a history as a troublemaker, Oswald Massingberd, broke into the house of a Maltese nobleman, beat him up, and abducted a female slave and her daughter.[40]

The list goes on. In 1554 two Knights, Adrien de Lugny and Claude Constant, were found guilty of throwing stones at the doors of the house of Constantia Venturina.[41] In 1556 a Knight named Torquato

Torto wounded Isabella Calli and was sentenced to a year in prison; the following year he attacked her again and was forbidden from having any contact with her in future.[42] Perhaps it was jealousy over a bride that drove two Knights in 1559 to violently disrupt a Greek wedding celebration.[43] Now and then some of the Knights' interactions with women, at least as they appear in the criminal record, seem to have been informed by a chivalric impulse: in 1556 three Knights helped Hieronyma Olivier to escape from her probably abusive husband; and in 1572 Alexandre Vagnon was punished for having sheltered Antonia Cardinale, a bandit and a fellow Knight's mistress, in his home.[44] More typical, however, was the sort of exploitative cruelty on show in perhaps the most unsettling case of all, when in 1536 an English Knight, Christopher Myers, was convicted – and executed – for killing a woman, in all likelihood a prostitute, who was described as *fere fatua*, 'well-nigh simple', which should probably be taken to mean that she was mentally disabled in some way.[45]

Although the pattern of violence against women seems to have been persistent, most recorded cases involved aggression against other men. The spare phraseology of the records means that it is usually impossible to examine motivations, but in some cases we are offered a little suggestive context. Litigation seems to have fuelled animosities that could readily spill over into verbal outbursts or physical violence.[46] Tempers could also flare in the performance of official duties, as might have been the case in a fight between Gerard de la Tour, captain of the artillery, and Michele Masso, captain of the slaves, perhaps because the slaves had been used to reposition cannon without Masso's permission.[47] Occasionally, it was a straightforward case of mugging or aggravated burglary: in 1566 a Knight named Louis de Marso broke into the home of another Knight, Gaspard Mallet, killed him and made off with a large sum of money and other valuables.[48] A combination of the stresses of life at sea, the very cramped and unsanitary conditions in a galley, and the usual presence on board of a group of young and inexperienced *caravanisti* helps to explain the significant number of violent incidents that are recorded taking place at sea or in ports of call.[49] At times, the claustrophobic world of the galley must have been the setting for very fraught moments of dissent that danced on the edges of mutiny. In 1559 two Knights on board the *San Filipo* started a fracas when they tried to prevent the captain from disciplining a soldier and clapping him in irons for disobedience.[50] In 1562 a fight between two Knights on the order's *Capitana*, or flagship, escalated into a brawl; it would seem that tensions over the distribution of goods illicitly seized from Christian vessels may have been a factor.[51] Sometimes violence simply begat violence in tit-for-tat acts of retribution: in December 1562 Martin des Moulins was wounded by Fernando de Heredia when he was set upon by a gang of four Knights; then in March 1563 Moulins was accused of having attempted to strike Heredia with his sword 'treacherously and insidiously', which probably means coming up suddenly from behind.[52] There are also indications that national rivalries could spill over into violence: a five-on-four brawl in 1563 was, to judge by the names of those involved, a case of French and Italian Knights coming to blows.[53]

Duelling was increasingly in vogue among the European nobility from around the second quarter of the sixteenth century, so it is not surprising to find some examples in the order's records.[54] Pre-arranged and staged combats seem to have been relatively unusual, however, although they may lie behind some of the references to wounds received to the hands, head or stomach.[55] Much more common in the records are incidents described as *rixae*, which typically involved armed confrontations between two men or small groups, but could also amount to serious incidents of group violence, as when in 1548 an argument between a number of Knights and some soldiers in the order's pay escalated to the point where the Knights chased their opponents into a tower and fired on them, ignoring orders to desist; three Knights were subsequently expelled from the order and seven more imprisoned.[56] The fact that several fights are described as breaking out in auberges, the Knights' principal venue for socializing, confirms the suspicion that drink lay

Violence, Vanity and Vocation: The Knights of Malta

behind a large number of incidents.[57] Gambling, which was widespread, was doubtless another routine flashpoint.

Although it was common for the Knights to visit violence on one another, it is important to bear in mind that their victims were often their social inferiors, which suggests that hierarchies of power and obedience were frequently at stake: there are many records of assaults on and the wounding of servants, slaves, merchants, brother-sergeants and soldiers (who sometimes fought back).[58] The assault by Jacques de Fanes de Salgues, a chaplain of the order, on a boy named Jean de Montpellier, in which he picked up a stone and struck Jean on the head so hard that it killed him, stands out as especially callous, but was far from atypical.[59] For the most part, the Knights wounded each other and third parties with weapons, occasionally firearms but more usually swords and daggers. Whether blood was drawn seems to have been an important criterion in judging the severity of an incident.[60] The records, however, also make frequent reference to assaults by means of the *alapa*, a word which could refer in general to any manual blow, in contradistinction to a wounding with a weapon, but in most cases would seem to have particularly denoted an open-handed slap or cuff as opposed to a straightforward punch. This could be used both on social inferiors by way of reminding them who was in charge, and on fellow Knights, in which case it was clearly something more than a spontaneous act; its aim was to humiliate and demasculinize one's opponent. The fact that assaults by *alapa* alone were punished, not only when they led to something else, suggests that those sitting in judgement in the Council well understood the theatrical quality of this gesture and the powerful meanings that attached to it.[61] The *alapa* is a reminder that the ways in which the Knights gave expression to their deeply ingrained propensity for violence lay along a broad spectrum, from crimes of passion and outbursts of raw rage to cool, semi-ritualized performances of aristocratic disdain.

One of the most troubled careers as a Knight to emerge from the records is that of the aforementioned John James Sandilands. In May 1557 he was sentenced to six months in close confinement for having provoked a *rixa* with his kinsman James Sandilands. Later that year James instigated an investigation into John James's noble credentials: one wonders what murky family history lay underneath this deep animosity. A dispute between the two over the succession to the preceptory of Torphichen followed in 1559, the same year in which John James got into a fight in which he was wounded in the ear and hand. In 1562 he was forced to sell his house in Birgu, as we have seen. In September 1563 he was involved in a bizarre incident when he and another Knight got into an argument while they were gambling in a church, the stakes for which they were playing – at cards or dice – consisting of an African slave and a gold cross. For this he was sentenced to two months in prison. He subsequently got into a fight with Oliver Starkey – a slice of Anglo-Scottish animosity transposed to the central Mediterranean – and was deprived of the habit of the order. It would seem, however, that this sentence was commuted, for in May 1564 he was still in Malta, involved with another errant Knight, Filippo Stagno, in a notorious act of sacrilege, the heist of precious objects from the church of San Antonio in Birgu. Having been tortured to secure a confession, and perhaps to give up the names of his accomplices, he was defrocked for a second time. He then absconded.[62] His eventual fate is unknown. Perhaps he was recaptured, in which case he would have been handed over to the secular authorities for execution, the order, as a religious institution, being unable to inflict the death penalty directly. If so, he would have been sewn into a weighted sack and thrown from a boat into Grand Harbour. But maybe he got away.

The worst form of punishment that the order could itself impose was to send miscreants to a tiny prison cell-cum-dungeon, the *guva*, the 'cage' or 'hole'. One of these was found by chance in St Angelo, one of the order's fortresses in Grand Harbour, in 1913. It is a terrifying, bell-shaped void, cut out of the rock, about four metres wide and three and a half metres deep, the only entrance a one-metre-wide opening at the top.[63] Around its walls are various graffiti carved by some of its many inmates, including coats of arms and a rather fine representation of what may be a hearse, as well as mysterious figures that may depict those in sacks awaiting execution.[64] One graffito was incised by John James during one of his periods of incarceration, a plaintive Latin poem which reads: 'John James Sandilands / Sent to prison / In this living tomb / The destruction of the good / The consolation of my enemies / A lesson for my friends.'[65] Was Sandilands a misfit who struggled to meet the standards expected of him as a member of a religious order, a troublemaker who invited the disapproval of his superiors as well as of his own family, a gambling addict driven to desperate measures, or an average sort of Knight who happened to be buffeted by historical forces beyond his control as the order's presence in his homeland collapsed? The records provide a stark and often troubling picture of the Knights' lives of easy violence, but this was born of contradictions which no Knight, however self-disciplined or high-minded, could ever have fully resolved. These were men who had been conditioned from a very young age to value their honour and status above all else, but who now found themselves caught between an instinctive urge for self-assertion and the obedience to which they had solemnly sworn. They were competitive as high-status men among men in a pressure-cooker homosocial environment, but they were part of a hierarchical, rule-bound organization that prized collaboration, conformity and the sort of buttoned-up self-control that Sabba da Castiglione had advocated. One must be careful not to take the Order of St John at its own estimation, but one should also avoid an easy cynicism about its many failures to live up to its ideals as a religious institution, ideals which it was never sufficiently equipped to meet. John James Sandilands and his travails are a glimpse into the human complexities that linger under the often troubled surface of the order's historical record.

2.

The Rewards of Relative Efficiency: The Ottomans

One of the most interesting figures to emerge from the history of the interactions between the Ottoman and Latin Christian worlds in the sixteenth century is Ogier Ghiselin de Busbecq.[1] A humanist scholar of note, he was chosen in 1554 by Charles V's brother Ferdinand, archduke of Austria and king of Bohemia, Hungary and Croatia, to be his ambassador to the Sublime Porte. Busbecq continued in that role when Ferdinand succeeded Charles as Holy Roman Emperor. He first arrived in Istanbul in early 1555, and would spend most of the next eight years in and around the Ottoman capital, recording his impressions of that place, its governing elites, its people and their customs in four Latin essays, 'The Turkish Letters', addressed to his friend and fellow diplomat Nicholas Michault.[2] Busbecq enjoys various claims to fame today. Diplomatic missions to the Ottoman court in the 1540s and 1550s were sometimes tantamount to humanist safaris, as scholars with various interests attached themselves to an ambassador's suite. It was when in such company, as he was travelling across Anatolia to catch up with the sultan, who was campaigning on the empire's eastern borders, that Busbecq is said to have discovered – from a western European standpoint, that is – the Monumentum Ancyranum, an inscription on the remains of a Roman temple at Ankara which preserves the fullest surviving version of the *Res gestae Divi Augusti*, the most important contemporary narrative source for the life and reign of the emperor Augustus. In fact the credit for finding the inscription and quickly grasping its significance almost certainly belongs to two of Busbecq's companions, Johannes Belsius, who was probably responsible for the transcription of the text that was made on the spot, and Hans Dernschwan. Nonetheless Busbecq was happy to insert himself into the story: 'We had it copied out by our people,' he loftily recorded.[3] Busbecq is also traditionally believed to have introduced the lilac and the tulip into western Europe, though again this may be a case of his name becoming attached to other people's achievements.[4] We are on more secure ground in noting that, as an avid collector and student of ancient coins, he was an important figure in the early development of numismatics as a subject of academic inquiry. He also did the future study of Germanic philology a great service by recording a short list of words in the Gothic language, which was still spoken in the Crimea in his day but has since become extinct.[5]

Busbecq was certainly no dove when it came to Habsburg relations with the Ottomans. In the 1570s he wrote a treatise entitled *Exclamatio, sive de re militari contra Turcam instituenda consilium* ('A loud appeal with advice about how to organize ourselves for war against the Turk').[6] His extended exposure to the Ottoman world, however, allowed him to develop a nuanced, even at times sympathetic, understanding. Like many western observers he was impressed and intimidated by the sultan's elite household infantry, the Janissaries, 'who carry such terror wherever they go'; but his account of being presented with flowers by the first group of Janissaries he encountered, in Buda, and of their antics in importuning him for a few coins, is light-hearted and almost affectionate.[7] In his dealings with the Ottoman government, he grew to appreciate one vizier, or senior minister, Ali Pasha, who struck him as cultivated, civilized and sophisticated.[8] For all their light and shade, however, Busbecq's letters contain several alarmist passages about what he believed was the Ottomans' overwhelming military strength: their armies were like 'mighty rivers swollen with rain' visiting 'infinite destruction' on their victims. He expressed very little faith in the ability of the Habsburgs, and by extension the larger club of western European princes, to offer any effective resistance.[9] In one particularly uncompromising passage Busbecq emphasized the contrast between the two sides' military capabilities. It is worth quoting one part of it, for the manner in which Busbecq framed his remarks is as important as their substance:

> I tremble when I think of what the future must bring when I compare the Turkish system with our own; one army must prevail and the other be destroyed, for certainly both cannot remain unscathed. On their side are the resources of a mighty empire, strength unimpaired, experience and practice in fighting, a veteran soldiery, habituation to victory, endurance of toil, unity, order, discipline, frugality, and watchfulness. On our side is public poverty, private luxury, impaired strength, broken spirit, lack of endurance and training; the soldiers are insubordinate, the officers avaricious; there is contempt for discipline; licence, recklessness, drunkenness, and debauchery are rife; and, worst of all, the enemy is accustomed to victory, and we to defeat. Can we doubt what the result will be?[10]

Busbecq was a highly accomplished Latinist; and here he is deploying a rhetorical technique routinely favoured by ancient Roman authors, which was to juxtapose starkly contrasting opposites. His aim is less to offer a dispassionate assessment of the Turkish state's military capacity than to persuade Christian rulers of the need for reform. But this sort of approach would not have had any purchase unless he and his readers did believe that, yes, the Ottomans were much tougher, more disciplined and better organized. Busbecq was by no means the only western commentator to pass this sort of judgement on the Ottomans' strength – a reaction that was one part jealousy, one part awe, one part frustration, and one part fear. Busbecq's close contemporary the Venetian Mario Savorgnano, a military theorist with experience of the Ottomans both on land and at sea, believed that the Turks were simply invincible; the best one could hope for in any conflict against them was to avoid defeat. Lazarus von Schwendi, the principal Habsburg commander in the Hungarian theatre in the 1560s, observed that one could only realistically aim to achieve modest, local successes against far superior forces.¹¹ Even if we make due allowance for the effects of exaggeration and cliché, were these fair assessments, and, if so, what did they mean in practice?

One way to approach this problem is to ask whether early modern Ottoman government and the society over which it ruled were specifically and predominantly organized for war. This sort of question has been posed of many premodern societies, for example the Frankish empire under Charlemagne and the borderlands of Spain during the *Reconquista*. To a certain extent it is one of those debates that historians confect by the very terms of reference that they devise. Was the Ottoman polity a war machine? It depends on what one means by that term. To a significant degree, however, the conviction that one finds expressed by the more reflective western observers – that there was a direct link between the Ottomans' system of governance and their ability to excel at warfare – was indeed borne out in many ways. The fundamental faultline that ran through Ottoman society vis-à-vis its relationship to public authority was that between an elite which did not pay tax and the mass of the general population, the *reaya*, which did. It is noteworthy that the members of the governing class favoured by this system were collectively known as the *askeri* – a word meaning 'soldierly' or 'warlike' – irrespective of whether they were actually 'military' in an occupational sense.¹² It is further significant that the governors of the basic unit of local government, the *sancak*, a word that revealingly means 'battle flag', 'standard', were, in addition to their administrative duties, expected to organize the mobilization of troops in their area and to serve as their commanders on campaign.

The most numerous elements among the Ottomans' frontline forces were the *sipahis*, who were remunerated by the grant of areas of land, *timars*, in return for equipping themselves as cavalrymen and presenting themselves for service when required, with mounted retainers armed at their expense if the size of the *timar* permitted. Although the *timar* is sometimes likened to the western fief, in the classic sense of a piece of land which constitutes the contractual *quid pro quo* for the performance of military service, it was in practice a hybrid of the fief proper and a money-fief, a grant of the right to draw an income from a specified source. In addition to exercising certain policing duties and overseeing agrarian arrangements as in effect the squire of his locality, the timariot collected the taxes paid by his *reaya* and put them to his immediate use, rather than remitting them up the chain of government. The predominant experience of the workings of the Ottoman state for many of its subjects was, therefore, to stump up cash and payments in kind for a local strongman, a cavalryman-on-standby.[13]

To a significant degree, also, the Ottomans' economic policies were keyed to what has been described as 'provisionism', a form of command economy in which supply and demand were substantially driven by those government operations considered vital to the public weal: building projects and civic works in Istanbul and other imperial centres such as Edirne in Thrace; the large imperial household and central bureaucracy; and the navy and army, including troops stationed on the empire's more vulnerable frontiers.[14] Western observers were frequently in awe of the resources that the Ottomans seemed to have at their disposal. A member of the French diplomatic mission in Istanbul in the 1550s, Jean Chesneau, expressed amazement that the sultan's head falconer had between 1,000 and 1,200 staff working under him, while the official in charge of the sultan's hunting dogs had 500 men.[15] Obviously such numbers were fed to foreigners by Ottoman officials in order to trumpet their power, but they also had a secure basis in fact. In a similar if more grandiose vein, Domenico Trevisano, the Venetian *bailo*, or ambassador to the Sublime Porte, reported in 1554 that the former grand vizier Rüstem Pasha (he would later resume that role) used to boast to him that the sultan's tax receipts were such that he commanded the resources to wage a major military campaign every year, without interruption, for eighty years.[16]

Clearly there was an element of diplomatic bluster or intimidation in such claims (though Trevisano for one was inclined to believe them). But Rüstem's emphasis on tax income as the decisive factor was judicious. Around the time of the Great Siege the equivalent of about 130 tons of silver was paid into the Ottoman treasury every year. We know that the government ran a relatively modest but sustained surplus until the end of the sixteenth century, which meant that it was able to maintain a strategic reserve that was regularly applied to military needs. Surprisingly, perhaps, the total income reaching the Ottoman treasury would seem to have been less than, albeit broadly commensurate with, that enjoyed by the French and Spanish crowns (though the fact that the taxes paid by the *reaya* to a timariot were collected and put to work at source means that the true tax burden borne by the Ottomans' subjects would have been significantly heavier).[17] The contrast with the Spanish Habsburg monarchy could not have been greater. Philip II largely paid for his many military commitments by borrowing against future income, as his father, Charles V, had regularly done. The debt burden that built up was enormous: the title of a detailed study of Philip's indebtedness, *Lending to the Borrower from Hell*, says it all.[18] It has been argued that in the long run the Ottomans' financial security bred a fiscal conservatism that inclined them to persist with traditional ways of raising money such as tax-farming, whereas western states prospered by learning to exploit manageably cheap debt.[19] But this would be to look too far ahead. At the time of the Great Siege, the relative strength of the competing powers in the Mediterranean was not a function of the raw amounts reaching the various governments' coffers, but of the cost efficiencies and effective organization that allowed the Ottoman state to punch substantially above its fiscal weight.[20]

Was the Ottoman state better governed than its European rivals? Machiavelli believed so: the sultan commanded the ingrained loyalty of his subordinates far more than did, say, the king of France; his standing army meant that he did not need to accommodate his subjects' wishes if he did not want to, provided he retained the loyalty of his elite troops; and the strength and continuity of the institutions of government were proof against the disruptions caused by a change of ruler.[21] Most other western writers concurred. They were especially struck by the fact that the viziers doubled up as military commanders, ensuring that the needs of government and of waging war were co-ordinated at the top. There was also an abiding fascination with the system of the *devşirme*, or 'collection'.[22] These were recruitment campaigns conducted on average every three or four years in those parts of the empire which had substantial Christian populations – mostly what are now modern Albania, Serbia and Croatia. Teams of collectors would travel between communities taking one child from a pre-determined number of households; in most cases these were boys, but some girls were taken to join the sultan's harem or those of members of the court elite. Most of the boys would face a long period of apprenticeship leading to membership of the Janissary corps or the household cavalry. A minority would be chosen for training in the imperial bureaucracy; those who made it all the way to the vizierate came from their ranks. Selection for this elite stream was on the basis of physiognomy and 'feel', not objective markers of intellectual ability such as an entrance exam. But for westerners of a humanist stamp, brought up in a world in which the social elites predominantly owed their positions to their birth, this was a fascinating exercise in meritocracy, in forging an aristocracy of service that it was believed gave the Ottomans an edge over their rivals.[23] One suspects that the Christian commentators had a point, although the advantage is difficult to quantify. The *devşirme* certainly contributed to a level of professionalism and an *esprit de corps* within the ranks of the Ottoman elite – though there could be bitter rivalries, of course – that were generally superior to those among the governing classes of western states. In a world in which the material and technological cultures of the Christian west and the Ottoman empire were fundamentally the same, any advantage in terms of political and organizational competence would make an important difference.

Although warfare in all its aspects, from growing the food that would feed soldiers and mariners to doing the fighting at the sharp end, permeated the lives of many Ottoman subjects, it would be prudent, as an eminent Ottomanist has argued, not to overstate the extent to which this was a society organized around war.[24] The Ottoman empire around the middle of the sixteenth century covered a vast area, stretching from central Europe to the Red Sea and from north Africa to the Persian Gulf. In this sprawling space of multiple ethnicities, languages, religious traditions and local economies, there lived twenty million subjects, far too many and too widely spread to have been touched by war in the same ways and to the same extent. The tax burden fell differently on different areas and on different groups of people. Additionally, the returns from war in the shape of booty did not have a significant impact on the economy as a whole, in contrast to its importance in the world of the Turks' distant cousins living in central Asia or on the Eurasian steppe. Nor, at least in the sixteenth century, was the Ottoman economy so geared to war that it could not ride out the inevitable negative effects of frequent mobilization – loss of production when men were taken away from their fields or workshops, falls in consumer demand, and a draining of the investment capital that might otherwise be available to stimulate growth.

In all this we need to be aware of the distorting lens of westerners' views of the Ottoman world, which, for all the rich human variety that travellers sometimes acknowledged and recorded, was believed to be energized by a palpable collective purpose characterized above all else by feelings of antipathy towards Christians in general and Latin Christians in particular.[25] In short, this, it seemed, was a world on a mission and everyone, or at least every Muslim subject of the sultan, bought into it in some way. The question of the impact of war on the economic and social life of the Ottoman empire, therefore, shades into a second question, which is the extent to which the sultan and his ministers pursued a grand strategy of conquest. Were they playing the long game to achieve their goals? Or were they, to use a phrase that Suraiya Faroqhi has borrowed from the idiom of British imperialists in later centuries, simply 'muddling through'?[26] Although these are not necessarily mutually exclusive propositions, the weight of evidence leans towards an ad hoc, opportunistic and largely reactive approach to warfare on the

Ottomans' part, one mindful of enduring traditions and ambitions but tempered by an appreciation of financial, technological and logistical constraints.[27] The notion that a society geared to war, to some considerable degree at any rate, must seek out new theatres of operation and new victims to sustain its sense of purpose and legitimacy is perhaps true, but trivially so. The absence, or at least relative unimportance, of a consistent strategy behind the Ottomans' programme of conquest is suggested by their tolerance of inconsistencies and anomalies. Cyprus, held by the Venetians, had lain astride the hugely significant supply route between Alexandria and Istanbul for more than fifty years after the Ottoman conquest of Egypt before it was invaded in 1570–71. Crete, the last piece of the jigsaw in the eastern Mediterranean, would only be taken from the Venetians after a drawn-out war in the middle of the seventeenth century. We shall see in a later chapter that there was a clear strategic element to the Ottoman decision to attack Malta, but that is not the same as saying that the conquest of Malta was part of a grand design, or that the Ottomans would have known exactly what to do with Malta had they acquired it.

As we have seen, many western visitors to the Ottoman empire in the decades before the Great Siege came away with a sense of irrepressible menace. In a considered review of the Ottomans' record of sustained military achievement, Domenico Trevisano observed that success had bred success and had been driven by its own internal logic.[28] To some extent, however, by the 1550s and 1560s the Ottomans were living off past glories, at least as far as campaigns on land were concerned. When Süleyman became sultan in 1520, the single greatest prize, Egypt and the other parts of the Mamluk empire, had already been won by his father, Selim I: it took some bedding in, and the defeat of rebellions, to make good on this spectacular addition to the Ottoman dominions, but by the mid 1520s, under the skilful direction of Süleyman's right-hand man Ibrahim Pasha, Egypt was becoming an integrated part of the empire. In the early years of his reign Süleyman kept up the pace of conquest: Belgrade in 1521, Rhodes in 1522.[29] The Hungarian king

The Rewards of Relative Efficiency: The Ottomans

Lajos II was defeated and killed at the battle of Mohács in August 1526, after which the Hungarian capital Buda soon fell. Vienna was besieged in 1529 without success, though the attackers came quite close. This setback is sometimes explained as a case of overreach on the Ottomans' part, but the fact that their army could mount such an ambitious assault so far to the west, and do so very late in the campaign season, between September and October, is itself significant. On the eastern front against Safavid Iran there was generally some measure of equilibrium, territorial gains alternating with retrenchments. The Safavid capital Tabriz fell to Ibrahim Pasha in 1534 but could not be permanently held. That same year, however, a major prize was won which proved to be of lasting importance, Baghdad: this and Basra, secured a few years later, granted the Ottomans access to the headwaters of the Persian Gulf.

Although there would continue to be local successes on the Hungarian and eastern frontiers, Iraq was Süleyman's last strategically significant terrestrial conquest. Western observers in the 1550s and 1560s detected a note of caution in the sultan and his less bellicose ministers: they would go to war, but only when provoked.[30] When making his final report in 1560 the Venetian *bailo* Marino Cavalli went through the motions by first observing that the Ottoman empire was a 'most warlike nation'. In the thoughtful analysis that followed, however, he suggested that the Ottomans' reluctance to wage war could be exploited by Venice to strengthen their mutually beneficial commercial relationship: whereas the Ottoman alliance with the French was predicated on France's military usefulness to the Sublime Porte whenever a state of war existed against their common enemy the Habsburgs, Venice would be better placed to benefit from peace as the Ottomans' principal trading partner.[31] Similarly, for all Busbecq's doom and gloom about the scale and imminence of the Ottoman threat, he introduced some interesting nuance towards the end of his final letter, written in December 1562, when he observed that the sultan was no longer achieving the kind of overwhelming victories that had characterized the early years of his reign. In remarking that Süleyman 'used to make an end of mighty kingdoms in a single campaign', but now had to be content with minor successes, Busbecq was in effect spotting that the Ottoman armies had reached the outer limits of their operational range, what is sometimes termed the action radius. This was dictated by how far an army travelling from the centre could travel in a single campaign season, allowing for time to make an impact commensurate with the cost and effort involved, and then get back home.[32]

Busbecq was principally concerned with the Ottomans' wars on land against the Austrian Habsburgs. Whether the Ottomans had reached their full action radius at sea was a more open question, however, for they had scored a significant amphibious victory over the Spanish Habsburgs on and around the island of Djerba, off the coast of Tunisia, as recently as 1560; Busbecq in fact witnessed the aftermath, when the fleet returned triumphantly to Istanbul with high-ranking Christian prisoners whom he did his best to help.[33] In the event, the decade between the assault on Malta and the reconquest of Tunis in 1574, which the Spanish had captured the year before, would establish what the operational range of a large Ottoman war fleet setting out from Istanbul in the spring could be. But there is evidence that already in 1565 the Ottomans were nervous about their chances of landing a quick knock-out blow in Malta and so instructed their ambassador to France to broach the possibility of their overwintering in a French port in case they needed to resume their offensive in the following year.[34] If they had not yet discovered their exact maritime action radius, they were well aware that they were nudging very close to it.

The caveats we have entered about the voracity and irrepressible strength of the Ottoman war machine should not be taken to suggest that the sultans' military might was anything less than formidable. The most practised western Ottoman-watchers in the period shortly before the Great Siege, Busbecq, the French ambassadors and the Venetian *baili*, were given to exaggeration and sometimes made the mistake of explaining in absolute terms what were in reality relative differences between the Ottoman and Latin Christian worlds. But they were not fools, and they were well aware

The Rewards of Relative Efficiency: The Ottomans

that the Ottomans' ability to wage war effectively and on such an impressive scale was grounded in several mutually reinforcing advantages: the power of the sultan and the effectiveness of his government, the state's largely (but not wholly) uncontested relationship with its subjects, the government's superior control of the nitty-gritty of warfare when it came to the mobilization of resources and attention to logistics, and the secure ideological foundations of the Ottoman regime.

When Venetian *baili* returned from Istanbul at the end of their period of service, they were expected to deliver a summative report. These were not simply memoranda filed with the Doge and Senate; they were read out in public performances attended by members of the Venetian elite, such was their fascination with the Ottoman world – a world part vital trading partner, part intimidating and enigmatic Other.[35] In view of this appetite to understand the Ottomans, it is significant that the *baili* almost always made a point of including in their reports a pen portrait of the sultan himself, for they and their audiences appreciated that any useful 'read' on the Ottoman empire as a whole had to start with him. This was not an altogether straightforward proposition, for the strict protocols that determined the layout of the imperial palace complex in Istanbul and controlled the movement of people within it meant that a western ambassador might only be in the same room as the sultan twice, on his arrival in Istanbul and then when he departed. Otherwise, his sightings might be limited to those times when the sultan appeared in public, typically on Fridays, when he rode to one of the imperial mosques in the city. It was on one such occasion that Busbecq was struck by Süleyman's impassive manner; he further noted that he had been told that when the victorious fleet had returned from the Djerba campaign, the sultan had shown no trace of emotion in the midst of the collective rejoicing, as if he had reached the point where he treated triumph and disaster the same.[36]

It was on the basis of such fleeting impressions, as well as of the mood of the capital and whatever they were fed by the viziers, that the ambassadors were required to construct a plausible portrait of the sultan. In 1558, for example, Antonio di Gabriele Barbarigo remarked that Süleyman was moderately healthy, of medium height, thinner than he once had been and pale, with an aquiline nose and big, dark eyes. Although he had been warlike in his younger years, his priority was now to enjoy the fruits of peace. He immersed himself in historical works, especially histories of the ancient Persians and of Alexander the Great – a remark consistent with Ottoman evidence that Süleyman took an interest in historians of his own time and assiduously attended to how future historians would remember him.[37] Barbarigo and others around this time believed that they detected a more observant religiosity in the sultan, a puritanical streak that gave rise to a crackdown on the sale of wine and a drop in the demand for expensive fabrics. Some attributed this more pious mood to Süleyman's advancing years, others to the influence of his hard-line first minister and son-in-law, Rüstem Pasha.[38] The sultan was noted as just, which is, again, consonant with internal evidence: it is significant that he was known for his attention to *adalet*, justice or equity, and that his regnal name was *Kanuni*, the lawmaker, in contrast to, most obviously, *Fatih*, the conqueror, the name that was attached to his great-grandfather Mehmed II.[39] Andrea Dandalo, the acting *bailo* in 1562, reported that the sultan was notably cruel to those who opposed him, but this was not a quality that most commentators emphasized, other than in their reactions to Süleyman's elimination of his sons Mustafa in 1553 and Bayezid in 1561.[40]

Whatever personal attributes and qualities commentators chose to mention, they were all in no doubt that Süleyman was highly competent and, ultimately, in charge. This is worthy of note because one can imagine a situation in which the constraints of elaborate court etiquette, and the fact that the sultan spent much of his time in the inner spaces of his palace complex removed not just from the gaze of the ordinary people but even from that of his senior ministers, might have favoured a system of governance that one finds in many guises in world history, from the mayors of the palace of Merovingian Francia to the shoguns of Tokugawa Japan:

that is, the relegation of the formal ruler-figure to a ceremonial role while real power is exercised by a kind of shadow-monarch or junta.[41] Subsequent sultans did retreat into a more inactive role; and it can be argued that Süleyman's reign was one of transition in this respect. He continued a practice that had begun under his immediate predecessors in not routinely attending the meetings of the *divan*, the executive cabinet of his senior ministers which gathered several times each week. But it was well known that the sultan could, if he chose, listen in on the viziers' discussions from a concealed window. In other words, he did not attempt to micromanage the empire, which would in any case have been beyond any individual: Philip II famously tried and failed to keep on top of the sprawling Spanish dominions from a small closet-study. The viziers acting in the sultan's name, however, would always have to assume that he was aware of what was happening.

Domenico Trevisano regretted that western rulers lacked the sultan's *dominio assoluto*. In doing so, he was making two points: that Süleyman's personal authority was unchallenged, and that his writ ran uniformly throughout his empire, in contrast to the clutter of overlapping jurisdictions and privileges that obstructed a European monarch in the exercise of power.[42] It was well understood that the sultan was not 'absolute' in the sense of ruling by personal fiat, for he stood at the head of a large and complex administrative apparatus. Western writers about the Ottoman world were often fascinated by the scale and intricacy of its bureaucracy, and would meticulously itemize the titles and responsibilities of various functionaries as well as their levels of pay. It was also understood that the sultan was screened to some extent by powerful ministers and subject to the rivalries and intrigues that formed around them. But it is interesting that western observers tended to focus on the influence over Süleyman that they believed was enjoyed by his wife, Hürrem, known to the Latin Christian world as Roxelana, and his daughter Mihrimah. This suggests that their understanding of the inner dynamics of the Sublime Porte was unequal to the intricacies of policy-making and factional rivalry, with the result that they fell back on misogynistic tropes about men under women's thumbs.[43]

For all the sophistication and relative efficiency of the government conducted in his name, Süleyman's personal authority was ultimately grounded in the prestige of the Ottoman dynasty and the near-universal acknowledgement among his subjects of its sole right to the title of sultan. The Ottomans maintained this dynastic monopoly of power by means of a generational cycle of fratricidal conflict. There was no system of primogeniture or designation to guide the sultanic succession; on a sultan's death his surviving sons would be expected to plunge into an internecine battle royale, the aim being to eliminate all of one's half-brothers – each the son of a different concubine in the imperial harem – and their male issue.[44] The daughters of the previous sultan and their male children were safe, because it was believed that a claim to the sultanate could not pass through the female line. The system fell out of favour from the end of the sixteenth century, following a particularly bloody cull of no fewer than nineteen half-siblings, some of them very young indeed, by Mehmed III (1595–1603). The violent contraction of the Ottoman male line in every generation carried obvious risks, of course, not least that the winner might prove to be vigorous but nonetheless incompetent or sterile; but in many cases the future competitors for the succession were sexually active before their father's death and had already become fathers themselves. The advantage of this system, for the winner, was a substantial degree of security from dynastic conflict during his reign, unless and until his sons began to compete for the eventual succession before his own death.

This is what happened to Süleyman. He had been fortunate, and unusual, in enjoying an uncontested succession. But his own sons went on to cause him problems. He had disregarded a long-standing tradition that a sultan should break off sexual relations with a concubine once she bore him a child. Instead he married his favoured concubine, Hürrem, with whom he entered into a monogamous relationship, or something close to it. In 1553 his son Mustafa, the son of a concubine named Mahidevran, was summoned to join him on campaign and was promptly put to death: it was believed that he had been the victim of intrigue fomented by Hürrem and her son-in-law Rüstem Pasha to ensure that one of her own sons would eventually succeed; it is also possible that Mustafa had become the figurehead of discontent within parts of the army. In 1559 one of Süleyman's sons by Hürrem, Bayezid, revolted, was defeated and took refuge with the Safavids in Iran. In 1561 Süleyman came to terms with the shah, Tahmasp, who allowed Ottoman assassins to be introduced into Bayezid's quarters.[45] Western observers struggled to understand the system of fratricidal competition or, as in Süleyman's case, filicide, but it had its own grim logic in the context of the Ottomans' insistence on their dynastic distinctiveness, and it probably prevented more bloody conflict within the borders of the empire than it caused.

The practice could even be the basis of a certain cultural snobbery. In 1573 a young Huguenot nobleman (and future diplomat and jurist of note) Philippe du Fresne-Canaye was travelling in the eastern Mediterranean to avoid the fallout in France from the St Bartholomew's Day Massacre. Arriving at Methoni in the Peloponnese, he came upon Hajji Murad, the Ottoman ambassador who had caused a diplomatic headache for the French by travelling to France at the time of the siege of Malta. Hajji Murad threw into the conversation the suggestion that if King Charles IX really wanted a quick and effective way to put an end to the Wars of Religion, he should simply invite Henri I, prince de Condé, one of the leaders of the Protestant cause, to court and have him quietly strangled.[46] Hajji Murad knew the French scene and its recent record of political violence too well to have been blithely advocating assassination for its own sake; the subtext of his remark was that although Condé was a distant cousin of the king, not a half-brother, he was nonetheless a 'prince of the blood', a direct descendant in the male line from Louis IX (1226–70), and thus deserved to die as a dynastic obstacle to Charles's untroubled exercise of power in much the same way as the sultans dealt with their rivals.

A leitmotif of western commentary on the Ottoman state was the sultans' ability to command obedience from disciplined and deferential subjects. One must always allow for an element of projection on the part of upper-class European observers who would doubtless have liked to have seen the same sort of social docility and respect for hierarchy back home. When Philippe du Fresne-Canaye marvelled at the Janissaries' self-control during an audience with the sultan attended by François de Noailles, the French ambassador to the Sublime Porte – they kept perfectly still like statues and made no sound whatsoever for seven hours – he must have been mindful of the political and social chaos back home in France.[47] But remarks of this sort crop up too often to have been mere wishful thinking. Obedience was observed at the general civic level: Daniele Barbarigo, for example, argued that the subservience of his people was, alongside the extent of his dominions, the true foundation of the sultan's power.[48] For Jean Chesneau, 'his subjects render such great obedience to their lord that they take great care not to break any of his ordinances and dwell in marvellous peace and concord'.[49] The inclination towards obedience was also spotted in particular contexts. Busbecq praised the discipline, self-control and capacity for endurance that he encountered in Ottoman military camps, in stark contrast to the chaotic behaviour of western soldiers; Jean Chesneau was similarly struck by the way in which the sultan's armies were well disciplined, maintained an orderly silence, and obeyed orders not to loot the places through which they marched.[50] The silence of the crowds watching the sultan process through the streets of Istanbul on Fridays made a great impression on du Fresne-Canaye; there existed 'a great concord and amity between rulers and ruled', and the fact that the people were schooled in respect and obedience, he supposed, was what made them powerful, something that should be a source of great shame for all Christians.[51]

Domenico Trevisano summed up the reactions of many commentators when he observed that the sultan enjoyed a form of obedience from his subjects that was wholly unlike that to be found in any other polity.[52] As always, we cannot take such comments

The Rewards of Relative Efficiency: The Ottomans

simply at face value. The western observers were prone to exaggeration and overgeneralization, and passed over or argued away evidence that contradicted their impressions: Busbecq, unusually, was willing to concede that, for all the Janissaries' formidable reputation, Rüstem Pasha had once admitted to him they could be turbulent and made the sultan and his ministers nervous.[53] There was also a tendency to attribute the results of practical arrangements to universal behavioural habits: the absence of looting by soldiers on the march, for example, was actually the result of co-opting tradesmen and suppliers to travel with the army, and a policy of avoiding towns, the most tempting targets.[54] We cannot penetrate the minds of twenty million Ottoman subjects to gauge how far obedience and deference came naturally to them. Nonetheless, for all their misconceptions, what the western observers mistook for a kind of cultural essence may be treated as evidence of people's broad assent to, and willing participation in, the political life of what was, by sixteenth-century standards, a conspicuously well-run and well-organized state.

The power of the Ottoman polity was aided by strategic good fortune. By the sixteenth century the expansion of the Ottoman empire had ensured that it not only had very large reserves of manpower on which to draw, but was also, to all intents and purposes, self-sufficient in the raw materials that sustained its military operations.[55] The Ottomans had access to all the metals necessary for war: iron, lead and copper, in addition to precious-metal deposits to pay for it all. They were largely self-supporting in tin, necessary for the bronze that had become standard in the manufacture of cannon, though here some had to be imported, particularly from England. The Ottoman government was accordingly able to develop a technologically sophisticated and productive gun-making industry, in artillery and small arms, to serve the needs of both the army and the navy.[56] Likewise there was no need to go beyond the empire to find the raw ingredients of gunpowder: saltpetre, sulphur and charcoal.[57] The Ottomans' large and effective navy is a particularly good indicator of the government's careful attention to matters of supply and logistics, because naval organization involved the intricate co-ordination of numerous moving parts. One might say, in fact, that operating a navy was the ultimate test of a state's competence and efficiency in the sixteenth-century Mediterranean. Here, once again, ample essential materials were to hand and their collection and transportation to the points of need the basis of well-practised administrative systems: timber, cloth for the sails, hemp for rigging, pitch and oakum for caulking, and tallow for waterproofing.[58] Visitors to Istanbul routinely commented on the arsenal across the Golden Horn from the main city; this was the main naval base in the empire, but there were several smaller facilities elsewhere.[59] There is a telling contrast between the Ottomans' careful attention to the production and distribution of biscuit, the basic foodstuff on galleys and thus ultimately the fuel that made them go, and the more haphazard arrangements to be found in the Habsburg fleet: letters written in the months before the Great Siege to and from García de Toledo, Philip II's naval commander-in-chief in the Mediterranean theatre, reveal the enormous difficulties that he was confronting in sourcing sufficient quantities of biscuit for his fleet and then getting it to where it was needed.[60] Likewise Toledo faced greater challenges than his Ottoman counterparts in exploiting the know-how of skilled craftsmen, always a precious resource, in the more loosely articulated Habsburg world. In January 1565, for example, he complained to the viceroy of Catalonia that the galleys under construction in Barcelona that he had ordered were being built by inferior local shipwrights, not the Genoese, 'the best there are', whom he had arranged to be sent to Spain.[61]

Similarly, with respect to armies in the field, there was notably superior attention than in western Europe to the need to keep men well fed and to ensure that their pay was regular: there were times when the Janissaries in particular could become restless, but there was nonetheless a clear contrast with the treatment of even the better organized and well-trained western armies.[62] The Spanish forces in the Netherlands in the final third of the sixteenth century, for example, routinely mutinied over backlogs in their pay that typically stretched back over several years.⁶³ It is significant that Ottoman forces avoided the orgies of destruction that were visited on cities such as Rome in 1527 and Antwerp in 1576 by unpaid, impoverished and disaffected Christian troops. Westerners sometimes clutched at straws to tell themselves that, for all the Ottomans' self-evident military superiority, this was a case of quantity over quality: it was often observed, for example, and the Ottomans themselves sometimes acknowledged, that Ottoman ship-makers laid down hulls using unseasoned, green wood, which meant that their galleys sat heavier in the water and were less manoeuvrable than those of western navies.⁶⁴ But the impulse to talk up localized advantages in such a way is clear evidence that the larger picture was very much in the Ottomans' favour.

Even as late as the sixteenth century, and indeed beyond, the legitimacy and prestige of the Ottoman dynasty were grounded in its origins as the leader from around 1300 of an aggressive confederation of Turkish tribesmen in north-western Anatolia. This was the launchpad for its first wave of conquests in the fourteenth and fifteenth centuries eastwards into central Anatolia and across the Bosphorus into Greece and the Balkans. Although in courtly and educated Ottoman circles the word 'Turk' came to be used pejoratively of an unsophisticated country-dweller, a boor, the dynasty's Turkic roots remained an important part of its deep cultural identity. In this the sultans had a good deal in common with the ruling elites of the two great Muslim polities to their east, Safavid Iran and Mughal India.⁶⁵ These roots are evident, for example, in the wonderful images to be found in one of the most impressive cultural achievements of Süleyman's court, the *Süleymanname*, an illustrated verse history of the sultan's reign between 1520 and 1555. Several of the sixty-nine illuminations depict scenes in which Süleyman and his entourage demonstrate qualities that would have been prized by their Turkish forebears: fine horsemanship, skill in the use of the bow, and a predilection for hunting.⁶⁶

As the Ottoman domains progressively expanded, however, the sultans' ideological repertoire grew as a reflex of the various traditions and sources of legitimacy with which they came into contact.[67] First, their myths of origins came to insist that they were the true heirs of the Seljuks, the predominant ruling dynasty in Anatolia between the eleventh and thirteenth centuries. Then imperial possibilities opened up thanks to the signal moment in the early history of the Ottomans' conquests, the fall of Byzantine Constantinople in 1453. With the defeat of the Mamluks in 1516–17 and the absorption of Egypt, Syria, Palestine and parts of Arabia, moreover, the borders of the Ottoman empire came to approximate those of the eastern Roman or early Byzantine state before much of it was swept away by the Arab conquests in the seventh century. It is not surprising, therefore, to find that when Charles V emerged in the 1520s and 1530s as the Ottomans' principal rival to their west, Süleyman began to be fashioned as the true successor of the Roman emperors, thereby undercutting Charles's own ideological appeal to the Roman imperial past as Holy Roman Emperor. What is often regarded as a decisive moment came in 1547: in that year Süleyman concluded a peace treaty with the Habsburgs in which Charles was dismissively termed as nothing more than 'King of Spain'.[68] The same technique of appropriating aggrandizing titulature and denying it to one's opponent was used against the Safavids to the east. Selim I's defeat of the Mamluks meant that the Ottomans could plug into a further source of legitimacy and prestige as the guardians of Mecca and the other holy places of Islam, Medina and Jerusalem. Abundant evidence points to the fact that Süleyman and his regime attached particular significance to their role as enablers and protectors of the *hajj*, the pilgrimage to Mecca enjoined on devout Muslims.[69] As we shall see, this probably played a large part in the decision to attack the Order of St John on Malta. Additionally, control of the holy places as well as of Baghdad, seat of the Abbasid caliphs until 1258, encouraged Süleyman to claim the caliphate, which conferred an imprecise but venerable form of leadership over the whole Dar al-Islam, the Muslim 'world of peace', even though the Ottoman dynasty could not lay claim to descent from the Prophet Mohammad, the essential qualification of the original caliphs.

The Rewards of Relative Efficiency: The Ottomans

In all this, Süleyman's reign has the appearance of the culminating moment in a process of ideological refinement that had been gaining momentum for two centuries. Another important strand of the sultans' ideology and self-fashioning – and one that we particularly need to address in the context of this book – was their ability to cast themselves as *ghazis*, holy warriors.[70] This was a rhetorical posture that any Muslim ruler might adopt according to need: it was exploited, for example, by the Mughals in India in their wars against Hindu rulers, and, albeit with some element of qualification, by the Sunni Ottomans against the supposedly heretical Safavids, who practised a form of Shi'ism. The notion of holy war in Islam found its most consistent and developed expression, however, in conflicts against Christians. It goes without saying that one does not need to look very far in the evidence for the sixteenth-century Ottomans' confrontations with Christians in central Europe and the Mediterranean, as well as Christian pockets elsewhere such as Georgia, to find, on both sides, frequent and virulent expressions of religious belligerence. Such articulations could take on an almost Pavlovian quality. Recent scholarship has tended to downplay the extent to which the Ottomans built holy war into their ideology of rulership and motivated their troops accordingly. On the whole, this sounds a salutary note of caution, for we need to avoid taking historical actors simply at their own estimation, especially when their public discourses had a kind of internal inflationary energy that pushed them towards extremes. Many of the sultans' loyal subjects, after all, were non-Muslims. On the other hand, we should not write holy war out of the story. Part of the problem is that historians often set the bar too high for what qualifies as an instance of religiously motivated conflict. Anything less than evidence of unremitting virulence and zealotry – and of course there will always be examples of inconsistencies, mixed attitudes and at least partial tolerance – is taken as an indication that the rhetoric of holy war was merely a gloss applied to conflicts played out for a variety of political, economic or other motives. But religious conflict is not a zero-sum proposition: it never exists in isolation, and it can insinuate itself into a very wide range of military confrontations, political interactions and cultural encounters. The Ottoman empire was – or more to the point could choose to present itself as – a *ghazi* state because such a posture was consonant with its other sources of ideological legitimacy and could be backed up by a comparatively well-organized governmental and military apparatus. The Great Siege, as we shall see, is a case in point.

3.
The Cruel Sea

One way in which to approach the Great Siege is as a particular moment in the drawn-out contest between two imperial hegemons, the Ottoman empire and Habsburg Spain, whose centres of gravity happened to be situated at opposite ends of the Mediterranean. Their relative strength was demonstrated at any given time by the location of the frontier zones between them – always fluid in maritime contexts – and the areas of contested authority. On this measure, the Ottomans in 1565 had broadly been in the ascendant for about three decades. Considered in the round, the siege turned out to be a case of military overreach on the part of a hitherto successful, confident, relatively compact, powerful and efficient empire. This overextension, in itself fairly modest but nonetheless consequential, allowed its more loosely articulated, weaker and more inefficient rival to mobilize just enough resources to enable it to avoid a grave defeat. As we shall see in a later chapter, moreover, it is impossible to understand the aims and priorities of the two imperial protagonists in the siege separately from their larger ambitions and strategies. Theirs was a global struggle. To this important extent, then, we need to understand the story of the siege on a 'macro', geopolitical level.

That said, the contest for dominance in the sixteenth-century Mediterranean seldom if ever came down to a straightforward collision of arms between the centrally organized forces of two monolithic empires. This was a war of composites, especially so on the Christian side; the maritime forces that the Habsburg kings of Spain could mobilize against the Ottomans were drawn from various parts of Spain, itself a plural state comprising polities with different traditions, and Italy, perennially divided between competing internal and external interests. Italian allies and clients who were not strictly speaking subjects of the Habsburgs' own Italian domains were an important additional element: much of the routine functioning of maritime communication between Spain and Italy, and of the projection of Habsburg naval might, was to all intents and purposes contracted out to a family of Genoese *condottieri*, the Dorias.[1] The famous Christian victory over the Ottoman fleet at Lepanto, off the coast of western Greece on 7 October 1571, was only possible because Spain had joined the Holy League in order to pool its naval resources with those of the papacy and, more importantly, Venice, the only other Christian power in the Mediterranean able to equip a large galley fleet.

Additionally, the two empires routinely played out their rivalry through smaller local proxies, maritime communities in north Africa, Italy, Sardinia and Malta. This complicated matters a great deal, for the proxies did not simply see themselves as waiting on standby to serve as the on-off instruments of distant imperial masters; they had their own interests to pursue and protect as traders, raiders, pirates and slavers. This means that the story of the Great Siege also has a significant 'micro' dimension. Viewed from such a perspective, from the bottom up and with local conditions in mind, the siege was a convulsive moment in the chaotic history of an unstable, fragile zone characterized by constant and intractable religious, political and economic flux. Malta was right in the middle of what one writer has appropriately termed 'the sea of fear'.[2]

Part cause, part symptom of this state of instability were the corsairs. The word derives from *corso* and its cognates, meaning a maritime expedition or raid. The formal difference between a corsair and a pirate resides in the fact that the corsair was, in theory at any rate, in receipt of some form of official warrant from those in authority. This often took the form of letters of marque or other sets of instructions specifying such details as the duration of the *corso*, the geographical parameters within which it could operate, and the types of targets that it could pursue. To this extent, Mediterranean corsairs were the cousins of the privateers licensed by Elizabeth I of England to harry Spanish interests in the Americas and, if possible, return with a handsome profit. In practice Mediterranean corsairs doubled up as merchants, smugglers and freebooters, often acting with the tacit approval of public authority but seldom directly answerable to it as a matter of fixed routine. That is to say, if they were not pirates pure and simple, they did a very good impersonation of them.[3]

Even when corsairs were subject to forms of official constraint, moreover, what actually happened once they were out to sea was all but impossible to police. A case in point is the frequency with which the Knights of Malta, active participants in the *corso*, preyed on the shipping of Christian Venice; the Venetians took a very dim view of those they considered nothing more than grandiose pirates. Such were the human scale and economic and cultural importance of corsairing that there was sometimes a blurring of the boundaries between it and the workings of public authority. This was the case most obviously in the principal corsair bases on the north African, or Barbary, coast. In Algiers, the largest and most active base, there was a complex distribution of power among various elements – local elites, representatives of the Ottomans and the corsairs themselves, many of whom were not Turks or Moors by birth but renegades, that is to say those who had converted to Islam from Christianity or, in some instances, Judaism.[4] It is noteworthy that in 1568 the Janissaries garrisoned in Algiers, who were increasingly becoming a fixture of local power structures rather than agents of the distant Ottoman state, were granted the right to take part in the *corso*, such was its economic, cultural and political centrality to the life of the city.

A similar impetus was felt in Malta. The Knights' small fleet existed to perform a variety of roles.[5] Its bread-and-butter responsibility was to transport or convoy people and supplies to Malta; not only did the Order of St John need the constant infusion of responsions from its priories in Europe, but Malta itself was far from agriculturally self-sufficient and therefore dependent on the regular import of food and other necessary supplies.[6] The order's galleys also operated as a military force, either as autonomous flotillas or as part of composite Habsburg fleets assembled from Christian ports around the western Mediterranean. Reconnaissance missions were another function; the order needed to be as well briefed as possible about the movements of ships in the Mediterranean. On top of all these uses of their naval resources, the Knights were also corsairs.[7] When considering the importance of the *corso* to the order's operations, it is important to bear in mind that the number of galleys and support craft at its disposal was modest: its normal complement of operational galleys around the time of the siege was four or five, sometimes topped up by one or two vessels operated by the Grand Master or a very wealthy Knight – typically those of independent means such as Leone Strozzi, the uncle of Brantôme's friend Filippo di Piero Strozzi, or François de Guise, the younger brother of another François, the duc de Guise, men whose relationship to the order could be semi-detached at best and who spent most of their careers away from Malta in the service of other masters.[8]

Nonetheless the Knights enjoyed, or perhaps more accurately assiduously cultivated, a reputation for punching above their weight, whether in terms of their seamanship, the quality of their galleys as war machines, or the heavy-metal impact of each galley's detachment of Knights and soldiers when it came to boarding an opponent.[9] Beyond a certain point, however, qualitative considerations unavoidably ran up against quantitative constraints. This central fact of the order's naval capacity made it particularly vulnerable to the effects of natural disaster or calamitous defeat. In 1555 four of the order's five galleys were lost in a freak storm in Grand Harbour, and the fifth, the *San Claudio*, was severely damaged. At Lepanto in 1571, although the Knights were of course on the winning side, their losses were disproportionate to their contribution to the Christian alliance.[10] A year before Lepanto, the galley fleet had performed so poorly and been so badly mauled in combat that its commander, François de Saint-Clément, was executed.[11] Given that its margins were so tight, the fact that the order not only entertained the possibility of exposing its precious naval resources to the hazards of corsairing, but also made it one of its principal activities, is clear evidence of the importance that was attached to this aspect of its operations.

The order's corsairing raids were concentrated in two principal areas. The Knights conducted relatively short voyages south to patrol the north African coast; here the prizes on offer included Muslim vessels carrying pilgrims to and from Egypt. Or they might sail to Greece, the Aegean and further east, in the process revisiting areas that had been familiar to them when their fleet had been based in Rhodes. These were now predominantly Ottoman waters, but, as Brantôme discovered when he was a guest on a *corso* expedition in 1566, the order could make use of a network of remote locations, in the Aegean and elsewhere, which were under the Ottoman radar and where the Knights could expect a friendly welcome from the local Christian people, take on water and supplies, and even careen their vessels.[12] The order's own efforts were complemented by independent corsairs based in Malta. Malta already had a long tradition of corsairing when the Knights arrived in 1530. Thereafter, far from being swallowed up or edged out by the order's official operations, freelancers flourished, thanks both to the development of Grand Harbour as a port area and the rise in consumer demand that the Knights stimulated.[13] In 1605 the order sought to regularize its relationship with the local independents by establishing a supervisory body, the *Tribunale degli Armamenti*, but the symbiotic relationship between the Knights and Maltese corsairs was already well established by that date.[14] There is a good deal of evidence from the seventeenth century that people of all walks of life in Maltese society invested money in *corso* voyages; and there is every reason to suppose that this sort of penetration of corsairing into the whole social and economic fabric of Maltese life was already in evidence around the time of the Great Siege, especially among the communities in the Grand Harbour area.

In all this Malta was simply participating in a system that extended across most of the Mediterranean. Generally speaking, corsairs had two kinds of targets. The first was shipping out at sea, the goods it was carrying and the people on board. Which of these three was most valuable to the corsairs who seized them varied from case to case. But the most prized target was usually the cargoes. There was enough high-value, low-volume material being moved around the Mediterranean – silks, spices, luxury commodities or bullion – to hold out the prospect of a big payday for an enterprising and well-equipped corsair. The odds were certainly shorter than those faced by French, Dutch and English privateers who dreamed of intercepting the Spanish silver fleet in the Atlantic. There were spectacular hits from time to time: as we shall see, one such, by the Knights at the expense of Ottoman vessels sailing from Alexandria, became a *casus belli* for the Sublime Porte in the build-up to the Great Siege.

In practice most cargoes were more modest, but valuable nonetheless. An important feature of the demography of the early modern Mediterranean, and of much of the world beyond it, was an often uneven fit between the concentrations of people, and hence the areas of greatest consumer demand, and the locations of the areas that grew the food to feed them. Given Malta's dependence on the import of food, which could easily be interrupted if the needs of the suppliers themselves took precedence or ships were lost, it was especially prey to famine; in such emergencies the order's galleys would intercept ships carrying foodstuffs and divert them back to Grand Harbour, where their precious cargoes would be impounded. The same slim margins were in evidence elsewhere. In a detailed report on the north African coast submitted to the order in 1587 by two Knights, Francesco Lanfreducci and Giovanni Ottone Bosio, it was observed that Algiers was a thriving city but wholly incapable of supporting and feeding itself without its community of corsairs.[15] Moving food by sea was the only practicable way to do so in bulk and cheaply given that land transport was permanently hobbled by the relatively small weight that each pack animal or cart could take, a mass of geographical and seasonal challenges, and a near-total lack of protection from bandits. Many of the corsairs' routine operations were, therefore, directed to the theft of food and other basic consumer items, such as cotton and linen, for which there was a guaranteed and constant demand.

The Cruel Sea

A sense of what it was like to be on the receiving end of a corsair's predations emerges from a letter written in August 1566 by an English sea captain, Roger Bodenham, to Anthony Penny, the owner of or an investor in his vessel.[16] Bodenham's tale was one of 'great misfortune'. On 29 July, just as dawn was breaking, his ship had been set upon off Cabo de Santa Maria on the southern coast of Portugal by several galleys crewed by those described as 'Turks' – the word tended to be used indiscriminately of all Muslims in the Mediterranean – from Algiers. He and his small crew had put up a brave fight, he insisted, but by noon further resistance had become impossible: several on board had been killed and all the rest were wounded. The assailants boarded the ship and stripped the survivors naked before bundling them onto their galleys. The ship was then systematically denuded of its more valuable cargo (Bodenham does not specify what this was, presumably because this was information well known to Penny) and its 'ordinans and takell', which is to say the light armament which had kept the corsairs at bay for several hours and all the sails, rigging and metal parts. The ship, picked over and effectively reduced to a hulk, was then cast adrift: Bodenham was at pains to reassure Penny that every effort had since been made to find her, but to no avail. Interestingly, he says that their captors did not press on back home to Algiers but stopped off at a Christian port, Cádiz in Spain, where they sold some of their prisoners, including Bodenham himself. This may have been a mixed blessing for any Protestant crew members: there is evidence of the Inquisition's taking an interest in seafaring heretics whom fate dropped into its lap. But Bodenham was only full of relief at his lucky escape, as well as deep anguish for the fate of those of his crew, including someone known to Penny called Waters or Walter, who had been 'carried away in sorrowfull captivitie'.

As Bodenham's experience makes clear, corsairs were scavengers in search of human as well as material bounty. People taken in circumstances such as these had two uses. First, they could be ransomed. Bodenham's captors had acted quickly by sailing the short distance to Cádiz and negotiating a price for those of their captives who, on the basis of their dress or bearing, looked like they would attract the highest prices. This was a hard-nosed business: Bodenham was redeemed by a friend for 700 ducats, a very substantial sum which he would have been expected to find in due course; 'howe I shall paye it again, God knows', he lamented. The other nine Christian captives whom Bodenham says were redeemed alongside him were probably not so lucky in having an acquaintance fortuitously on hand, and their ransoms were most likely paid by local speculators with the intention of re-ransoming the men at a profit. To be held for ransom was generally believed to be the 'least worst' outcome for those seized by corsairs, but that is not to say that it did not inspire fear and dread. When ships were about to be boarded, it was not uncommon for the more affluent passengers to discard indications of their wealth such as jewellery and fine clothing, their hope being that they would avoid attracting a ransom amount set so high that it would deter those back home expected to pay it.[17] Ransoming was well organized and an important source of the cashflow in corsairing economies, Malta included. There was, for example, a flurry of lucrative ransom activity in 1564, soon after the Knights had taken large prizes in the eastern Mediterranean.[18]

Second, captives represented a valuable source of labour.[19] Those taken could be put to work in a variety of ways, including domestic service – the fate of many female captives – or cottage industries. If their captors discovered that they had a trade or possessed a particularly prized skill, such as military engineering, shipbuilding or weapons manufacture, their expertise would be exploited. There are many recorded cases of artisans in this position carving out new lives for themselves in relatively free and comfortable conditions. The prospects for most of those taken, however, were much more grim: they had little to look forward to other than hard, unremitting labour. There were not by and large the sorts of agricultural gangs that would become a common feature of Atlantic slavery, though slaves in some of the north African port-cities were often put to work, individually or in small groups, tending their masters' *masseries*, plots of land beyond the city walls. Heavy construction work was the fate of many; the Knights, for example, exploited a great deal of slave labour when building Valletta in the years immediately following the siege.

Work of this sort was often combined with rowing on galleys in the sailing season between late spring and early autumn. The demand for human motive power to propel oared vessels was probably the single biggest driver of the sixteenth-century Mediterranean slave trade. The various political communities around the Mediterranean that ran substantial navies pursued a number of strategies, singly or in combination, to populate their *ciurme*, the complements of oarsmen in their galleys and other oared vessels.[20] They might recruit professional rowers serving for pay, or they might use some form of conscription to raise levies. Some oarsmen served under a system known as *buonovoglia*, an arrangement whereby the galley-owner provided a lump sum to pay off an oarsman's debts in return for a specified period of service at sea. Some were convicts. Others, in many cases the majority, were slaves. This was a mixed economy. The Order of St John was heavily reliant on enslaved oarsmen, interspersed with *buonovoglia* recruits and convicts supplied by Naples, Sicily, the papal states and even France.[21] Galleys from the north African corsairing ports tended to rely on slaves, though those running the various diminutives of the galley type, which did a lot of the routine work of hunting down smaller trading craft and conducting lightning raids ashore, made greater use of volunteers and hired men. As a general trend, an expansion of the numbers of galleys in the Mediterranean over the course of the sixteenth century, in conjunction with a constant shortage of labour and the high mortality rate among oarsmen, meant that even those naval powers such as Venice and the Ottoman empire which had traditionally set their face against a reliance on convicts or slave labour were forced to revise their policies to some extent: Venice began to use convicts, and the Ottomans convicts and slaves.[22] Christians tended to exaggerate the number of their co-religionists enslaved on Ottoman vessels, but the presence of significant numbers is confirmed by the fact that as many as 15,000 Christians, mostly Greeks, were freed from the galleys captured at Lepanto; many more must have died during the battle. It is confirmed too, though on a much smaller scale, by evidence of Christian slaves, described in the documentation as oarsmen, who escaped from the Ottoman fleet during the Great Siege.[23]

The enormous demand for slaves explains why corsairing extended beyond acts of piracy out at sea to raiding on land, where potential victims were more numerous.[24] Here there was an element of asymmetry: the human cost of raids by north African corsairs on Christian shores was substantially greater than that of Christian raids on Muslim lands. The Knights sometimes raided ashore and took captives in the process, but this was not their preferred *modus operandi*: there were relatively few secure, and discreet, anchorages on the north African coast, and there were also many dangerous shoals. Up to the decade or so after Lepanto, many of the slaving expeditions undertaken by the north African corsairs were conducted in concert with the operations of the Ottoman galley fleet. When such resources could be brought to bear, the result would be a highly organized operation in which a base was set up on or near the targeted coast for several days, or even weeks, from which systematic and wide-ranging sweeps for captives would be conducted through the surrounding countryside. The numbers could be very large: for example, 7,000 taken from the Bay of Naples in 1544, 'only' 400 from Augusta in Sicily in 1551, and 4,000 from Granada in 1566.[25] As we shall see in the next chapter, nearly the entire population of Gozo, Malta's second island, perhaps 5,000 men, women and children, was swept up and whisked away in 1551. After about 1580, the rhythm of corsairing reverted to a 'small war' of frequent, darting raids. But these had always been going on; it is probable that even in the period of the large-scale trawls, most of the victims of corsairs who were seized on land were taken in opportunistic smash-and-grab raids conducted by the crews of perhaps one or two vessels.

The economic and social impact of these raids, big and small, was reflected in significant changes to settlement patterns along the most affected coastlines in Italy and Spain. There was widespread abandonment of coastal villages and relocation of communities inland. There were attempts to develop defences and warning systems in the form of watchtowers and fortified places of safety as well as patrols on land and sea.[26] But these were usually inadequate – even more so in Spain, on the whole, than in Italy – in large part because of the sheer length of coastline that needed to be protected, and partly, too, because governments calculated that whatever manpower and resources they committed to coastal defence would end up being spread too thinly.[27] The corsairs' agility and excellent knowledge of familiar coastlines usually kept them one step ahead. Something of the anguish of those on the front line emerges from their pleas for help. In 1551 the Castilian *cortes* appealed to Charles V to address 'the great harms which the infidels visit upon the coast of the bishopric of Cartagena' – the area of the Spanish mainland closest as the crow flies to Algiers. The petitioners, clearly suspecting inconsistent treatment, were prepared to be frank: such 'abominations' were the direct result of a failure to guard that area adequately, in contrast to Granada further to the south-west. Galleys that could operate as a defensive screen, it was claimed, were stationed elsewhere or sitting idle in Seville. In an interesting implied reference to the activities of the Knights of Malta, the petitioners wondered why it was that the three Spanish military orders, Santiago, Calatrava and Alcántara, which were under royal control, had not developed naval arms. The orders should base themselves in Cartagena, Almería and Gibraltar and learn to sail galleys.[28]

In 1559 petitioners in the *cortes* offered a despairing conspectus of all the harms that corsairs were able to visit upon their victims: they were severely disrupting trade to such an extent that no ships from the Levant could evade them, and their haul of both captives and goods was making them rich beyond compare; there was 'great destruction and desolation' on the coast of Spain all the way around from Perpignan, on the Mediterranean border with France, to Portugal in the Atlantic; and a coastal belt to a depth of about four or five leagues (as much as approximately twenty kilometres) had become a no-go zone in which farms had been abandoned, with a consequent loss of rents and incomes for landowners. It was a source of ignominy, no less, that such great harm could be done to Spain by 'a single frontier town like Algiers'. Given such stresses, it was understandable that isolationism would creep into the petitioners' thinking: the king, they suggested, spent large amounts each year on his galleys only for these forces to be deployed elsewhere (that is, around Italy and in the central Mediterranean), whereas they should properly be stationed along the Spanish coast, where they could both offer adequate protection and – another implicit acknowledgement of the activities of the Order of St John – go on *corso* themselves.[29]

The greater part of our evidence for the activity and impact of corsairs dates from after the Great Siege, but we may, with due caution, apply this later material to the earlier period whenever it is consistent with sources such as the petitions to the Castilian *cortes* in the 1550s. One should also be alive to an imbalance in the evidence in favour of Christians' experiences and perceptions as against those of Muslims and also Jewish communities. If one keeps these caveats in mind, one can nonetheless gain some sense of corsairing's significance as a shared, trans-cultural experience shaped by its distinctive Mediterranean setting. It is true that corsairing could extend beyond its traditional zones of operation. Bodenham's ship, for example, was intercepted west of the Straits of Gibraltar. As he noted, corsairs in unprecedented numbers were being drawn into the Atlantic in the search for richly laden ships coming from the Spanish Americas. 'The lyke,' he believed, 'was never sene in these partes.'[30] In 1586 a nine-year-old from the Scilly Isles, Peter Dein (Dean?) was seized by corsairs when his uncle's fishing boat strayed into dangerous waters off Cabo de São Vicente in the Algarve, the most south-westerly point of Portugal.[31] The remarkable limit case of the penetration of Atlantic waters by Mediterranean corsairs was a raid on Iceland in 1627 in which about 400 captives were taken.[32] But these were overspills; the centre of gravity of corsair activity was the Mediterranean and the social and economic structures that sustained it, and it was in consequence there that its impacts on people's lives were greatest.

The Cruel Sea

The most accomplished writer to have experienced the sea of fear at first hand, and indeed to have been a victim of it, was Miguel de Cervantes Saavedra (1547–1616). When he was in his twenties Cervantes served as a soldier in Italy and around the Mediterranean; he fought at Lepanto, where he lost the use of his left hand.[33] In 1575 he was returning to Spain from Naples when his galley became detached from its convoy in stormy weather and was intercepted by Barbary corsairs off the coast of Catalonia. Cervantes was made captive and taken to Algiers, where he would be held until he was ransomed in 1580.[34] His experiences in Algiers, which was the most active corsair base in north Africa and contained the largest population of Christian captives and renegades, informed one of his first works, a play entitled *El trato de Argel* ('The Algiers Deal'), and subsequently his other *comedias de cautivos* ('captive comedies'), including a revisiting of the scene of his captivity in *Los baños de Argel* ('The Slave Compounds of Algiers').[35] The years spent as a prisoner also inspired a nested narrative within the inn sequence in Part I of Cervantes' most famous work, *Don Quixote*, in which a traveller, who has arrived with a mysterious female companion, is prevailed upon by the other guests at the inn to tell his story. The narrative that then unfolds is one of servitude in and escape from Algiers.[36]

The traveller's tale departs from Cervantes' own experiences in several respects. Most obviously, and in ways that resonate with Cervantes' skilful mobilization of literary clichés, this is a story of chivalric romance and derring-do in which the protagonist rescues a Muslim maiden-in-distress and would-be Christian, Zoraida, the daughter of one of the most powerful men in Algiers. The traveller cuts a more heroic dash than his creator: he is not captured out at sea, but because of a mistimed act of bravado at Lepanto; and he is not ransomed at the end but gets away by organizing a daring and elaborate escape. (We know that Cervantes tried and failed to escape several times.) In a nice metafictional moment, Cervantes acknowledges the degree of separation between his own persona and that of his *alter ego* by having the narrator observe in passing that in Algiers he had known of a particularly upright and fearless captive named 'something or other Saavedra' – none other than Cervantes himself, of course.[37] In many other ways, however, the traveller's tale nudges closer to autobiography and evokes aspects of the author's experience as a captive in Algiers which seem to ring true. There is the acute distress of hunger, and also the loss of dignity when one has to go without adequate clothing; the casual and often brutal violence to which captives are regularly subjected; and a powerful sense of having been pitched into a disorienting and threatening world turned upside down, a place where 'the most dreadful and amazing events are witnessed every day'.[38]

In addition, the traveller describes an environment in which hard-and-fast binary oppositions are, if never wholly effaced, complicated in numerous subtle ways. He reveals, for example, that he was helped by a renegade who had originally come from Murcia in southern Spain. Not only does this renegade have a reputation for treating Christians better than others, it also turns out that he has tenaciously and surreptitiously clung on to his own Christian faith despite his ostensible conversion to Islam; he reveals a crucifix that he has always worn in secret under his shirt.[39] French and Spanish merchants are described coming to Algiers to do business, and there is a community of Christian Spanish oarsmen living in the town who, it is implied, offer their services to corsairs for pay.[40] Interestingly, when the traveller is surprised by Zoraida's father as he reconnoitres the villa from which he intends to rescue her, they are able to converse, with a measure of polite and respectful decorum, in *lingua franca*, the Romance creole with an admixture of words from Greek, Arabic, Turkish and other languages in which masters and slaves communicated with one another in the corsair communities along the Barbary coast. Interestingly, too, Zoraida, though the plot requires that she has lived a very cloistered life, is also able to converse in *lingua franca*, if not quite so well; the narrator observes that the strict social conventions that governed a Muslim woman's interactions with a Muslim man were relaxed when she found herself in the company of a male Christian slave.[41]

The abiding sense of categories confused and boundaries blurred persists even after the traveller, Zoraida and their companions make their escape. En route to Spain they are set upon by French corsairs from La Rochelle (an interesting suggestion that the possible returns from corsairing in the Mediterranean could attract sailors from Atlantic ports); and when the fugitives reach the apparent safety of the coast of southern Spain, they are still terrified of being seized in a lightning raid by Moroccan raiders from just across the strait in Tétouan. For good measure, before they are finally recognized and welcomed home, they are mistaken for Muslim raiders themselves.[42] This is a predatory, threatening world shot through with conflicting and fluid identities.

The doleful picture of captives' fates found in *Don Quixote* is corroborated by the monumental *Topography and General History of Algiers* written by a Portuguese cleric named Antonio de Sosa; his period of captivity there (1577–81) overlapped with that of Cervantes, and the two men became close.[43] Many of Cervantes' themes are further echoed in a captivity narrative written by Diego Galán.[44] In 1589 Galán, still only in his early teens, was captured at sea en route to the Spanish *presidio* at Oran, having fallen in with a soldier and been talked into volunteering. He served as a slave on public works and at sea on the galleys, before fetching up in Istanbul, where he was bought by an Ottoman sea captain. When not serving in his master's vessel he was given responsibility for looking after his children. He also got to travel to various parts of the Mediterranean. In 1599 he escaped when his fleet was watering on the coast of Negroponte (Euboea) and was for a time hidden by Greek Orthodox monks before being smuggled back to Spain via Crete and Sicily. In one of his most evocative passages, Galán recalls the fear and humiliation that he felt when he first arrived in Algiers and was taken to the *bezistan*, or market, where he was subjected to a long, close and dehumanizing physical inspection; he had to parade around so that would-be buyers might check for lameness or other defects. This, he observed, was exactly the sort of treatment that animals sent to market received in Spain.[45]

The experiences of Cervantes and Sosa, in contrast to that of Galán, were fairly unusual in that they had the means and connections to entertain the hope that they might eventually be ransomed. The fate of such captives was, at least some of the time, not to be worked as hard as their fellow Christians from humbler backgrounds; in *Don Quixote*, the traveller has the time and space to develop a relationship with Zoraida because he and a few companions are regularly left to their own devices when the majority of the inmates of his *baño*, or prison compound, set out in the morning and are put to work around the city. Captives with some means could pay a fee, the *gileffo*, to be excused work. Galán's origins were more modest, but he was unusual in eventually finding some degree of protection, as a privately owned slave, in his ability to forge a close relationship with his high-status master. It is interesting that his eventual decision to escape was motivated by his master's refusal to countenance negotiating a ransom because Galán had become such a valued member of his household. For most of the captives who fetched up in Algiers and the other Barbary corsair cities, ransom was a remote possibility at best, which meant that they faced the prospect of a lifetime in servitude. The worst off were those who, like Galán before he got his lucky break, were not owned by private masters but were public slaves; these formed between a third and a half of the 25,000 or so captives believed to be living in Algiers.[46] Often they were put to work on civic projects, such as dragging stones from the quarry outside the city to repair the vital Mole, the large breakwater in the harbour, making ropes or cutting timber. These were the wretches at the very bottom of the heap, living in cramped and squalid conditions in the *baños*.[47]

There is some debate about the relative severity of the conditions endured by slaves in Algiers and the other north African corsair port-cities. *Grosso modo* they were most probably no worse off than slaves in other parts of the Mediterranean, and in some cases perhaps more favoured; the conditions in which slaves worked in the Spanish mercury mine in Almadén, for example, were notoriously terrible. Nor is a direct comparison with the treatment and predicament of those who came to be caught up in Atlantic slavery realistic or appropriate. But the argument that the masters did not abuse their captives because they coveted their ransoms would only have applied to a minority of those enslaved; and the notion that those who did hard labour were not routinely mistreated because of the value to their owners of the work that they did merely recycles a rather worn truism that is more or less applicable to all slave-owning societies. Especially when there was a glut of new slaves, for example after a major Christian naval defeat, this calculation would scarcely have applied. This was a brutal and brutalizing world.[48]

It is important to remember that slaving and slavery were facts of life in most communities around the Mediterranean, on both sides of the religious divide, Malta included. As we have noted, when the Knights arrived in 1530 they could build on the existing corsair tradition in the archipelago as well as memories of their own naval exploits in Rhodes. It is significant that corsairing became an important strand of their operations very quickly, even as they adjusted to their new circumstances. As early as 1531 two of the order's galleys were collaborating with forces from Genoa and Sicily in a raid on Methoni in Greece; more than 800 captives were taken.[49] By the 1540s and 1550s raids on coastal targets and the capture of vessels at sea had become standard features of the Maltese flotilla's operations.[50] Many slaves were taken to man the order's galleys: several hundred were in Malta during the Great Siege, and were put to work repairing defences, sometimes cruelly herded into the most exposed positions. Before he became Grand Master, La Valette was actively involved in slaving raids. He also owned slaves himself. In 1549 he was investigated for bringing over from Tripoli an African slave whose servile status was disputed. Perhaps this was the same person, Abdullah, whom La Valette freed in 1564 as a reward for his many years of service.[51] Similarly, in March 1566 it was the dying wish of a Spanish Knight, Hernando de Bracamonte, that his two African slaves be freed, Ynes de Bracamonte, aged about forty-five, and her daughter Maria, aged about thirty-two. One wonders whether Maria was in fact Hernando de Bracamonte's daughter.[52] It is intriguing to find captives being freed or ransomed just a few weeks before the Great Siege began: a Turkish tailor named Mehmet was freed as a reward for ten years' service on 14 March 1565, and a Jew named Samuel ben Iomtov was ransomed on 16 April. Did they have time to get off Malta before the arrival of the Turkish fleet on 18 May?[53] In sum, the Malta of the Knights was a place easily familiar with, and to a large extent reliant upon, slavery and captivity on many levels.[54]

Our knowledge of who was enslaved in the sixteenth-century Mediterranean, how they came to be captured, and how they fared is skewed, as noted earlier, by an imbalance in the surviving evidence in favour of Christians taken by Muslims. There are many reasons for this. There are fewer Muslim captivity narratives, at least from this period, a reflection, it has been argued, of a greater reticence about revealing one's inner self to strangers in early modern Muslim culture; and a consequence, too, of the relative absence from Islamic religiosity of the sort of emphasis on redemptive suffering which informed many Christian captivity stories.[55] There was also no Muslim equivalent of the Inquisition, the records of which are a mine of information about captives, slaves and renegades who found themselves in the marginal spaces between two opposing cultures and belief systems. One exception to this general rule is an account of his two years of captivity in Malta by Macuncuzade Mustafa.[56] Macuncuzade was a *kadi*, a judge, who was travelling to Cyprus to take up an official position. As his ship neared the island it was intercepted by four Maltese vessels: the clear implication is that the assailants were galleys of the Order of St John, not native Maltese corsairs. After a stiff fight, in which, we are told, more than eighty of the attackers lost their lives, Macuncuzade, his slave and his surviving companions, who included several other Ottoman officials, were taken prisoner. Having endured nearly a month at sea, during which time his captors pressed on with their *corso*, seizing a further twelve vessels, they arrived at Malta in June 1597. In all more than 280 prisoners had been taken.[57]

The story that Macuncuzade tells of the captivity that awaited him makes mention of many of the challenges that he faced. The physical hardships, as one might expect, are emphasized: he was particularly struck by the dark, cramped, unsanitary and foul-smelling conditions in the dungeons in which the captives were placed, the filthy water and the inadequate food.[58] Of perhaps greater interest, however, are the clues that his account offers about Macuncuzade's evolving mental state, as his initial shock and disorientation shifted to a more resigned coming to terms with his predicament. He was fortunate in being supported by a captive family, which took him under its wing. He also benefitted from the companionship of an old acquaintance, a judge named Hasim el-Hasimi, who had already been a prisoner in Malta for seven years. He was made to do hard labour in construction work on Malta's fortifications, and he was badly affected by it, though such severe physical demands seem to have been intermittent. He also spent time in solitary confinement, some of his fellow inmates having informed on him about some transgression to the guards.

Macuncuzade's account is particularly interesting in its description of his interviews with a panel of Knights to agree on a figure for his ransom; this would seem to have been a deliberately drawn-out process in which psychological pressure was applied to browbeat Macuncuzade into agreeing a higher price than he originally claimed he could afford. Also of note are a few hints in his narrative as to the ways in which the unequal and brutal power dynamic between captor and captive was, if not exactly mitigated, at least complicated. He observes that after a time the guards settled into a less aggressive routine, which suggests that the particularly harsh initial reception that he describes was a deliberate breaking-in of new arrivals when they were at their most psychologically vulnerable. The captives were not completely forlorn: they could receive letters from the outside world; and Macuncuzade mentions that when he fell ill, he was treated in the 'hospital of San Giovanni', by which he must mean the Sacra Infermeria, a reminder of the paradoxes running through the Order of St John's religious vocation. In December

1598 he learned that arrangements were in hand to secure his release, and he left Malta the following year.[59]

In one, in the end decisive, respect Macuncuzade was extremely fortunate in being very well connected back in Istanbul, with the result that pressure could be brought to bear on the Ottoman elite to facilitate his release. Indeed the sultan himself, Mehmed III, took an interest in his situation and ordered that a Christian captive be freed in a prisoner exchange.[60] In this Macuncuzade more closely resembles Christian prisoners such as Cervantes and Antonio de Sosa, who were likewise educated, literate and sufficiently important to entertain the hope of liberation. The large majority of those swept up in the corsairing net were, in contrast, poor people with far fewer prospects of anything other than a lifetime of servitude in front of them, at least until, on the Christian side, the religious orders devoted to the redemption of captives, the Mercedarians and Trinitarians, expanded the scale of their operations in the seventeenth century. Most of these victims are nameless and lost to history. We are therefore fortunate in having written evidence for a small minority, at least, of the many hundreds of thousands taken captive in the sixteenth-century Mediterranean in the form of investigations conducted by the Inquisition or, in places in which their rulers did not allow the Inquisition to operate, similar procedures undertaken by local clergy. The Inquisition was principally concerned with the investigation of heresy, which is the formal denial of the authority of the Catholic Church. This central remit was expanded, however, to address many forms of heterodox belief and practice, and also apostasy, the abandonment of one's membership of the Church. It was this last category of offence which brought before inquisitorial panels around the Latin Christian Mediterranean a steady stream of confused, pathetic, defiant or desperate people who, in their various ways, were all victims of the cruel sea.

It is important to bear in mind that many of those who came before the Inquisition, and typically the most problematic, were not those who had simply been enslaved, clung on to their Christian identity, and somehow managed to find their way back to

Christian territory. For the majority of those enslaved in north Africa, conversion to Islam was never a possibility, and was in any event usually discouraged by slaves' masters; manumission did not automatically confer freedom, but it was believed it might make the freed slave less productive.[61] A minority, however, of those seized in raids on their communities or at sea were forced, or volunteered, to go through a simple ceremony, including circumcision for the males and the cutting of one's hair for females, by means of which they signalled their conversion to Islam. In so doing they detached themselves from their former co-religionists; there was in fact a widespread belief that these renegades were harsher towards their Christian slaves than native-born Muslims because they felt the need to vindicate their new identity in aggressive ways. That said, the renegade who helps Cervantes' traveller to escape was not a wholly exceptional figure. There is evidence that some renegades continued to identify with Christian captives to the extent that they helped them come up with their ransoms.[62] Some of those who prospered re-established ties with their natal families, even to the extent of promoting their interests.[63] It is because they inhabited a complex liminal zone between cultural certainties that the renegades' experience can tell us so much about the tensions and paradoxes that ran through the larger system of Mediterranean slavery and corsairing.

One of those caught up in this twilight world was a Sicilian named Giovanni Fabricio Ferlito, who had been taken by the 'Turks' but managed to find his way back to Sicily and was reconciled by the Church. He then voluntarily switched sides again, participating in a raid on Sicily in which he used his local knowledge to hunt down and enslave some of his former neighbours. He was then himself taken captive in 1582, brought before the Inquisition and handed a life sentence as a galley slave.[64] The same sort of shuttling between Sicily and north Africa characterized the life of Bartulo Marcelo, who was first captured in 1564 at the age of thirteen. Having escaped during a raid on Corsica, he returned to Marsala, only to be captured at sea many years later and taken to Tunis a second time. He subsequently contributed his local knowledge to a raid on Sicily, lingered there for a while, and then returned to Tunis before finally being captured, in his early sixties, by the viceroy of Sicily in 1612. During his time moving back and forth he had picked up two wives, the first in Sicily and the second, bigamously, in Naples, and also had a family with a female renegade in Tunis.[65] A Genoese, Gian Battista known as Bairan, was seized as young child in a raid and sold in the slave market of Algiers. He converted to Islam and pursued a career as a corsair, only to be captured by the Spanish and made a galley slave. He escaped by stealing a boat from Cádiz, in the process kidnapping two children whom he sold when he reached Larache in Morocco. Resuming his life as a corsair, he was captured a second time in 1579 and given a life sentence in the galleys.[66]

Ferlito, Marcelo and Bairan come across as adaptable survivors whose ruthlessness was a matter of ingrained acculturation, an easy dog-eat-dog cruelty that extracted as much advantage as possible from a world that had stacked the odds against them. Others who found themselves in a similar position seem more like victims buffeted by the twists and turns of fate. Jean Canassa from Pézenas in southern France, for example, was captured at sea in about 1550 when he was in his early teens. He was, he later claimed, forced to abjure his faith and was circumcised. He spent the next seventeen years in Algiers, before taking part in a *corso* which ran into a detachment of Spanish galleys. The cultural conditioning of his many years in Algiers – his only adult experience – ran too deep for him to be treated by his captors as anything other than a Muslim. He was therefore made a galley slave; it was as such that he found himself in one of the Spanish galleys that fought at Lepanto. Ten years later, his galley called at Lisbon, and he made a desperate appeal to avail himself of the papal amnesty for renegades who had contributed to the Christian victory. Only then, by now in his forties, was he able to regain his freedom.[67] Léon de Olivier, from Marseille, was thirteen and aboard a merchant ship carrying silks and other fabrics to Algiers in about 1581 when he was captured by a corsair known as 'Five Teeth'. Five Teeth took a particular liking to Léon – there is a good deal of evidence that younger victims were often singled out by their captors – and allowed the others on the ship to go free. Léon was taken to Bizerte in Tunisia and sold on to a Janissary named Murad, who beat him daily to force him to convert. In 1593 he was captured when his frigate was surprised by a large force of Christian galleys and ran ashore near Rome. Through all this, Léon insisted to the panel of inquisitors, he had remained a good Christian, avoiding meat on Fridays and Sundays, saying his Pater Noster and Ave Maria, and never entering a mosque. When asked by the inquisitors to recite these prayers, he stumbled through them with some mistakes; the Credo and the Salve Regina he could not recall at all. His fate is not recorded, but the chances are that he did not convince his interrogators and he was consigned to the galleys.[68] There are many other such sad tales in the surviving inquisitorial sources.

The people who emerge from these stories seem either to have succumbed under the crushing weight of ill luck and powerlessness, or to have devised desperate ways in which to carve out some agency for themselves in unforgiving environments. In both cases they found themselves in a marginal space between two cultures, the traces of which it was difficult to efface even if one were determined to do so. A Portuguese, Francisco de Zamora, who had been captured in 1576 when he was about sixteen, but had subsequently escaped, decided to go on pilgrimage to Rome and had got as far as southern France when his bearing and manner of speech aroused the suspicion of local people and he was arrested. The fact that he was found to have been circumcised sealed his fate, and he was sold to Genoese slave traders. He spent the next twenty years as a galley slave, and only regained his freedom when he was in his mid fifties.[69]

Not all those who came before the Inquisition had returned to Christendom voluntarily, and even those who expressed relief to be back home had to overcome suspicion. The Church was particularly exercised by the question of apostasy: it could not treat it exactly the same as heresy, which resides in a voluntary act of denial, because those facing the Inquisition would routinely claim, though not always truthfully, that they had been forced to abjure. Most of those who went through this process, moreover, were poorly educated, with little understanding of religious faith in the abstract, at least in the sorts of terms that the inquisitors would have acknowledged as legitimate. This led the Inquisition to direct the majority of its questions to matters of external culture, such as dress and diet, as markers of Christian identity or the loss of it.[70] On the other hand, the fact that many of those investigated argued – or were coached by sympathetic clerics to claim – that, for all their superficial participation in the outward trappings of Muslim culture, they had always remained Christian deep down in their hearts suggests that a capacity for some degree of interiority, self-possession and agency was acknowledged even in the uneducated. It was, and is, easy to be cynical about renegades. Cervantes' traveller observes that renegades in Algiers would secure letters of accreditation from Christian captives, some in case they managed to return to Christendom as they hoped, but others in order to give them a cover story if they ever found themselves on a Christian shore involuntarily.[71] One should not underestimate, however, the difficult choices and cultural ambiguities that renegades were forced to confront in extremely stressful and disorienting circumstances, often under duress.

The early modern Mediterranean offers up many cross-currents and paradoxes. As the research of Amy Remensnyder has shown, the small island of Lampedusa, roughly midway between Malta and the coast of Tunisia, was the site of a remarkable long-term experiment in religious syncretism and (to a degree) tolerance. In a limestone cave there was both a shrine to the Virgin Mary and the tomb of a Muslim holy man, a *marabout*. Here mariners of both faiths would leave offerings, which doubled up as helpful supplies for those who fetched up on the island as escapees or because of shipwreck.[72] As the picaresque traveller and adventurer Alonso de Contreras, who visited Lampedusa at the beginning of the seventeenth century, noted, however, there were limits to the ecumenical spirit. When a vessel was spotted offshore, anyone on the island would be very careful to check whether it was one of 'theirs'; the fear of being taken captive still predominated in this most exceptional of places.[73] That said, the fact that such co-existence was possible at all, albeit in a remote, thinly populated and liminal space, is noteworthy.

A very different, and more typical, picture emerges from Antonio de Sosa's account of the authorities' reaction to severe drought and famine in Algiers in 1579. Having sought advice from religious leaders, the city's ruler, Uluç Ali Pasha, banned the saying of mass for Christian captives and ordered that three *imágenes* which had been taken from captured Christian galleys, and which were on display hanging upside down near the harbour, should be taken down and destroyed.[74] These were most probably three-dimensional representations.[75] One was of St John, seized from the Hospitaller galley the *San Giovanni* in 1570, a second had been taken when another Hospitaller galley, the *San Paulo*, had been captured (with Sosa on board) in 1577, and the third was from a Sicilian vessel taken the following year. They had been deliberately placed so as to be readily visible to large numbers of people, and had been accompanied by no doubt triumphantly worded explanatory placards. As Sosa remarked, for as long as the *imágenes* were on show they were a source of great pride to the local people and of offence to their Christian captives. In the authorities' reaction to the crisis in 1579 we see a shift from one stark contrast, that opposing self-congratulatory victor and abjectly humiliated loser, to another that insisted on religious separation: Algiers should be absolutely cleansed of the corrupting traces of Christian practice and belief. But the net effect was the same: an emphasis on ultimately irreconcilable difference and bitter conflict as basic facts of life. The cruel sea that first put the *imágenes* on display as a means to taunt a defeated opponent and then destroyed them as a source of religious contamination did not cause the Great Siege, but it was the basic source of the immanent and fissile tensions, contradictions and hatreds that underpinned the events of 1565.

4.
1551: The Precursor of the Great Siege

In June 1524, when the Order of St John was first looking for a new home after its expulsion from Rhodes, it appointed an eight-man team to visit Malta and Tripoli and to submit a report on their respective suitability – the guiding assumption being that, far from fundamentally reinventing themselves and their vocation, what the Knights were seeking was as close an approximation as possible to Rhodes as a base for continued naval operations.[1] Although the commissioners were slightly more favourable towards Malta than Tripoli, their verdict was nonetheless forbidding: the existing defences were inadequate and would be very expensive to improve; the castle in Grand Harbour was overlooked by positions from where an attacker could rain down artillery fire; the island was poor, lacked natural resources and was very dry; and it could only feed itself for a third of the year, with the result that it was largely dependent on food brought over from Sicily. Gozo was not a practicable alternative because, although a little more fertile, it lacked a suitable harbour and its one fortress was of a redundant design that would be unable to withstand a determined assault. There would seem to have been a pervasive mood of vulnerability hanging over the islands: Malta, the commissioners reported, 'is wretchedly subject to the rapacity and depredation of infidel corsairs' whose slaving raids were frequent.

Nonetheless, and despite all these formidable disadvantages, the commissioners, when pushed by the Grand Master and Council, were prepared to concede that Malta, unlike Tripoli, *might* just satisfy the order's needs, provided that the favourable terms under which food was brought cheaply from Sicily without taxes and tolls were allowed to continue. This was prescient: paying for imported food to keep Malta going would become one of the order's main expenses in future years. The reason why the commissioners were willing to qualify their negative verdict was simple: Malta had two excellent harbours adjacent to one another, Marsamxett and Grand Harbour, praise of which formed the only positive part of their report. In the event, the order opted for Malta and Tripoli as a combined package a few years later. But the initial lack of enthusiasm is notable. It suggests that despite the advantages of the two largest and most secure harbours – and there are several other good bays and inlets, particularly on Malta's northern and eastern coasts – Malta was still a hard sell.

The order's hesitation largely flowed from its assessment of Malta's strategic strengths and weaknesses as a possible naval base, given especially that the island's existing defences against amphibious assault were inadequate, water and food were scarce, and there was no woodland to provide the basic raw material for shipbuilding, a point that the commissioners emphasized. This assessment was in turn informed by an underlying appreciation of the maritime 'ecosystem' of the sixteenth-century Mediterranean. What people could or could not do in and with the Mediterranean was shaped by a combination of geography and technology. Modern means of transport have accustomed us to thinking of the relationship between two places as principally a function of the straight-line distance between them. Viewed in these terms, the fact that the Maltese archipelago is almost exactly equidistant between Gibraltar and the eastern end of the Mediterranean, and also the same distance between Trieste and the Gulf of Sidra, the northernmost and southernmost points of that sea, seems compelling.[2] Who would not want to control these islands, given also that they lie just to the south-east of the Sicilian Channel or Narrows, the narrowest point in the Mediterranean separating the Levant and Ponant? The answer, however, depends on the technology available to a would-be Mediterranean hegemon. The fact of Malta's east-to-west equidistance only became a central strategic consideration during the period of British rule in the nineteenth and twentieth centuries, and even then not immediately; significantly, British appreciation of Malta's value as a naval base only took firm hold with the opening of the Suez Canal in 1869, coupled with the growth of steam-powered ships. It was the naval link connecting Gibraltar, Malta, and Alexandria/Port Said that was at stake in the dogged defence of Malta in 1940–43 – the other 'great siege'. The irony of that remarkable moment in Maltese history is that it itself heralded a new quantum shift in military technology – submarine warfare and air power – which would change the strategic calculus applying to military domination of the Mediterranean once more.

In the ancient and medieval periods, Malta's relationship to naval technology could not have been more different. Ships plying the Mediterranean would cleave close to land as far as possible, with the result that, although Malta had some role as a stopping-off point for traffic between Sicily and north Africa, vessels travelling along the east–west axis would largely pass it by. The thrust of the story of St Paul's shipwreck on Malta around the year AD 60, as told in the Acts of the Apostles: 27–28, is that he and his companions are blown to such a remote place that even the sailors struggle to recognize where they are. By the sixteenth century developments in naval technology had made navigation out of sight of land more commonplace, with the result that islands such as the Maltese archipelago, which lies approximately one hundred kilometres from Sicily, the nearest landmass, became less isolated. The vessel *par excellence* that connected the nodal points of military, and to some extent commercial, competition in the Mediterranean was the galley, complemented by an array of smaller oared craft – in descending order of size the galliot, brigantine, frigate, felucca and fusta.[3] Far from being a throwback to an earlier age, the galley, rigged with lateen sails to complement the motive power of its *ciurma*, was optimally suited to Mediterranean conditions, and was reaching the peak of its technological development around the time of the Great Siege.[4] The design characteristics that optimized a galley's performance – its narrow hull, shallow draught and low freeboard – could cope with the relatively calm weather in the Mediterranean between March and October, though it was unwise to push one's luck: Charles V's invasion fleet off Algiers was badly undone by a violent storm in October 1541.[5] In addition, the Mediterranean is microtidal: its tidal reaches are less than two metres, among the smallest in the world, which made it easy to pull galleys onto beaches and moor them there or to careen the hulls, which had to be done frequently. The modest tides and the manoeuvrability that oars permitted also made entry into ports much less hit-and-miss than it was for sailing vessels confronting the much heavier seas and shifting winds of the Atlantic or North Sea.[6]

A war galley's banks of oars made it impossible to furnish it with broadside armament, except perhaps some small anti-personnel artillery pieces. The heavy metal of a galley's firepower was located at the bow, with one, three, five, even seven forward-facing guns. These could be deployed against a weaker craft that a galley was chasing down, as well as against enemy galleys. They also equipped galleys to come close into shore to cover the disembarkation or embarkation of troops, or to bring their guns to bear on coastal fortresses, either on their own account or in support of forces on land. The sleek dimensions of galleys, and the presence on board of perhaps 200 or more oarsmen, crew and soldiers crammed uncomfortably together, placed severe limits on storage capacity. Finding room for sufficient quantities of biscuit, the staple diet for the oarsmen, was a particular challenge. But an even greater constraint was the storage of water, which the *ciurme*, engaged in hard physical labour in the heat of the Mediterranean summer, would need to consume at a very high rate if they were to remain healthy and efficient; they typically rowed all the hours of daylight, unless a fresh wind was directly astern, which would have been unusual. This meant that a galley's operational range was determined by the time it could travel before having to take on water, and whether and where there were friendly places for it to do so. It has been calculated that the outer limit was about two weeks on the open sea, though in practice a prudent captain would avoid going down to the wire if possible.⁷

This constraint, in conjunction with the galley's offensive capacity that we have noted, meant that naval power in the Mediterranean was a function of one's control of those strongpoints where galleys could take on supplies and be refitted; these places would ideally be well fortified to protect one's own naval assets and deter one's enemy from attacking them. In such circumstances, one cannot speak of the Habsburg and Ottoman empires and their respective surrogates competing for actual control of the sea in the sixteenth century. The days when naval technology and supply infrastructure had reached the point where, for example, Nelson could spend two years between 1803 and 1805 out at sea blockading the French naval base at Toulon without once touching land lay far in the future. The sea as such was not at issue in the sixteenth century: it was simply an expanse that connected the real pieces in the game, fortified coastal positions, their harbours and the resources of their hinterlands.

The question that confronted the order in the 1520s was where to situate itself as a small but not insignificant element in that system. The unknown at that point was the extent to which conflict with the Ottoman state would follow it westwards into the central Mediterranean. When the Knights had been based in Rhodes and its outposts, they had been tight up against Ottoman territory and sea lanes, and the conflict that this geographical proximity encouraged had duly dominated their sense of mission. As we have noted, the commissioners in 1524 identified Malta's vulnerability to frequent corsair raiding and its human costs; and the order would have understood that, if it decided to settle in Malta, dealing with that threat would have to be one of the first orders of business. But what if a hostile state actor which commanded much greater resources than the north African corsairs were to insert itself into that part of the Mediterranean? With the benefit of hindsight we know, as the Knights could not in 1524, or 1527, when Charles formally offered them Malta and Tripoli as a package, or 1530, when they relocated to

1551: The Precursor of the Great Siege

Malta, that between the 1530s and 1550s the Ottomans would come to assume a more aggressive and expansive role in the central and western Mediterranean. As always in such circumstances, we should be careful not to see this development through the eyes of anxious contemporary westerners: this was not an inexorable and relentless programme of conquest pursued for its own sake by implacable opponents. Rather, we should think in terms of an expanding zone of opportunity and reactivity on the Ottomans' part: opportunity in the sense that the Sublime Porte forged alliances with those – France and the corsairs – who in their different ways shared their hostility towards the Habsburg dominion; reactivity in the sense that the sultans, for the most part, only acted when provoked or when they believed that their strategic interests in the eastern Mediterranean were threatened. For the Knights, the result was that, if back in the 1520s they were mostly conscious of the differences between Rhodes and Malta, by the 1540s and 1550s they could be in no doubt that they once more occupied a position on the front line.

By the mid sixteenth century, the Ottoman state had long since made the transition from a land-based power to one that combined effective naval might with a formidable military apparatus.[8] The navy had played an important role in Mehmed II's conquest of Constantinople in 1453. In 1480 an Ottoman amphibious force besieged and held Otranto, on the back of the heel of Italy; local forces slowly organized some resistance, but it was principally news of the death of Mehmed in May 1481 which persuaded the Ottoman forces to withdraw. At the time the occupation of Otranto was something of a one-off, but it and the first siege of Rhodes, also in 1480, seemed to portend some sort of programme of aggression in the future. Clearly momentum lay with the Ottomans: between 1499 and 1503 their navy overcame the Venetians in a series of conflicts which ensured that when the commercial relations on which the Venetians relied came to be resumed, they would be on terms favourable to the Sublime Porte. As with so much else, the conquest of Egypt and the other Mamluk territories in 1516–17 was the turning point in the Ottomans' approach to naval power, for not only did they significantly extend their coastline around the eastern Mediterranean, they also acquired a direct strategic interest in the trade route passing up the Red Sea, the need to protect their supply lines between Alexandria and Istanbul, and an imprecise but ideologically resonant responsibility for the protection of pilgrims travelling to the Hijaz, including those from the south-western shores of the Mediterranean, whose journeys would take them close to Malta and Tripoli.[9]

It was at this significant juncture in the 1510s that the sultan, Selim I, received the submission of a corsair, Oruç Reis. Oruç and his brothers, originally from Lesbos, had begun their careers as corsairs in the Levant, but had relocated their base of operations to Djerba, just off the Tunisian coast, and had thereafter concentrated their efforts in the Maghreb.[10] In 1516 their seizure of Algiers announced their emergence as a powerful force in the region. In receiving Oruç's submission, Selim was being handed formal, if at this stage only notional, control of territory far to the west of the reach of Ottoman power up to that point.[11] When Oruç was killed by the Spanish at Tlemcen in 1518, his position of leadership was assumed by his brother Hayreddin, widely known as Barbarossa. Increasingly secure in his base in Algiers, especially after the Spanish were dislodged from its *peñón*, or offshore fortress, in 1529, Hayreddin became the predominant naval figure in the central and western Mediterranean up to his death in 1546. He incited a mixture of raw terror and romanticized awe in his Christian opponents. (It will be his protégé and successor, Turgut Reis, whom we shall see assuming an important, if brief, role in the Great Siege.) In 1533 Süleyman made a bold move in appointing Hayreddin as *kapudan*, high admiral of the Ottoman fleet. In the short term this was partly a like-for-like reaction to the Genoese *condottiere* Andrea Doria's defection from the French in 1528 and his appointment as admiral by Charles V. In the longer run, Hayreddin's elevation inaugurated a fruitful, if sometimes fraught, relationship between the Sublime Porte and the north African corsairs; it increased the Ottomans' naval strength, and more importantly it gave them the benefit of unrivalled knowledge of the waters of the central and western Mediterranean. The harnessing of the corsairs' energy and expertise soon began to pay off: Hayreddin captured Tunis from its Hafsid ruler in 1534, prompting Charles V to launch a large expedition that took the city in the following year. In 1538 he commanded the fleet that dealt a devastating blow to an allied force of imperial, papal and Venetian vessels off Preveza on the western coast of Greece; in 1540 he ranged as far west as Gibraltar, one of the factors that decided Charles V on his ill-fated expedition against Algiers in 1541; in 1543–4 Hayreddin's fleet overwintered in Toulon, which the French had made available thanks to their alliance with the Ottomans, and created havoc along the western coast of Italy on his return voyage; and in 1545 he raided as far west as the Balearic islands.

By the mid to later 1540s, therefore, the Knights on Malta could be under no illusion that the expansion of the Ottoman zone of operations, either directly or through their corsair surrogates, had now placed them in a more exposed position. One of the first acts of Turgut Reis after Hayreddin's death was to raid Malta in July 1547; he had already descended on the islands regularly in recent years, and had led a slaving raid on Gozo in 1546.[12] In 1547 Turgut landed his forces at Marsaxlokk and worked inland as far as Żejtun before being chased off by the Knights, though he still managed to hang on to about half of the 300 captives he had seized. In 1548 he captured a Hospitaller galley, the *Catarinetta*, en route from Marseille with a very large sum of money, 70,000 *scudi*, that had been raised in France.[13] Initially Turgut would seem to have been acting largely on his own account. But the Knights knew that sooner or later, if he reached an accommodation with the Sublime Porte as Hayreddin had done, his personal interest in the Maltese islands would draw in the main Ottoman fleet.

Sure enough, Turgut did enter into a closer relationship with the Ottoman government between 1548 and 1550, and in 1551, in conjunction with another experienced corsair, Salah Reis, he collaborated with the Ottoman fleet under the command of Sinan Pasha, the brother of the grand vizier, Rüstem Pasha, in direct attacks on the Knights' positions in the central Mediterranean. The challenge that the order faced in 1551 was without doubt the most perilous in its history between its arrival in Malta and the Great Siege. It is therefore worth examining the events of that year in some detail because, far from being just one more instance of the predation of the Maltese islands that was becoming commonplace around that time, they exposed the vulnerability of Malta and Gozo as never before. If not quite a trial run for the Great Siege, the joint Ottoman–corsair assault on Malta and Gozo in 1551 was its most significant antecedent, a foretaste of many of the opportunities and challenges, on both sides, that would be at stake in 1565.

1551 is particularly important because it was in that year that what had become a kind of running feud between Turgut and the Knights became definitively subsumed within the naval competition between the Ottoman and the Habsburg empires. As we shall see, matters were complicated further by an attempt to reanimate the on-off alliance between France and the Sublime Porte, which in turn worsened divisions within the order along national lines. In 1547 a truce had been agreed between Süleyman and Charles V, but local conflicts, driven by the corsairs' own interests, continued to break out in the southern Mediterranean. In early 1550 Turgut seized Monastir and Mahdia on the Tunisian coast from their Hafsid rulers, who were, after a fashion, Habsburg clients. Charles V's response was to send his principal naval commander, Andrea Doria, with a taskforce that besieged and captured Mahdia in September; the Knights contributed to the operation, with the loss of thirty-six of their number.[14] The question then became whether the Ottomans would choose to interpret Doria's aggression as a provocation and breach of the truce, and in the process exploit Turgut's difficulties to project their own power into Tunisian waters, with a view to threatening Habsburg control of Tunis itself. The French ambassador in Istanbul, Gabriel de Luetz d'Aramon, was certainly advocating for such a reaction, as well as holding out the possibility of French naval collaboration.[15] The Habsburg response was to insist that Doria had simply been conducting a police operation

1551: The Precursor of the Great Siege

against notorious thieves, a right in natural law which lay beyond the scope of the truce; this was a clever distinction, but one that allowed the Ottomans to play the Habsburgs at their own game by claiming that, while likewise remaining true to the spirit of the truce, they were free to avenge the loss of Mahdia.[16] So when news began to reach western courts in 1551 that the Ottomans had assembled a large fleet, an obvious inference to be drawn was that Mahdia was the objective, though whether this would be with or without active French support remained an open question.

In the meantime Turgut had pulled off a spectacular coup. Doria had tried to catch him by surprise on the island of Djerba, 'the nest and lair of every thief and corsair' in Bosio's words, but had been humiliated when Turgut cut a channel out to the sea in order to slip away from the narrow inlet where Doria believed he had him trapped; Bosio remarks that Doria was utterly amazed and deeply depressed by Turgut's ingenuity and daring.[17] From there Turgut sailed to join forces with the Ottoman fleet, offering up a hint of his future intentions en route by landing on Malta on 17–18 April and sacking Siġġiewi before being chased off by local cavalry.[18] By early July Sinan Pasha had brought the combined Ottoman–corsair force to stand off Reggio in Calabria and had begun negotiations with the viceroy of Sicily, Juan de Vega. Sinan Pasha insisted that Mahdia be returned. Vega stalled by claiming, correctly enough, that he was unable to accede to such a demand without first consulting Charles V. But the fact that Sinan Pasha kept his fleet in Sicilian waters for nearly a fortnight, with the end of the campaigning season only about two months away, suggests that he held out hopes for an agreement.[19] The Habsburg apologist Pedro de Salazar observed of this interlude that interactions remained tense but courteous and controlled: the Ottoman fleet took on, and paid for, supplies brought out to it by local merchants.[20] Only when Sinan Pasha finally lost patience did the fleet move off, sacking Augusta on the eastern coast of Sicily – Turgut played an active role – by way of signalling that it had now shifted into an aggressive register.

The fleet, which comprised approximately one hundred galleys in addition to galliots, smaller craft and supply vessels, sailed south, arriving off Malta on 18 July. This was a decisive moment, for what Sinan Pasha did next would establish whether the reconquest of Mahdia remained his priority. The worst fears of the Knights and the Maltese were duly confirmed when the fleet took up position off the entrance to Marsamxett and began to land troops on the Sciberras peninsula, the tongue of land between that bay and Grand Harbour. They occupied the small church on the site of the future fortress of St Elmo and, showing great discipline, used the cover of stone walls to work their way into positions looking out onto Grand Harbour. Meanwhile, in a nice illustration of the different styles and priorities of the two military cultures harnessed together in the Ottoman armada, Turgut led a force of azabs, or irregular infantry, and Levantine corsairs in looser order into the interior of the island towards Qormi and Birkirkara. They burned everything as they went along and were only slightly impeded by the harassing tactics of a cavalry detachment under the command of an English Knight, Nicholas Upton.[21] By this stage many thousands of refugees were pouring into Birgu, the main settlement in the Grand Harbour area, and Mdina, the old capital of the island: if Bosio's figures of about 12,000 in each place are correct, this would have amounted to the great majority of the population of the island.[22] On the 19th Sinan Pasha disembarked his elite troops, 3,000 Janissaries, but was soon persuaded that an assault on St Angelo, the Knight's fortress in Grand Harbour, was impracticable, even though, significantly, Turgut urged him to press on. There may have been countervailing voices in his high command and among some of the other corsairs arguing that Tripoli was a more promising target.[23] Rather than abandon the Maltese islands altogether, however, and perhaps as a gesture to Turgut, Sinan Pasha moved the fleet a few miles westwards; most of his vessels relocated to St Paul's Bay, and a detachment took up position in St Julian's Bay. His troops disembarked once more and made their way inland towards Mdina, sacking several places – Naxxar, Birkirkara, Mosta, Attard and Lija – as they went.[24]

Mdina, or Città Notabile, stood on high ground that offered some protection on its steeper flanks, while the walls facing its suburb, Rabat, were tolerably strong. In places, however, the defences were very weak. It had supplies to hold out for two months, but its greatest vulnerability was a shortage of water if, as now seemed to be an imminent threat, a besieging force cut off the sources of water in Rabat on which the inhabitants of Mdina mostly relied. The governor, the Knight Giorgio Adorno, was able to call on only about one hundred experienced soldiers; this forced him to cobble together a militia from all the local men capable of bearing arms. Thanks to snatch-squads sent out to capture Turkish prisoners for interrogation, Adorno was in a position to anticipate the enemy's moves to some extent and to mount an effective defence against a force of about 8,000–10,000 men.[25] By rationing the water, conserving his gunpowder and preventing anyone from slipping away who might be taken prisoner and reveal the defenders' weaknesses, Adorno established some measure of discipline and control. In this he was assisted by a timely boost to the defenders' morale when a nun was reported to have had a revelation that the city would be saved through the intercession of St Agatha.[26] The arrival of an experienced French Knight, Nicolas Durand de Villegagnon, with a handful of colleagues also reassured the defenders that they had not been forgotten.[27] The attackers began dragging their cannon into position and building trenches, but, almost as soon as they had arrived, on the 21st they began to pull back towards St Paul's Bay. The interrogation of further captives, as well as of fugitive renegades, provided no clear explanation for the sudden volte-face. Some suggested that the Turks were nervous about the movements of Doria's fleet. Others, nearer the mark as it proved, believed that when Turgut had recently intercepted a boat carrying gunpowder and gunners from St Angelo to Gozo, he had concluded that the second island must be very poorly defended, making this an opportune moment to restage on a more devastating scale the predatory raids that he had conducted there several times in the past.[28]

On 22 July the Ottoman forces disembarked, again, at Mġarr on Gozo and moved inland towards the island's central fortress, the

Castello, in what is now Rabat/Victoria, where most of the island's population had taken refuge; Bosio says that he had spoken to old Gozitans who were still able to recall the mood of terror that gripped those within.[29] The defences were, if anything, weaker than those of Mdina, and resistance was further hampered by the fact that the governor of the island, the Knight Galatiano de Sese, seems to have experienced some sort of breakdown. When the one gunner who was able to lay down effective counter-fire, an Englishman, was killed, there was no one to replace him. On the 25th de Sese sent an Augustinian friar to negotiate the surrender of the castle in return for allowing 200 of the most prominent people in it to go free with whatever possessions they could carry; Sinan Pasha knocked the number down to forty. The following day de Sese duly delivered the fortress, which was promptly sacked. According to Bosio, whose figures are probably quite reliable, between 5,000 and 6,000 Gozitans were enslaved. In a cruel, or, as he would have seen it, clever twist, Sinan Pasha chose forty of the island's oldest inhabitants to be the ones left behind under the terms of the capitulation, while de Sese was sent straight to the galleys; he would eventually be redeemed, but not for five years. Several days were spent scouring the remoter parts of Gozo for further victims: some evaded capture, Bosio stating that a number of local people successfully hid in caves. In truth, however, the main return of human booty had already been secured, in that, much more than was the case in Malta, a large proportion of the population of Gozo lived in and around the fortress, even if their livelihoods took them out into the countryside. Although the island does not seem to have been quite as denuded as Bosio's lachrymose account suggests, there can be no doubt that this was a demographic disaster of the first order, one that would take many decades and a good deal of immigration from Sicily and Malta to correct.[30] Turgut's relentless targeting of Gozo as perfect slaving country had reached its dreadful apotheosis.

Now it was Tripoli's turn, the Ottoman forces settling into a siege in early August.[31] This too had inadequate defences, though its substantial complement of artillery pieces was able to inflict some significant damage on the enemy. There were only a few dozen Knights among the defenders, some of them convicted offenders who had been released from prison to serve as relatively expendable cannon fodder; in addition, a hastily recruited contingent of untrained soldiers, most of them terrified and disaffected Calabrian peasants, proved much more of a hindrance than a help.[32] The Ottoman gunners' effective concentration of their fire on certain weak points meant that the defenders' position soon became untenable, and on the 15th the governor, a French Knight named Gaspard de Vallier de Chambert, who was believed to entertain ambitions to become Grand Master, was forced to surrender.[33] He and 200 of the oldest and weakest defenders, including some of the French Knights but none of the Spanish, were saved by the intervention of the French ambassador, d'Aramon.[34] On their arrival in Malta, however, Vallier and a number of his lieutenants were immediately clapped in irons. On 4 November, Vallier and the others were found guilty of cowardly dereliction of duty and punished with expulsion from the order. (Vallier would subsequently be rehabilitated when his former associate, Jean de La Valette, became Grand Master some years later.)[35]

D'Aramon's intercession on behalf of those whom the Ottoman command was willing to spare was the latest twist in an intriguing subplot which had been playing out for several months, and which came to influence the ways in which contemporaries perceived the dramatic events of that year. D'Aramon had found himself a spectator at the fall of Tripoli because, as the French ambassador to the Sublime Porte, he had been tasked by King Henri II to continue to stimulate Ottoman interest in the Franco-Ottoman alliance. This alliance, forged between Süleyman and François I in 1536, had always been an on-off affair, a tactical diplomatic option for both sides if there were some immediate advantage to be gained, but not a central structural principle of their respective strategies.[36] There was sometimes talk of co-ordinated action against the Habsburgs in order to stretch the enemy's resources, but this usually underestimated Charles V's ability to manage more than one threat at any one time. The overwintering of the Ottoman fleet at Toulon in 1543–4, which shocked opinion in Habsburg Europe, did not establish a regular pattern of close collaboration, and may indeed have unsettled the French.

Venetian *baili* in Istanbul, always among the most acute observers, routinely took a measured view of the alliance, arguing that the Ottomans cynically exploited it when it suited them but entertained few illusions about the strength and value to them of French naval power.[37] In 1550–51, however, there were signs that the alliance was entering its next active phase. Having originally been less of an enthusiast than his father, François I, Henri warmed to the possibilities of collaboration with the Ottomans when he saw Charles V gaining ground in his conflict with the Protestant princes in Germany as well as in Italy, the perennial cockpit of competition between the Valois and the Habsburgs.[38] D'Aramon, himself a great believer in the value of the alliance as the best way to protect France from Habsburg aggression, had done his utmost to stoke Ottoman indignation over Doria's conquest of Mahdia, with the result that in January 1551 he set out from Istanbul bearing a letter of friendship from the sultan to the king, and hoping to interest Henri in the idea of joint operations with the Ottoman fleet in the Mediterranean.[39]

Henri was indeed interested, and sent d'Aramon back to liaise with the Sublime Porte. At this juncture a number of delays intervened, the cumulative effect of which was to ensure that d'Aramon would always be playing catch-up vis-à-vis the Ottoman fleet's movements and its commanders' evolving priorities during the crisis months of July and August. First he stopped off at Avignon to visit his wife, whom he had not seen for ten years; he was then detained in Marseille by a long illness; finally he had been instructed not to proceed directly to Istanbul or make contact with the Ottoman fleet, but to begin his mission by sailing to Algiers in order to involve its governor, Hasan Pasha, Hayreddin's much weaker son, in whatever joint endeavour might subsequently emerge. This is an interesting indication that the French saw Algiers, correctly, as a

1551: The Precursor of the Great Siege

political and military entity in its own right, not merely as an extension of Ottoman power; and that their own parochial interests in and around their home waters were always part of the equation. When d'Aramon's party arrived in Algiers towards mid July, it was well received at first, but relations soon turned sour when Christian slaves began to swim across to the French vessels and their owners demanded their return. Hasan Pasha, whose control over the *reis* – the corsair captains – in the city was insecure, sought to bolster his position by sabre-rattling and trying to coerce the French into handing over military supplies. At one point the French had to stand to arms because they feared an imminent attack, and in the end d'Aramon had to come up with a substantial amount of cash in order to extricate himself and his group.[40]

It was as d'Aramon sailed east from Algiers that he learned, first at Bône (Annaba), then on Pantelleria, of the Ottoman fleet's actions in Sicilian waters and its assault on Malta. He arrived in Malta on 1 August, just missing the Ottoman fleet as it made its way south from Gozo. Having first been received by La Valette and Villegagnon – a clear signal that he was much more welcome to the French Knights than those whose sympathies lay with the Habsburgs – he was then dined, courteously enough, by the Aragonese Grand Master, Juan de Homedes. It was when d'Aramon was told the story of the recent Ottoman raid on the islands, and reacted by grandly claiming that this news would horrify Henri II, who only had the very best interests of the order at heart, and that if he, d'Aramon, had been there he would have done his utmost to deflect Sinan Pasha from his plan, that Homedes archly suggested that perhaps he could sail to Tripoli and work his magic there.[41]

After only one night in Malta, therefore, d'Aramon's party set out for Tripoli. In a meeting with Sinan Pasha on 6 August, d'Aramon expressed surprise, on behalf of his king, that the armada had not proceeded to Mahdia as had originally been expected. His objections, however, were summarily batted away. Now disabused of the notion that the Ottomans were acting with any meaningful reference to the French, and sensitive to the optics of his being present at an assault on a Christian fortress commanded by a Frenchman, d'Aramon asked for leave to depart for Istanbul, where, he said, he hoped to persuade the sultan to redirect his armada against Habsburg interests. Given the time it would have taken him to sail to Istanbul, negotiate with the government and then get back to Tripoli to save the defenders, whose prospects were almost certainly to be measured in days or weeks, not months, this suggestion was obviously a diplomatic fiction, and Sinan Pasha knew it. He initially refused d'Aramon permission to leave, thereby forcing him to bear witness to the siege operations and their climax on the 15th.[42] Unsurprisingly, therefore, when d'Aramon did return to Malta around 18 August with those he had been able to save, his reception was much cooler than before. Denied a ceremonial salute, he was at first refused entry into the harbour; La Valette had to ferry supplies out to the French vessels. A series of frosty meetings with the Grand Master and the Council ensued, at which it became clear that the Spanish and Italian Knights believed that d'Aramon had aided and abetted the loss of Tripoli, and had perhaps even contrived it himself by suborning Vallier. The mood became so toxic that when d'Aramon's party eventually sailed on towards Istanbul, it believed that the order would tip Andrea Doria off so that he could intercept the French vessels en route.[43]

The 1551 assault on the Maltese islands is sometimes described as a tentative raid or a reconnaissance in force, but it felt like more than that at the time. The immediate reaction among the defenders was a mixture of both profound relief and apprehension that the Ottoman fleet might return to finish the job on its way back from Tripoli; there was also puzzlement as to why the Turks had suddenly abandoned what seemed to be a winning position.[44] Although the Maltese islands were the victims of frequent raids, it was surely the memory of 1551 in particular that came to inform the panic that would grip the people of Malta in May 1565. The events of 1551 also galvanized the order into accepting that its future, strategically, economically and emotionally, did indeed lie with Malta, without the counter-attraction of Tripoli chipping away at its sense of purpose.

Pierre de Bourdeille, seigneur de Brantôme, *c.* 1580.

Malta as rendered in Matteo Perez d'Aleccio's wall paintings in the hall of the
Grand Master's Palace in Valletta, *c.* 1578: the map serves as an 'establishing shot'
for the detailed visual narrative of the Great Siege that wraps around the room.

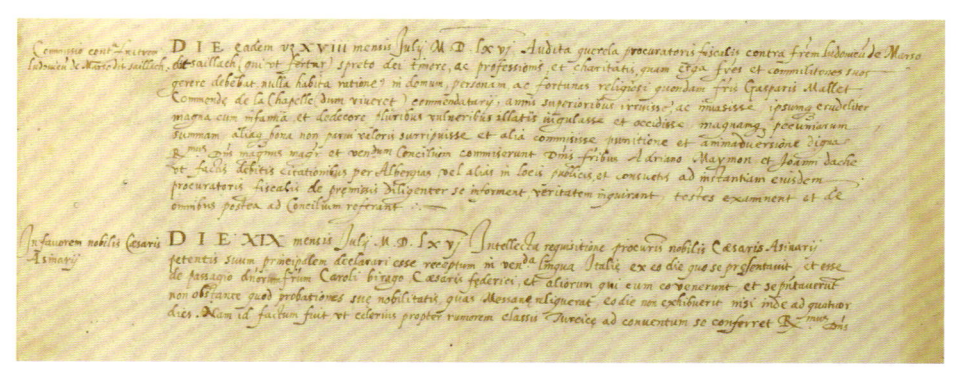

A record in the Order of St John's archives concerning Louis de Marso,
one of many Knights found guilty of violent crimes including, as here, murder.

John James Sandilands's poem incised onto the wall of the *guva* in St Angelo, the mournful lament of a troubled Knight.

A wheeled vehicle, probably a depiction of a hearse, among the many graffiti carved by prisoners consigned to the St Angelo *guva*.

The Siege of Rhodes, 1522, as depicted in the *Süleymanname*, an illustrated verse celebration of Sultan Süleyman I's achievements up to 1555: from the Ottoman perspective one significant military success amongst many, but for the Knights a defining moment.

Süleyman I depicted in the *Semailname*, a genealogy of the Ottoman sultans (1579).

Istanbul as a great imperial metropolis and naval hub, as seen across the Golden Horn from Galata, 1559: a section of a much larger panorama of the city by Melchior Lorichs (Lorck), who was for a time attached to Ogier Ghiselin de Busbecq's embassy.

A Janissary off to war, as depicted by Nicolas de Nicolay, a companion of Gabriel de Luetz d'Aramon, French ambassador to the Ottoman court.

Süleyman I confers with Barbarossa, as depicted in the *Süleymanname*: the image reflects the strategic importance of the close relationship between the Sublime Porte and the Barbary corsairs.

Matrakçi Nasuh, the overwintering of the Ottoman fleet in Toulon, 1543–4: a provocative demonstration of the reach of the Franco-Ottoman alliance that caused great unease in Habsburg Europe.

Anon. (attributed to Jooris van der Straeten), Philip II of Spain, *c.* 1565: for Habsburg apologists the successful defence of Malta was an achievement that truly belonged to *Hispania victrix*, 'Spain the victorious'.

Matteo Perez d'Aleccio's depiction of the mortal wounding of Turgut around 17 June during operations against St Elmo.

1551: The Precursor of the Great Siege

One important consequence of this shift in, or enforced clarification of, perceptions was that, as we shall see in the next chapter, the configuration of fortifications in the Grand Harbour area that greeted the Turks in 1565 was substantially the result of a programme of building, some of it rushed and panicked, that was motivated by memories of the ease with which the Ottomans had preyed on Malta and Gozo in 1551.

The near miss of 1551 helps us to anticipate the story of the Great Siege in various ways, and primes us to look out for certain significant features of what would happen in 1565. The evidence for the events of 1551, for example, is a reminder of the enormous difficulty that Christian observers typically experienced in reading the Ottomans' intentions and goals. In 1551 this straining after understanding is most evident in authors' reactions to the precipitous withdrawal from Mdina, but it hangs over their treatment of the whole episode. An extension of this is something we have already noted, a tendency to oversimplify Ottoman objectives and to cast them in stark, 'existential' terms that permitted of no nuance. The self-image that the Knights cultivated made them especially prone to this sort of language: even before the Turkish armada had arrived off Malta, on 16 July 1551, the Council was telling itself that the fleet was coming to 'overcome and annihilate this our Religion and knighthood of Jerusalem'; the theme of imminent extermination was resumed in a letter sent to the king of France in August.[45]

In reality, Ottoman naval policies, and the wider strategic objectives that they subserved, were adaptable and fluid. To be sure, large armadas were not organized, paid for and set on their way in the hope that something might turn up. But nor were they unresponsive juggernauts. Sinan Pasha's willingness to stand off Reggio until he was persuaded that the Habsburgs would not hand over Mahdia is one indication of the ways in which options and priorities could evolve *in medias res*; the subsequent decision not to attack Mahdia, perhaps because there were reports that the Habsburgs had strengthened its defences, is another;[46] the likelihood that one reason why Sinan Pasha opted to besiege Tripoli was overtures from local interests, especially Murad Agha, ruler of Tajoura, is a third.[47] As with short-term naval objectives, so with larger strategic goals: in 1551 the Ottomans were not rolling out a grand strategy as much as they were reacting to a provocation, the seizure of Mahdia, and an opportunity, the indications that the French were interested in reanimating their alliance. In the event, neither the recovery of Mahdia nor the possibility of linking up with the French governed where the armada went and what it did, but that was precisely because Sinan Pasha was not locked into an inflexible, all-or-nothing plan of campaign. If the Knights were too quick to 'make it all about them' in 1551, the irony is that in 1565, as we shall see, the destruction of the order almost certainly *was* the Ottomans' principal war aim. Even so, when we encounter, in the sources for the Great Siege, the same sort of black-and-white explanatory tropes that were readily wheeled out in 1551, we need to exercise due caution.

Additionally, the events of 1551 alert us to some of the questions and challenges that would confront the Knights fourteen years later. One was the role of the Grand Master in uniting an often fractious and fissile order. It is unsurprising that Villegagnon's account of this episode, *De bello Melitensi* ('The Maltese War'), an exercise in talking up his own role in the defence of Mdina and absolving the French from any responsibility for the loss of Tripoli, takes a dim view of Juan de Homedes as a pusillanimous and divisive leader whose stubborn misreading of the Ottomans' intentions impeded preparations for the invasion until it was almost too late.[48] But it is noteworthy that Bosio, who was more even-handed and willing to acknowledge whenever Homedes acted as befitted a Grand Master, shared some of these reservations, the implication being that Homedes allowed the situation to get away from him in July 1551.[49] Would La Valette, who had after all been a partisan figure in 1551, associating himself with Villegagnon and defying the Grand Master over his treatment of d'Aramon, be able to do a better job when it came to the crunch?

A further question was what relationship the Knights in 1565 would choose to forge with the approximately 25,000 inhabitants of the Maltese islands, and how this might improve their shared

1551: The Precursor of the Great Siege

chances of survival. A tone of aristocratic hauteur is evident in many sources back in 1551, for example in Villegagnon's expression of disdain for the common people's ability to withstand danger and to strive for victory; one also comes across it in the order's letter of 12 August 1551 to Charles V narrating recent events, which comes close to intimating that the people of Gozo somehow brought their misfortune down upon themselves.[50] Homedes' earlier insistence, just before the Turks' arrival, that two boats carrying desperate Gozitan refugees to Malta should be forced to turn around, because otherwise it would set a bad example, likewise speaks to the very different value systems that separated rulers and ruled on the islands.[51] On the other hand, Adorno's mobilization *in extremis* of poorly trained but willing local militiamen in Mdina pointed the way to what the order would need to do if the islands were ever threatened again. Similarly, Bosio's repeated insistence in his account of the events of 1551 that there were voices in the order presciently expressing concern about the fate of the inhabitants of Malta and Gozo looks, on one level, like an exercise in being wise after the fact, but it also suggests that, even many years later, there were enduring sensitivities about how badly the Knights had let the people down.[52]

1551 was not simply a foretaste of 1565 on the level of events; it also helps us to understand some of the ways in which memories and stories would come to form around the Great Siege and suffuse the sources at our disposal. One finds, for example, a gravitational pull towards anecdotes that nicely illustrate pluck and initiative: there is a striking equivalence between Bosio's account of Adorno's decision, when the Turks began to work their way towards Mdina, to order every inhabitant of the city, women and children included, to the walls in order to fool the enemy about the number of soldiers at his disposal, and the resort to precisely the same ruse, in the same place and in much the same desperate circumstances, in 1565.[53] One also encounters a tendency to latch on to specific moments that, it was supposed, captured the essence of more intricate and wide-ranging processes. A story that soon became embedded in the master narrative of the devastation of Gozo, for example, concerned a long-time Sicilian resident of the island who, rather than allow his wife and two daughters to fall into the attackers' hands, killed them one after the other before arming himself to the teeth with an arquebus, crossbow and sword and throwing himself suicidally at the enemy.[54] This anecdote was especially powerful in that it served as both an encapsulation or microcosm of Gozo's dreadful fate and in some sense a critique of it, insofar as the interest-value of the Sicilian's actions was enhanced by his being one of the very few who, it was supposed, had actually tried to fight back. This neatly anticipates a tendency that we shall find in the narrative sources of the Great Siege, which was to take particular note of the contributions of lower-status inhabitants of the Maltese islands when the signal being sent to the reader was that their actions conformed to aristocratic ideals of honour, self-sacrifice, physical bravery and resourcefulness: they were good chaps who had done their bit. But who indeed did their bit, on both sides, in 1565 will only truly emerge from the story of the Great Siege itself, to which we now turn.

5.

The Great Siege Begins

One of the first things that strikes someone coming to the study of Christian Europe in the sixteenth century is how much time and energy people were willing to expend in coming up with fanciful plans, or in straining after some elusive advantage that they believed would shake them loose from an irksome stasis. There was a particular strain of overoptimism, or, in more elevated terms, idealism, specific to elite male culture which found expression in innumerable letters, memoranda and petitions advocating various schemes, or 'enterprises', a great many of which were very far-fetched. One might be forgiven for thinking that there was a kind of collective bicameral mind which allowed high-status men to be grounded in a common-sense instinct for what was practicable within the constraints of the world that surrounded them moment by moment, while also entertaining fantasies that experience should have shown them were wholly unrealistic. At the very least, a dogged fondness for indulging hope over reason was embedded in elite culture. Numerous instances of this tendency can be cited. It emerges, for example, in the various plots against Elizabeth I of England, which tended to be undone not only by Francis Walsingham's espionage networks but also by their sheer complexity, which required so many moving parts to work in perfectly choreographed co-ordination that something was bound to go wrong.[1] It is significant that it was the unpredictable fanatic or unhinged lone wolf, not the cunning plotter, who came to represent the greatest personal danger to European rulers in the later sixteenth century. The same idealist impulse is also in evidence in Philip II's doomed attempts in 1588 to micromanage the Spanish Armada from afar while failing to address the most glaring flaw in his plans, which was a fatal vagueness about precisely how Medina Sidonia's fleet would link up with Parma's invasion force waiting for it on the Flemish coast.[2] Perhaps the acme of misguided overoptimism was prompted by the first flush of Spanish contact with Chinese merchants and products when the Spanish established a base in the Philippines in 1565 (a development that is considered in a later chapter). Very soon there emerged various schemes for nothing less than the conquest of China itself, which, it was argued, would only take a few thousand soldiers, such was the supposedly parlous state of China's fortifications and the unwarlike quality of its people. The point about these risible proposals is that they were not mere dinner-table bravado, but the substance of formal dispatches submitted, from halfway around the world, to Philip II himself and his officials. In this instance, the common-sense half of Philip's bicameral mind prevailed, and the schemes were summarily rejected.[3]

This constant tension between realism and overreaching idealism helps us to understand what we might term the 'mood music' of events in the central and western Mediterranean between the raids on Malta and Gozo in 1551 and the Great Siege fourteen years later. This is especially so because the predisposition in European elite culture to hope for the best in the best of all possible worlds had a negative corollary that came to the fore in times of acute stress: a tendency to overread and overdramatize an opponent's intentions, to dwell on one's own disadvantages, to assume that the worst imaginable outcome was in fact the likeliest, and to foresee deleterious domino effects stretching out into the distant future. We shall see that many of our sources are informed by this sort of perspective; some, when written by more sober-minded observers such as García de Toledo, Philip II's principal lieutenant in the central Mediterranean, readily exploit it as a rhetorical posture. The line between overstatement and alarmism as conditioned cultural reflexes and as a kind of discursive game is not always easy to discern.

The immediate reaction of the Knights to the raid in July 1551 was informed by a healthy dose of realism. As early as 4 August the Grand Master, Juan de Homedes, and the Council were revisiting the question of where to find the money to improve Malta's – and still, at this stage, Tripoli's – defences and to pay for the soldiers who would garrison them. It was agreed that a sum of 30,000 *scudi* would be raised from the order's priories. It is interesting that this matter should have exercised the order's leadership while it was still confronting an immediate crisis; it was believed that the *armata turchesca* would soon return, and only the day before it had been agreed that women, children and other 'useless persons' should be encouraged to evacuate to Sicily.[4] Since the early 1530s a succession of Italian military engineers, the acknowledged experts in fortress design, had been consulted about the defence of the Grand Harbour area as well as the order's other important positions. In 1533 a Florentine engineer named Piccino had suggested that a fortification should be built at the far tip of the Sciberras peninsula, the site of a watchtower and a chapel dedicated to St Elmo, so as to command the entrances to both Grand Harbour and Marsamxett; in 1540–41 Charles V's favoured expert, Antonio Ferramolino, who had been invited over to Malta while conducting an inspection of fortifications in Sicily, recommended much the same. On both occasions the costs had been a deterrent to further action.[5] Now the scheme was revived with a newly found sense of urgency. Another engineer, Pietro Prato, was recommended by Juan de Vega, the viceroy of Sicily; and work began on the fortress, which took its name from the chapel that stood on the site, in January 1552. The suspicion that operations were rushed is confirmed by the frantic efforts made to co-opt as many workers as possible, not just expert masons shipped over from Sicily, but also every able-bodied Maltese male over twelve and even the *ciurme* of Leone Strozzi's galleys. The fortress was completed and its garrison of Knights, soldiers and gunners in place by September. Two years later, probably on the advice of another engineer, Nicolò Bellavanti, who was in Malta doing work on the defences of Senglea, a polygonal cavalier, or raised position that could act as a gun platform, was constructed at St Elmo;

subsequently an outerwork was built on the Grand Harbour side; and shortly before the siege a ravelin, or detached, triangular structure, was hurriedly begun on the western, Marsamxett side, the more vulnerable flank.[6]

Meanwhile work had begun to strengthen the interior of Grand Harbour. Since at least as early as Ferramolino's time on the island, visiting engineers had confirmed what the team of inspectors had first spotted in 1524: that the only durable solution to Grand Harbour's security would be the construction of a fortress centred on the highest point of Mount Sciberras – in other words a version of what in due course would become Valletta. The cost was prohibitive, however, with the result that most of the resources that could be scraped together were directed towards the defences of the two parallel peninsulas across Grand Harbour from Sciberras and perpendicular to it. The tip of the more northerly peninsula, closer to the harbour's entrance, was the site of the only fortification there – the *Castello a mare* – that the Knights had inherited in 1530. Rechristened St Angelo, this served as the location of the order's convent and consequently became the focus of the early defensive improvements: Ferramolino built an internal cavalier and dug a water-filled ditch between the fort and the settlement that occupied the rest of the peninsula, Birgu.[7] The second peninsula, L-Isla, was much emptier. In the mid 1540s a small position was constructed at the tip to guard one end of the enormous chain, commissioned from Venice at great cost, which stretched across to St Angelo in order to control movement in and out of what is now Dockyard Creek. (This would be replaced by a new chain shortly before the Great Siege.)[8] In the 1550s a star-shaped fort, St Michael, was built on the landward end of the peninsula, now renamed Senglea after Grand Master Claude de La Sengle (1553–7); ramparts were also constructed along the base of the peninsula and around the western shoreline, the side, that is, facing what is now French Creek away from the protection of the chain and St Angelo's guns.[9] This tripartite defensive arrangement of St Elmo, St Angelo/Birgu, and St

Michael/Senglea – its footprint broadly similar to what the visitor sees today – would be what awaited the Turks in 1565.

If the efforts to fortify the Grand Harbour area were mostly informed by careful assessments of the delicate balance between what was needed and what could be afforded, in contrast the tension between realism and idealism, tinged by ill luck, continued to play out in the order's naval endeavours and in the larger Habsburg initiatives to which the Knights frequently contributed. The stimulus in all this was the fact that between 1551 and 1560 the working alliance between the Sublime Porte and the Barbary corsairs entered its most active and expansive phase. In 1552 a force led by La Valette and Leone Strozzi raided Zuwara, 100 kilometres west of Tripoli. It is uncertain whether the principal objective was to snatch slaves to work on the fortifications in Grand Harbour or to gain a foothold in Tripolitania with an ultimate view to regaining Tripoli itself. The raiders were surprised by local forces and badly mauled: ninety-eight Knights, their names solemnly listed by Bosio, were killed, and several others gravely wounded. When Juan de Homedes was told the news, he remarked, 'his eyes filled with the most abundant tears', that this was the gravest setback to have befallen the order since the loss of Rhodes.[10] The elements, too, seemed to be on the enemy's side. In October 1555 a freak storm overturned and wrecked four of the order's galleys riding at anchor in Grand Harbour. Many of their crews and oarsmen were lost. Mathurin d'Aux de Lescout, known as Romegas, the rising star of the order's naval operations, was rescued from one of the overturned vessels: it was believed that his hands shook for the remaining twenty-six years of his life. When the galleys were righted, the salvage parties found the pitiful evidence of the doomed attempts of the *ciurme* to save themselves. Three of the galleys were reparable, but Philip II had to give the Knights two more so that they could maintain their fighting strength.[11]

The order's travails were matched by those of Spain. In 1558, as if to provide an object lesson in the triumph of improvident ambition over practicality, Philip's regency government in Spain while he was away in the Netherlands authorized a poorly conceived expedition to strengthen the Christian position in western Algeria. A large force, under the command of Martín Alonso Fernández de Córdoba, count of Alcaudete, set out from the *presidio* of Oran towards Mostaganem, only to be roundly defeated by Hasan Pasha, *beylerbey* of Algiers. Antonio de Sosa was later told that more than 11,000 Spaniards were taken prisoner; many in fact took service with their captors, and there would seem to have been a sudden spike in the numbers of both captives and renegades in the city.[12] In 1560 the Habsburgs suffered an even greater defeat at Djerba in an ill-considered effort to deprive Turgut Reis of one of his principal bases and to relieve pressure on Tunis. A combination of cumulative delays, poor planning, plague, desertion and bad weather meant that an initial mobilization in 1559 had to be carried over into the following year. In March 1560 a substantial body of Spanish soldiers was finally landed on the island of Djerba, but in May the supporting fleet, under the command of the young and inexperienced Gianandrea Doria, was surprised and largely destroyed by an Ottoman armada under Piyale Pasha. The losses were enormous. The order managed to extricate its galleys from the debacle, though one was subsequently lost trying to pick up some of the wounded from Djerba. The troops now stranded on the island held out grimly until late July, but eventually had no choice but to surrender. Many thousands were enslaved: we saw in an earlier chapter how Busbecq witnessed the Ottoman fleet's triumphant return to Istanbul and the public humiliation of the captives. As John Francis Guilmartin has argued, the true disaster for the Habsburgs at Djerba was not so much the toll in vessels or soldiers, grave as this was, as the loss of maritime expertise in the form of *oficiales*, the skilled mariners from the captains down to the boatswains who made the galleys of Spain and her allies 'go'.[13] There would be something of a lull in the central Mediterranean after 1560.[14] But from the perspective of an observer soon after Djerba, the progressive shift in the balance of power between the Habsburgs and the Ottomans would have seemed obvious, and well-nigh irreversible.

The Great Siege Begins

The Ottoman decision to regroup may have partly been driven by circumstances: there were outbreaks of plague in Istanbul, and the ageing sultan was sometimes ill. But partly it was strategic, as if to suggest that it was understood that the reach of Ottoman power in the central and western Mediterranean was nearing its effective limits. Henceforth Ottoman policy in that region would be reactive, confronting provocations as they emerged.[15] But if the falling away of proactive Ottoman interest after 1560 means that the events of 1565 cannot simply be explained as a natural continuation of the momentum and energy generated by the victory at Djerba, then why did the Ottomans mobilize in such strength in 1565 and why did the Great Siege take place?

Part of the explanation is to be sought in the recovery of the Habsburg navy after its nadir in 1560.[16] This was, to be sure, a slow and fitful process: in October 1562 twenty-five vessels that Spain could ill afford to lose were wrecked in a storm off La Herradura near Málaga.[17] A substantial rebuilding effort was nonetheless made possible by Pope Pius IV's grant to Philip II, in addition to generous papal subsidies, of the *Cruzada*, a privilege that dated back to the later Middle Ages which essentially gave the kings of Spain free rein to mulct the Spanish Church in return for prosecuting holy war against the infidel.[18] After the Treaty of Cateau-Cambrésis in April 1559 had ended the long-running and expensive war between Spain and France, Philip II showed that he was willing and able to direct more of his attention to the Mediterranean. Evidence of a more joined-up approach to the co-ordination of logistics and operational command is seen in the appointment in February 1564 of García de Toledo as Captain General of the Sea, in effect commander-in-chief of the Habsburgs' dispersed naval resources in the Mediterranean, and subsequently in October as viceroy of Sicily.[19] In that same year the decision was made to announce the re-emergence of Spain as a naval power by means of a campaign – in reality more a parade – directed against the remotest Ottoman outpost in the western Mediterranean at Peñón de Vélez de la Gomera, a fortress on a tied island on the Moroccan coast which the Spanish had taken in 1508 but lost in 1522. The unnecessarily large armada, including perhaps one hundred galleys and 16,000 soldiers, appeared off the Peñón on 31 August; and a week later the tiny garrison of a few dozen men wisely fled. (The Peñón remains a modern Spanish exclave, its eighty-five-metre border with Morocco forming the shortest international frontier in the world.)[20]

Some western observers in Istanbul such as Antoine de Petremol, the French ambassador, believed that the loss of the Peñón exercised the Ottomans and was one of the reasons why they decided to mobilize the following year.[21] This is very unlikely: it would seem that the decision to launch a naval campaign in 1565 had been taken by the Ottomans by early October 1564, too soon for news of events at the other end of the Mediterranean to have reached Istanbul, or at least to have made a significant difference to the Sublime Porte's calculations. In any event the Spanish victory at the Peñón was of little strategic importance in itself. Brantôme, who attached himself to the Spanish forces as an independent adventurer, persisted thereafter in regarding this moment as a notable achievement.[22] But the campaign was really an elaborate sideshow: a large hammer to crack a tiny nut, its outcome as much as anything the result of the local sultan's growing dissatisfaction with the Ottoman garrison on his doorstep. If the victory at the Peñón did anything it would have been to confirm in the Ottomans an emergent sense that the Spanish recovery was gaining momentum.

In this connection, it is perhaps no coincidence that, as we shall see in a later chapter, the earlier 1560s witnessed efforts on the part of Philip II's regime to improve the arrangements for the safe and effective transportation to Spain of the silver mined in Mexico and Peru, now that technological advances in the extraction of the silver from its ore had begun to produce much greater yields. By the mid 1560s these changes were beginning to pay off. In 1565, for example, a report circulated that the Indies fleet had arrived at Seville with one and a half million ducats' worth of precious metal; the rumour was exaggerated, but the fact that it did the rounds in the first place is what is most significant.[23] We cannot be sure how much the

The Great Siege Begins

Sublime Porte understood of the operational details of Spain's silver fleets. Did it know how much of the silver actually found its way into royal hands, and did it realize that most of the king's share went straight to the crown's creditors? But the Ottomans had more than enough eyes and ears in the western Mediterranean to have suspected that something was afoot, and that this had a bearing on the early but unmistakable signs of a Spanish naval recovery. This can only be a suggestion. But it is reasonable to argue that the root cause of the Malta campaign in 1565 was Ottoman unease that American silver would increasingly shift the balance of power in the Mediterranean. In this the Sublime Porte would have been only partly correct: the silver did not give Philip II a free hand to go on the offensive against his enemies at will, merely more collateral against which to borrow and stave off bankruptcy for as long as possible. But perceptions in Istanbul would have been what mattered, and the conclusion to be drawn in the mid 1560s may well have been that, if the Sublime Porte had any unfinished business in the central and western Mediterranean, now would be the time to address it, before the Spanish grew in resources and confidence.

But what unfinished business? Why Malta? And why then? It was one thing for the Sublime Porte to be anxious about a Habsburg recovery, another to identify and justify a specific target. A clue to the Ottomans' thinking is provided by the main eyewitness chronicler of the Great Siege, Francesco Balbi da Correggio, who sets the scene for his narrative by claiming that the sultan was angered by the many campaigns that the Knights had conducted against him, both on their own account and as a part of larger Habsburg enterprises. More specifically, according to Balbi, Süleyman delivered a speech to his senior officials in which he identified several pressing reasons for his decision to attack Malta: the order's actions against Ottoman interests in the Aegean, in particular an attack on Monemvasia in the Peloponnese; Romegas's capture off Alexandria of a ship carrying pilgrims en route to Mecca, including an elderly and high-ranking lady, 'Giansever', whose relations were now petitioning the sultan for redress; Romegas's further capture of another ship in the same area carrying the *sancakbey*, or governor, of Alexandria; and in 1564 the seizure by the full complement of the order's galleys, under Pierre de Giou and Romegas, of a large ship belonging to the Kapi Aga, the chief eunuch of the court, en route to Venice with a valuable cargo of silks, copper and other items valued at more than 80,000 ducats. In addition the sultan recalled that his wife (Hürrem, who had died in 1558) had often advocated the total destruction of Malta because its ships disrupted the movement of pilgrims to the tomb of the Prophet in Medina (and thus, by extension, the Hijaz in general); on her death she had bequeathed a large sum of money to contribute towards a future expedition against Malta. Balbi goes on to suggest that news of the fall of the Peñón also exercised Süleyman: as we have seen, this in itself is unlikely, but Balbi's further remark that Hasan Pasha in Algiers and Turgut in Tripoli had expressed their anxieties about the resurgence of Spanish naval power does ring true. Finally, Balbi adds, two letters had come to the sultan's attention, one from the captive *sancakbey*, the other from all the slaves in Malta, in which he was reproached for not having taken action against a small island that was now weak but which might become stronger in the future.[24]

There is obviously much that is confected in Balbi's version of these events: given that in his two accounts of the siege he made a point of emphasizing his own status as an eyewitness, he needed to contrive a surrogate, a source of information in the form of a spy sent by the Grand Master who was conveniently able to eavesdrop on discussions at the very heart of the Ottoman government. But Balbi was almost certainly correct in his basic assumption that the Order of St John was the connecting thread between the various problems that moved Süleyman to act. His assessment shrewdly identifies three interrelated concerns on the Ottomans' part: the order's disruption of pilgrimage traffic; its threat to the empire's most important maritime route of communication, between Alexandria and Istanbul, as well as that between Istanbul and Venice; and its predation of commercial vessels in which members of the Ottoman elite had financial interests.[25] In the later 1550s and earlier

1560s, once the burst of building activity prompted by the invasion of 1551 was coming to an end, the order had put aside its dream of a *revanche* in Tripolitania and had adopted a more realistic policy of concentrating on frequent *corso* expeditions, some towards north Africa but most to the Levant; in this way its limited resources could be put to most effective and profitable use.[26] It is unsurprising, therefore, that the sultan's list of grievances finds some corroboration in the order's records as well as in the pages of Bosio, who provides, for example, a detailed account of the capture of the *Sultana*, a merchant ship bound for Venice, in 1564.[27]

The suggestion that it was the maritime activities of the Knights that triggered the Ottoman mobilization against Malta is confirmed by some of the sultan's pronouncements in his *fermans*, or formal decrees. Only a few of the mandates that directly refer to the Malta campaign survive; it was in the nature of their rhetorical style to be short and peremptory; and they were written from a position of absolute authority, meaning that they did not need to expatiate on or justify the sultan's reasons for a given action. All that being said, however, one or two offer revealing glimpses into the Sublime Porte's motivations. Probably around December 1564 a *ferman* sent to Hasan Pasha in Algiers stated:

> I intend to conquer the island of Malta and I have appointed Mustafa Pasha as commander of the campaign. The island of Malta is a headquarters for infidels. The Maltese have already blocked the route utilized by Muslim pilgrims and merchants in the East Mediterranean, on their way to Egypt.[28]

The fact that this relatively full and candid mandate was addressed to one of the principal Barbary corsairs, who knew conditions in the central Mediterranean very well, and whom Süleyman wished to contribute to the campaign, is surely significant. Around March 1565 the sultan was equally forthright in a letter sent to his vassal the khan of Crimea, which explained why he was unable to send him troops and ammunition to help him resist his Russian enemies:

'This is impossible at the moment. The reason is that I have decided to send an armada to occupy the island of Malta. The Maltese attack Muslim pilgrims and merchants frequently.'[29] In other pronouncements what was envisaged was represented more straightforwardly in terms of the acquisition of territory. In early December 1564 Süleyman simply declared that 'I have decided to send an armada that includes many warships to occupy Malta'; several subsequent decrees refer to an assault on or conquest of the island.[30]

Clearly the conquest of Malta and the defeat of the Knights were complementary goals, in much the same way that Balbi imagined Hürrem wishing for the destruction of Malta when what she really meant was the eradication of the order. But these two war aims were not co-extensive, for each might in theory be attained without the other: there could be a repeat of the Knights' retreat from Rhodes; or the Knights on the island might be eliminated to a man, leaving behind a debilitated rump dispersed around the order's European commanderies, at which point the Turks might simply choose to leave Malta to its own devices as surplus to strategic requirements. So Süleyman's various pronouncements raise important questions about what, if anything, the Sublime Porte wanted beyond the destruction of the order, and what larger objectives may or may not have been on its mind.

At this point, we run up against the fact that the fullest evidence at our disposal for the Ottomans' broad strategic aims comes from western observers, and is therefore characterized by the tension between realism and idealism that we noted earlier. Most of what Europeans thought and said on this matter was, moreover, simply ill-informed. Western ambassadors in Istanbul often filled their dispatches with lists of possibilities rather than committing to a definitive 'read' of what the Sublime Porte was thinking and doing at any given moment; so if experts on the spot found it difficult to understand the Ottomans' intentions, one can readily imagine how much those back in Christian Europe found themselves groping in the dark. In such circumstances, as news of the Ottoman mobilization between October 1564 and March 1565 filtered west, a capillary effect took hold which encouraged increasingly inflated and doom-laden assessments of where all this was heading. This in turn opened up possibilities for the alarmist mood to be exploited for rhetorical purposes. For example, García de Toledo, often one of the more measured voices in 1565, was happy to play on Philip II's fears that the fall of Malta would represent a mortal threat to the Habsburg dominions around the Mediterranean. He did so because he understood that this was the best – and perhaps the only – way in which to prod the cautious king into committing more men, ships and resources.[31] La Valette likewise was motivated to argue that the Ottomans' intentions transcended the immediate threat to his own order.[32] Similarly, Pope Pius IV, when drumming up support for the defence of the Maltese islands, could summon up a nightmare vision in which the loss of Malta would expose Italy and Spain to the likelihood of conquest. On the other hand, when in the relatively sober atmosphere of his own consistory, or cabinet meeting with his cardinals, he looked ahead to the less apocalyptic, if still troubling, prospect of an Ottoman Malta forcing the Christian Mediterranean to live in a state of constant high alert.[33]

Pius's more measured prognosis as to the implications of an Ottoman conquest of Malta was sensible because it implicitly differentiated between two very different types of outcome: increased coastal raiding, in which both the Ottomans and their corsair allies were of course well practised, so it would be a case of more of the same only worse; and the out-and-out conquest of Sicily, Italy or Spain, which the Ottomans could not have realistically entertained as a strategic ambition, at least in the short-to-medium term. But the problem remains that most other western observers seldom if ever arrived at realistic assessments of the extent of the Ottomans' resources, their strategic priorities and sense of what was possible, and the cost-benefit judgements that they made when weighing up their military options. This raises the question: once the Knights were dealt with once and for all, what *would* the Ottomans have wanted to do with Malta? A valuable piece of evidence is tucked away in the order's records in the form of a memorandum concerning the pension that was awarded to the most high-ranking defector who came over to the Christian side during the Great Siege, a *sipahi* who took the name Filippo de Lascaris when he converted to Christianity.[34] As we shall see in the next chapter, the Christian chroniclers made a good deal of this man, especially Balbi, who was one of those on hand to help him when he made his move by trying to swim across from Sciberras to Senglea; Balbi subsequently renewed their acquaintance when the two men ran into one another in Naples.[35] After the siege Lascaris was presented to the pope and to Philip II, who gave him a position to support himself in the kingdom of Naples. But clearly money remained a problem, for Lascaris petitioned for, and received, an additional pension from the order in August 1566; in July 1567 he asked that it be confirmed.[36]

In the narrative accounts, Lascaris's immediate value to La Valette when he defected is said to have been the intelligence that he provided concerning the Ottoman high command's intentions at a critical juncture, between the fall of its first objective, St Elmo, and the beginning of the next phase of the assault. But the note concerning the pension adds that, just before he had changed sides, Lascaris had been present at a high-level meeting in the Ottoman camp in which a sealed instruction from the sultan had been opened. This had suggested further targets in other parts of the Mediterranean for the armada, the implication being that Süleyman assumed that once St Elmo had fallen, the rest of Malta's defences would quickly follow suit and it would be possible to redeploy the fleet elsewhere before the end of the campaign season. La Goletta or Corsica, which was in revolt against its Genoese rulers, were mentioned. In the meantime, the sultan's letter added, Malta should be held by 10,000 men under the command of what the document calls the 'captain' of Rhodes, which must mean the deputy on that island of the *kapudan* Piyale Pasha in his capacity as *beylerbey*, or regional governor, of the Archipelago.

The connection to Rhodes and to the jurisdiction of the *beylerbey* of the Archipelago, which stretched across the Aegean, would seem to suggest that Süleyman envisaged a future for Malta at the intersection of the Ottomans' provincial organization and its naval command structures. But already there is in this document a suggestion that holding on to Malta would present a severe challenge. A garrison strength of 10,000 was probably intended as a short-term measure to counter a possible Habsburg invasion of about the same size as the relief force that we shall see actually did materialize in September 1565. But even if the garrison were maintained at around half that strength thereafter, it would have become an enormous and permanent drain on Ottoman resources. We know, moreover, that the Ottomans came to Malta well briefed about the islands, on top of the experience gained in 1551 and at other times. There are references to spies taking measurements of the fortifications in 1564, and to the consulting of models and images.[37] The Ottomans would therefore have known that exactly the same topographical considerations would apply to them as had led a succession of Italian engineers to nag the order about the inadequacy of its harbour defences. If the Ottomans were serious about holding on to Malta over the long term, they would have appreciated that the existing combination of the three fortified positions in the Grand Harbour area, even when duly repaired and improved after the damage that they themselves visited on them, would be inadequate. At the very least, as new masters of the islands they would need to build an approximation to the future Valletta, and perhaps the Floriana Lines beyond it, in order to secure control of Mount Sciberras. They would also have been wise to construct defences similar to the seventeenth- and eighteenth-century Santa Margherita and Cottonera Lines in order to negate the fact that Birgu and Senglea were overlooked by the very high ground that their own artillery had exploited during the siege.

New fortresses and their garrisons were hugely expensive, however: it has been suggested that when the Ottomans expanded into southern Georgia in 1578–90, the annual cost of garrisoning three new fortresses there with the same number of men as had been initially earmarked for Malta, 10,000, represented 10 per cent of the government's income even before one allowed for the cost of provisions. The Ottomans stretched their resources along the long Hungarian frontier by deploying only about 20,000 troops and moving them from place to place as need arose – an option that would obviously be unavailable on Malta.[38] The core elements of Ottoman garrisons in the most exposed border fortresses were, moreover, Janissary units, so how many of its elite troops would the Sublime Porte be willing to park on a remote and vulnerable frontier island? Malta would have been like an exposed and costly Spanish *presidio* in reverse and on a larger scale. In short, did the Ottomans *want* Malta that much? Would it be more trouble than it was worth when the hunter became the hunted?

Finally there was the wild card represented by the Barbary corsairs. As the record concerning Filippo de Lascaris suggests, simply handing the Maltese islands over to the corsairs to govern was not on the cards. Who would have got what? And what would need to change as and when Tunis, the most obvious pairing with Malta on the north African coast, was taken from the Spanish, as would indeed happen in 1569 and again, definitively, in 1574? In making the eastern Mediterranean an Ottoman lake, the Sublime Porte had succeeded in pushing the Levantine corsairs out to the margins, as demonstrated by the fact that they were offered amnesties to make modest contributions to the Malta expedition.[39] But the Barbary corsairs were an altogether different proposition, a self-standing and powerful liminal quantity half in, half out of the structures of Ottoman provincial government. Those structures were, moreover, modified – especially in Algiers, somewhat less so in Tripolitania – to accommodate local interests at the expense of control from Istanbul.[40] This kind of arm's-length approach is reflected in the fact that the Ottomans never sought to develop a naval arsenal west of Egypt. In such circumstances, perhaps the greatest unknown surrounding the Great Siege is the extent to which a successful outcome for the Ottomans would have forced them to revisit their relationship with the Barbary corsairs and to revise their policies towards the governance of north Africa beyond Egypt. That some significant recalibration would have been necessary is beyond doubt. But exactly what it would have entailed we shall never know.

The more one is drawn into counterfactual speculation about the consequences of an Ottoman victory on Malta, the more one simply has to accept that the conjunction of disquiet about a silver-fuelled Habsburg revival and the vendetta against the order sufficed to get the armada in motion in 1565. Perhaps, too, a combination of an ageing sultan and the sort of reactive policy that we have noted meant that the Ottomans chose *not* to look too far ahead. Theirs was a part-maritime empire whose most important supply lines and prestige were threatened by a smaller naval foe which had been allowed to punch above its weight for too long and now needed to be expunged; and that was all there was to it.[41] (In a later chapter we shall find another empire, the Spanish, thinking in exactly the same terms, at exactly the same time, in relation to *its* vital strategic interests in another part of the world.)

Süleyman split the command of the expedition against Malta in acknowledgement of the fact that this would be a complex amphibious undertaking requiring careful co-ordination between its naval and military elements. As general of the forces on land the sultan appointed Mustafa Pasha, a veteran soldier; the *kapudan* Piyale Pasha, a much younger man, would assume command of the navy. After the death of Hayreddin, the Sublime Porte had reverted to appointing admirals from the ranks of the Ottoman establishment, men who were not experienced mariners. Piyale Pasha had been one such choice, though he had worked hard to become an effective naval commander, as his bold strike against Gianandrea Doria's fleet off Djerba had demonstrated; and he had a reputation for getting on well with corsairs.[42] The Christian sources often invoke disagreements and personal ill-feeling between Mustafa and Piyale as explanations why the Ottomans made various poor judgements as the siege progressed; ultimately indeed their fraught relationship became accepted as one of the fundamental reasons why the attack failed.[43] But we need to be cautious. Some degree of disagreement and rivalry between Ottoman commanders was typically tolerated, even encouraged, as a source of creative tension – though this was riskier when the sultan was not himself present on campaign to impose his ultimate authority. There was, moreover, a clear hierarchy of status, and this mattered: Mustafa was a vizier, a member of the uppermost tier of the elite below the sultan; Piyale was not (yet).[44] In a number of his surviving pronouncements, Süleyman was perfectly clear that it was Mustafa who was the *serdar*, the commander-in-chief, and it was he whom the sultan asked for updates once the campaign had begun.[45] In truth, we do not have enough evidence to penetrate the complexities of the relationship between the two men and the extent to which this may have influenced the course of events. Friction between them may well have existed, but it was also an easy device for Christian writers to fall back on as they struggled to understand their often opaque opponents.

In late 1564 and the first months of 1565 westerners in Istanbul were in no doubt that a very large expedition was in prospect. In a letter to Catherine de' Medici dated 20 January 1565, Petremol stated that 'great preparations' were under way to assemble the largest force 'that a Turkish emperor has ever put to sea in terms of the number of galleys and other large vessels, munitions, and artillery'.[46] This was an exaggeration, but it was the perception that counted, and others shared it. The size of the Ottoman armada cannot be established with certainty because observers' estimates varied. There is, however, a reassuring correspondence between the figure of 129 galleys reported by a representative of the Fugger bank, careful Ottoman-watchers, as the fleet left home waters, and the 130 mentioned by La Valette in a letter dashed off to the pope when the fleet arrived off Malta.[47] We can thus take this as a working total for the core element of the Ottoman force. Accompanying the galleys were assorted other vessels, the types and numbers of which vary from source to source: perhaps twenty or thirty galliots, the next size down from galleys, and around the same number of large cargo vessels of various kinds, as well as a host of smaller auxiliary craft.[48] In any event the Ottoman fleet was never a fixed entity during the siege: it would always have been in flux, as corsairs arrived from north Africa, supply ships plied back and forth, and galleys were broken up for siege materials as oarsmen and crews died off.

The question of the number of people that these vessels delivered to Malta is more uncertain, thanks to the tendency of the Christian accounts, pretty much our only sources of detailed information, to exaggerate the David-and-Goliath quality of the siege.[49] That writers could be perfectly aware of what they were doing is suggested by the fact that when the printing of a second edition of his history of the siege presented Balbi with an opportunity to introduce a greater note of realism, he substantially revised his estimate of the number of Ottoman combatants down from 45,000 to 28,500.[50] On the basis of the exhaustive analysis of the various sources by Stephen Spiteri, the foremost military historian of the Great Siege, one might tentatively suggest that between 20,000 and 25,000 troops were brought to Malta with the fleet, of whom approximately 16,000 were elite warriors: around 6,000 Janissaries, representing about half of their total corps, and 10,000 *sipahis*. The remainder would have comprised irregular and light infantry, including those soldiers who served on galleys, as well as volunteers. There would also have been corps of artillerists, trench-diggers and sappers. The number of corsairs who subsequently arrived in various waves probably peaked at around 4,000 or 5,000 at most.[51]

The number of combatants is an important consideration of course, especially given that we shall find the siege settling into a grim war of attrition. But the complement of expert, or at least willing, combatants is only part of the story, for the most important total was the number of mouths consuming food and water on an island that offered little in the way of either. The fleet was mostly powered by thousands of oarsmen: some were Christian slaves, others conscripted men, the great majority of whom would have had no military background. One hundred and thirty galleys at a bare minimum of 144 oarsmen gives us a total of nearly 19,000, but this probably underestimates the numbers by several thousand. The other vessels must have accounted for at least 5,000 men. In other words, there were about equal numbers of combatants and non-combatants in the fleet that arrived off Malta, and perhaps more of the latter. The *ciurme* were not useless; it was they who dragged the cannon into position and performed other labouring duties; and in the latter stages of the siege, as the Ottomans grew more anxious, some of them were thrown into the front line. But Piyale Pasha would have been concerned to keep as many of his oarsmen as safe and well as possible, because without them the army would be marooned; they could not be treated as mere cannon fodder from the start. The fact that the Ottoman armada was operating close to the limits of its operational range exposed the inescapable calculus that the further the fleet travelled from its main bases of supply, especially in hostile waters, the more it needed to approach self-sufficiency. This meant more vessels carrying supplies and propelled and sailed by non-combatants, which is to say more mouths which would in due course need to consume a large proportion of those very same provisions. The Ottomans could hope for but could not absolutely rely on additional resources from the Barbary corsairs. And we know that further supplies were shipped out during the campaign. But it would seem that there was considerable anxiety about the length of time that the Turks could sustain themselves on Malta. On the armada's outward voyage a large supply ship sank off the Peloponnese, with the loss of several hundred *sipahis*, and two other vessels got into difficulties and ran aground. It is possible that the Ottoman ships were especially vulnerable to mishaps such as these because they had been overloaded in an effort to squeeze as many men, munitions and supplies on board as possible.[52]

As western observers in Istanbul had watched the armada taking shape, it had remained open to debate where it would be sent: Malta or La Goletta, the fortress in the harbour of Tunis which allowed the Spanish to dominate the city and its rulers, were the best bets, but no one could be certain. García de Toledo kept his options open, and it would only be after the armada had begun the assault on Malta that Philip II would finally concede that La Goletta, which more directly touched the interests of the Spanish crown, was not the Ottomans' principal target.⁵³ By January 1565 at the latest, however, the Knights were convinced that Malta would probably be attacked, and arrangements were put in place for the recruitment of mercenaries in various parts of Italy. In February plans for the upcoming general chapter of the order were suspended because of 'the rumour of the Turkish fleet'.⁵⁴ In such uncertain and tense circumstances, no precautions would ever be perfect, of course. But it is difficult to escape the conclusion that the Knights' preparations were both rushed and severely hampered by a shortage of funds: desperate orders were given to scour the island for both cash and foodstuffs; instructions for the further recruitment of mercenaries went out too late; there was recourse to the well-established model of raising 30,000 *scudi* from the commanderies, but again too late to make an immediate difference; it was believed that significant improvements to the fortifications still needed to be made; and although the evacuation of non-combatants had first been considered in January, it had scarcely got under way by the time that the Turks arrived four months later.⁵⁵

The armada left Istanbul towards the end of March and worked its way steadily south then west, rendezvousing with the troops who had mustered in the empire's European territories at Navarino (Pylos) in the western Peloponnese. The fleet sailed from there on 12 May to cross the first substantial stretch of open sea that it had faced, the approximately 700 kilometres to Malta. It was spotted off Cape Passero, the southernmost tip of Sicily, on the 17th, and it arrived off Malta the following day, taking up position close to the large harbour of Marsaxlokk on the south-east coast of the island.⁵⁶ It is noteworthy that one of the first things that Balbi mentions when the fleet appeared, and warning guns were fired, is the flight of ordinary Maltese to the fortified positions with their families, livestock and possessions; he makes the shrewd observation that memories of 1551 remained fresh.⁵⁷ La Valette sent out a force of 1,000 men, including about one hundred Knights, to oppose any landing, but the fleet stayed out to sea, working westwards along the southern coast of the island while the defenders tracked its movements. By nightfall it had taken up positions off the bays to the west of Mġarr and in the Fliegu, the channel between Malta and Gozo. Overnight twenty galleys slipped back to Marsaxlokk, and on the 19th troops began to disembark.[58]

Meanwhile reconnaissance parties had come ashore on the western beaches, and a detachment of horsemen was sent to investigate under a French Knight, Adrien de La Rivière. The rash actions of a young Portuguese Knight, Vendo de Mesquita, exposed La Rivière's position, leaving him no option but to attack. In the ensuing mêlée, Mesquita was mortally wounded and La Rivière was unhorsed and taken prisoner, the valiant efforts of a Maltese to carry him to safety proving unavailing. So ended the first clash of arms of the Great Siege.[59] Its particular interest lies in the fact that, in addition to the Christian sources that narrate this incident, there is in a register of the rewards granted to Ottoman soldiers who had performed conspicuously on Malta a record to the effect that a Mehmed bin Mustafa had acted bravely at the very beginning of the campaign, when he overturned one of the horses of a party of infidel horsemen and took the rider prisoner.[60] We cannot prove that this refers to the same incident but it seems very likely. That there should be such an intriguing intersection between the Christian and Ottoman sources so early in the campaign makes it all the more disappointing that there are fairly few conjunctions of this sort thereafter.

The main part of the fleet now returned to Marsaxlokk and on the 20th the disembarkation began in earnest. The Ottoman forces moved north, pressing on to Marsa, the furthest inland point of Grand Harbour, where they set up their main camp. They then began to bring up their artillery. Marsa was a position of great significance, for it was the site of one of the most important sources of water on the island; the defenders had attempted to foul the cisterns there, but evidently not with complete success. On the 21st the Ottomans made a reconnaissance in force towards Birgu, which La Valette countered by sending out about 700 Knights and soldiers flanked by cavalry. There followed what Balbi described as a 'ferocious and hard-fought' encounter lasting five hours, at the end of which, the same author claims, more than one hundred Turks, including a *sancakbey*, lay dead as against ten defenders – the first of the many 'scores' that conclude Balbi's and other chroniclers' accounts of engagements.[61] La Valette's decision to expose some of his men in this manner served no obvious tactical purpose; it must have been meant as a signal to the Ottomans that they could expect stiff resistance, and as a way of galvanizing his own troops before they withdrew for good inside the fortifications. The forces at La Valette's disposal in the Grand Harbour positions were few, but not hopelessly so: approximately 530 Knights and sergeants; about 2,000 soldiers, more or less evenly split between better-trained troops supplied by the Habsburg authorities and mercenaries, as well as those soldiers who served on the order's galleys; and perhaps 4,000 or 5,000 Maltese, some of whom had received some basic training in their village militias.[62] There were also about 1,000 slaves, who could be put to work doing the most arduous and dangerous jobs such as repairs to exposed fortifications.

By 23 May it was clear from the movement of a portion of the Ottomans' artillery from Marsa towards Mount Sciberras that the first target would be St Elmo. Sufficient pieces were in position by the 28th to begin firing on the fortress, as well as across Grand Harbour at St Angelo; and on the 31st the first full bombardment began. The Turks deployed eighteen large cannon and half a dozen smaller pieces, in all a little more than a third of the total artillery train that they had brought to the island; more pieces may have been introduced later as the assault dragged on.[63] The gunners had the advantage of the higher ground afforded them by the down-slope of Mount Sciberras towards St Elmo, though an area of relatively flat land between the fortress and the foot of the incline meant that the guns had to inch forward from an initial position several hundred metres from their target, well beyond their optimal range.[64] The targets of the early bombardments indicated that the Turkish gunners had correctly identified the outerworks, especially the ravelin, as the fortress's most vulnerable points. These were also the focus of the first major assault. On 3 June thousands of troops were thrown forward in waves, and the ravelin, which the Turks had first begun to secure the night before, fell; the Christian sources blame the defenders' inattention or poor judgement, but in truth the ravelin was so weak in its design and construction that it was all but inevitable that it would be taken in the first determined attack.[65]

Meanwhile reinforcements had begun to arrive: towards the end of May Turgut's protégé Uluç Ali, with several galleys from Alexandria and 600 men; and on 2 June Turgut himself with thirteen galleys and two galliots from Tripoli.[66] Several Christian sources stage a scene in which, while one or both of the commanders defended their choice of St Elmo, the newly arrived Turgut expressed surprise and dismay that the first order of business had not been the reduction of Mdina, as well as of Gozo, so as to ensure control of the islands in the rear and to prevent any Christian relief force from attempting a landing.[67] This moment has become central to what we might call the Turgut myth: the idea that if only he had arrived in Malta a few days earlier and brought his superior acumen to bear on the high command's decision-making, the whole outcome of the siege would have been very different. But we need to be cautious. If indeed there was any disagreement when Turgut arrived – and there is some evidence to suggest that St Elmo had been identified as the first objective even before the fleet left Istanbul – the fact was that both arguments had merit, and that the Ottomans were already having to confront difficult choices because they lacked the resources to cover all their bases.[68] The plan that the sources ascribe to Turgut was sensible, in that it was reasonable to expect that the eventual fate of Malta would be decided on land – if, that is, the Habsburgs were able to disembark a force that could bring the besiegers to battle. This was certainly emerging as the received wisdom among experienced military observers on the Christian side. On the other hand, the elimination of St Elmo would enable the Ottoman fleet to relocate to Marsamxett, which was a much more secure and suitable harbour than Marsaxlokk. The sources present Piyale Pasha in particular as preoccupied by the need to preserve the fleet that the sultan had entrusted to him. But we do not need to resort to personal anxieties on the *kapudan*'s part to explain the choice of St Elmo, for it was informed by what amounts to the first law of amphibious warfare, which is to keep one's naval and land forces as close together as possible. In addition, control of all the surface area of the islands was not a priority in the short term because it would be some time before a Christian relief force could be organized and landed. Turgut had arrived too late to influence a decision that needed to be made promptly. On balance, Piyale Pasha and Mustafa Pasha had made the right call.[69]

The ferocity of the assault on 3 June and the number of casualties would seem to have unnerved the defenders.[70] And the danger continued to mount: the Turks began work on increasing the height of the ravelin by means of goatskins filled with cotton, wool and earth, and soon they would be able to fire down from it into the interior of the fort. At the suggestion of Juan de Miranda, a respected captain who had recently arrived from Sicily and had slipped into St Elmo before crossing to St Angelo, La Valette sent over pay and wine in an attempt to bolster the defenders' morale.[71] Miranda confirmed what La Valette had already been told by Juan de la Cerda and Gonzalo de Medrano, two of the captains commanding the soldiers who formed the majority of St Elmo's garrison: that the fort's prospects were very bleak. Then, on the 8th, he received a fatalistic message from uncomfortably closer to home in the form of a letter signed by fifty or so Knights among the defenders in St Elmo – if not all of those there, then the great majority. The letter stated bluntly that, although the defenders had put up a stout resistance up to that point, both they and the defences were in such a parlous state, and the enemy's forward positions so advanced, that the fort must soon be lost. It would be futile to send further reinforcements, they insisted. In such circumstances, the Knights concluded, they had no choice but to withdraw, if boats could be sent over from St Angelo, or failing that to sally out self-sacrificially against the enemy and meet their certain deaths.[72]

The wording of the letter, as Bosio reports it, came close to suggesting that the Knights, now that they had been placed *in extremis*, looked on themselves as free agents who had been released from their duty of obedience to the order. The order was familiar with murmurings against the Grand Master and those in authority almost as a matter of course: soon after the siege, for instance, La Valette would crack down on Knights who were voicing criticism of him, probably over his conduct of the defence of the island. But such an act of mass semi-defiance in wartime was unusual and troubling. The Grand Master had the upper hand over the dissenting Knights, however, if what they were doing was trying to negotiate, in that he controlled the movement of boats between St Angelo and St Elmo, the vital link that for the time being was keeping St Elmo alive with infusions of new men and supplies. In the event, La Valette faced the near rebels down by standing on his authority and appealing to their sense of aristocratic honour. That he was clearly unnerved, however, is indicated by the fact that he promptly sent over a fact-finding commission of three Knights to report on the situation in the fort. The three were an Italian, Costantino Castriota, a Spaniard, Francisco Ruiz de Medina, and a Frenchman, Antoine de Flotte de La Roche, whom we last met holding forth before the Valois court at Plessis-lèz-Tours five and a half months later.

What happened next, once the three Knights had got across to St Elmo under cover of darkness, is the basis of one of the most stagey scenes in the narrative sources. That there was some sort of tense confrontation is, however, certain. In some versions of events the verdicts of the three Knights about the defenders' prospects lay along a neat continuum: Castriota was the most upbeat, La Roche somewhere in the middle, and Medina very pessimistic. In other tellings, while Castriota remains optimistic, his two colleagues are equally convinced that further resistance is out of the question.[73] Castriota's gung-ho confidence, and the news that the Grand Master was not organizing an immediate evacuation, clearly grated with the defenders, whom the three Knights had found on their arrival spiking their guns and making other preparations for what they assumed would be their imminent departure.[74] The three Knights

The Great Siege Begins

were confronted by an angry crowd, and the way back to their waiting boat was blocked. Medina and La Roche would seem to have given a poor account of themselves by weakly pleading that, because they shared the defenders' gloomy prognosis, they should be allowed to return to St Angelo so that they might argue the case for evacuation before the Grand Master and Council. Eventually it was only the quick thinking of one of those in command of the fort, Melchior d'Eguaras, who rang the alarm bell to make the defenders stand to arms, that defused the tension and allowed the three Knights to slip away and get back to St Angelo. La Valette was relieved that Castriota, at least, offered a bullish assessment. But he would have known that this had been more than a momentary outburst of grass-roots frustration: one of those who had been most vocal in his hostility towards the three commissioners had been one of the senior Knights in command, Pierre de Massuez-Vercoirin, known as Colonel Mas. A relief force of 200 men was organized by La Valette in response to the defenders' anxieties; Castriota expressed the wish to be put in charge, but command went instead to a less contentious but equally energetic Knight, Melchior de Monserrat.

By mid June the Ottomans were increasing the pressure on the fort. A significant attack on the 15th was followed by an even larger mass assault on the following day.[75] Although the Ottoman casualties were high, the rate of attrition nonetheless favoured the attackers. The assault was relentless: by this stage it was reckoned that the Ottoman cannon had fired 13,000 shots at St Elmo, and by the time the fort fell the estimate would have risen to 18,000 or 19,000.[76] Belatedly the Turks realised that they needed to cut off the defenders' lifeline to St Angelo, and by around the 18th they had worked their trenches down to the point where the supply boats landed, thereby sealing the fort off from any further relief. There was some good news for the Christians at this time when Turgut was mortally wounded: accounts of what happened vary, but the most widely accepted version had it that he was struck on the head by rock splinters when a cannon that he was trying to re-sight fired too low and the shot ricocheted off the counterscarp near where he was standing. He would linger in Mustafa's tent before dying some days later, on the 23rd.[77]

However significant Turgut's incapacitation and death might prove for the subsequent prosecution of the siege, it made no practical difference to the immediate prospects of those trapped in St Elmo. A particularly hard-pressed and bloody general assault on 22 June left most of the defenders dead – perhaps as many as 500 out of 600 – and although it did not give the Ottomans possession of the fort, as had seemed all but inevitable, the end was now clearly in sight.[78] The handful of survivors, almost all of them wounded, were very short of gunpowder, meaning that they would have to face the final onslaught with swords, pikes and whatever tools lay to hand. Sure enough, they were soon overwhelmed when another attack was launched on the following day. As the last survivors pulled back to the chapel in the interior of the fort to make a last stand, one of the order's standards was being seized by none other than Mehmed bin Mustafa, the probable captor of Adrien de La Rivière thirty-five days earlier.[79] Almost all the defenders were cut down. A handful of Maltese and soldiers tried to swim to safety: some reached St Angelo, others drowned. Meanwhile a few Knights were lucky enough to be taken alive by corsairs with an eye to ransom – the Ottoman troops themselves gave no quarter.[80] Once the fort was taken, there followed some form of organized humiliation and desecration of the Christian dead. The fact that the Christian accounts differ as to what was done to the corpses – decapitated bodies nailed onto crosses and floated out into Grand Harbour became the canonical image – should warn us that we are in the blurred territory between what may have actually happened and what Christian writers wanted to believe of a despised Other.[81] In any event such cruel taunting of a besieged opponent was commonplace in sixteenth-century warfare. La Valette may have responded in kind, ordering that the Turkish prisoners who had been taken since the beginning of the campaign should be executed.[82] But there was no amount of psychological tit-for-tat that could disguise the fact that the defenders had suffered a grave setback.

The Great Siege Begins

The stock narrative of the Great Siege has it that the defence of St Elmo was, from the beginning, a heroic act of sustained self-sacrifice on the part of its defenders to stall the Ottoman advance and to buy Birgu and Senglea precious time. Likewise the standard image of La Valette, which has its roots in the hero-worship that he began to attract even as the siege was in progress, is of a resolute and implacable leader willing to make difficult decisions for the greater good. There are grounds for believing, however, that once the Ottomans showed their hand by moving on St Elmo, the situation was more fluid, and the Grand Master more indecisive and vacillating, than the orthodox narrative would have it. The fact, for example, that Miranda persuaded La Valette to send pay over to the soldiers around 4 June suggests that at that point the defenders anticipated that the fort would be evacuated sooner rather than later. Likewise the busy preparations for departure that greeted the three-man commission do not speak to a group of men stoically accepting their fate as sacrificial heroes. As late as the night before the final denouement, Romegas and others made frantic but unavailing efforts to get the remaining garrison out on five boats.[83] La Valette emerges from this phase of the siege as someone whose authority could be fragile: he tended to favour those such as Monserrat and Castriota who agreed with him and to freeze out, even humiliate, those such as Juan de la Cerda who did not.[84]

What is more, the letter from the fifty Knights was either an attempt to negotiate with a hesitant leader or a vote of no confidence. La Valette's anger at what he believed to be the failure of the Knights known to have assembled in Sicily to sail to Malta on the two Hospitaller galleys that were still at large, not trapped in Grand Harbour, points to a weakness for clutching at straws – the irony being that such attempts were indeed made.[85] And what soon became the routinely rehearsed position, that La Valette had prolonged St Elmo's agony simply because he was expecting the relief force that García de Toledo had promised him to arrive at any moment, looks like special pleading and a shifting of blame.[86] The month or more that the defence of St Elmo bought the defenders of

Birgu and Senglea probably did contribute to their eventual survival, but we cannot be certain. What is clear is that St Elmo became a second Thermopylae less by noble design than because of a series of half-measures and prevarications.

A number of themes that we shall see recur in the latter stages of the siege first appear in the accounts of the Ottomans' arrival and the assault on St Elmo. One notes, for example, the importance attached to the sort of liminal figures that we encountered in an earlier chapter in the form of renegades, escaped slaves and defectors. These could be important sources of intelligence for both sides.[87] La Valette was exercised by the thought of defectors briefing the Ottomans on the defenders' numbers and defences.[88] For the defenders especially, who were starved of information, incoming escapees and renegades were a valuable resource. Bosio tells the intriguing story of a Knight who came up with a plan to slip over to Mount Sciberras and blow up the Turks' main ammunition dump there; in this he would be aided by a relative, a Genoese renegade who was probably acting as a double agent in the Ottoman camp.[89] One also sees the beginnings of a new willingness on the part of the elite defenders to value the contributions of the Maltese. Balbi, for example, conceded that during the major assault on St Elmo on 16 June, the Maltese, along with the convicts and oarsmen pressed into action, gave their lives 'with as much spirit as any person worthy of greater esteem'.[90] Most of all, one sees the bedding in, at least among the defenders, for whom we have the most evidence, of an obsession with relative casualty rates. Who was dying off faster, our side or theirs? By the end of June the running score was indeed forbidding. St Elmo had accounted for a very large number of casualties, perhaps 4,000–5,000 attackers, around a quarter or fifth of their total number of combatants; and as many as 1,500 defenders.[91] The problem was compounded by the fact that, on both sides, the casualties were disproportionately heavy among the elite warriors in their respective forces. How long such fearsome rates of attrition would or could be sustained now remained to be seen.

6.
The Guns of July and August

The immediate consequence of the fall of St Elmo was that Piyale Pasha was able to bring his fleet around from Marsaxlokk to the more secure Marsamxett. On or about 30 June the Turks constructed a pontoon barrier across the mouth of Grand Harbour to isolate the defenders still further. St Elmo itself was now of no particular significance. A detachment of Ottoman troops was stationed there to guard the entrance to Marsamxett, but no attempt was made to repair or refortify the site, which remained ruinous; after the siege, when the defenders returned, they would find a number of their cannon buried in the rubble. More than twenty pieces had been captured by the Turks, however, an indication that La Valette had gambled by deploying a significant proportion of the artillery and expert gunners at his disposal in an effort to prolong the resistance. The guns were sent to Istanbul as trophies.

The Ottoman command began to redeploy its forces very soon after its victory at St Elmo, though for a few days there was something of a pause which gave both sides time to regroup. For the attackers this largely meant attending to matters of supply: on the 26th a large transport ship was sent to Tripoli with wheat to be baked into biscuit; there were obviously insufficient ovens and fuel on Malta to do the job. Another vessel sailed to Djerba at about the same time with the same mission. In early July ships were sent to the empire's European territories to stock up with foodstuffs, gunpowder and ammunition.[1] Turgut's body was taken back to Tripoli by Uluç Ali, ostensibly so that he could be granted an honourable burial, but in reality to ensure that Turgut's great personal wealth could be appropriated, Ottoman influence in Tripolitania reasserted with the appointment of a new *beylerbey*, and the vital supply line secured.² For the defenders the options were much more limited: work could continue on improving the defences of Birgu and Senglea, while an attempt was made to compensate for some of the human toll at St Elmo by ordering that the companies of local militia from four villages which had been stationed in Mdina should be sent down to the Grand Harbour positions before the Ottomans sealed Birgu and Senglea off from the land side.

While four batteries were set up on Sciberras to fire at the Christian positions from across Grand Harbour, the greater part of the artillery that had been used against St Elmo was dragged back down the peninsula towards Marsa to join those cannon, the majority of those brought to Malta, which had been held back up to that point. It then became a question of hauling the pieces towards the east and then north-east, or from the perspective of the defenders right to left, to form an arc of 180 degrees around Birgu and Senglea. The Turks' great advantage was what had long preoccupied the order and its visiting engineers, and which will be familiar to any visitor to modern-day Valletta who has looked across Grand Harbour from the Upper Barrakka Gardens: that Birgu and Senglea are overlooked by a sweep of higher land to their rear and flanked by two promontories, Corradino (Kordin) and Kalkara. In addition, the tongue of land that forms the south-eastern end of the mouth of Grand Harbour, up to what was then known as Gallows Point, extends sufficiently far beyond Kalkara to offer an unobstructed line of fire towards St Angelo. The Ottomans pressed ahead with a sense of urgency: already by 29 June La Valette could write to Don García de Toledo describing the progress that the Turks were making in positioning batteries at various points on the arc.³

The outer fortifications of Birgu and Senglea, facing south-east towards the central positions taken up by the Ottoman artillery, were located a little way up their respective peninsulas, which meant that they did not form a single defensive line. An overspill suburban area, Bormla, broadly modern Cospicua, had grown up in part of the interjacent stretch of land. The fact that the two positions were not contiguous was a possible source of weakness for the defenders because it would limit their ability to deploy men to the points of greatest need in an emergency – a problem that we shall see came to be addressed by means of an improvised bridge across Dockyard Creek. On the other hand, it forced the Turks to divide their artillery strength, as well as their forces when assaults were made on both positions simultaneously. Senglea, dominated by the fortress of St Michael at the landward end, was the weaker of the two positions, but its land frontage was much narrower than that of Birgu. This meant that it was proportionately more vulnerable to concentrated artillery fire, especially from Corradino, the Mandra, which was a hill at the base of the peninsula, and Bormla, but it also ensured that assaults on it would be funnelled into tight areas that the defenders might hope to contain.

An Ottoman gunner in position on the heights of Santa Margherita, just beyond the central point of the arc, would thus have seen two lines of fortifications, each fronted by a large ditch and separated by the innermost point of Dockyard Creek. He would have recognized the familiar zigzag of *trace italienne*, the signature feature of early modern fortress design in which angular bastions were configured to eliminate dead zones where attackers might be sheltered from the defenders' fire.[4] The Knights' fortifications were by no means state of the art, in large part because the overlooking heights and the narrowness of the peninsulas militated against the optimum arrangement, which was low, wide, very thick defensive works which absorbed or deflected incoming artillery fire. There were also blind spots, which the Turks would come to exploit. But the order had invested substantial amounts in the defences, especially on the land front, and to some extent also on the outer flanks of the two peninsulas. As events would prove, they were just about adequate. The most vulnerable points were at the outer corners of the two positions, where the land defences met their respective flanking creeks. This would be where the Ottoman artillerists would direct much of their fire, and the location of the main killing zones in the hand-to-hand fighting.

The Knights apportioned responsibility for sections of the defences, or posts, to the various langues, the national or, in the French case, regional groupings into which members of the order were divided. The langues were not regiments or organized military units as such, but this arrangement was suggested by earlier sieges, and at least had the advantage of giving the Knights and the soldiers and civilians under their command a clear sense of where they should be. It also promoted a sense of collective solidarity and mutual responsibility that was proof against frequent changes at the top as those in command were killed or incapacitated and had to be replaced by new men. Intermediate posts came to be named after the captain in command or the place of origin of a group of soldiers serving there. The langues of England – a token courtesy because it was effectively defunct – and of Germany – represented by only a small number of Knights – were put in charge of the least critical positions, on the outer flank of Birgu facing across the creek towards Kalkara. The land-facing defences of Birgu were assigned, reading from north-east to south-west, to the langues of Castile (one of the highly vulnerable corner positions), Auvergne, France, Provence and Aragon. Italy, the langue with the single largest complement of Knights and sergeants in Malta when the siege began, was given responsibility for Senglea. Its numbers were supplemented by companies of soldiers, many of them themselves Italian, as well as Maltese militiamen.[5]

The Christian narrative sources punctuate the period of transition after the fall of St Elmo with reference to two incidents, each in its different way setting the scene for the resolute spirit of defiance that, it was believed, came to animate the defence thereafter. First, on 29 June, just as the Turkish gun emplacements were nearing completion and the defenders had been forced to abandon frantic efforts to demolish buildings in Bormla so as to deny the enemy cover, a group led by a mounted figure, an Ottoman emissary, or *çavuş*, worked its way up from Marsa and drew to a halt some distance back from Bormla under the white flag of truce. When a squad of men was sent out from Provence to investigate and came upon an old Spanish slave, he revealed that he had been ordered, by none other than the pashas themselves, to ask the Grand Master to receive the *çavuş*. The slave was blindfolded and taken before La Valette. He reluctantly revealed that the *çavuş* had been instructed to offer terms of surrender: if the Knights abandoned the island, they and the other defenders would be allowed to sail to Sicily unmolested and with all their property; they could even take their artillery with them.[6] At this point the Grand Master lost his cool and threatened to have the slave put to death, before being prevailed upon to change his mind. Balbi suggests that this was a piece of theatre meant to demonstrate both the Grand Master's magnanimity and his determination; but if so, it was quite a show to put on for a decrepit and terrified slave. La Valette had a record of being febrile and violent, and one wonders whether the tension of the moment got the better of him before he regained his composure. The slave was told that the *çavuş* would not be received, nor would any negotiations be considered in future. He was then returned to the no man's land in Bormla, his blindfold having been removed in the ditch so that he might take back word of the looming strength of the defences. He and his party then made their way back to Mustafa's headquarters at Marsa. One hopes that, as Cirni supposed, he was rewarded for his efforts with the freedom that he had been offered.

The narratives turn this incident into a confrontation between two old men, one powerful, the other abjectly powerless, and by extension between two ways of viewing the siege as a conflict between irreconcilable opposites. The powerful old man would brook no compromise, no blurring of dividing lines. But the powerless old man embodied that very blurriness, all the ambiguities and smudged identities of the cruel sea. Whose side was a Spanish slave running errands for the enemy's high command *really* on? That being said, what was actually going on in that moment? If, as was argued in the previous chapter, the Sublime Porte's main war aim was the destruction of the order, the Ottoman commanders were on the face of it taking a big risk in telling La Valette that, in Balbi's words, 'they wanted nothing other than the empty island'. They may have calculated that the order was already so weakened that it could no longer pose a threat to Ottoman interests, at least for many years; or that, once Malta was lost, the order would have run out of places where it might rebuild itself as a naval operation capable of functioning in the central and eastern Mediterranean. Most probably the pashas correctly anticipated the Grand Master's reply, the point being that the rejection of a formal offer of terms meant that the defenders could expect no quarter as and when they were overwhelmed. Unlike at Rhodes, the niceties were being got out of the way early. One wonders, too, whether the choice of go-between was a calculated insult, designed to elicit the very response it received, and La Valette knew it: it was not unusual for a *çavuş* to be preceded by a more expendable cat's paw when negotiating with an enemy, but surely there were other candidates for the role to be found in the Ottoman camp, multilingual men of higher status?[7] If La Valette was indulging in theatre, as Balbi supposed, so too were the pashas. The Christian authors understood this and that is why they included this incident. For La Valette and the Knights, on the other hand, this was a moment of clarity. The surrender of Rhodes had loomed over the order like Banquo's ghost for more than forty years, but now the ghost could be exorcised.

The second incident was touched on in the previous chapter: on 30 June a *sipahi*, probably called Mehmed bin Davud (holder of a *timar* in the Peloponnese) or Memi Çelebi, came down to the shoreline of Sciberras opposite the tip of Senglea and gestured to those stationed there that he was desperate to cross over. Balbi was one of the company manning that position. There was no boat outside the chain that could be sent over in time, so the *sipahi* had no choice but to strip off and swim for it. Getting into difficulties halfway across, he was saved by three of Balbi's colleagues, who dived in and pulled him to safety while covering fire pinned down the Turks on Sciberras who had spotted what was happening. After the fugitive had composed himself – and Balbi had given him a pair of his trousers – he was taken to the Grand Master.[8] He told La Valette that he wished to revert to the Christianity of his forebears: this rings true insofar as many higher-status families in south-eastern Europe had converted to Islam in order to adjust to the Ottoman conquests in the fourteenth and fifteenth centuries. His choice of baptismal name, Filippo de Lascaris, may suggest some ancestral memory of a connection to a Greek aristocratic family. As we have seen, he survived the siege, was presented to the pope and Philip II, and made a new life for himself in Naples with a little help from the order's coffers. The net flow of people and their information over the course of the siege was probably from inside to out, at least until the last few days of the campaign; so a knowledgeable and high-status defector of this sort was a real coup for La Valette. His immediate value for the defenders lay in the intelligence that he could pass on about the Ottoman high command's intentions, in particular plans for a large amphibious assault which, as we shall see, came to be launched on 15 July.

According to Balbi, the defector also had very encouraging news to which he alone was privy: that a Christian relief force had landed on the island and had reached Mdina. The dating makes it uncertain whether he could have known this; Balbi may be conflating two separate events that happened in fairly quick succession.[9] But something definitely was afoot around this time. The prevalent view in Habsburg circles was that if the Ottoman occupation of Malta was to be overcome by force from outside, this could not be achieved by means of a naval confrontation, which would play to the enemy's particular strengths, but on land, where the skill, experience and close-order discipline of the Spanish *tercios*, the elite corps, could, it was hoped, be brought to bear. Before this decisive conflict could take place, however, the question remained whether García de Toledo, as commander-in-chief of the Habsburg forces in the Mediterranean, should marshal all his resources for one big push – as late in the campaign season as he dared in order to allow time for Turkish numbers on Malta to be depleted by the attrition of the siege – or drip-feed troops into the island to sustain the defence pending a final showdown.[10] The Ottomans' patrolling of the seas around Malta meant that disembarking forces in one of the island's more secluded bays was fraught with danger, while thoughts of blasting one's way into Grand Harbour ram-raid-style, though entertained, were wholly unrealistic; indeed, when one such attempt was nearing its target in July, the Grand Master signalled that it should be aborted.[11]

García de Toledo had been given the green light by an always circumspect Philip II, in a letter dated 18 June, to proceed with the organization of a relief expedition.[12] But, as was often the case given the king's fondness for imprecise utterance, much remained to be settled. The viceroy was juggling conflicting pressures. If an interim relief force were to be organized, it would need to be sufficiently large to make a difference to the defence of the island, but small enough to be able to evade any Ottoman patrols. The Knights who had arrived in Sicily hoping to contribute to the defence of Malta, and who were forming themselves into an effective and vociferous lobby, were pushing for prompt action. But when would enough troops be available? García de Toledo's dilemmas reflected the fact that, for all the sense of remoteness and cultural unfamiliarity that European visitors to the Maltese islands sometimes expressed, geopolitically the archipelago amounted to an extension of Italy.[13] This meant that its fate in 1565 would ultimately be decided by the extent to which Italy's political fragmentation could be transcended in the interests of saving its southern outlier. The Habsburg Mezzogiorno, the kingdoms of Sicily and Naples, were the most secure sources of men, supplies and ships, but even here Naples was a semi-detached entity whose viceroy could not be treated as García de Toledo's subordinate.[14] As one moved north from Naples, one entered an even more complex political landscape – simplified to some extent by the absence of French interest in Italy after the Treaty of Cateau-Cambrésis, but still a kaleidoscope of Habsburg clients, allies and more independent polities, in addition to the papal lands and finally Venice, which stood aloof. The tangled account of the mobilization of troops in various parts of Italy that is provided by Cirni, the chronicler most au fait with Italian conditions, reflects the complex process whereby, over the early summer, various contingents recruited by Italian rulers fitfully made their way from north to south, sometimes ferried part of the way by Gianandrea Doria's galleys.[15] Faced with this bitty mobilization delivering him men in fits and starts, García de Toledo could not simply accumulate troops in Sicily against some future decision to strike. Who would pay these soldiers if their leaders' money ran out, and how would they be fed? A poor harvest had meant that food in Sicily was scarce – an issue that had come up in April in discussions between the viceroy and La Valette about sending foodstuffs to Malta. Should García de Toledo stick or twist?

The answer that emerged was informed by the combination of calculated policy, ad hoc reaction to events, hoping for something to happen, and balancing of interest groups that seems to have characterized much of the rolling Habsburg response to the Malta crisis. It was decided that four galleys, including the two belonging to the order, would deliver 600–700 men onto the island, about half the number that La Valette was hoping for.[16] The commander would be Melchior de Robles, an experienced and widely respected soldier and a Knight of the Spanish military order of Santiago. The force included about forty Knights and approximately the same number of gentleman volunteers. Companies raised by Pius IV either did not arrive in time or were excluded, much to the pope's subsequent irritation.[17] The dates provided by the sources are not in agreement, but it is likely that the galleys disembarked the troops at Pietra Negra, on the southern coast of the island, on or about the night of 30 June–1 July.

The landing is the subject of one of the set-piece vignettes in the narrative sources that are put to use to illustrate the defenders' resourcefulness and determination. Juan de Cardona, the captain-general of the Sicilian fleet in command of the galleys, had been ordered not to disembark the men if he heard that St Elmo had fallen. When a French Knight, Esprit de Brunefay-Quincy, went ashore and learned about St Elmo's fate from some local Maltese, he swore them to secrecy and suppressed the news.[18] The subterfuge was sustained until the troops reached Mdina and discovered the truth. Now beyond the point of no return, Robles gambled on keeping his force together in a single column: easier for the Turks to spot, but better able to defend itself if necessary. Under the cover of darkness, probably on the night of 3–4 July, his men made their way from Mdina in a wide anti-clockwise arc that took them around the rear of the Turkish positions. Reaching Rinella, the spur of land at the south-eastern end of the mouth of Grand Harbour, they were ferried to Birgu in small boats. In due course this expedition would become known as the *piccolo soccorso*, the small relief. But in the moment it was no small matter. Fewer men had arrived than had been lost at St Elmo, but most of them were experienced fighters. Other attempts to land more men on Malta around this time proved unavailing, so by default the *piccolo soccorso* became the sole means whereby the defence of Malta would be prolonged, for the time being at least.[19]

In the meantime the defenders' priority had become coping with the artillery bombardment, which was growing in intensity and destructive efficiency as the Ottoman gunners perfected their positioning and their range-finding. Balbi reports that the Grand Master ordered the demolition of the more exposed houses in Birgu and the construction of stone barricades to obstruct the trajectory of incoming cannonballs.[20] By around 6 July boats were being dragged across the neck of the Sciberras peninsula from Marsamxett to Marsa, confirmation that the amphibious assault about which Lascaris had warned was now in prospect. By the 10th, according to Balbi, there were about sixty boats, and soon thereafter eighty or more.[21] Given that a chain guarded the entrance to Dockyard Creek, as we have seen, and that any attempt by the Turks to bring their boats around to the outer shore of Birgu would force them to pass close up by St Angelo, the defenders' strongest position, it was clear that their target would be the flank of Senglea facing out onto what is now French Creek. As a counter-measure, a barricade was constructed along this flank about ten metres out from the shoreline: reinforced stakes were driven into the seabed at intervals of about twelve metres and connected by an iron chain (perhaps part of the

The Guns of July and August

old Dockyard Creek chain that had recently been replaced) and planks.[22] Balbi optimistically believed that the barrier could stop a galley in its tracks, but this was not put to the test; its principal purpose was to prevent the Turkish boats from reaching the shore and thereby reduce the impetus of the assault. The attacking troops would be especially vulnerable as they laboriously waded ashore, and their firearms and gunpowder would, it was hoped, become soaked. On 11 July the Turks countered the counter-measure by sending in a group of swimmers equipped with axes to break the chain; they in turn were intercepted by four Maltese, who killed one assailant and drove the others away before the chain could be damaged. Balbi records the names of the four Maltese, a sign of the significance attached to this small but nasty struggle: they were Pietru Bola, Martin, Gianni tal-Pont and Frangiscu. In one of the pleasing if rare symmetries afforded by the Ottoman evidence, moreover, we know that one of the attackers who survived was a mariner named Salih bin Mahmud.[23] A subsequent attempt to drag the chain out of position by means of ropes hauled by slaves on the far side of the creek was similarly frustrated, with the result that the barrier was in place when the great blow fell on the 15th.

The account of the events of the 15th by Balbi, who was in the thick of the fighting on Senglea, forms one of the two most intensely autobiographical sequences in his history of the siege. (The other concerns the defection of Filippo de Lascaris, in which he played a role, as we have seen.)[24] Balbi's eyewitness testimony tends to draw our attention particularly to events in Grand Harbour, but the simultaneous land assault on St Michael, focusing on the vulnerable post that had recently been placed under Robles' command and lasting some five hours, was among the hardest-fought of the whole siege. As many as 8,000 Ottoman troops were thrown forward in waves, including many of the surviving Janissaries. Meanwhile the fleet of boats was making its way up the length of the harbour from Marsa. There were between 2,000 and 3,000 fighting men on board, many of them Barbary corsairs, including those from Algiers who had newly arrived in Malta, on the 12th, in twenty-five galleys under the command of Hasan Pasha.[25] As the boats neared French Creek, they split into two groups, all but ten bearing to starboard towards the flank of Senglea and its protective barricade. The principal target of the larger group was the weakest point of the peninsula, its spur, which was poorly fortified; all that confronted the attackers, once they forced their way ashore, would be a low platform and improvised parapets manned by sixty soldiers, Balbi included, under the command of an Aragonese Knight named Francisco de Sanoguera.[26]

As Balbi tells it, the Turks' onslaught came on quicker than the defenders had expected, with the result that two mortars which had been set up to fire on them were never deployed. There was bitter hand-to-hand fighting as the attackers tried to bring up ladders to surmount the platform. With so few defenders to hand, individual mishaps could assume great significance: in attempting to light an incendiary weapon, probably a fire pot or bag of gunpowder, a Christian soldier accidentally set fire to the rest of his supply, burning himself and others around him. Soon the defenders were resorting to throwing stones at the enemy. The Turks picked out Francisco de Sanoguera from the quality of his knightly armour – a recurring motif in the story of the siege – and although his cuirass protected him from a shot to the chest, he was felled by an arquebus fired up from the foot of the platform into his groin. There then followed a macabre tug of war, as Balbi and some of his companions tried to heave Sanoguera's body away from the edge, while a group of Turks took hold of his legs and tried to pull him down.[27] They only managed to get his shoes, Balbi records, one of those inconsequential details, remembered of moments of great peril, that one finds in many war memoirs. The problem of moving reinforcements between Birgu and Senglea had been addressed only a couple of days earlier by the construction of a bridge across Dockyard Creek made from spars and planking and floated on barrels; this would now prove its worth as fresh troops came over from Birgu to stiffen the resistance both on the land front and at the spur.[28] Gradually the assaults petered out, Balbi and others chasing the retreating Turks back to the shoreline before they in turn were forced to retire by covering fire.

Meanwhile the ten boats that had carried straight on made for the end of the spur. Their intention may have been to destroy the position, just around the tip of the peninsula, where the Senglea end of the chain across Dockyard Creek was secured. They may simply have meant to come ashore just before the chain and attack Sanoguera's post from the side. As they swung around, however, they exposed themselves to the five guns of a battery under the command of Francisco de Guiral, one of the order's galley captains. This was positioned just above sea level at the foot of St Angelo's inward-facing defences so as to guard the entrance to Dockyard Creek. It is often supposed that the Ottomans had simply overlooked this position when planning their assault – Balbi says as much – though this is not altogether easy to believe. The Turks may have gambled that Guiral's guns could not be brought to bear without imperilling the defenders on the spur of Senglea – in which case their geometry was off, just. Or they simply underestimated the damage that the guns could do in the time that it would take for them to effect an unopposed landing while the defenders were occupied elsewhere. If so, they were badly mistaken. In perhaps the most critical two or three minutes of the entire four-month siege, Guiral spotted the ten boats coming around the tip of Senglea, sighted his first volley of lethal anti-personnel grapeshot – links of chain, iron spikes, pieces of stone – and chose his moment to fire. The effect of the first salvo and those that followed, at a range of about 250 metres, was devastating. Nine of the ten boats were destroyed. Many of those not killed on impact drowned; in all about 800 lost their lives (an indication that these boats had been especially tightly packed with men).[29] A story that crops up in several narrative sources is that Piyale Pasha had deliberately chosen men for this mission who could not swim so as to concentrate their minds.[30] This sounds like the sort of baroque reasoning that Christian writers sometimes liked to impute to the Ottomans. But it does capture something of the wonder occasioned by this moment of sudden and decisive carnage. Balbi believed that Guiral's battery, in preventing the spur from being overrun, was 'on that day, in the judgement of all, the salvation of the island'. The close shave is a motif that crops up frequently in the narrative accounts of the siege. But in this instance Balbi was almost certainly correct.

We cannot tell how badly the Ottoman command was shaken by the failure of the 15th. Within a few days it became apparent, as the boats began to be dragged back from Marsa across to Marsamxett, that there would not be another amphibious attack. In fact the next large-scale assault would not be launched until early August. The Turks needed to regroup, and were probably waiting on the arrival of supplies; there may also have been illness in their camp.[31] In the meantime the contest settled into the now-familiar rhythms of a war of attrition, as the attackers resumed their bombardment and worked to secure positions of tactical advantage closer and closer to the front line – the ditches and outer fortifications – while the defenders improvised ways to negate the enemy's efforts through a constant process of trial and error. The Ottoman guns resumed their bombardment the day after the amphibious assault, and by 22 July had reached a new level of intensity: it was believed that they could be heard as far away as Sicily. Batteries that were particularly effective against the weakest points of the defences, especially those on Is Salvatur firing on Castile, were strengthened.[32] Ottoman sappers, an expert corps, drove trenches towards the counterscarps of the ditches, while blind spots and areas of particular vulnerability in the ditches themselves were identified and targeted.[33]

It was by working their way right up to the fortifications that the Turks were able to begin to dig mines – tunnels which could be packed with gunpowder, which when detonated would cause a stretch of fortification to collapse, or might enable troops to surprise the enemy from the rear. On 18 July Robles was told that his post, one of the weakest points of the defences, was being mined; a counter-mine was hurriedly dug, the sappers discovered within it were killed and the entrance was sealed. About ten days later, in one of the close shaves beloved of the chroniclers, a mine in the same stretch of fortifications was detected when one of the engineers supervising its construction tested its depth by prodding upwards with a pointed probe; a sentry named Bartolomé Gonzalo spotted the earth near his feet subside a little, the alarm was raised, an entrance was swiftly dug, and a party of Knights and arquebusiers led by Robles' ensign, Andreas de Muñatones, entered the tunnel and chased off those inside.[34] Another tried-and-tested tactic in siege warfare, already attempted against St Elmo, was the construction of a bridge over a defensive ditch. This was one of the Ottoman command's first resorts after the failed amphibious assault: by 17 July work on a bridge on the St Michael front had begun, and the following day it was already supported by five strong piers. The frantic efforts that the defenders made to destroy the bridge as quickly as possible are a measure of the grave threat that they believed it posed. On the 18th a demolition squad led by the Grand Master's nephew, Henri, achieved very little and Henri was killed – the visibility to Turkish snipers of a Knight's showy armour proving fatal. Then another party tried to set fire to the supports; although the piers were coated in damp earth, this time enough damage was done to bring down part of the bridge.[35]

As these small but keenly fought contests illustrate, the dynamic of the siege by this stage was one in which the Ottomans enjoyed the initiative. They could ring the changes on the well-practised techniques of siege warfare – towards the end of the campaign they would even build siege engines – and force the defenders to react. The defenders' ability to survive, therefore, depended on the extent to which they could anticipate whatever the Turks might devise. They were fortunate in that they enjoyed the services of a team of inventive military engineers led by an Italian, Evangelista Menga from Brindisi; one of those under him was a Maltese, Girolamo Cassar, who would go on to play an important role in the construction of Valletta.[36] Thanks to the skills of these engineers, as well as the experience of several Knights who were known as specialists in siege warfare, the order could make good on a number of 'textbook' counter-measures. One such was the building of retrenchments, additional defensive positions set back from the edge of the fortifications. Another was the packing of earth behind the fortifications to form a terreplein able to absorb the impact of artillery fire; when a shot from one of the Ottomans' monster guns, a basilisk, was able to penetrate all the way through one such mass of earth measuring twenty-one feet, this seemed especially worthy of note.[37] Additionally, and as was often the case in sieges in this era, one had to be ready to improvise. A barrier of the sort that had saved Senglea on 15 July was not practicable on the far side of Birgu, so boats loaded with stones were sunk to hinder an amphibious assault across Kalkara Creek. Overnight repairs to fortifications which had been battered over the course of the day made use of mattresses, ropes, spare pieces of wood and whatever else was to hand that might impede the progress of oncoming troops. Sails were used as awnings to deny the Ottoman gunners a clear aim on those making frantic repairs. Even the clothes off the backs of dead slaves were put to use to make sacks.[38]

For all the skill and ingenuity with which the defenders were able to mobilize their diminishing resources, the question remained whether relief would ever arrive, especially now that communication with the outside world was becoming more hazardous and infrequent. Perhaps because he was reduced to allowing the wish to precede the thought, or was gambling in order to boost morale in the short term, La Valette had made it known that he confidently expected a major relief force to arrive by 25 July. This was the feast day of St James, Santiago, the principal military saint venerated in Spain. Surely Philip II and García de Toledo, who was himself a Knight of the Order of Santiago, would time their moment so as to redound to the greater glory of the Spanish crown?[39] When the 25th came and went, however, a fatalistic combination of fight-them-on-the-beaches bloody-mindedness and resigned isolation seems to have taken hold. La Valette gave a briefing to the effect that the defenders' only hope now lay with God; Balbi's observation that this speech was then 'spread' suggests that a deliberate effort was made to disseminate it by word of mouth. Starved of news and useful intelligence, and in a near-hopeless position, La Valette could only hope to galvanize the defenders and maintain his authority over them by trying to shape the collective mood.[40]

By the beginning of August the Ottoman forces had regrouped sufficiently to increase their pressure on the defenders. A massive artillery bombardment on the 1st was resumed the following morning. Then, around noon on the 2nd, a large number of troops began an assault against the most vulnerable points on the Senglea frontage, the posts of Robles and the Knight Carlo Ruffo (who died in the fighting).[41] The attack lasted five hours before the Turks retreated. Balbi picks out one climactic moment in particular, which, though clearly demonstrating how bitter and bloody the fighting on the walls could be, provides a clue as to why, in assaults such as this, the defenders were able to offer effective resistance despite their numerical inferiority. When twenty or more Turks had managed to clamber up onto the highest point of Robles' post, Robles, Muñatones and three arquebusiers made a rush at them with pikes or poles that had flammable material at the end, one of the types of incendiary weapon that were a feature of the siege. Several of the Turks were killed and the rest withdrew. That five men, armed with unconventional as well as conventional weapons, could hold the line reveals that, although the sources routinely state that the numbers of attackers in general assaults were in the several thousands, in practice the Turks moved forward in smaller groups. As they did so, they were picking their way up towards the Christian positions through a rubble field created by their own artillery. By early August, the Ottoman guns were not so much punching holes in the defences as rearranging debris and gradually flattening mounds of collapsed masonry. In such circumstances tight, packed formations were not feasible, nor could the attackers come on at a sustained rush. The Ottoman command's advantage lay in its being able to send in successive waves of troops in the hope that cumulatively these would achieve what the first loosely arrayed detachments to scramble towards the front line probably could not. The defenders did not have this option; their hope lay in effecting repairs to the fortifications in such a way that at the point of contact the enemy would be funnelled into manageably compressed killing zones, while a system of holding reinforcements in reserve, progressively refined through a process of trial and error, enabled them to react to sudden crises wherever and whenever they arose.[42]

After this assault on the 2nd the Turks reverted to the standard pattern of heavy bombardment, as much a psychological as a tactical weapon, and the digging of trenches ever closer to the front line so that attacks launched from them would have greater impetus. On 7 August, the fairly brief interval since the previous large assault perhaps a sign of mounting impatience and concern on the Ottoman commanders' part, they decided to go again. Perhaps 12,000 men were sent in against both Castile and Senglea.[43] It would seem that the Turks tried to tighten their formations in an attempt to gain a greater advantage from their weight of numbers. Although more men were thrown in at Senglea, the narrative sources direct most of our attention to events in Birgu. There the attackers were able to force their way up through what was left of Castile's defences and over into the forward Christian positions. A Knight brought the news to La Valette, who was with the reserves in Birgu's piazza. Disregarding the objections of the team of senior Knights which typically accompanied him, La Valette made up his mind to meet the danger in person: Castile itself was too risky because it was exposed to enemy guns, so he took up position at a lower point from where he directed arquebus fire up against a group of Turks which was establishing itself on a raised platform.[44] Eventually La Valette, wounded in the leg and surrounded by a pile of bodies, was prevailed upon to withdraw. The whole assault, according to Balbi, lasted nine hours – about five was more typical – during which the Ottomans showed great *furia y pertinacia* in sending in a dozen or more waves of attackers.[45] The numbers and the duration would suggest that this was the single most determined effort at a knockout blow that the Ottoman command attempted over the course of the siege.

That it did not succeed was, it was believed, thanks to a *deus ex machina*, an unexpected intervention from outside that caused the Turks to panic and pull back just as victory seemed assured. We always have to be cautious in assessing the evidence because of the Christian sources' predilection for the motif of the near miss that we have already noted; once last-gasp denouements are baked into the narrative structure of the memories that form around an event and the stories that perpetuate them, they are very difficult to unbake. Nonetheless it would appear that the sources' insistence that there was a very close shave on that day was essentially correct. The key to the drama that unfolded was Mdina, the Christian position in the rear which, it was supposed, Turgut would wisely have targeted first had he arrived in time to influence the Ottoman strategy. Ever since the order had arrived in Malta and had chosen to set up its headquarters in Grand Harbour, not Mdina, or Città Vecchia, the old city in the interior of the island, its relationship with Mdina and the remnants of the formerly dominant political class who lived there had been less than straightforward. As the events of 1551 had shown, the Knights had a vested interest in building Mdina into whatever system of defence in depth that the geography of the island made possible; but the allocation of resources to fortification projects after the scare of that year clearly demonstrated that Grand Harbour was their priority. Before the siege a Portuguese Knight named Pedro de Mesquita had been appointed governor of the city: he had very few fellow Knights stationed with him, and, as we have seen, his initial complement of local militia forces was depleted in order to reinforce Birgu and Senglea. But he seems to have been skilful in his cultivation of good relations with Mdina's urban elites, and this meant, crucially, that the small force that he was able to maintain in the city included a cavalry corps which mostly comprised local men.[46]

By August, Mdina had already demonstrated its strategic value to the defenders of the island. It was the principal route through which messengers smuggled letters in and out of Grand Harbour. And it had served as an invaluable staging area for the *piccolo soccorso*, a role it would go on to repeat when a larger relief force arrived in

Malta in September. Mesquita's small but mobile forces had, moreover, become practised in disrupting Turkish foraging expeditions and supply lines, sometimes probing as far as the main enemy positions.[47] The story of one such raid, as recounted to Balbi by a Greek resident of Mdina, Michalis Cali, had clearly grown in the telling. Sixty Maltese who were living in the caves of Għar il-Kbir south of Mdina, either as refugees or because they were an established troglodyte community, were discovered by the Turks. When the Turks were in turn ambushed by the cavalry from Mdina, a *sancakbey* tried to abduct one of the Maltese women in the caves; cornered and unable to get away, he petulantly beheaded the woman before himself being shot and killed.[48] The other Maltese were rescued. It is a curious anecdote to have lodged itself in the larger story of the siege, but it does illustrate the tactical mobility, speed and effectiveness of Mesquita's cavalry.

On 7 August, Mesquita could see, thanks to the view of Grand Harbour afforded by his elevated position in Mdina, that something significant was happening, and he therefore sent one hundred horsemen and as many infantry down to investigate. Most of the sources suggest that there was already a plan to attack the Turks in the rear in their camp at Marsa, but it is more likely that this was an on-the-spot decision made by one of the commanders, a French Knight named Jean de Lugny, once he realized that no guards had been posted – presumably because every available soldier had been pressed into service for the assault on Birgu and Senglea about three kilometres away. There were only the sick and non-combatants in the camp. Lugny's small force launched a devastating attack, burning tents and killing everyone in their path. A domino effect of misapprehension was then set in motion within the Ottoman ranks. A group of Turks stationed on Mount Sciberras had the best view of what was happening, but having first decided to investigate they quickly changed their minds and stopped dead in their tracks, perhaps because they were afraid that a relief force had landed and they did not wish to become separated from the ships in Marsamxett. They in turn were spotted by those across Grand Harbour, first by those attacking Castile and then those along the Senglea front. Rumours of the arrival of a Christian army began to spread, the assaults petered out, and mass panic set it. Mustafa Pasha attempted to regroup his forces at Santa Margherita, but the momentum of the attack was by then irretrievably dissipated.[49]

The Ottoman riposte was quick in coming, though it was probably too hastily planned to be effective. Shortly after the failed assault – Balbi says as soon as the 8th – a large detachment of soldiers was sent to round up cattle grazing on the low ground below Mdina so as to provoke a response from the defenders and draw them into an ambush. Lugny, Vincenzo Anastagi (who has left us a valuable account of the siege from the perspective of those stationed in Mdina) and Vincenzo Ventura led out the Christian forces and retrieved the cattle, but then came close to being cut off and had to fight their way clear, losing several men and horses in the process.[50] Ventura and those with him were forced to hide until they could make their way back to the city under cover of darkness. Balbi complacently records this incident as another victory on points for the defenders, but it would seem to have significantly reduced the fighting strength of the Mdina garrison and its number of available mounts.[51] Piyale Pasha, in command of this expedition, followed up by bringing his forces close to the walls of the city. Although an attack was made on a section of the defences, it was unlikely that, without cannon, the Turks would be able to force their way in. Mesquita was nonetheless sufficiently worried to repeat the ruse that had been used back in 1551, dressing civilians in military outfits and positioning them ostentatiously on the ramparts so as to convince the Turks that the garrison was much stronger than it was in reality. Piyale was most probably not fooled, but he knew that the prudent course of action was to withdraw. Mdina survived. Its great importance for the defenders' cause would be confirmed one month later, as we shall see in the next chapter.

Although there was always the chance that the tide could turn very suddenly in the Ottomans' favour, by the middle of August the siege was settling into some sort of equilibrium. Neither side could be said to be winning; rather, they were losing at about the same rate. Balbi makes the telling observation that the sounds of the shouts, musical instruments and drums that preceded assaults would have unnerved the defenders had they not grown accustomed to them.[52] All the various groups that the siege had thrown together were finding ways to survive. The experiences of the Ottoman rank and file are the hardest to capture, because they are not embedded in detailed narrative sources. Our best way into their world is through the *Ottoman Campaign Register*, a document which largely comprises notes of the actions taken to reward those who had performed conspicuously well in Malta and to reallocate the *timars*, incomes and positions of those who had died there. The entries are mostly brief and to the point, but in some cases a little circumstantial detail is included, thereby offering up tantalizing glimpses on an individual level of what happened to some of those in the Turkish forces.

From the register we learn, for example, that Pir Mehmed, son of Salih, from the Dardanelles cut off many heads in what was probably the final assault on St Elmo and was rewarded with a posting to a fortress close to his home; while Mehmed, son of Hüsrev, was severely injured and burned in an attack on the same fortress.[53] Ali, a timariot from the Peloponnese, was killed by cannon fire during the 'battle of the Malta fortress', that is, in the Senglea–Birgu theatre; another Ali, from north-western Anatolia, was wounded in the same area; so too a *sipahi* named Piri, who was struck by a cannon.[54] Mustafa bin Abdullah, a freed slave who served one of the senior officers in the Janissary corps, fought alongside the Janissaries in a battle at the fortified position of *Değirmenlik*, 'the place of the mills', in other words Senglea; the reference may be to the amphibious assault on 15 July. A *sipahi* named Sarrac Ali had been captured and enslaved at Djerba in 1560, and presumed dead. He was then released, in circumstances which are not explained, and went on to fight in Malta. Mustafa, son of Mehmed Reis, did excellent work as a tunneller before he was wounded; Ali bin Hüseyin captured an infidel and brought him back alive; and Behram, son of Abdullah, worked as a surgeon tending to those wounded at St Elmo and Senglea–Birgu and was rewarded with a pay rise.[55]

Although the siege staged, and in staging accentuated, an us-and-them sense of separation on both sides, there were those who tried to find a way across that boundary, whether voluntarily, opportunistically or out of sheer desperation. A marquee defection such as that of Filippo de Lascaris was newsworthy because it was unusual; the circumstances of most of those who crossed the lines were much more humble. Nonetheless all were useful. Several who fled to the Christian side were put to work making ammunition, for example.[56] For the defenders, incoming renegades and escapees, most of them probably slaves from the galleys in Marsamxett or Barbary renegades harbouring second thoughts, were an important source of information about what was happening in the Ottoman camp; they are probably responsible for many of the suspiciously elevated and rounded figures that chroniclers give for the number of enemy casualties in the various engagements. One suspects that most of those who tried to cross the lines never made it, like the old Greek man living in Mdina who, for reasons that the sources do not properly address, tried to slip away to warn the Turks of the arrival of the *piccolo soccorso*, was spotted, caught, interrogated and thrown to the people of the city to be done to death.[57]

One of those who did get through was Stephano di Castra from Lombardy, a kind of mirror image of Sarrac Ali in that he too had been captured at Djerba. He was enslaved as a *rimego*, an oarsman in the galleys, and five years later found himself in Malta. In the opening phase of the campaign, as the Turks were beginning the bombardment of St Elmo, Stephano made his escape and managed to reach Birgu. It is possible that supervision of the galley slaves was loosest early in the campaign, when the armada was moored in Marsaxlokk at some remove from the main concentrations of Ottoman troops. Or he may have been one of those dragging the cannon up Mount Sciberras. Stephano must have had experience as a cavalryman in his previous life, for after he escaped he was sent to Mdina, where he served in Mesquita's mounted unit, survived many dangers, and was given leave to return home to northern Italy in December 1565. The fact that he was reconciled by the bishop of Malta may suggest that at some stage after his capture he had converted to Islam, probably in an attempt to improve his circumstances: if he was still an oarsman but no longer chained in 1565, it might help to explain how he managed to get away.[58] As Stephano's experience reveals, the siege was for many an opportunity to make the most of the cards that fate had dealt them. One of those in that position was Istemad, most probably a Greek Jew, who decided to convert to Islam while he was serving in the Ottoman forces on Malta. He took the name Yunus and was promised a position as a fortress guard close to his home. Perhaps he survived the siege and was able to embark on his new life, but he may be the man of the same name, also described as a guard from Greece, who is recorded among those killed during the assaults on St Elmo. (He may also be the Istemad from Methoni who we are informed asked the Ottoman authorities for a safe conduct for himself and a colleague called Todoro – Theodoros, a Christian name – to transport Christian captives from Malta.)[59]

For both sides, incoming would-be converts and renegades reclaiming previous identities were a welcome vindication of their sense of superiority over the enemy and of the justice of their cause, though people on the ambiguous margins of a conflict believed to be between right and wrong still had to be handled circumspectly; the defenders would detain incoming renegades unless and until they proved trustworthy; and at one point Mustafa Pasha grew so suspicious of the renegades in the Turkish camp that he ordered that they should be made to sleep in the galleys.[60] Outbound fugitives, on the other hand, were doubly troubling: not only could they pass information on to the enemy, the very fact that they could contemplate crossing over in the 'wrong' direction destabilized the binary oppositions that structured the mental world of the siege. A case in point was a Spanish soldier named Francisco de Aguilar, a Lascaris in reverse who went over to the Turks on 6 August. The fact that Balbi devotes a great deal of space to Aguilar's defection just before his account of the great assault on the 7th is an indication of how much he and the other defenders were unsettled by it. In Balbi's telling, Aguilar was a soldier, with a wife and children on Gozo, who served under Francisco de Guiral, the Knight whose battery had saved the day on 15 July. Aguilar had a falling out with his commander, having already earned a reputation for disobedience that had come to the notice of La Valette himself. He subsequently found a new patron in Melchior de Robles, and in gaining his confidence became privy to high-level tactical discussions. Then, on the 6th, he made a run for it from Aragon towards Bormla.

Mustafa Pasha, we are told, was delighted when Aguilar was brought to his tent and poured out everything he knew about the Christians' plans and the state of their defences; Balbi's statement that Aguilar also impressed upon Mustafa the Christians' willingness to persevere to the bitter end can only be wishful thinking.[61] The Grand Master promptly ordered the firing of four mass arquebus volleys from the ramparts as an act of defiance, but the fact that he did so reveals that Aguilar's defection was taken very seriously; indeed Balbi is willing to break into his hagiographical treatment of La Valette to acknowledge how anxious he became. What is perhaps most interesting about Balbi's account of this incident is the absence of any reflection on what motivated Aguilar, in contrast to the considerable amount of space devoted to his actions. We are told, as a matter of routine, that Aguilar was inspired by the devil. And there are suggestions that he was a disaffected troublemaker. But that is about it. Aguilar almost certainly had very good reasons for coming to such a momentous decision and taking the risks that he did; he had probably come to the conclusion that the defenders' cause was hopeless and he had no choice but to take his chances elsewhere. But for Balbi such reasoning was either unthinkable or could not be acknowledged without compromising the very cause and worldview for which the defenders were fighting and dying.

The people who were probably most changed by the siege were the Maltese, at least on the level of perceptions. La Valette and other Knights came into the siege with a generally poor opinion of the

Maltese as pusillanimous and inert; their bands of village militia could make up the numbers to an extent, but everyone else was dead weight.[62] Likewise García de Toledo criticized La Valette in a letter to Philip II's secretary Eraso for failing to evacuate more non-combatants before the arrival of the Turkish armada; the immediate problem was the extra mouths to feed, but the subtext was that the Maltese, the large majority of whom were low-status peasants, artisans and sailors, had nothing significant to contribute to the coming struggle.[63] As the siege dragged on, this tone of aristocratic disdain gradually softened into something closer to appreciation; not even an epic siege could wash away ingrained class divisions, but one detects a new warmth emerging from the shared experience.[64] This registered itself in two ways. First, there was a more effective mobilization of the energies of Maltese men, women and children inside the fortifications; they brought supplies up to the front line, performed other auxiliary duties, and when necessary joined in the fighting.[65] La Valette's decision in August not to accede to the advice of some of his team to pull back into the redoubt of St Angelo, and thereby leave the Maltese in Birgu and Senglea to their fate, may have been informed in part by a new sense of solidarity.[66] Although some Maltese served in St Elmo, and a few escaped the final defeat, the majority of those who had fought and died there were outsiders: Knights and some of the soldiers who had been brought to Malta. In contrast the struggle for Senglea and Birgu, especially the latter, was, in simple demographic terms, much more of a 'people's war'.

Second, certain individual Maltese are singled out in the sources as making noteworthy contributions to the defenders' cause. It is significant that they are often named, for this more than anything signalled their inclusion, a kind of honorary membership, in the elite male value system of physical bravery, valour and fortitude that permeates the evidence. We have already met the four Maltese who swam out to protect the barricade in French Creek. Another Maltese elevated to the status of the named was Toni Bajada, who did very important – and remarkably brave – work running messages and letters between Birgu and Mdina. It is interesting that Balbi makes a point of suggesting that Bajada was the one person who shrewdly saw through Francisco de Aguilar.[67] The willingness of the Knights and their chroniclers to acknowledge the achievements of individual Maltese was anchored in their growing confidence in the loyalty of the people as a whole. Shortly after the embassy to Birgu involving the Spanish slave, another approach was made by letter to the citizens of Mdina, offering them the freedom to govern themselves and pursue their accustomed way of life if they abandoned the Knights and surrendered the city; Mesquita was anxious, but the offer was rebuffed.[68] In a similar vein, Balbi and other writers refer to an incident in which, during a lull in the fighting, a Maltese renegade called across to some former acquaintances and tried to entice them into abandoning their support of the Knights; this too was firmly rejected.[69] Bosio describes La Valette rousing the Maltese by invoking faith, freedom, family and fatherland; the list has a rhetorical feel to it, but some permutation of these four ideals was probably decisive for most Maltese in determining where their sympathies lay.[70] References in the narrative sources to Turkish prisoners being thrown to the vengeful local people, even groups of children – Cirni talks of the *furor di popolo* – do not speak to a mood of ambivalence.[71]

In contrast, for the Knights the siege was about playing a role: a deadly serious form of role-play to be sure, but an opportunity above all else to put into practice the paradigms of channelled aggression, personal courage and aristocratic affect that Sabba da Castiglione had set out for them, and in which they had been schooled since their youth. As we have seen, however, this was an order in which reality often fell short of the ideal. What became of those who had most conspicuously strayed from that ideal is therefore a powerful index of the siege's capacity to re-energize the order's vocation and invest it with a renewed sense of collective purpose. In short, did the bad eggs come good? There are indications in the order's records that the commutation of punishments for serious offences was becoming more frequent from around 1560, perhaps because La Valette's regime was nervous about losing numbers that it might need at some later date; and it would seem that this policy was amplified in the few months before the siege. If one cross-matches the evidence for criminal acts committed by Knights between 1562 and 1565 against the lists of those who survived the siege or died during it to be found in the pages of Balbi, Cirni and Bosio, there are several intriguing correspondences. Without romanticizing the situation unduly, one might say that the siege represented an opportunity for self-affirmation on the part of the Knights which found potent expression in the re-absorption of some of their recently errant *confrères* into the fold. In 1563, for example, an Italian Knight named Giovanni Battista Pagano killed a surgeon of the order named Giovanni Spilioti at Żurrieq; and in February 1564 he was sentenced to two years' imprisonment. In August, however, it was reported that he had absconded from his prison on Gozo; and in January 1565 it was decided to proceed to his expulsion from the order. Exactly how he found his way back into the order's good graces is unknown; but he fought in the siege, was wounded in St Elmo and was killed in Birgu.[72]

There were several others in a similar situation, both Knights who were still in trouble in May 1565 and those who had served their punishment but still lived under the cloud of their recent crimes. Claude de Tarsac de Lambres, who was convicted of brawling in January 1563 and sentenced to six months' imprisonment, was a member of the final relief force that landed in Malta in September 1565. So too was Ruy Breo da Silva, who had been deprived of the habit in January 1563, at which point he had succumbed to a madness (*furor ac dementia*) so severe that custodians had to be appointed to watch over him. He made a recovery and was readmitted to the order in June 1564.[73] Georges de Hautoy de Récicourt was one of the last Knights to be convicted before the siege: on 6 April 1565 he was sentenced to two years for assaulting two of the order's servants. He died in the defence of St Elmo.[74] On 11 September 1564 Pierre de Loubès was deprived of his habit when he was found guilty of theft both from the conventual church of St Lawrence and from his own langue; exactly one year later he was among the survivors of the siege. So too his fellow Knight from the langue of Auvergne Guy de Morgues la Motte, who had been convicted of killing another Knight in November 1563.[75] Bernardo de Cabrera was convicted in October 1562 of taking part in a brawl, and in August 1563 of fighting with another Knight. For the latter offence he was sentenced to three months. In 1565 he became a leading figure in the defence; he was wounded at St Elmo; he fought valiantly on 15 July; he was wounded again in the great assault of 7 August; and it was at his post that the basilisk shot penetrated twenty-one feet of earth, killing several soldiers standing next to him. Bosio thought Cabrera was 'judicious and brave'. He survived the siege.[76] Perhaps the greatest act of redemption worked by the siege concerned Gregorio de Adorno. Adorno had committed a murder in Naples and in February 1564 was sentenced to one year's imprisonment; he must have been released early, because in December he was punished for brawling aboard a galley. Sentenced to two years, he was once more let out early and fought in the siege. Balbi singled him out for his conspicuous bravery during the assault on Senglea on 15 July. Wounded, like Cabrera, on 7 August, and again on the 21st, he too made it to the end.[77]

7.

Relief

The Christian narrative sources present the three weeks or so after the raid against Mdina as a period of decline in the enemy's fortunes, a growing state of, in Cirni's words, *molta confusione* characterized by dissension within the ranks, competition and disagreement between the commanders, and resort to increasingly desperate measures to break the deadlock before the end of the campaign season.[1] But the chroniclers were being wise after the event, of course, or at the very least imposing a pattern that those caught up in the moment would not have discerned as clearly. Although the Ottomans almost certainly grew more anxious and frustrated as August wore on, and their numbers were now significantly reduced, they retained the upper hand until at least the last of their major assaults, on 21 August, and probably until the 31st, when Mustafa Pasha effectively signalled that he was running out of ideas by making a second, rather half-hearted attempt on Mdina that was easily driven off by Mesquita's garrison.[2] For most of August the triangular pattern of siege warfare continued: artillery bombardment, assaults and hard-fought competition for tactical advantage on the ragged front line. Whereas much of the Turks' energies since the fall of St Elmo had been directed against the weakest points of Senglea's fortifications, it would seem that Castile was now especially identified as a target: in places its walls had all but entirely collapsed into a near-horizontal rubble field. This meant that the defenders, the number of more or less fit troops now down to a few hundred, would continue to be severely stretched along the whole of the Birgu–Senglea frontage.

It is significant that the Ottomans were willing to go back on the offensive soon after the failure of their assault on 7 August. On the 9th they made a feint attack against both Birgu and St Michael, and also indicated where much of their future efforts would be directed by throwing stones into the ditch in front of Castile, so as to displace the water in it, as well as pushing new trenches forward.[3] On the 10th a two-hour assault was launched against St Michael in the morning, and another in the afternoon. Balbi observes of the earlier attack that because the Turks lost more than a hundred men, this just about satisfied his definition of a true *assolto*, which may suggest that the depletion of the Ottomans' ranks was now reducing their ability to throw men forward in the large waves of the past. But the defenders had severe manpower problems of their own.[4] In order to make an assault on the cavalier at Castile on the 13th, the Turks came armed with picks and shovels, not so much rushing the enemy's position as digging their way up towards it. In response, La Valette ordered the construction of a retrenchment, which proved its worth two days later when it was the only obstruction still of use to the defenders when another attack was beaten off.[5]

There then followed what proved to be the last phase of sustained assaults. Although there was growing dissent among the Janissaries, the precise reasons for which are unclear, Mustafa Pasha was able to contain the situation to the extent that he could launch a series of attacks on 20 August against both St Michael and Castile; the fact that, although an old man, he chose to lead the assaults in person may suggest nervousness on his part about his men's morale.[6] Balbi remarks that in preparation for this attack the Ottomans had been reduced to dressing their irregulars in the clothes of dead Janissaries and *sipahis* so as to fool the enemy; these men were also offered promotion to the Janissary corps if they fought bravely (but contrary to the system whereby the Janissaries were recruited). If Balbi believed that this demonstrated the straits to which the Ottomans had been reduced – his point is vividly illustrated by his description of Mustafa, his turban knocked off by gunfire, having to take cover in a ditch until dark – he also had to concede that one of these attacks 'was among the fiercest that the enemy launched against us during the whole siege'. The fact, however, that even after several hard-pressed assaults the Turks were believed to have lost only 200 men, in contrast to the thousands often cited with reference to earlier engagements, is a further indication of the contracting scale of the fighting.[7] Such were the reduced margins indeed that an attempt to launch another attack on Castile on the 21st, before the defenders could fully regroup, was repulsed after four hours, even though the numbers of those defending the position and those who could be brought up as reinforcements were, in Balbi's estimation, perilously small. In a restaging of the events of 7 August, La Valette's flying squad of only a few dozen men, held in reserve in the piazza of Birgu, had been forced to move up to the front line, as indeed had been the case on previous days.[8]

It is significant that from around the second week of August the narratives of Balbi and other closely contemporary authors dwell a little less than before on the grand staging of the siege, the bombardments and assaults, and more on a kind of close-up-and-personal trench warfare fought along the front line. The Turks, for example, continued to dig mines.[9] They also tried to repeat a tactic that had worked well at St Elmo, which was to gain height advantage over the defenders by building up a platform of wool and cotton sacks.[10] An indication, perhaps, of the much reduced numbers on both sides is the suggestion that even larger assaults could turn on the outcome of a contest between two small groups of men, even a one-on-one fight to the death. For instance, according to Balbi the decisive moment during the assault on 21 August had been a confrontation between a Turk and a defender, both carrying firearms: each man's gun had set fire to nearby piles of incendiary weapons and the attack broke down in the resulting confusion.[11] Stealing the opposition's tools and food or making small-scale gains with impermanent results, such as a night-time raid on the 15th on the Turks' entrenchment at the Castile cavalier, became achievements worthy of note, almost as psychological rather than tactical victories; in the same spirit, the taking of enemy heads became a marker of success.[12] As gunpowder became ever scarcer on both sides, tussles for possession of a few barrels assumed a new significance.[13] At some points the two sides' forward positions were so close that renegades in the Ottoman ranks could call across to their former co-religionists, using allusive language disguised as derogatory remarks in order to pass on encouraging news about the poor conditions in the Turks' camp.[14] Food was also thrown between the two lines so as to give the impression that there were abundant supplies; the trenches were so near to one another, Balbi remarks with only a little exaggeration, that the men in them could even have shaken hands.[15]

After the failure of the assaults on the 20th and 21st, a note of desperation, or at least of rush, is evident in the Ottomans' subsequent efforts. After a desultory attack on 29 August, what proved to be the last push of any consequence, against St Michael on the 30th, was fought off with few losses on the defenders' side: Balbi's description of it is almost dismissively brief.[16] By this stage the Turks were resorting to old-fashioned siege engines: first a *manta*, or mantelet, a reinforced covering under which a group of men could work its way up to the walls while protected from small-arms fire and missiles thrown from above; then a more elaborate siege tower. In both instances they were destroyed by cannon hidden until the last moment in a concealed embrasure.[17] On or about 25 August the weather became colder and wetter, making the use of firearms difficult; La Valette's solution was to distribute protective shawls made of matted grass along with relatively rain-resistant crossbows, which the order had in abundance because they had until quite recently been standard issue on the galleys.[18] It is probably no coincidence that it was at this juncture, the last week of August and the first few days of September, that the defenders, for the first time, seem to have been able not only to gain but to maintain a clear tactical superiority on the front line.[19] Bernardo de Cabrera, whom we met in the previous chapter as a former offender channelling his aggression into the siege, specialized in leading out snatch-squads to capture unwary Turks or to behead their corpses in order to demoralize the enemy.[20] The defenders even fired a mine, something the Ottomans never seem to have succeeded in doing, as if to demonstrate that they could afford to use up the very large amount of gunpowder that such a detonation required.²¹

It is important to bear in mind that the siege took place before the reform of the Julian calendar decreed by Pope Gregory XIII in 1582 in the bull *Inter gravissimas*, which corrected what had by then become ten days of misalignment between the solar cycle and calendar time. In other words, early September in 1565 corresponded, meteorologically speaking, to what we would now understand as the middle of that month.²² The pressure was thus on the Ottomans, if they did not overcome the defenders very soon, either to make arrangements to overwinter in the central Mediterranean, which would have been extremely difficult, or to disengage and return to the Levant before the end of the safe sailing season in October. At some point either side of 1 September – the Christian sources vary – the defenders began to notice what was at first a gradual and discreet Turkish withdrawal from their camps and forward positions. That the mood was shifting seemed to be confirmed by a spate of fugitives and renegades crossing over to Birgu and reporting on the poor shape, low morale and depleted numbers of the Ottoman forces. In the event, however, the Ottomans were denied the option of simply disengaging from the siege on their own terms, for on 7 September lookouts on the highest points of St Angelo observed a galliot hurriedly enter Marsamxett from the north-west. A man was then seen crossing over by boat from St Elmo to Rinella; Balbi records the curious detail that he was so agitated that he killed the horse that was offered to him when it proved difficult to mount.²³ He made his way to report to Mustafa Pasha's tent in Kalkara. Soon afterwards, a large detachment of galleys exited Marsamxett to take up position outside its entrance. Clearly something significant was in the offing.

What had so agitated the Ottoman messenger was the arrival of a Christian relief force, the *gran soccorso*, numbering about sixty galleys and approximately 9,000 fighting men. This was the culmination of the efforts directed by García de Toledo to assemble an armada that could either persuade the Ottomans to quit Malta or, if they

Relief

chose to stand and fight, to dislodge them from it. As we noted in the previous chapter, the organization of this force was a fraught and cumbersome process, a reflection of both Italy's fragmented political landscape and the many logistical challenges that confronted García in the absence of the sort of relatively centralized war economy that aided the Ottomans. Because Spain was the predominant Christian power in the western Mediterranean, it would be a necessary part of any realistic attempt to relieve Malta; but its resources were insufficient for it to act alone. For this reason García was faced with a delicate challenge: how to build an alliance of willing partners, and make the most of the manpower and military experience that they brought to the mix, while maintaining his control over the whole enterprise.

The laborious process of assembling men and resources over the summer, all while solicitously keeping a distant Philip II in the loop, was finally showing results by around mid August. As we have seen, taking the Ottomans on at sea had been ruled out: even a depleted Ottoman navy would outnumber whatever Christian fleet could be assembled. When it came to thinking about putting boots on the ground in Malta, the forces that gradually became available to García in Sicily were of three types. First, and much the best option, were the *tercios*, the Spanish Habsburgs' elite military units. In the event, *tercios* from Lombardy, Naples and Sardinia, also a Habsburg territory, would comprise the single largest element of the *gran soccorso*. This was to some extent a leap of faith, for even though Spain and the Ottoman empire had been bitter rivals for several decades, there had been few toe-to-toe confrontations on land between their respective elite formations: in recent memory, neither Mostaganem in 1558 nor Djerba in 1560 served as direct points of comparison, and in any event both of them had been disasters from the Spanish perspective. Nonetheless the *tercios* were the nearest thing that the Habsburgs had to well-disciplined, practised and hardened soldiers whose tight formations, it was hoped, would hold up against the typical Ottoman tactic of isolating and picking off enemy units.

Second, there were the various groups provided by the Habsburgs' assorted Italian clients and allies, including the papacy. These were a mixed bag: some were local levies and rulers' retainers, many more were mercenaries. A great deal depended on the experience and charisma of whoever was in command of a given group of men, and the depth of their pockets. It is revealing that Philip II and the Spanish ambassador in Rome lobbied very hard for the renowned *condottiere* Ascanio della Corgna to be released from a papal prison, where he had been committed on charges of conspiracy, and to be put in charge of the force recruited by the pope. Pius IV agreed, with an ill grace, but he was right to do so because Ascanio was precisely the sort of rare person who could galvanize a disparate collection of soldiers into something resembling an effective corps.[24] The number of galleys and barges available to transport the relief to Malta, as well as, of course, questions of cost, gave García licence to weed out the weaker elements as they arrived in Sicily. One solution was to use soldiers of this sort to release *tercio* units from garrison duties in the Habsburg domains.

Third, there were gentlemen adventurers, self-financing (at least in theory) independents who attached themselves to military ventures that caught their interest. It was in such a capacity that Brantôme had latched on to the Peñón campaign in 1564. It is tempting to dismiss these men as footloose hangers-on engaged in a kind of upper-class combat tourism. They were certainly an eclectic group: one of their number was an Englishman, Captain 'Marcos de Toledo', an exiled relative of Jane Dormer, the duchess of Feria, formerly Mary Tudor's senior lady-in-waiting, who had married the Spanish ambassador to England and relocated to Spain when Elizabeth I came to the throne.[25] But it is noteworthy how much the narrative sources talk up the motivations and contributions of the gentlemen adventurers – Balbi, Cirni and Bosio include lists of all those whose names they knew in their honour rolls of the *gran soccorso* – because they could be presented as embodying and vindicating the same ideals that the Knights liked to believe animated their own vocation: trans-national Christian solidarity, self-sacrifice, physical bravery and the complex of elite masculine qualities captured in the elusive but potent Italian word *virtù*. They were like aristocratic Christian Europe coming to save its own.[26] Nonetheless, and for all his own impeccably noble origins, García had the adventurers' measure: he banned them from taking up valuable space on the relief's transports by bringing their baggage and servants.[27]

After the siege García attracted criticism for delaying the *gran soccorso* and thereby both prolonging the defenders' sufferings and increasing the chances of an Ottoman victory. But this is unfair. Although he was the man on the spot, there were limits to the resources or authority that he enjoyed to improvise solutions to problems as they emerged and to revise strategy on his own account. He was scrupulous in consulting Philip II, although their correspondence was of necessity conducted with time lags of several weeks. More than that, he had in Philip a king who was never fully persuaded that saving Malta was worth the risks involved. As Philip had written to García on 27 July, keeping the Spanish fleet intact 'was more important than the relief; for if Malta were to be lost, which God forbid, there are other ways to go about recovering it'.[28] When the news of the Turkish armada had begun to circulate in the spring of 1565, moreover, Philip had been much more exercised by the threat to La Goletta, the Spanish harbour fortress that controlled Tunis, than that to Malta, and this order of priorities was still in evidence as late as July.[29] Between chivvying a cautious and sceptical king into decisive action and herding the cats of Italian politics, García did about as good a job as anyone could have managed in the circumstances.

When the preparations for the relief were still in their early stages, and García and others had addressed the question of the optimal number of troops to land on Malta, figures of 10,000–12,000 had been suggested.[30] It was an impressive achievement, therefore, that the numbers of those who had actually assembled in Sicily towards the end of August came close to that ideal: probably about 9,600 men. Of these about 4,500 were drawn from the *tercios* of Lombardy and Naples (the single largest contingent). There was also a regiment from Sardinia, as well as about 1,500 Italian troops, probably the pick of the 4,000 or so who had been recruited in Tuscany.[31] In addition to assorted other groups of soldiers, and the adventurers, there were about 200 Hospitallers and thirty-five Knights of St Stephen, members of a military order founded by Cosimo de' Medici, grand duke of Tuscany, as recently as 1561 in imitation of the Knights of St John. When Don García summoned a council of war to discuss the forthcoming campaign, there were, according to Cirni, twenty-seven men in the room, a clear indication of the composite and disparate nature of the force.[32]

Similarly, the fleet that had been assembled to convey the soldiers to Malta comprised vessels from Spain itself, Naples and Sicily, Savoy, Florence and Genoa, as well as the two galleys of the order that had not been trapped in Grand Harbour at the beginning of the siege.[33] Balbi and Cirni agree that the final number of galleys that gathered to carry the relief force was fifty-eight; shortly before departure García had discarded some of those in poorer condition and redistributed their *ciurme* in order to strengthen the manpower in the more robust vessels.[34] The numbers were fewer than the Ottoman fleet – in addition to raw cost, García's greatest constraint had been the number of available oarsmen – but the galleys were overall in good shape. Many of the soldiers were to be conveyed in barges towed behind the galleys. An average of about 160 troops per galley-barge pairing was a quite relaxed concentration; they were not packed in like sardines.

On 24 August, García travelled down from Messina to Syracuse, and the fleet sailed on from there the following day.[35] Almost immediately, however, it was pitched into a complex combination of bad weather, missed rendezvous and missed opportunities that would cumulatively ensure that the relief troops would not set foot on Maltese soil for almost another fortnight. The galleys had only travelled a few miles when they ran into heavy seas, the result of the same weather system that was suggesting to La Valette that he should break out the crossbows.[36] The fleet stood to in order to ride out the storm, allowing some of the adventurers who had been left behind – perhaps deliberately – to catch up in frigates and other small craft.[37] When the storm abated the galleys aimed for Cape Passero, the southern tip of Sicily, which they cleared on the morning of the 26th.[38] At first the signs were propitious: the vanguard chased down and captured a ship from Ragusa (Dubrovnik) which had been blown off course between Djerba and Malta carrying a large cargo of munitions and 500 *cantara*, or about sixty cubic metres, of biscuit as well as rice – enough, Cirni calculated, to have fed the Ottoman forces for several days.[39] From García de Toledo's perspective, so far, so good.

Rather than head directly south, the fleet bore south-west towards the island of Linosa, about 140 kilometres to the west of the Maltese archipelago. This made good sense: it would reduce the chances that it would be spotted by Ottoman patrols, and as always with galley warfare – there would have been about as many oarsmen and crew as there were passengers – the abiding concern was to stock up on water wherever and whenever possible. García was also keen to make contact with Gianandrea Doria, whom he had sent on ahead to reconnoitre and perhaps to make a feint towards the Barbary coast; Linosa was their agreed contact point. Then everything started to go badly wrong when the fleet, already battered by worsening weather, was caught in an unusually severe storm on 28 August: when Don García wrote to the king on the 30th he stated that 'neither I nor the others of like mind have ever seen the like'.[40] The mood of the landlubber soldiers being towed in the barges can only be imagined. The fleet was helplessly blown north to Favignana, one of the Egadi islands, off the western tip of Sicily. Some of the galleys were badly damaged, but remarkably none had been lost. The men were allowed a short interval on shore to recover – there was time for hunting both deer and some of the crew of a Turkish vessel at large on the island – and then the fleet crossed over to Trapani on the Sicilian mainland.[41] From there, on 1 or 2 September, it set out once more for Linosa in search of Doria, only to find two or three men whom Doria had left on the island with a letter for García narrating his own movements up to that point.[42]

Doria had sailed from Syracuse with a small fleet on 23 August and made straight for the Maltese islands. Entering the Fliegu, he dropped off a Spanish soldier, Juan Martinez de Oliventia, whose task it was to set up a system of signal fires on Gozo which would alert an approaching Christian fleet as to whether there were Ottoman vessels in the vicinity, and if so their location and strength.[43] He then sailed west to Linosa, stocked up with water, returned to the Maltese islands and checked that the signals were in operation in the Fliegu before heading back towards Sicily. He was approaching Cape Passero when he was informed that García was en route to Linosa. Doria turned around and set off once again in search of the main fleet, zigzagging his way across the Sicily Channel. When he stopped off at Lampedusa to take on water, his landing party came off badly when it was attacked by the crews of two Turkish brigantines. Extricating himself from this difficulty, he then crossed to Linosa before returning to Sicily.

Meanwhile García's fleet had come very close to completing its mission, only to miss its chance at the last moment. Having come upon Doria's men on Linosa, García had pressed on to the east, arriving off Malta on the night of 3–4 September. Unable to see any signal fires, and nervous that the weather was unfavourable and his fleet had become too dispersed, García decided that he had no choice but to return to Sicily.[44] Cirni does his best to excuse his actions, arguing that this had been an invaluable reconnaissance mission that made the ultimate success of the relief possible; but he does acknowledge that there was criticism of García's timidity. Unsurprisingly, there was also discontent, as well as sickness, in the ranks: back in Sicily guards had to be posted to deter desertions, and detachments of troops were sent ashore to round up those who had tried to drift away.[45] Finally García tried again on the 6th, swinging his fleet around to the west so as to approach the Maltese islands from the Gozo side. The fire signals confirmed that it was safe to proceed, and so at dawn on the 7th the galleys and their barges entered Mellieħa Bay, Malta's northernmost large inlet. Shortly after daybreak the men, their supplies and arms were disembarked in quick order.[46]

Relief

In recognition of the fact that this was predominantly a Spanish exercise, the man placed in overall command of the relief force was Álvaro de Sande, an able general with experience of north African conditions, the closest analogy to Malta that those planning the expedition could imagine.[47] There was also an element of personal vindication at stake: Sande had led the stubborn but doomed resistance at Djerba and had been taken captive to Istanbul, where he had been fortunate to have Busbecq on hand to help him. Ascanio della Corgna was made *maestro di campo*, effectively second in command; and further responsibilities were distributed so as to reflect the politically composite nature of the relief and, as far as possible, to satisfy the competitive sensibilities of the various Italian noblemen and *condottieri*.[48] One thing was clear: this was not intended as a smash-and-grab raid to deliver a swift knock-out blow. Provisions were landed sufficient for one and a half months. Particular attention had been paid to the supply of biscuit: if the relief could not feed itself it would make impossible demands of an impoverished and war-torn island. García had planned that each soldier would need to carry a burden of seventy or eighty pounds; and it is noteworthy that when the relief began to make its way south to Mdina, and a great many soldiers discarded their packs of biscuit by the side of the road because of the heat, they were brusquely forced to pick them up again.[49] In the event, the campaign would unfold quite quickly, and the relief's work would be done in less than a week. But this was not what had been anticipated at first.

Pedro de Mesquita sent porters and pack animals down from Mdina to help with the laborious process of carrying the relief's supplies and munitions up to the city.[50] Meanwhile in Grand Harbour the defenders had more grounds for optimism. After the arrival of the agitated messenger on 7 September, any lingering doubt that a Christian relief force had landed was removed when García, calculating that the element of surprise was no longer important and confident that the Ottoman galleys would not set out in pursuit, brought his fleet around to the east so as to be visible from the defenders' elevated positions in Grand Harbour. To make his point doubly clear, he fired a series of salvos before turning to the north, his intention at this stage to pick up further troops in Sicily.[51] At this point the piecemeal breaking up of the Ottoman camp which the defenders had already been observing went into overdrive: baggage was packed, tents were folded up, battery platforms burned and cannon hauled away; a single large cannon in Bormla stubbornly refused to be shifted. The Turks sensibly withdrew onto Mount Sciberras in order to be close to their fleet; the efficiency with which this tactical withdrawal was executed is demonstrated by the fact that soon some of those in Mdina were able to go down to the Grand Harbour area without running into the enemy.[52] Only one detachment of Turks stayed behind for a time on what had been the front line, guarding the immoveable big gun.[53]

The celebrations in Birgu and Senglea on 8 September that followed the appearance of García de Toledo's fleet and the Turkish withdrawal – Balbi writes of the euphoria that greeted the jubilant ringing of church bells – certainly did not mean that the siege was over.[54] In many ways the Ottomans still enjoyed the advantage: they had the larger fleet, in uneven condition to be sure but still a formidable weapon if marshalled carefully, especially now that García had helpfully offered up a demonstration of his own fighting strength; and the relief force would still be strung out along the road between Mellieħa Bay and Mdina. As renegades reported to the defenders, moreover, the Ottomans' confidence had revived after their initial panic because they were persuaded that the relief was manageably small, many of its troops were ill from the sea-crossing, and its leaders were divided.[55] It made good sense, therefore, to deal with the relief column before it had a chance to dig in around Mdina. As always, the Christian sources insist that the process of decision-making in the Ottoman high command was riven by bitter disagreements and jealousies, but we should be cautious about taking such statements at face value. The pashas would have known that if the relief force could be destroyed – and surely there could not be another on such a scale – they could return to Grand Harbour at their leisure to finish off what would by then be the utterly demoralized and forlorn defenders. For the moment the Ottomans could keep their options open. But their immediate priority was access to a secure and sufficient supply of water, so the whole Ottoman army boarded the vessels in Marsamxett and the armada sailed up to St Paul's Bay.

The relief force had taken until 10 September to bring all its supplies up to Mdina and to set up a camp in Rabat just outside the city.[56] At this stage, as Ascanio della Corgna later told Balbi, the hope was that a show of force would suffice to persuade the Turks to evacuate the island.[57] The distance between Mdina and Grand Harbour and the lack of water until one reached the spring at Marsa, which the Turks were likely to have fouled anyway, meant, moreover, that an immediate push eastwards towards the Ottoman camp was out of the question. On the 11th a large number of Ottoman troops, probably all those still available, were disembarked at St Paul's Bay and began to make their way purposefully towards Mdina to the south. Ascanio della Corgna argued that the Turks should be allowed to come on, become stretched out and lose their impetus against the inclines and walls of Mdina, but the predominant mood in the Christian army was in favour of meeting the enemy head-on in open country.[58] Balbi, who had taken the opportunity to travel up to Mdina, describes the difficulty that the officers had in gathering and organizing their respective squadrons; he puts this down to overenthusiasm on the part of the soldiers, but it was more likely to have been a consequence of the composite nature of the relief and its improvised command structures.[59]

The accounts to be found in the narrative sources of the running battle that ensued between Mdina and St Paul's Bay are not altogether clear because they are in the business of anticipating the final Christian victory and of celebrating what was believed to have been the wide disparity between the numbers of casualties on the two sides.[60] But it would seem that for several hours the struggle was hard fought and the outcome in the balance. As the relief moved north to engage the Ottoman army, the initial contest was for areas of higher ground that would confer a tactical advantage.

Here the fighting appears to have been particularly intense, its effects worsened by the great heat; Balbi says it was the hottest day of the whole siege.[61] The Ottoman vanguard was gradually beaten back, but Mustafa Pasha was able to cover his retreat quite effectively; in this he was aided by the experience and resilience of the Barbary corsairs Uluç Ali and Hasan Pasha. At some points the Ottomans were able to score minor victories. Eventually, however, the fact that fairly fresh troops were pitted against those who had been through a gruelling four-month campaign began to tell, and the Ottomans were forced back towards St Paul's Bay. There the pursuit descended into a rout as the Turkish troops waded into the bay and scrambled onto the boats that Piyale Pasha sent in to retrieve them.[62] Covering fire from the Ottoman galleys halted the momentum of the onslaught, the last survivors clawed their way to safety, and the attention of the victors turned to looting the dead. The Ottoman fleet pulled away from the coast to regroup. It was still offshore on the 12th and may have lingered, weighing its options and reorganizing its *ciurme*, until the 13th.[63] Eventually, however, it withdrew. The corsair contingents veered off to return to Africa, and the main armada disappeared over the north-eastern horizon. So ended the Great Siege of Malta.

As the siege concluded, a number of the Christian principals wrote to the pope, Philip II and others to give an account of recent events and to begin the process of situating themselves favourably within the emerging narrative.[64] Around the same time a number of lesser figures, with fewer axes to grind, committed their thoughts to paper, in the process giving us some precious insights into both the impression that the siege made on those who had experienced it and the themes and motifs, the memory hooks, that would shape the story of what had happened as it came to be told in the coming months and years. Martin Crova, who may have been a member of the *gran soccorso* and would seem to have had a connection to Naples, concluded his brief but well-informed narrative with the observation that a siege that had pitted so many against so few would become 'one of the most renowned and memorable that there has been for many centuries'.⁶⁵ In a letter written on 11 September, even as the final act of the siege was still being played out, Antonio Cressino, the prior of the order's conventual church of St Lawrence and thus one of the senior clerics in Malta, anticipated the debate that would be staged two and a half months later at Plessis-lèz-Tours by observing that this siege had been more demanding and more perilous than that of Rhodes in 1522 according to those who had been through both.⁶⁶

For Francesco Guevara, an Italian Knight who gained a reputation during the siege as something of an action man – Bosio pictures him in the thick of the action, a crucifix in one hand and a sword in the other – the material and human costs were intertwined. Not only had 'this wretched island of Malta' been left burned and ruined, with no walls and no food, the order had suffered grievous losses: 313 of its members had been killed, another eighty were severely injured in their hands, feet or faces, and were mostly expected to die, and the mere thirty or forty who had escaped wholly unscathed were 'aged and bent', men broken by their experience and incapable of waging war.⁶⁷ One finds in these and other writers a reaching for ways to measure, and in measuring to understand, what had just happened. Casualty figures, on both sides, were of course the most obvious metric. Another was the number of times that the Ottoman artillery had fired. Guevara tells us that he had made a point of counting the sounds of cannon fire during the siege of St Elmo – 19,000 – and that the final total was a minimum of 68,000; 70,000 became a standard figure.⁶⁸

One also finds in the early verdicts on the siege an underlying tension. On the one hand this was a great victory to be celebrated, the work of a powerful and merciful God and a vindication of the justice of the defenders' cause. On the other, however, this had been a very close-run thing; and the validity of the maxim that for those on the inside of a siege winning comes down to not losing had been pushed to its limits. The defenders had indeed 'won', but at enormous cost. Why, then, did the siege play out as it did? This is a very difficult question to answer satisfactorily because our evidence does not reach evenly into all the possible factors. We should also be wary of straying too far into counterfactual speculation about what might have occurred but did not – what-ifs can be used to 'prove' whatever one wants them to. Yes, if the Great Siege were played out in ten parallel universes, it would be reasonable to imagine that the Ottomans would emerge as victors in seven or eight and there would perhaps be some kind of stalemate at the end of the campaign season in one more. But all we have to work with is what actually happened.

One can adduce various underlying structural reasons for the outcome of the siege, though none in isolation serves as a satisfactory explanation. The Ottomans, we know, were fighting on the outer limits of their operational range, and this must have softened the punch that they were able to deliver. But we also know that in 1574 a similarly large and ambitious armada made short work of reconquering Tunis, which the Spanish had briefly reconquered the year before. There is also good evidence that the Ottomans planned carefully for the reprovisioning of their forces in Malta during the 1565 campaign; though always under some strain, these arrangements seem to have worked until very late in the siege, as illustrated by the large Ragusan cargo vessel, one of several supplying the besiegers, which the *gran soccorso* captured off Sicily.[69] One suspects that the reason why Christian sources make so much of the loss of one of the transport ships off the Peloponnese as the armada sailed towards Malta is not so much that this was the first intimation of a doomed enterprise, but the authors' fear of the Ottomans' formidable command of logistics; any setback was a small mercy. If the tiny margins of the siege had played out just a little differently and the Turks had prevailed, we would now most probably explain their success with reference to their impressive ability to push their operational limits and supply chains to the edge and *still* come out on top.

Three particular considerations stand out in relation to the outcome of the siege: not reasons *why* things happened as they did, but factors that nudged the odds a little in favour of the defenders. First, there were what appear to have been disproportionately heavy losses among the Ottomans' best troops, the Janissaries and the *sipahis*, early on, in the St Elmo phase of the campaign; this may have been compounded by the deaths of a significant number of newly arrived and fresh corsairs in the amphibious assault on 15 July. If we view the siege through the lens of First World War-like human attrition – which side was dying off more slowly relative to its total available manpower – the Ottomans were just about 'winning' the numbers game against their opponents up until the arrival of the *gran soccorso*. But the disproportionate depletion of their elite units must have made a difference to the intensity and efficiency of the assaults launched in the later stages of the siege. When Christian writers describe the lengths that Mustafa Pasha and his subordinates had to go to from around the middle of August to make assaults possible at all – dressing irregulars in the clothing of dead elite troops, making lavish promises of promotion and driving reluctant soldiers forward with batons – we are on one level observing the tendency of Christian authors to depict the Turks in over-the-top, cartoon-like terms.[70] But there was probably enough basis in fact to suggest that there was a real problem. On balance it took more skill with weapons, tactical savvy and combat experience, as opposed to raw energy, visceral courage and sheer desperation, to attack a fortified position than to defend it. The Ottomans' reserves of expertise drained too quickly.

Second, the defenders never quite ran out of the essentials.[71] For all the element of rush that attended the Knights' preparations before the arrival of the armada, they got certain things right – or, rather, just about right enough. Although one of the order's powder mills blew up in St Angelo in June – sabotage was suspected but it was probably an accident in what must have been an extremely hazardous environment – there would seem to have been sufficient stocks of the ingredients of gunpowder and secure places to mix them to sustain a basic level of supply throughout the siege: never enough to confer an advantage, but just about enough never to be reduced to helplessness.[72] This is particularly significant in that, for all that crossbows had to be distributed when it rained and the Knights typically liked to go into combat aristocratic sword in hand, the order had invested heavily in firearms as the weapons of choice for its galleys and garrison troops.[73] Its ability to sustain the defence therefore depended to a large extent on the effectiveness of that technology. Food and water were getting scarce by the latter stages of the siege, but again supplies held out: a spring discovered in Birgu was greeted as a miracle, but the real value lay in the cisterns, which the Knights had been careful to build and maintain since their arrival in Malta, and which proved resistant to the Ottoman bombardment. Perhaps the most significant factor of all, in spite of all the privations that the defenders had to endure, was the absence of epidemic disease inside the fortifications – unlike in the Turkish camp. Any outbreak would surely have doomed the defence. Yes, the Infirmary would have been of some help, but it was doubtless overwhelmed during the siege anyway, and sixteenth-century medicine was, needless to say, unequal to the task of treating and containing contagious diseases. To understand what was at stake, one has only to consider the way in which the English defence of Le Havre against a besieging French army in 1563 was wholly undermined by the outbreak of plague: 500 men a week were dying at its peak. To compound matters, when the survivors returned to England they took the plague with them: 20,000 people died in London.[74] The defenders of Malta were presented with many ways to die, but not the one way that would have absolutely guaranteed their defeat.

Third, there were the Maltese inside Birgu and Senglea. As we have seen, they came to make many important contributions on both an individual and a collective level. The willingness of large numbers of Maltese to aid in the defence lowered the ratio of effectives to about four or five attackers to one defender, about a par score for survival in a sixteenth-century siege. More than that, the visibility and industry of the Maltese communicated to the Knights that they were in the business of defending a place and its people, not just themselves; La Valette's refusal to withdraw the Knights into St Angelo and raise the drawbridge was probably the single most consequential decision that he took during the whole siege. We should not imagine the kind of dissolution of social and cultural barriers that one sometimes finds within besieged populations in modern, total wars – sixteenth-century Europe was a highly stratified, deeply hierarchical world – but the very willingness of the sources to notice the Maltese, albeit on the edges, suggests that their active involvement was at the very least hugely important and in all likelihood what made the difference.

When pondering why events played out as they did, one always comes back to the countless moments in the killing zone on the front line that may well have been decisive but about which we know nothing – incidents that turned on the precise angle of a slightly deflected blow, a fractionally misaimed arquebus shot, an ounce more or less gunpowder packed into an incendiary weapon. They were the difference between the domino effects that did happen and those that did not. When the chroniclers chose to describe a particular life-or-death tussle on the ramparts, they were in part resorting to a well-worn narrative technique: they were dramatizing what was at stake by making it personal. But they were also acknowledging the fact that such moments of intimate, small-scale confrontation did indeed have the potential to change everything. The margins were so extraordinarily fine. When La Valette conspicuously placed himself near the front line during the major assaults on Castile in August, this was spun after the fact as evidence of his iron resolve and selfless heroism. But one wonders whether, in the moment, what truly motivated him was a resigned refusal to be taken alive, given that the outcome of any one of the many fights to the death playing out right in front of his eyes might trigger a series of cascading events that would spell final disaster. In the end, the defenders in the Great Siege just about held on because they were very, very lucky.

8.

Meanwhile . . .

When we think about the Great Siege as an event that took place in 1565, we should bear in mind that we are applying a dating system that only became the world's universal standard in later centuries. Measuring the passage of time by means of solar years counted from a starting point fixed at *Anno Domini* was just one method among a host of others in use around the world in what we conventionally think of as the sixteenth century. Although dating by *Anno Domini* was, by around the time of the siege, becoming the most geographically widespread system, it was used by states that ruled over only 10 or 15 per cent of a global population of approximately 500 million. There is the further complication that the numbering of consecutive years *Anno Domini* did not always run from 1 January: for most people 1565 did not start until the Feast of the Annunciation on 25 March, on Easter Day or some other date. As long as we remain mindful of these caveats, however, we may still profitably appeal to the notion of '1565' as a discrete block of time, framed in our modern January-to-December terms, which helps us to gain some sense of the Great Siege's larger setting and significance. What else was going on? And how might events taking place elsewhere aid our understanding of what was happening in the central Mediterranean?

1565, so understood, was certainly a momentous year, not just in the Mediterranean but around the world. If we limit ourselves in the first instance to events in, say, north-western Europe, we find, for example, that in this year Peter Breughel the Elder created perhaps his most famous painting, *The Hunters in the Snow*. Probably a week or so after the Great Siege had concluded, in Edinburgh, the

Meanwhile . . .

future James VI of Scotland/James I of England was conceived towards the end of the brief honeymoon period enjoyed by his parents, Mary, Queen of Scots, and her cousin Henry Stuart, Lord Darnley, before their marriage descended into disastrous acrimony. Earlier that year, on 20 March, in Whitehall Palace, Elizabeth I had been unusually and no doubt artfully candid in seeming to confide to the Spanish ambassador, Diego Guzmán de Silva, her most private thoughts on the most pressing problem in English public life at that time, the vexed question of the queen's marriage and the royal succession:

> . . . if I could today appoint such a successor to the Crown as would please me and the country I would not marry, as it is a thing for which I have never had any inclination. My subjects, however, press me so that I cannot help myself, but must marry or take the other course, which is a very difficult one. There is a strong idea in the world that a woman cannot live unless she is married, or at all events that if she refrains from marriage she does so for some bad reason . . . But what can we do?[1]

On a larger canvas 1565 presents us with several vivid demonstrations of the mutability of dynastic and political fortune, the impermanence of regimes and the grave consequences of military adventurism. In Ming China, Yen Sung, formerly the predominant figure in the grand secretariat of Chu Hou-ts'ung, the Chia-ching emperor (1521–67), met his end. An old man in physical and mental decline, he had been dismissed from office through the machinations of his great rival Hsü Chieh in 1562. His son and intended political heir, Yen Shih-fan, was executed for treason in April 1565; and Yen Sung, now a broken outsider demoted to the status of mere commoner and deprived of all his property, died later in that year – a spectacular fall from grace for someone who only a short time before had been the ruthless power behind the throne in the most populous and powerful state in the world.[2] In Japan the Muromachi bakufu, the military government that had existed since the 1330s, began a steep and terminal decline when in June 1565 the shogun, Ashikaga Yoshiteru, was assassinated in Kyoto. This played into the hands of Oda Nobunaga, the most powerful *daimyo*, or regional warlord, whose support was sought by the emperor, Ōgimachi, as well as those competing for the shogunate. In 1568 Nobunaga occupied Kyoto by force in the name of the emperor, and in 1573 defeated and exiled the last of the shoguns of the Ashikaga clan, thereby inaugurating the final phase of the Sengoku ('warring states') period of civil war during which Japan would be dominated by a succession of rival strongmen.[3] Elsewhere in 1565, in January in southern-central India, the forces of the powerful and rich Hindu kingdom of Vijayanagara were heavily defeated in battle by an alliance of the five Muslim Deccan sultanates to the north. The ruler of Vijayanagara, Rama Raja, was killed, as were many of his kingdom's elites. The capital city was then sacked so completely that later attempts to repopulate it failed, and it was left in ruins, an enduring monument to the fragility of overweening military and political ambition.[4]

Such a list of global events could, of course, be extended. There are, however, four notable moments or episodes which are especially helpful in situating the Great Siege in a larger context. Of these, the one in which a connection to events in Malta was most apparent to contemporaries themselves concerned developments in the Netherlands, which were part of the dominions of Philip II of Spain. On 8–12 September 1565, which is to say exactly the interval between the arrival of the *gran soccorso* in Mdina and the departure of the Turkish fleet from Maltese waters, a meeting of discontented nobles was held at the castle of Vianen, near Utrecht, which belonged to Henry of Brederode.[5] Present at the meeting were various Netherlandish grandees, including William of Nassau, prince of Orange, Lamoral, count of Egmont, and Philippe de Montmorency, count of Hornes, as well as German nobles with family ties to the principals and interests just across the imperial frontier in north-western Germany. (One of these was William of Jülich-Cleves-Berg, the brother of Henry VIII of England's fourth wife,

Anne.) There had been earlier meetings of lesser nobles over the summer, but the higher status of those assembled at Vianen represented a significant shift. Further meetings would follow in the following months at which members of the Netherlandish political elite discussed a posture of resistance against Philip II and the government conducted in his name by his regent and half-sister, Margaret of Parma.[6]

With the benefit of hindsight, we know that the growing disenchantment of a significant portion of the Netherlandish governing class would lead to a revolt against the Spanish in 1568.[7] That revolt in turn, though dealt with efficiently and harshly by the authorities in the short term, would prove to be the first of a long series of conflicts, a bitter and costly 'Eighty Years' War' which would result in the division of the Netherlands between the Dutch Republic and an area to the south in which Habsburg rule endured. We further know that as the Dutch Revolt, as this drawn-out process is generally known, played out, it became progressively more characterized as a religious conflict between a Protestant north and a Catholic south – though in practice these differences were never consistently observed nor grounded in hard-and-fast demographic divisions. Back at Vianen in 1565, however, confessional conflict was not in itself the issue: the host, Henry of Brederode, was a hotter sort of Protestant, but some of his guests were Catholic or like William of Orange, the future leader of the revolt, a latitudinarian influenced to a degree by the Lutheranism of his Saxon in-laws. Religion did matter at Vianen, however, insofar as Philip II and the harder-line advisors around him who were in the ascendant in 1565 were growing increasingly alarmed at the spread of heresy in the Netherlands – Calvinism, Lutheranism and Anabaptism – and were insisting that the local authorities act against it in strict accordance with recent and uncompromising anti-heresy enactments, the so-called *placards*. In this way the question of the toleration or suppression of Protestant heresy had become a sensitive index of the reach of direct Habsburg power in the Netherlands from Spain, as against the ambitions of local notables to exercise a substantial degree of autonomy through a council of state working with the regent in Brussels. In the spring of 1565 Egmont had travelled to the Spanish court and had returned in May with what soon proved to be a wildly overoptimistic impression of Philip's intentions. If doubts still lingered among those gathered at Vianen in September, they would soon be disabused when, in October, Philip restated his firm position on heresy and the subordinate role of the council of state in a series of letters issued from his country retreat at El Bosque de Segovia.[8]

As is often the case, political unrest was bound up with social and economic distress. The winter of 1564–5 had been especially severe: Breughel's *The Hunters in the Snow* was informed by a grim topicality.[9] The harvest in 1565 had been poor and food prices had inevitably risen. A recent trade war with England had gravely disrupted the supply of wool, the essential raw material for the Flemish cloth industry. And warfare in the Baltic had dislocated the rhythms of maritime trade and cut off an important source of the foodstuffs that the urbanized and densely populated Netherlands needed to make up the shortfall in its homegrown supply. In such circumstances, it is not surprising that the pressures building up in the Netherlands were too complex and too intractable to be eased by a mere insistence on firm governance on Philip's part.

After 1565 events, by sixteenth-century standards, moved quite quickly. While the disaffected nobles began to organize themselves further, Calvinist preachers, drawing larger crowds than ever before, succeeded in arousing their audiences to such an extent that they created a wave of iconoclastic rage – the *beeldenstorm,* or 'picture storm' – against religious images and the trappings of Catholic devotion in local churches. This in turn confirmed Philip in his determination to deal with the Netherlands decisively; and in 1567, in one of the famous set-pieces of European military history, 10,000 troops were sent up the 'Spanish Road' from Milan to the Netherlands under the command of Philip's hard man of choice, Fernando Álvarez de Toledo y Pimentel, duke of Alba.[10] Alba had for some years been politically marginalized, but his recent readmission to Philip's inner circle – it was he who, alongside the queen, had represented the king in the summit meeting with the French at Bayonne in June 1565 – was an indication that attitudes were hardening. A notably tough and effective commander, Alba dealt with the invasions launched by various of the grandees from beyond the Netherlands' borders, as well as suppressing internal resistance. Egmont and Hornes were publicly executed in the Grand Place in Brussels in June 1568, while Orange sought refuge on his German ancestral estates. A semblance of peace and order was, for the moment, restored.

For our immediate purposes, what is most striking about the emerging troubles in the Netherlands is the frequency with which observers made a connection to Malta's predicament. While Egmont was at the Spanish court between February and April 1565, for example, he had presciently reported back to his colleagues that Philip's attention to the Turkish threat would prevent him from travelling to the Netherlands that year, as had been mooted; and he restated this judgement when he returned in May.[11] That same month Margaret of Parma received letters from Philip concerning the execution of Anabaptists and other heretics which also stated that his close attention to the situation in Malta meant that he would not be able to travel north that year.[12] As early as March Philip had confided to his secretary of state, Gonzalo Pérez, that he was feeling overwhelmed and torn in different directions: 'I have so much on my mind that I scarcely know what I am saying or doing.'[13] People joked that, never mind the relief of Malta, it would take the capture of Istanbul before Philip would properly attend to the situation in the Netherlands.[14]

Does it follow that Philip himself precipitated the Dutch Revolt because he took his eye off the ball in 1565 when events in the Mediterranean consumed all his energies? Probably not, for the revolt had many complex roots stretching back many years. Philip may have sent out mixed signals and prevaricated for some months before the El Bosque de Segovia letters, but this sort of cautious approach was not unusual: his typical *modus operandi* was to weigh problems carefully, and then, when a decision had been reached, to entertain overly optimistic expectations that his instructions would or could be carried out promptly and without deviation. The belief on the part of the king's supporters, and even some of his opponents, that his presence in the Netherlands would in itself solve their problems was certainly naïve; had he travelled north, the result would most probably have been a variant of the tough regime subsequently instituted by Alba. We know, moreover, that over the course of 1565 Philip worked hard to stay abreast of events in the north: Margaret of Parma sent him numerous detailed reports, and he conversed at length with Lorenzo de Villavicencio, an Augustinian friar who since 1561 had been his most trusted eyes and ears on Netherlandish conditions. On the other hand, the fact that a connection with Malta was made is itself of interest. Even if we make allowance for an element of 'groupthink' settling on a simple answer to a complex question, it at least suggests that Philip did indeed take the situation in the central Mediterranean very seriously and was reluctant to be diverted from it. It also reveals that the sheer extent and variety of Philip's dispersed domains meant that, for all the strategic ambitions that guided Habsburg policy, much of the routine of rulership came down to fighting fires one after another. Netherlandish commentators might not welcome the fact, but in 1565 Malta was indeed the bigger fire.

 A letter sent from Margaret of Parma in Brussels to Philip II in central Spain would normally take about three or four weeks to reach its destination. In stark contrast, in late May 1565 a packet of correspondence addressed to the king was put together on the island of Cebu in the Philippines which those sending it knew would take many months, perhaps more than a year, to arrive, if indeed it ever arrived at all.[15] The man chiefly responsible for assembling the sheaf of reports was a Basque sea captain, Miguel López de Legazpi, who in that moment was the most remote servant of the Habsburg monarchy anywhere in the world. In keeping with his more hands-on interest in the conduct of Spanish trade than that of his father, Charles V, Philip had instructed the viceroy of New Spain, Luis de Velasco, to equip an expedition to locate what were vaguely described as the 'western isles' adjacent to the Spice Islands, the Moluccas, or Maluku Islands, in what is now eastern Indonesia, and to explore the possibilities for trade.[16] An air of subterfuge attended the whole enterprise when Legazpi, with the assistance of a well-known pilot, Andrés de Urdaneta, set sail from Navidad on the Pacific coast of Mexico in November 1564; their written instructions were only to be unsealed when they were well out to sea because of the sensitivities and uncertainties surrounding the location somewhere in the Pacific of the line of demarcation between the Spanish and Portuguese spheres of interest. At Tordesillas in 1494 the two kingdoms had agreed a north-to-south dividing line in the Atlantic, the Spanish to the west, the Portuguese to the east. The logic of their treaty, of course, was that sooner or later, if their respective imperial expansions continued apace, they would run up against one other on the antimeridian of the line on the far side of the globe; where this might be had been discussed in the 1520s, but at that stage the issue was still largely hypothetical. The moment of decision, however, was now approaching. The tiny Spanish settlement on Cebu, which relocated to Manila in 1571, soon realized that it could not muscle in on the spice trade, which was jealously guarded by the Portuguese to the west. But the Spanish told themselves (not altogether correctly) that the Philippines lay in their zone of operations as granted them at Tordesillas. They consequently set about inserting themselves into the existing trade networks that connected the Philippines to China and Japan; and as a result their base became an important entrepôt for the onward shipment of mostly Chinese goods – silk, porcelain and manufactures of many kinds – bound for American and European markets.[17]

In theory Spanish ships collecting this merchandise could have returned to Europe with it by travelling west. But this would have been to intrude upon the Portuguese sphere of operation, and it would have been impossible without the chain of supply bases that the Portuguese had patiently constructed over many decades to make the trade route around the Cape of Good Hope feasible. Part of Philip II's instructions to Legazpi in 1564 had therefore been to find a way back across the Pacific to New Spain – in other words, to develop a new route while staying within the Spanish zone as established by the Treaty of Tordesillas. The west-to-east crossing of the Pacific was the missing link of sixteenth-century global navigation. The east-to-west crossing was itself a formidable undertaking, of course, but was at least aided by favourable currents and prevalent easterlies blowing on or just above the Equator. To fight against those same currents and winds for thousands of miles in the opposite direction, however, was out of the question; and if a reverse route were indeed possible, it was understood that it must lie somewhere substantially to the north. There had been several abortive attempts; but it was only in 1565 that the navigational code was finally cracked. In fact it was cracked twice, first, in a remarkable act of seamanship, by a tiny forty-ton patache, the *San Lucas*. Having become detached from Legazpi's flotilla, probably deliberately, about ten days out from New Spain, the *San Lucas* reached the Philippines, missing – or evading – Legazpi and Urdaneta coming up behind, and then sailed east on a latitude of about 40°N, arriving at Navidad in August. Returning to Spain, the captain, Alonso de Arellano, was just about to claim the reward offered for the first such crossing when Urdaneta, the bearer of Legazpi's packet of reports, also turned up and challenged his right to the prize. Accompanying Legazpi's grandson, Felipe de Salcedo, in one of the expedition's larger vessels, the *San Pablo*, Urdaneta too had discovered a northerly route, reaching Acapulco in October after more than four months at sea.[18]

The two extraordinary west-to-east crossings of the Pacific of that year inaugurated one of the most significant and unusual institutions in the early history of global navigation, the Manila Galleons.[19] Every year until the early nineteenth century between one and four ships – in time the norm became two – would set out from the Philippines bound for Mexico crammed with merchandise. The 129 days taken by Salcedo and Urdaneta proved to be one of the quicker crossings: to be out at sea for only five or six months

Meanwhile...

came to be considered lucky, eight months was not unusual, and more than a year not unknown. There were no stops midway: remarkably, the Hawaiian islands remained undiscovered by Europeans until James Cook in 1778, because they lay between the galleons' eastbound and westbound routes, and freelance exploration was strongly discouraged, such was the vital importance of the sailings as an economic lifeline.[20] Conditions on board the galleons, especially on the west-to-east voyages, were infamously gruelling – and extremely cramped because priority was given to squeezing as much merchandise as possible on deck as well as below it. Hundreds of water containers swung from the rigging. Vermin were everywhere, including in all the food. Those who wrote about their experience remarked on the unnervingly unremitting sound of waves pounding against the hull day after day.[21] The worst-off of all were the Filipino crew, most of them drafted men with little or no experience of the sea: it is unsurprising that many chose to settle in New Spain rather than face the return journey home.[22] The travails of various sailings became the stuff of legend. In 1600 the *Santa Margarita* spent eight months fruitlessly beating back and forth in the South China Sea, unable to pick up the right wind; in that time, of the 260 on board, more than 200 perished. Galleons would simply disappear without trace on average every eight or ten years, sometimes in clusters. One such was the *San Antonio* in 1603, reputed to be carrying the most valuable cargo to date. In 1657 the *San José* inexplicably overshot Acapulco and was found drifting off Huatulco. Every single person on board was dead.[23]

Thanks to the vastness of the ocean in which they could hide, only one galleon before the eighteenth century had the ill fortune to be intercepted by a predator: in 1587 off the coast of what is now California two small English ships, the *Desire* and the *Content*, commanded by a Suffolk gentleman-turned-adventurer, Thomas Cavendish, managed to track down and capture the *Santa Ana*.[24] According to the inventory handed to the captors, she was carrying silks, damasks, musk, civet, pearls and 122,000 pesos of gold, though the true amount, most of it kept off the books, must have been much higher. The total value of the cargo was estimated at two million pesos. There was so much loot that the English took about a week to transfer the cargo to their vessels and had to burn what they could not carry.[25] The 190 crew and passengers of the *Santa Ana* were put ashore with food, water and arms to defend themselves. On the return voyage, the *Content* was either lost or chose to disappear. But Cavendish successfully found his way back to England on the *Desire* in September 1588 after more than two years at sea, to be greeted by the national euphoria following the recent defeat of the Spanish Armada. The *Desire* was moored at Greenwich for Elizabeth I and her court to admire, and Cavendish received the queen on board. Meanwhile such was the impact of Cavendish's booty that the price of gold fell significantly on the London market.

Of all the things that happened around the world in 1565, the creation of the Spanish colony in the Philippines – their control scarcely extended beyond their main base and a few other posts – and the voyages of the forerunners of the Manila Galleons arguably represented the most important global development in the long run. Courtesy of the decline of the Ming navy since the fifteenth century, the Spanish were able to establish an outpost which came to function as an economic outlier, not of the far-distant imperial metropolis in Spain itself, but of China and the Spanish Americas, which became a significant market for the goods delivered by the galleons.[26] It was silver mined in Peru and Mexico that paid for those goods; the quantities involved sometimes exceeded those crossing the Atlantic to Spain. Most of the silver passing through the hands of the Chinese mercantile community that dominated the Spanish Philippines – it substantially outnumbered the Europeans – found its way back to China itself, and this played a significant role in monetizing the Chinese economy.[27] The Chinese had begun to use silver currency in the fifteenth century, and this new source confirmed them in that policy; this would equip them to plug themselves more fully into global commercial networks in subsequent centuries. It was with good reason that the Spanish monarchs were known to the Chinese as 'the kings of silver'. In saying all this we are of course

Meanwhile...

getting ahead of ourselves. But it is fair to say that in 1565 the world became significantly more joined up than ever before – albeit by means of a perilously thin thread stretching across thousands of kilometres of empty ocean.

In late November and early December 1566, a Jesuit named Lourenço Peres wrote two letters from the Portuguese outpost of Malacca, in what is now southern Malaysia; the first was to a colleague, Gomes Vaz, in Goa, the second to no less a figure than the superior general of his order (and future saint), Francisco de Borja. The letters addressed various matters of report, including a gruesome story of torture and martyrdom that had played out 'this past year' (*ho anno passado*); this probably meant some time in 1565 or early 1566.[28] According to Peres, when a Portuguese merchant ship had called at Aceh, on the northern tip of Sumatra, those on board had been prevented from trading – almost certainly for pepper – as they had anticipated. They became, instead, the unwitting victims of a diplomatic incident contrived by someone whom Peres described as 'an ambassador of the Turk'. This mysterious figure accused the Christians of behaving discourteously towards him and then subjected the ship's captain to a severe beating. To compound matters, the Muslim sultan of Aceh, Ala'ad-din Ri'ayat Syah, sided with the Ottoman ambassador and gave orders that the members of the crew should be seized, whereupon they were offered the choice between conversion to Islam or death. Surprisingly, perhaps, only two chose to abjure their faith; it is interesting that Peres makes a point of noting that these were a mixed-race *mestiço* and a Fleming, as if to register that they were outsiders in some way. The rest of the crew were made to suffer dreadful torments: some were crucified while others were flayed alive and their bodies tossed near the foot of the crosses.

What had prompted this violent incident? Peres's accounts offer various clues. The first is the fact that the instigator was a representative of the Sublime Porte, which raises interesting questions about what an Ottoman official was doing, evidently wielding authority and influence, on the far side of the Indian Ocean. Independent evidence suggests that the 'ambassador of the Turk' was an experienced sailor and Ottoman agent named Lufti.[29] The second clue is that, as Peres noted in his letter to Francisco de Borja, the sultan of Aceh had hostile designs on Malacca, and to this end had sought military aid from the Ottomans. The third is Peres's description of this sultan as 'the lord of pepper'. Finally there is the strong suggestion in Peres's letters that the executions of the Christian sailors were staged in such a way as to accentuate their religious symbolism and, by extension, to send out a powerful message that confessional differences should supersede commercial interests when it came to Muslim–Christian relations in the Indian Ocean. In sum, the grim fate of the unsuspecting Portuguese mariners offers a glimpse of a powerful conjunction of political, military, economic and religious imperatives drawing the Ottomans into the Indian Ocean world around the same time as they were launching their forces against Malta.

A question that is sometimes asked is why the Ottomans never chased the Spanish across the Atlantic. Granted, Spain was better situated geographically to become an ocean-going power, but it is not too fanciful to imagine a situation in which the Ottomans made it a priority to stiffen their imperfect authority in the Maghreb, push west into Morocco and develop ports on the Atlantic beyond the Straits of Gibraltar. The answer to the question is that it was simply not necessary for the Sublime Porte to become an Atlantic power, because with the conquest of Egypt in 1516–17 it had gained access to the Red Sea and the Indian Ocean beyond.[30] That is to say, two years before Hernán Cortés's expedition inaugurated the Spanish conquest of Mexico, the Ottomans had already acquired the potential to become an oceanic power where it mattered most, close to the biggest economic prizes. The conquest of Iraq in 1534, followed by the creation of a seat of government and naval base at Basra in 1546, cemented this opportunity by giving the Ottomans a second means of access to the Indian Ocean through the Persian Gulf.[31]

Because we are aware of the importance of the Americas to world history in subsequent centuries, it is easy to fall into the trap

A detail from one of Matteo Perez d'Aleccio's wall paintings depicting Dockyard Creek (with protective chain, improvised pontoon bridge and a merchant vessel captured by the Knights before the siege), Birgu and St Angelo, and the Ottomans withdrawing most of their cannon from the Sciberras peninsula after the fall of St Elmo.

The amphibious assault against Senglea on 15 July and the carnage wrought by the battery at the base of St Angelo: a moment of acute crisis that came to be treated as the climacteric of the whole Malta campaign.

The arrival of the *gran soccorso*: Matteo Perez d'Aleccio's rendering of this decisive moment emphasizes the ability of the Christian fleet to disembark its troops without interference from the Ottoman galleys, the composite nature of the force that was landed (the contingent of Knights is shown to the fore), and the strategic importance of Mdina.

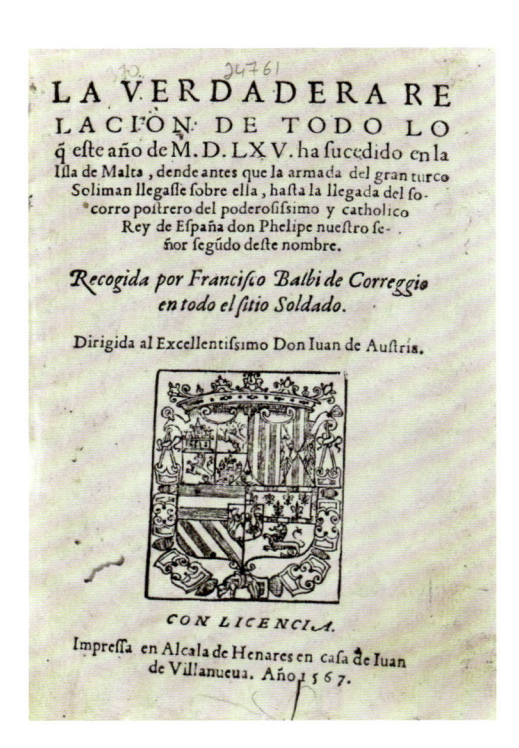

Title page of the first edition of Francesco Balbi da Correggio's *La verdadera relación*, 1567: Balbi could lay claim to being the only author of a book-length history of the siege to have been an eyewitness throughout.

Giovanni Bandini, portrait bust of Grand Master Jean de La Valette, *c*. 1566: probably commissioned as a gift to La Valette, it speaks to his heightened prestige after the siege.

Ottoman vessels in the Gulf of Aden.

Fort Caroline engraved by Theodor de Bry in Jacques Le Moyne's history of the French expeditions to Florida.

The conspectus of the Great Siege in the Galleria delle Carte Geografiche in the Vatican, *c.* 1581: its positioning both situates the siege in an Italy-centred vision of history and suggests a close connection to the Christian naval victory at Lepanto in 1571.

Giuseppe Caloriti, an aerial view of eighteenth-century Valletta and its surroundings: the image captures the enormous changes wrought to the human landscape after 1565.

The memorial to Daphne Caruana Galizia at the base of Antonio Sciortino's Great Siege Monument in Valletta.

of supposing that sixteenth-century Europeans already had an intimation of where this would lead in future. True, they had originally been drawn across the Atlantic, from Columbus onwards, by the hope of gaining unmediated access to the sources of the eastern spice trade. But did they not, sooner or later, come to appreciate that they had stumbled on something much more significant and beneficial to their interests than a long-distance trade route? The answer is: only to a certain extent, slowly and fitfully. After the initial predatory phase of Spain's expansion into the New World – which reached its peak in Pizarro's orgy of looting of the Incan empire, part of the booty from which substantially paid for Charles V's grandiose expedition against Tunis in 1535 – Spanish enthusiasm for the Americas began to level off, even to cool. As we shall see later in this chapter, for example, by 1565 the Spanish had been frustrated by several failed attempts to reconnoitre and create settlements on the American mainland north and east of New Spain. True, the opening up of silver mines in Mexico and Peru in the middle decades of the century, in conjunction with improvements in the technology used to extract the silver from its ore, heralded a new, long-term regime of profitable exploitation. But as Philip II's decision to send the Legazpi–Urdaneta expedition goes to show, in the European imagination around the time of the Great Siege, America was still substantially conceived as an obstacle to the riches that lay beyond it, or at best as a staging-post to somewhere else.

That 'somewhere else' was the point of origin of the spice trade, the beating heart of the global commercial economy. The ultimate prize was access to the Moluccas, the only source in the world at that time of nutmeg and cloves. But there were other valuable commodities to pursue. The largest concentration of the trees whose bark is the source of cinnamon was to be found in Ceylon. Pepper was more widespread, from India down to the Indonesian island chain. It was the cheapest bulk item among the spices, but nonetheless a valuable resource: witness the close connection between the sultan of Aceh and pepper made by Lourenço Peres, the result of official policy since the 1530s to plant and exploit large plantations.[32]

The harsh treatment of the Portuguese traders is to be understood as one dramatic moment in the Ottomans' evolving relationship with this world of spices, not only on an economic level – though the stakes here were very high – but also in terms of the extension of their ideological soft power into parts of the Muslim world that had been remote from them before the 1510s. The Aceh incident was, it has been argued, a 'stunt' intended to underscore an incipient alliance between the local sultan and the Sublime Porte and to use religious antagonism to galvanize local feeling against the Portuguese, who had been trading with the Acehnese for some time and had even come to look on them as one of their more reliable commercial partners in the region.[33]

The key to understanding the Ottomans' expansion into the Indian Ocean is the fact that by 1516–17 the Portuguese had beaten them to it by about fifteen years.[34] Every policy and initiative was consequently informed by the Portuguese presence and judgements as to whether confrontation or some sort of guarded but mutually beneficial collaboration was the better option in any given moment. The Ottomans' sphere of interest in the Indian Ocean came to consist of two connected zones, the perennial question that they faced boiling down to whether control of the first, which was a strategic imperative, required or encouraged expansion into the second. The first zone was the inner geographical core, control of which ensured that the terminal points of the Indian Ocean trade routes were securely in their hands. This meant making the Red Sea an Ottoman lake and extending the sultans' lordship along the southern Arabian coast, even though areas such as Yemen were often disturbed and could prove difficult to dominate, and then around the Arabian Sea into the Persian Gulf. Control of the Gulf was complicated by the presence there of Portuguese strongpoints, especially the island of Hormuz, which meant that some sort of *modus vivendi* with the Portuguese was often necessary to facilitate the movement of shipping to and from Basra. The Red Sea was more important than the Gulf, however, both in terms of commercial value and because it was the route taken by Asian pilgrims to Mecca and

Meanwhile...

Medina. The second zone was the larger Indian Ocean world beyond, an enormous space of shifting alliances, political conflict and cut-throat commercial competition into which Ottoman soft power could be projected by various means, including the dispatch of military hardware and experts to willing Muslim rulers and the formal submission of local potentates to Ottoman overlordship.[35]

For the Portuguese the aim was simple: to carry as much of the Indian Ocean trade as possible. The route that their ships had to take to and from the sources of the spices, around the Cape of Good Hope, was very time-consuming, hazardous and expensive. It could only be profitable, therefore, if the Portuguese were able to strangle the traditional trade routes across the Indian Ocean and around the northern shores of the Arabian Sea that led to the Red Sea and the Gulf. In the early decades of the century, this policy was proving effective. In 1517 Portuguese ships entered the Red Sea and attacked Jeddah; it was even feared that they would strike against Mecca itself, only about sixty-five kilometres inland.[36] In 1525 a report on the strategic situation in the region submitted by Selman Reis, an experienced mariner who had served both the Mamluks and the Ottomans, commented on the effectiveness of the Portuguese in establishing a chain of fortified bases around the Indian Ocean rim despite the fact that they were very few in number; as a result of this policy, Selman observed, the substantial revenues which had been raised from tolls and taxes in the past had now dried up.[37] The Portuguese interdiction of the traditional routes reached the point that in 1530 Venetian merchants in Alexandria complained that they were unable to come by any spices at all.

The Ottoman priority was, therefore, to break the Portuguese naval blockades of the Gulf and the Red Sea. Their first significant military action with this in mind was a campaign in 1538 against the Portuguese outpost at Diu in Gujarat in north-western India, which was besieged without success.[38] In 1541 it was the turn of the Portuguese to take the initiative, though an ambitious raid up the Red Sea all the way to the Ottoman naval base at Suez did not succeed in delivering a knock-out blow.[39] In 1546 Diu survived a second epic siege.⁴⁰ In 1552 the Ottomans launched an ambitious attack on Hormuz; its failure led to the execution of the expedition's aged commander, the celebrated geographer Piri Reis.⁴¹ Naval encounters in 1553 and 1554 were fought to a tie that significantly weakened both sides, after which there was something of a lull.⁴²

The events at Aceh, however, were an indication that Ottoman interest in the Indian Ocean was reviving. It is noteworthy that when Daniele Barbarigo, the Venetian *bailo* in Istanbul between 1561 and 1564, made his final report in early 1565 – in the process capturing the mood in the Ottoman capital just as preparations for the attack on Malta were getting under way – he departed from the normal running order of such documents by beginning with a detailed analysis of the competition between the Ottomans and the Portuguese in the Indian Ocean and its implications for the movement of spices through the Red Sea.⁴³ In 1562 the sultan of Aceh had approached the Ottoman government asking for military assistance; and Lufti's exploratory mission in 1564–6 had been the result. A positive response from the sultan – his letter, almost certainly the work of Lufti himself, offered formal submission to the Sublime Porte and held out the prospect of future military collaboration – in turn led to the organization of a substantial Ottoman expedition in 1567.⁴⁴ In the event, only part of the planned force reached Aceh the following year, after which the local sultan launched two expeditions against Malacca with the men and resources that the Ottomans had been able to spare; both proved unsuccessful.⁴⁵ With this, the status quo returned to the region for the time being.

How did the Indian Ocean compare with the Mediterranean as a cockpit of conflict between the Ottomans and their Christian adversaries? There are some intriguing similarities. For example, when Süleyman issued his instructions to the commander of the 1538 expedition against Diu, Hadım Süleyman Pasha, the language of holy war and the emphasis on the need to protect the pilgrimage routes to the holy places closely resemble the official rhetoric that one encounters in pronouncements concerning the assault on Malta.⁴⁶ The appointment in 1560 of the leading corsair adventurer

Meanwhile...

in the region, Sefer Reis, as admiral of the Red Sea fleet, and the co-opting of his skills and knowledge of local waters, recall the use that the Ottomans made of Barbary corsairs such as Sefer's close contemporary Turgut.[47] In other respects, however, there were clear differences between the two theatres. Naval conflict in the Indian Ocean region centred on the establishment of blockades and attempts to break them, not the amphibious attacks on coastal fortresses which were the bread and butter of warfare in the Mediterranean; it is significant that on the two main occasions when the Ottomans and their allies did launch Mediterranean-style assaults, on Diu, very small garrisons were able to hold out against much larger forces. In addition, and as the above brief narrative of major engagements suggests, the rhythm of conflict was more intermittent than in the Mediterranean, and there was always greater scope for establishing working relationships with the enemy: it is striking that in 1564, exactly the time, that is, when we have seen that a more forward policy against Portuguese interests was taking shape in Istanbul, Süleyman wrote to King Sebastian I of Portugal offering peace if Muslim pilgrims and merchants were allowed to pass freely through the areas that he controlled.[48]

The conflict in the Indian Ocean was, moreover, seldom conducted on the same sort of scale. In 1561, for example, what amounted to an unusually large expedition for the region was organized by the Portuguese in an attempt to track down Sefer Reis. The force that was assembled was nonetheless small by Mediterranean standards: twenty-three oared vessels, two sailing ships and 650 soldiers. For his part Sefer was at that time operating with only three galleys.[49] There is also the question of effective action radius relative to the great expanse of the Indian Ocean: it is significant that the ambitious expedition to Aceh planned in 1567 was in the event substantially frustrated by the need to divert resources in order to deal with a rebellion much closer to the heart of the Ottomans' strategic interests, in Yemen. In time, the Ottomans discovered that they did not need to mobilize Mediterranean-level military resources in the Indian Ocean to achieve their essential aims. By disrupting the always precarious Portuguese system of widely dispersed bases, by cultivating links with well-disposed local rulers, and by establishing a regime of taxes and tolls that, while highly lucrative, did not deter traders from returning to the traditional routes, they succeeded in rediverting much of the spice trade back through the Red Sea and Gulf by around the middle of the sixteenth century.[50] The Aceh incident in 1565/6 was in one sense, therefore, a flash in the pan, a kind of contrived performance predicated on a more expansive and aggressive policy in the Indian Ocean than the Ottomans ultimately needed to pursue. But it is a salutary reminder that conflict between the Ottomans and Christians was not confined to its principal theatres, the Mediterranean and central Europe; and that in fact the Great Siege took place at a time when the Ottomans were experimenting with a more capacious understanding of what might be achieved by combining holy-war ideology and strategic competition.

On 8 September 1565, the day on which the *gran soccorso* began to settle into Mdina and Rabat, Pedro Menéndez de Avilés, *adelantado* of Florida, was rowed ashore on Florida's Atlantic coast to be greeted by a large crowd of no doubt puzzled and apprehensive Native Americans. After the celebration of mass in honour of the Virgin Mary, for this was one of her feast days, Menéndez took formal possession of the land for Spain in a ritual that had been played out many times over the course of the Spanish exploration and conquest of the Americas.[51] The ceremony gave expression to the expectation that as *adelantado*, or royal licensee of the right to settle and exploit a territory on behalf of the Spanish crown, Menéndez would establish a community with prescribed legal and administrative structures and an orderly system for apportioning land. This was to be no free-for-all, and the hope was that the settlement would prove permanent. Previous Spanish attempts to explore and colonize Florida, the term applied by contemporaries to the whole of what is now the southeastern United States, not just the state of that name, had fared badly and there was some reluctance to persist in trying. But perhaps things would now be different.[52]

Meanwhile . . .

Menéndez had in fact waited a day for his big moment: his small fleet had arrived at that point on the coast on the 7th, and 300 soldiers had been landed to reconnoitre and identify the best location for a defensive stockade. In the event, this proved to be the site of a successful settlement. The name it was given was inspired by the fact that the harbour on which it lay had first been discovered by Menéndez on 28 August, the Feast of Saint Augustine. Today St Augustine lays claim to the title of the oldest continuously occupied European settlement in the United States (notwithstanding the fact that it was sacked and burned by Francis Drake in 1586). One's first reaction might be that Menéndez's actions were simply the latest manifestation of Spain's insatiable appetite for new territory in the Americas. But this would be to oversimplify the subtleties of the situation. The Spanish had become wary of overextending themselves and taking on unprofitable commitments: this had been the main reason why the possibility of expansion from the Caribbean into Florida had not been pursued more intensively up to that point. Menéndez was only there as a reactive measure. He was digging in on what is now Florida's 'First Coast' because he and his master, Philip II, were panicking.

The root cause of their panic is to be found in the system that the Spanish had developed, and recently refined, to exploit the mineral resources of the Americas to their fullest extent and to overcome the formidable physical challenges that this presented. When Europeans first came upon the Americas, and especially after Cortés's conquest of Tenochtitlan in 1519–21, the dream of easy riches had been centred on purloined gold. Pizarro's conquests in Peru in 1532–4 represented the *ne plus ultra* of this conquest-as-looting phase. From the 1540s, however, the emphasis switched to silver, generally only about one tenth or one twelfth of the value of gold but available in much greater quantities.[53] The turning points were the discovery in 1545 of large silver deposits at Potosí in Peru (now modern Bolivia) and in 1546 at Zacatecas in central Mexico, followed by other Mexican sites. The yield of the mining operations that developed would be transformed by the introduction to the

Mexican mines in the mid 1550s of the mercury amalgam technique, using mercury mined at Almadén in Spain.[54] This process, which inflicted terrible suffering on those condemned to mine the mercury or work it into the ground silver ore in large treatment beds, or *patios*, came a little later to Potosí, after a source of local mercury was discovered at Huancavelica in 1563–4; but thereafter it overtook the output of the Mexican mines. A boom town soon sprang up, and although it would have felt like the roof of the world, more than 4,000 metres above sea level in the high Andes, Potosí would become the most populous city in the whole Spanish empire.[55] Since the sixteenth century it has produced more silver than any other mine in world history.

The yields from the American mines would increase enormously in the 1570s and 1580s, but they were already growing significantly by the early 1560s. There is a popular image of sixteenth-century Spain drowning in American silver, but this is overdrawn. The Spanish crown's share of the silver crossing the Atlantic – the traditional *quinto*, or fifth, in the case of Peru, somewhat less in the case of Mexico – represented only about 10 or 15 per cent of its direct income (though it also stood to benefit indirectly from increased receipts from taxes and tolls thanks to the quickening of the economy that the silver, as well as luxury items imported from the Americas such as dyes and pearls, stimulated). As we have seen, however, Philip II ran his government and fought his many wars largely on credit, with the result that the margin represented by the silver premium made all the difference. Not only was the hypothecation of future income from silver imports the most secure way to insure against Philip's shaky creditworthiness, the crown's creditors became stakeholders in the system themselves. For example, the Fuggers, the firm of German bankers which was one of Philip's main sources of credit, was for a time granted control of the Almadén mercury mine itself.[56]

Given the push of growing silver production and the pull of demand for it on the part of a Spanish crown beginning to take a more hands-on interest in the Americas, it made sense to place the

Meanwhile . . .

transportation of the silver on a secure footing. In 1561, therefore, a royal ordinance sought to create a single, joined-up system for the movement of the silver from the mines to embarkation points on the coast, and thence across the Atlantic to Seville; this was refined in 1564.[57] One of the architects of the system, the *flota*, was Menéndez himself, whom Philip particularly trusted as a maritime expert. According to the revisions made in 1564, two fleets, accompanied by escorts part of the way, would set sail from Seville every year: the *flota* proper in April bound for New Spain, and the *galeones* in August headed for Tierra Firme, i.e. the South American mainland, in particular Cartagena de Indias in modern Colombia. They would collect shipments of silver brought to the coast – in the case of the Peruvian loads after they had been transported up the Pacific coast to Panama and then carted overland across the isthmus – and then rendezvous at Havana in Cuba. From there they would set out for Spain in March of the following year, ahead of the hurricane season, and pick up escorts off the Azores for the final leg of the voyage back to Seville. Needless to say, the co-ordination of so many moving parts, the slowness of communication and the vagaries of the weather meant that things seldom went strictly according to plan. But broadly speaking the system was as sophisticated an operation as could be attempted given all the logistical difficulties, and *grosso modo* it did its job well. French, English and Dutch privateers dreamed of intercepting the silver fleet on its return journey, and sometimes picked off one or two stragglers; but when the famed Dutch admiral Piet Heyn succeeded in capturing the whole New Spain *flota* in 1628, about fifteen ships in all, this was a big story precisely because it was exceptional.[58]

Back in 1565 Menéndez and Philip II had good reason to hope but could not yet be wholly confident that the *flota* system would prove successful in the long run. Their doubt and unease on this score were ultimately a reflection of the hydrography and meteorology of the Atlantic Ocean between approximately 10°N and 50°N. The Spanish Atlantic was, like the Pacific, not a two-lane highway. It was, on the contrary, an enormous clockwise churn of currents and prevailing winds that severely limited seafarers' options, in some instances making a long-distance voyage relatively straightforward, and in others making direct travel between two places that look close to one another on the map all but impossible.[59] Spanish ships headed for the Caribbean would first have to work south-southwest to the Canaries and on towards the approaches to the Cape Verde Islands, before picking up the North Equatorial Current and the prevailing easterly trade winds which together would carry them across the ocean, sometimes in a matter of a few weeks. A vessel in, say, Havana, however, intending to return to Spain would need to take a very different route: rounding the Keys to arrive off Florida's Atlantic coast, it would then bear north, passing through the channel between Florida and the northern islands of the Bahamian archipelago and then sailing up the coast of what is now the south-eastern United States. The intention would be to nudge as far north as was practicable: too far and one would run up against the contrary flow of the Labrador Current, while there might also be northern European privateers lying in wait. The ideal was to use the Gulf Stream to reach a latitude a little shy of the North Carolina Outer Banks, and then ride the prevailing westerlies and the continuation of the Gulf Stream, the North Atlantic Drift, to the Azores and onward to southern Spain. Once out in the open expanse of the Atlantic one could reasonably hope to avoid predators, while the final leg from the Azores was quite well patrolled. The most fraught part of this route, therefore, was in the early stages: the Bahama Channel was poorly mapped and its shoals and reefs were notoriously hazardous; and more dangerously still any hostile presence on the coast between modern-day Florida and the Carolinas would be like a finger pressing on the carotid artery of Spain's silver lifeblood. Menéndez and Philip II were nervous in 1565 because they were persuaded, with some measure of justification, that this nightmare was in fact coming true.

    The threat had emerged over the previous three years. In 1562 an expedition sponsored by one of the foremost noblemen in France, Gaspard de Coligny, and led by an experienced mariner named Jean

Meanwhile . . .

Ribault, had crossed the Atlantic by taking an unconventional northerly route in order to steer clear of the Spanish Caribbean. Reaching what is now northern Florida in late April, Ribault's two ships laid claim to the area by erecting a marker stone near the mouth of the St Johns River. Working their way north, they repeated this exercise on the shore of a sound they christened Port Royal, and a simple fortification was constructed on what is now Parris Island, close to the modern border between South Carolina and Georgia.[60] A garrison of thirty men was left to consolidate the settlement, which was named Charlesfort after King Charles IX, while Ribault sailed back to France, having promised to make a prompt return with reinforcements and supplies. The outbreak of the first of the Wars of Religion in France in 1562, however, meant that Coligny, a leading figure in the Protestant cause, could not spare the time, energy or resources to attend to his colonial venture, with the result that no further sailings could be attempted before 1564. In the meantime discipline in Charlesfort had begun to break down; the situation reached breaking point when the man left in command, Captain Albert, hanged one of the soldiers and expelled another from the fort. Albert was then murdered and one Nicolas Barré chosen to take his place. Short of supplies and despairing of ever being rescued, the garrison somehow managed to confect a makeshift vessel, cobbled together from local materials, even though none of them had any shipbuilding experience, nor indeed any knowledge of navigation. In August 1563 twenty-three desperate men set out on what would become one of the most remarkable epics of survival against the odds on the open sea. Remarkably, only one had died, chosen by lot to be eaten by the others, by the time that they were discovered by an English ship off the coast of Brittany.[61]

The conclusion of the first civil war in France allowed Coligny and Ribault to organize a second, larger expedition in 1564. By now aware that there was nothing waiting for him at Charlesfort, Ribault returned to the St Johns and established a new settlement, Fort Caroline, on a site on the river in what is now the outskirts of

Jacksonville. As before, Ribault promptly sailed back to France, leaving his deputy, René de Laudonnière, in command. Laudonnière's account, 'The Notable History of Florida', is our fullest source for what happened next, although the author's impulse to put himself in the best possible light must always be borne in mind. The Fort Caroline settlement was a more considered and ambitious project than Charlesfort, which Ribault may in fact have improvised in the moment. Initially positive interactions with local Timucuan communities, and the arrival of a supply ship in September, meant that the French were in reasonably good shape heading into the winter. In due course, however, tensions began to emerge. Relations with the Timucuans cooled. Mutinous elements seized some of the vessels that had been left behind by Ribault and used them to prey on ships and coastal communities in Cuba – in the process alerting the Spanish in the Caribbean to the presence of unwanted guests to their north.[62] Food became short, and by the summer of 1565 the situation for the settlers had become desperate. They were offered a respite by the arrival of a group of ships under the command of the English privateer Jack Hawkins, who gave them one of his vessels in return for most of the French artillery. A few weeks later, Laudonnière was just on the point of abandoning Fort Caroline when out of the blue Ribault arrived with supplies and new settlers. They had, so they thought, been saved.[63]

News of Ribault's preparations had reached the Spanish court, and a taskforce was organized under Menéndez's command. Depleted by a troubled crossing of the Atlantic, what survived of Menéndez's flotilla located Ribault's ships and Fort Caroline on 4 September.[64] After an inconclusive stand-off, Menéndez withdrew to the south in order to regroup; the founding of St Augustine took place in this interval. Meanwhile Ribault had rashly disregarded the advice of his more sensible followers and decided not to dig in and strengthen the fortifications at Fort Caroline in anticipation of an attack. He chose instead to pursue the Spanish by sea; his intention may have been to track down and neutralize the threat of the *San Pelayo*, the largest and most powerful of the Spanish ships. As the

Meanwhile...

French vessels made their way south, however, they all came to grief in a hurricane.[65] Back at St Augustine, Menéndez assembled a force to march north to Fort Caroline; overcoming very difficult swampy terrain and terrible weather, the Spanish reached their target on the 19th and attacked at dawn on the 20th, massacring most of the defenders. Some, including the future chroniclers of these events Laudonnière, Jacques Le Moyne and Nicolas Le Challeux, managed to escape and eventually found their way back to France in the vessels that had been left behind in the St Johns under the command of Ribault's son, Jacques.[66] Having returned to St Augustine, over the next few days the Spanish came upon two large groups of survivors from Ribault's wrecked ships, huddled and starving on sandbars. Lured across to dry land, probably by deceitful promises of fair treatment, they were all, with a few exceptions, put to death. Ribault was among the victims.[67]

As news of these events trickled back to Europe between December 1565 and February 1566, the Spanish and French courts threw themselves into an ill-tempered diplomatic squabble over the rights and wrongs of what had happened. As was often the case in the back-and-forth of early modern diplomacy, any and every argument that seemed pertinent was thrown into the mix at some point. But in essence the question over which the two courts fought came down to legal title.[68] For the Spanish, the Treaty of Tordesillas had granted them sovereignty over all the area at issue; the French were trespassing, irrespective of the fact that the rightful owners had not yet exercised their right to occupy that particular stretch of land. For the French, effective possession was nine tenths of the law; Fort Caroline, moreover, lay in territory that was theirs by reason of French explorations of the Atlantic seaboard earlier in the sixteenth century. Florida was also – the level of geographical understanding that informed this dispute was consistently very poor, especially on the French side – some sort of southerly extension of a very ill-defined area to the north known as the 'coast' or 'land of the Bretons' which the French had come upon, and crucially named, in years past. Such were the irreconcilable legal positions; the Spanish had the better argument by their lights, and they knew it.

As the crisis had played out, however, the Spanish had been exercised by two further considerations. The first was religion. The brief French presence in Florida has traditionally been seen as a kind of Plymouth Rock before the fact, an attempt to find a new land on the part of those – in this instance Huguenots – who were suffering religious persecution at home. This is, for example, the thrust of the tourist information supplied at the modern reconstruction of the fort at the Fort Caroline National Memorial. Matters were not so straightforward, however. Coligny, Ribault, Laudonnière and most of the principals were Huguenots, but the Florida project would not seem to have been conceived as a Protestant refuge, even though this notion may have progressively gained some traction sailing by sailing as religious tensions intensified in France between 1562 and 1565. The Huguenot character of the expeditions may to some extent have been incidental: much of the recruitment for them was undertaken in and around Dieppe and other Norman ports, places where Protestantism had taken a particular hold. One of the complaints voiced by those in the 1564 group as Laudonnière's authority began to falter was that there were no Protestant ministers, which suggests that the spiritual needs of the colonists and evangelization of the Timucuans had not been a priority in the planning of that expedition.[69]

On the other hand, the account of the massacres of the shipwrecked French by Gonzalo Solís de Merás, our fullest eyewitness source, suggests that those stranded on the sandbars were overwhelmingly Protestant, and, more to the point, unable or unwilling to pass themselves off as Catholics in order to save themselves: in the first massacre eight out of 208 were spared for this reason, in the second four out of 150. (Another twelve were saved because they were young members of the expedition's military band, which the Spanish chose to keep for themselves.)[70] If some ambiguity attached to the relative importance of religion from the French perspective, however, the more important point was that the Spanish had no

Meanwhile...

doubts whatsoever on this score. They were waging what, according to Solís de Merás, Menéndez insisted was 'a war of blood and fire' against dangerous heretics: if the interlopers were not stopped, they would spread the contagion of their new religion to the Native Americans and even incite rebellion among the slaves in the Caribbean.[71] Menéndez, who regularly employed religious ritual and rhetoric to enhance his authority with his men, was convinced that he was a man on a mission.

The second consideration turned on the strategic needs of the Spanish in the Atlantic that we have considered. As Menéndez insisted in his reports to Philip II, if a French or English settlement were to put down roots in Florida, this would pose a grave risk to the passage of the Indies fleets and, ultimately, to the Spanish hold on their possessions in the Caribbean.[72] For their part, the French sources are a little coy on this matter, in part because the official line throughout was that they were scrupulously avoiding treading on Spanish toes. The French colonists brought a variety of hopes and ambitions to their participation in the expeditions, and they never quite succeeded in working out where their priorities lay. As Nicolas Le Challeux observed rather high-mindedly:

> They were guided by various motives; some were urged on by a praiseworthy and honest desire to increase their knowledge of the world... hoping that the expedition would profit them later. Others also came who wished with heart and soul to wage war... Others were encouraged by the spread of a rumour that Florida was able to furnish all that a man could wish on earth, for that country had received a particular favour from heaven.[73]

By contrast John Sparke, who was with Hawkins when the English arrived at Fort Caroline in August 1565, painted a much more unfavourable picture of listless gentlemen and soldiers who had become disillusioned by the absence of the easy riches that they had hoped to find – whatever gold they had come across actually came from Spanish wrecks – and were unwilling to do their bit for the survival of the community by learning how to fish or do agricultural work.⁷⁴ It would seem that the French fell into a trap that caught out several other early European attempts at settlement in the Americas – including the English 'Lost Colony' on Roanoke in the 1580s – which was that it was almost impossible to achieve a working balance between the needs of a secure military garrison and the creation of a self-sustaining agricultural community.

Given these contradictions, and the fact that many of the colonists were looking for a quick profit, it is more than likely that predation of Spanish shipping, especially the *flota*, did indeed enter their thinking. The testimony of Guillaume Rouffin, who refused to get on the makeshift boat at Charlesfort in 1563 and was later discovered and interrogated by the Spanish, suggests that already at the time of the 1562 reconnaissance the French were planning in such terms: the aim, he said, had been to discover 'a good location for going out into the Bahama Channel to capture the fleets from the Indies'.⁷⁵ Perhaps Rouffin's captors worked him for the answer they wanted to hear. But it is significant that those who rebelled against Laudonnière chose to prey upon ships and coastal communities in the Caribbean rather than sail back home, which suggests that this was something they had had in mind from the beginning. More broadly, it is inconceivable that, had Fort Caroline survived and prospered, the French would have resisted the temptation to go after the *flota*. What would happen, too, if a state of war were to exist between France and Spain? The Spanish may have overstated the immediate threat that Fort Caroline presented, but their reading of the longer-term strategic danger was fundamentally correct.

The Great Siege was not a world-historical sideshow, but we limit our understanding of it if we ignore the global context, which offers up compelling connections and points of comparison. Like the assault on Malta, the emerging tensions that would lead to the Dutch Revolt, the Ottoman confrontation with the Portuguese in the Indian Ocean and the Spanish elimination of Fort Caroline speak in different ways to the power of religious hatred to animate and exacerbate conflicts with roots in political and economic

Meanwhile...

competition; they are a reminder of the ideological benefits that regimes could reap by presenting themselves to their subjects and allies as guardians of religious orthodoxy. The tentative beginnings of the Manila Galleon are an indication that this was a world that was becoming increasingly integrated by complex circuits of production, trade and consumer demand. The Mediterranean remained an important element in these larger global circuits, but the strategic interests of the powers that sought to dominate it could no longer be limited to it alone. Perhaps the most intriguing comparison is that between the Great Siege and the denouement of the Spanish reaction to the French presence in Florida, for although the human scales were very different – tens of thousands of combatants in Malta, several hundreds in Florida – the same basic strategic calculus was at work. In both instances an expansive and aggressive power was reacting violently to the uncomfortable realization that its most important maritime supply line was threatened by a dangerous predator, weaker to be sure, but nonetheless capable of inflicting disproportionate damage on the Achilles heel of the economic system that sustained its imperial hegemony. Separated by 8,500 kilometres, Malta and Fort Caroline told essentially the same story at exactly the same time. In such circumstances, informed contemporaries were alive to the connection. For the Spanish in particular their assessments of the relative importance of the two places were not always what we might expect. As Raimond de Beccarie de Pavie, baron de Fourquevaux, the French ambassador to Philip II, observed to Charles IX in February 1566, when the Spanish had heard of Menéndez's destruction of Fort Caroline, the news had been greeted with undisguised delight: 'And the court rejoiced more than if this had been a victory won over the Turk. For they used to say, and still do, that Florida matters much, much more to them than Malta.'[76]

9.
And in the End

One of the most distinctive art spaces in the world, walked through by countless visitors to the Vatican as they make their way to the Sistine Chapel, is the Galleria delle Carte Geografiche. Along both sides of this corridor, built for Pope Gregory XIII (1572–85), there are forty painted maps of Italy, two of the whole area, the others of specific regions.[1] To walk along the gallery is effectively to travel the length of the Italian peninsula, depictions of areas facing the Adriatic to one side, of those facing the Tyrrhenian and Ligurian Seas to the other. The paintings, created by a team of artists working under the supervision of Egnazio Danti between 1579 and 1581, are large, measuring some four metres by three. Parts of the built environment of each region are shown, and in about half of the images there are historical vignettes, predominantly battles. On the ceiling further panels depict scenes from biblical and ecclesiastical history. The guiding principle informing the images as a complex is the beneficent reach of papal power in Italy. On the northern end of the corridor, however, the far end for the tourist heading for the Sistine Chapel, there is a change of scale. The door through which one exits the corridor is flanked by two depictions, of the Great Siege to the right, and of Corfu and the Christian defeat of the Ottoman fleet at the Battle of Lepanto in 1571, which took place near that island, to the left. These are not mere space-fillers: the inscription which guides the viewer in how to understand the whole schema of the gallery is placed between and above them. Both images resume the theme of the popes' authority, for the papacy contributed galleys to the Holy League that fought at Lepanto, and, although Malta as a place was not a papal fief, the Order of St John as an organization was directly answerable to Rome. By way of

And in the End

reinforcing this point, Malta's connection to the history of the papacy is further emphasized by three images on the ceiling directly above the door portraying St Paul's stay on the island.[2]

For all that the two images tie into the space as a whole, they also stand out from it in important ways. They are smaller than the regional maps, easier for the viewer to take in up close. While the same interest in the cartographical representation of space is in evidence, the emphasis is much more on conflict, which is rendered in greater detail and with more attention to historical specificity than the rather wispy depictions of combat in the main images along the corridor. There is also, from the perspective of a viewer when the images were first created, a notable difference in contemporary resonance. The battles depicted in the regional maps were mostly fought in Antiquity, especially during the Punic Wars, and only a few are medieval or early modern: the most recent is that fought between the French and the Spanish at Ceresole, in Piedmont, in 1544. In contrast the Great Siege and Lepanto would have still been recent history, an impression reinforced by the use of a *trompe l'oeil* effect which plays on their topicality by creating the illusion that the representations of the siege and battle have been painted on paper and pasted onto the wall as later additions.

The Great Siege is depicted by means of a bird's-eye view of Grand Harbour and Marsamxett, the composition centred on the Sciberras peninsula. It offers a conspectus of several phases of the siege, not a freeze-frame moment. St Elmo is shown being bombarded while a cluster of boats near the tip of Senglea evokes the amphibious assault on 15 July; the barricade in French Creek is clearly depicted. The image was not wholly original. It almost certainly drew on a print of the siege produced in 1565 by Antoine Lafréry, a French cartographer and engraver resident in Rome. It also has close affinities with some of the images in Matteo Perez d'Aleccio's famous pictorial rendering of the story of the siege in the Grand Master's Palace in Valletta, in particular a scene labelled *Dimostrazione di tutte le batterie* (Depiction of all the batteries). It is closer still to the corresponding image in Aleccio's prints of the Valletta wall paintings, which he published in 1582.[3] If that print was indeed a source for the Vatican artist, who may have been Antonio Tempesta, a member of Danti's team who was a specialist in the depiction of group scenes such as hunts and battles, this might suggest that the north-door panels were painted slightly later than the gallery as a whole.

Be that as it may, the important point to make is that the depiction of the siege in the Galleria is not a derivative recycling of other artists' visions: it has an interpretation of its own to communicate. In particular, it departs from its probable sources in placing less emphasis on the Ottoman artillery, apart from the batteries pounding St Elmo, and more on the size of the Turkish fleet, which is not only packed into Marsamxett but also stretches out towards the horizon. Ships, even more than guns, call to mind the power of the Ottoman state; they also establish a connection to the naval battle of Lepanto depicted on the matching panel on the other side of the door. There is no *gran soccorso* sweeping across the Maltese countryside to save the day – a possibility that Aleccio had made available had the artist wished to draw on it. In the Vatican image, the story of the siege is that of a very tight space subjected to, but resisting, the might of a very large enemy. As represented, this was not so much a victory as a dogged holding operation, the full significance of which would not play out until Lepanto – *the* victory, or so it was supposed – six years later. The rendering of the events of 1565 in the Galleria suggests that, even fifteen or more years after the fact, the question of the significance of the Great Siege was still open to debate. Yes, the siege had an epic quality, and that must surely mean that it was important. But in what ways? For how long would it make a difference? And on what sort of political or human scales were its impacts most in evidence? The Galleria suggests an answer by saying, in effect, that if one wishes to understand the Great Siege properly, the event in itself will only reveal so much; one has to look ahead to what happened *next*.

The Galleria's pairing of the Great Siege with Lepanto picked up on a connection that had been made since 1571, and which has continued to hang over the events of 1565: Malta and Lepanto, it seems, are joined at the hip. The siege is imagined as the 'one' of a one-two

And in the End

punch that stopped the Ottomans' expansion in the Mediterranean and was the tipping point in their fortunes, heralding their subsequent military and political decline. There are three compelling arguments against such a view. The first is that Lepanto ended up being all heat and no light. In the moment it appeared to be a crushing victory for the Christian allies, as measured by the large number of Ottoman galleys sunk or captured. And it certainly had a significant impact on the collective psyche of a Christian Europe beleaguered by a long history of Ottoman military success: in *Don Quixote*, Cervantes, who fought in the battle, has his *alter ego* the captive remark that Lepanto was that happy day which cast down the Ottomans' pride and disabused Christendom of its belief that the Turks were invincible at sea.[4] In practical, strategic terms, however, Lepanto changed very little.[5] The Ottomans rebuilt their fleet remarkably quickly, and although the defeat made subsequent expansion into the western Mediterranean less likely, their control of the eastern Mediterranean as their 'lake' remained unthreatened. Second, it is raising all sorts of questions to suppose that the 1560s and 1570s were the high point of Ottoman power or success, after which the only way was down. Power and success as measured against what criteria? The Ottoman polity had a great deal of life left in it. Third, the pairing of the Great Siege and Lepanto can all too easily get folded into a tired narrative about the 'clash of civilizations' between Islam and Christianity. Framing the siege in such overblown terms does a disservice to all the people who were caught up in the events of 1565 or affected by them in some way; the human richness, variety and in-the-moment actuality of their experiences do not reduce to such trite slogans.

In what ways, then, was the Great Siege significant? Its most enduring impact was the transformation of the Grand Harbour area. The siege had cruelly confirmed the need to fortify the peninsula between Grand Harbour and Marsamxett that had been apparent to the order since 1524. After the raid of 1551 the building of St Elmo had been a cost-effective way of securing the entrances to the two harbours; but as the events of June 1565 had shown, control of the higher ground above it was essential.[6] The highest points of the peninsula are a plateau, Mount Sciberras, and what is now Castile Heights to the south. The dimensions of their combined space, and the contours of the peninsula as a whole, meant that a relatively compact fortress, a kind of larger, stronger twin to St Elmo below it, would not suffice. The size of the area that the new fortifications would need to contain meant that whatever was built would perforce become inhabited as well as defended space, a blending, on a larger scale, of the functions of Birgu and St Angelo. The plans submitted to the order by two visiting Italian military architects, Bartolomeo Genga and Baldassare Lanci, in 1558 and 1562, respectively, had already envisaged the creation of what amounted to a new city. Genga was the more ambitious, proposing that the defensive line on the land side – the single most important part of the fortifications – should be drawn beyond what is now the suburb of Floriana. If this plan had been adopted, the surface area of the future Valletta would have been about twice its eventual size. Lanci's proposal was more practical, establishing the defensive line at the highest point about halfway up the peninsula; and it was broadly his vision that was followed by the architect who actually got to build on Sciberras, Francesco Laparelli.[7]

La Valette had always been a particular advocate of fortifying the peninsula, and now the siege presented him with an unrepeatable opportunity. There was, however, disagreement on this issue. It was possible to argue in the immediate aftermath of the siege that the priority was to rebuild on the footprint of the existing fortifications. Much needed to be done: visitors to Grand Harbour from the *gran soccorso* had expressed amazement at the ruinous state of the defences. With a Turkish *revanche* expected in early summer 1566, and with funds limited, it could be argued that it did not make sense to divert precious resources to the building of a wholly new site: in addition to sucking in money better spent elsewhere, it would be many years before such a large fortification was fully functional, and in the meantime the people building it and the soldiers who would be needed to guard them would be extremely vulnerable to a Turkish assault. La Valette therefore needed to act quickly to exploit the wave of sympathy created by the siege. European rulers were solicited for funds and in some cases actually made substantial contributions; and it was agreed with Pope Pius IV that he should send Laparelli, his own principal military architect, to Malta. Laparelli arrived in December, an indication of the element of rush, and had already submitted two reports about how best to proceed by the end of January 1566.[8]

Even as progress was being made towards securing the Knights' future in Malta, however, La Valette was sending out contrary diplomatic signals to the effect that the order was willing to abandon the island, or at least substantially scale down its presence there. There was talk of withdrawing most of the convent to Sicily and leaving a reduced garrison in Malta as a forward position, much as Tripoli had been. Failing that, the order might relocate in its entirety to Sicily or elsewhere: Corsica had been suggested in the past, and the French believed that La Valette had his eye on the Îles d'Hyères, just off the southern French coast near Toulon.[9] There was a good deal of scepticism in European courts about such threats, but they were not idle rhetoric.[10] They meant that Valletta was begun, not so much as a bold step into a brighter future, but rather as a tentative, provisional exercise, an option that could be abandoned at any moment. Only gradually, as the money from abroad started to come in, and many hundreds of masons and labourers from Sicily were shipped over to complement the Maltese workforce, did the new city become a kind of self-fulfilling prophecy. Laparelli's clarity of vision, as well as his ability to reassure a frequently anxious and wavering La Valette, proved vital. Various grandees, including the duke of Alba and Ascanio della Corgna of *gran soccorso* fame, had muddied the waters by suggesting different schemes; but the support of Laparelli on the part of the well-connected military expert (and Knight of the order) Gabrio Serbelloni, who had been Laparelli's patron, proved decisive.[11] On 28 March 1566 the first stone of Valletta – the decision to name it after the Grand Master had already been made – was ceremoniously laid; and in November 1569 the General Chapter of the order formally decreed what everyone already took as read, that the convent would soon be relocated from

Birgu to the new city. The official transfer took place in March 1571.[12] Valletta would develop into a complex and vibrant urban space – the filling in of buildings along its distinctive grid pattern of streets was largely complete by the mid to late 1570s – but it was also in effect a monument to the siege. And so, in some ways, it remains.

A visitor to Valletta today, on seeing the impressive defences, would be forgiven for coming away with the notion that here is evidence of a confident and revitalized order, reconnected to its historical sense of mission and newly assured that Malta was its true home. Taking the long view, such an impression would broadly correspond with the image of itself that the order cultivated in the seventeenth and eighteenth centuries. Valletta, the rebuilt Great Siege fortresses and in due course further fortification programmes allowed the Knights to imagine that Malta was nothing less than the *propugnaculum*, the bulwark or forward defence, of Christendom. Admirers of the order endorsed this view.[13] But the picture that the sources present of the first few decades immediately after the siege is not so straightforward: what emerges is a fractious and fragile group of men, struggling on a psychological as well as an economic, military and demographic level to come to terms with the effects of the siege. There was an element of delayed reaction, for the exigencies of the siege in the moment had encouraged a sense of solidarity that was sustained by the shared experience of acute danger. It is significant that, other than criminals on the run, only one member of the order, a senior Aragonese Knight named Luis de Salcedo, is known to have fled the island before the arrival of the Ottoman armada; in early May 1565 he hid himself on a Spanish galley and made it to Messina, where he was discovered and packed off back to Malta by one of the order's representatives in Sicily, Rafaele Salvago. He survived the siege and, in part thanks to a generous donation towards the cost of building works, was able to resume positions of responsibility thereafter.[14] If others were tempted to follow Salcedo's example, considerations of honour and reputation would have been a powerful deterrent. Chains of military command also helped to hold things together. As we saw in an earlier chapter, La

And in the End

Valette just about kept on top of the near-mutinous mood among the Knights who had sent him the letter from St Elmo in June, the most serious and organized challenge to his authority during the siege. But once the immediate threat passed on 12 September, all sorts of unresolved tensions and animosities could now surface.

It is noteworthy that some of this came from the top. As early as October, La Valette and the Council were initiating disciplinary action against Knights who, it was supposed, had failed to obey the summons to Malta before the siege; there is a suggestion that in some cases these were marked men with a reputation for disobedience before 1565, but the siege now raised the stakes, and the pursuit of the supposed no-shows had an unmistakably vindictive edge to it.[15] By 1567 there is evidence of emerging dissent among some sections of the order; this would seem to have found expression as criticism of La Valette's conduct of the defence against the Turks and his governance of the order. *Libelli diffamatori*, booklets or posters displayed in public places, began to be circulated.[16] The Grand Master came down on the dissenters and their supporters unusually hard, evidence, perhaps, of insecurity and a fear that the mood of dissatisfaction extended substantially beyond a handful of malcontents.

The fact that those Knights known to have been most vocal in their criticism were Spanish suggests that the sorts of national tensions that had been in evidence in the past, for example in 1551, were now making themselves felt once more. This receives some oblique confirmation from Brantôme's comment that when he travelled to Malta with a party of noblemen and soldiers in 1566, La Valette was especially pleased to have an opportunity to spend time with his fellow Frenchmen.[17] More direct evidence is provided by the exceptionally harsh punishment handed down to a senior Castilian Knight, Antonio Maldonado, for having aided the rebellious brethren. Maldonado was a prominent figure in the order, an experienced naval commander and diplomat with close connections to the Spanish court: in January 1566 it was he who was sent to Philip II to raise funds, a particularly important mission, and he had returned with a magnificent gift from the king for the Grand Master, a golden sword and dagger (now in the Louvre).[18] He had also taken part in the *gran soccorso*. But his service in the siege availed him little. He was sentenced to deprivation of the habit, perhaps as a precursor to his being handed over to the secular court for the passing of the death penalty. This was then commuted to ten years in prison on Gozo, an unusually long sentence; particular care, it was stipulated, should be taken to ensure that the locks to his cell were secure at all times.[19]

Although it is difficult to establish a direct connection, it is tempting to see the ripple effects of the siege in the most convulsive moment of crisis to beset the order in the years after 1565. In 1581 the Grand Master, Jean de La Cassière, was deposed in a coup by a cadre of disaffected Knights. Romegas, a hero of the siege and the order's most famous sea captain, was prevailed upon by the plotters to be their front man, though he himself seems always to have acted towards La Cassière scrupulously and with honour.[20] This was a moment of acute crisis: the viceroy of Sicily, Marc Antonio Colonna, was so worried that Malta would be left defenceless while the order turned in on itself that he shipped a substantial body of troops over to the island. The immediate trigger for the revolt, unsurprisingly perhaps, was a puritanical edict to expel the prostitutes and courtesans from Valletta. But its deeper roots lay in what it was claimed were La Cassière's authoritarian and high-handed methods, and more deeply still in his wish to re-emphasize the religious vocation of the order, as against the ethos of military, masculine bravado that had become attached to and validated by the memory of the siege, and which a figure such as Romegas personified so well. National antagonisms, by now an almost automatic corollary of tensions within the order, were also at play.[21] Both La Cassière and Romegas went to Rome to present their cases to Gregory XIII, and both died there, Romegas perhaps the victim of poisoning. This was a bitter dispute that split the order down the middle: the future historian of the order Giacomo Bosio, who supported La Cassière, killed a Knight of the opposing camp in a duel. In the end it was the implacable imposition of papal authority that suppressed the revolt.

And in the End

The pope threw his weight behind the order's ruling elite, and the next Grand Master, Hugues de Loubens de Verdalle, was able to restore calm to some extent while at the same time vigorously reconstituting the sort of top-down governance of the order that had been his predecessor's undoing.[22]

If the siege contributed to disequilibrium and tension within the ranks of the Knights, there was also the more prosaic fact that, for all its success in surviving the Turkish invasion, the order's slender human and logistical margins continued to make it as vulnerable to serious setbacks as it had always been before 1565. This was most clearly demonstrated in 1570, when the order's four operational galleys, under the command of the captain-general François de Saint-Clément and with a larger than average complement of Knights on board, went on manoeuvres in Sicilian waters in conjunction with Gianandrea Doria's fleet. Rashly disregarding intelligence that a force of twenty Algerian galliots under Uluç Ali was prowling nearby, Saint-Clément sailed his flotilla out to sea from Licata; several Knights, as well as some sailors, were so opposed to this course of action that they stayed ashore. The order's galleys were jumped by Uluç Ali's fleet off Gozo, and two, the *Santa Anna* and the *San Giovanni*, were captured; in the case of the *Santa Anna* poor seamanship had compounded its difficulties.[23] (As we have seen, the representation of St John on the *San Giovanni* would go on public display in Algiers, hung upside down in a gesture of humiliation.)[24] For his part, Saint-Clément in the *Capitana* tried to make a run for it but ran aground, and his galley too was captured, though most of those on board were able to scramble to safety. Only the *Santa Maria della Vittoria* escaped. About eighty Knights on the *Santa Anna* and *San Giovanni*, perhaps a quarter of all those resident in the convent at that time, were killed or taken prisoner.

Saint-Clément compounded his error by abandoning the order's standard, a powerful taboo, as he made his escape; it was retrieved and taken back to Malta by a Maltese made of sterner stuff, Michele Calli. Pius V insisted that Saint-Clément, at large in Italy and naturally reluctant to face the music, should return to Malta and stand trial. He did so and was found guilty, stripped of his habit and condemned to death by the secular court. There was a great deal of agitation against Saint-Clément among the population of Grand Harbour, which had lost so many of its own in the disaster. For this reason, perhaps, he was discreetly strangled in his cell, after which his body was rowed out to sea under cover of darkness and thrown overboard in a weighted sack. He was not the only one to pay with his life. His pilot, the Maltese Orlando Magro, had been a hero of the siege, bravely running messages to and from Sicily. Captured by the Turks, in late July 1565 he had been made to approach the front lines at Provence and shout out an offer of terms if the defenders surrendered: Balbi tells us that Magro made it abundantly clear from the awkward intervals between his sentences that he was mechanically repeating what he was being forced to say. Magro must have escaped from his captivity at some point and returned to his employment with the order. Bosio tells us that people regretted that someone who had rendered such conspicuous service during the siege should be caught up in the disaster of 1570. But in the end this was of no help to him, and he was hanged, his death an indication that the afterglow of the siege, a mere five years after the fact, only counted for so much when the order lashed out at those whose mistakes had exposed its underlying weaknesses.[25]

In contrast to the order's experience, the Ottoman empire had the sheer size, the human and financial resources, and the traditions of respect for higher authority to ride out the consequences of the siege, and by extension to come to terms with its failure. True, there is evidence immediately after the siege of panic in parts of the Muslim Mediterranean; and in October 1565, as the fleet returned home, Antoine de Petremol, the French ambassador in Istanbul, remarked that it was unsafe for any Christian to be seen in public when news of the defeat reached the city, such was the public mood of vengeful grief.[26] Malta was a setback to be sure, the more galling for being unusual and coming after the euphoria that had greeted the victory at Djerba, but no more than that. As we have seen, the recuperative powers of the Ottoman military apparatus were soon in evidence as new galleys were constructed to bring the fleet back up to strength. This rejuvenated force announced itself in 1566 by taking Chios, a soft target to be sure, and sailing into the Adriatic, where it caused a great deal of alarm.[27]

Clearly there was an imperative to reassert the Ottomans' military reputation, for in the same year a large campaign was undertaken in central Europe. In a sense, Süleyman was an indirect casualty of the siege of Malta, for, stung into action, he chose to lead his army in person for the first time since the early 1550s. He died in his tent as his army besieged the Hungarian fortress of Szigetvár in September 1566. The fratricidal contest for the succession had already been played out during Süleyman's reign, and experienced viziers were at the helm, so the accession of the new sultan, Selim II, proceeded smoothly. Some Christian writers, indulging in the cliché of the Ottoman polity as a violent despotism, liked to suppose that Mustafa Pasha and Piyale Pasha would forfeit their lives when they brought their defeated forces back to Istanbul. But this did not happen; Mustafa accompanied the sultan on the Hungarian campaign, and Piyale prospered, in due course being promoted to the vizierate.

On the Christian side, García de Toledo took an active part in the flurry of activity immediately after the siege, arranging for reinforcements to be sent to the island in case the Ottomans were minded to return, commenting on the plans for fortifying Sciberras and advising Philip II. But he was soon replaced as viceroy of Sicily, and would seem to have been eased out of public life thereafter, in part, perhaps, because he had attracted rather unfair criticism of his organization of the reliefs. Jean de La Valette lived long enough to galvanize the efforts to defend and prop up Malta in the years immediately after the siege, and to see the city that bore his name begin to take shape on Mount Sciberras, but not long enough, other than in his harsh suppression of dissent among the Knights, to have to confront the aftershocks of the events of 1565. He died, probably of a stroke, in August 1568.

By that time La Valette's status as a military hero had become secure. Although one sees in the burst of contemporary historical writing about the siege an emerging tension – was the victory an achievement that belonged to the Knights, to *Hispania victrix* (Spain the victorious) or to a reinvigorated Counter-Reformation Catholic world in general? – there was a widespread consensus that La Valette personally had had a very good war.[28] One glimpses this, for example, in Brantôme's adoring recollections of his encounters with the Grand Master in 1566: here he is elevated to the status of a paragon of noble virtue.[29] La Valette certainly did a lot right during the siege, especially in his efforts to sustain St Elmo for as long as possible; but his reputation benefitted from the tendency of observers to treat collective endeavours as the individual achievements of those in charge, and those individual achievements as manifestations of aristocratic values. Because events turned out as they did, La Valette's actions could be spun to conform to this pattern: when he exposed himself to danger during the assaults on Castile in August, for instance, what was probably in the moment a resigned acceptance of the near certainty of defeat could be reworked as once-more-unto-the-breach leadership at its finest. Any competent Knight steeped in the traditions of the order could have conducted the defence of Malta as well as La Valette, if not better. But he was the man on the spot when the storm broke; he just about held things together; and he got a city named after him to prove it.[30]

Rather like the Battle of Lepanto on the other side of the north door in the Galleria delle Carte Geografiche, the Great Siege of Malta was a momentous, epic event that changed very little. The Ottomans' recovery after 1565, and even more so after Lepanto, demonstrated that they remained the predominant power in the Mediterranean.[31] The resources brought to bear on the conquest of Cyprus in 1570–71 and the reconquest of Tunis in 1574 made this abundantly clear. When Spanish overtures for a ceasefire were first entertained in 1573 and developed into a formal truce by the end of the decade, this was not an admission of weakness on the Sublime Porte's part. Spain's programme of galley-building since before the siege had reached the point that the two powers found themselves caught in an expensive arms race that neither wanted or needed.[32] For the next few decades, moreover, the Ottomans' military priorities were in the east against Iran and on the central European front. Spanish attention, meanwhile, was drawn more to its wars in the Netherlands, and, as an extension of that primary conflict, competition with England. But on neither side could this be characterized as a retreat from the Mediterranean, still less an acknowledgement that this sea was declining in economic and geopolitical significance.[33] The Mediterranean still mattered and remained a vital part of the world economic system: witness the appearance there from around 1580 of Dutch and English ships muscling in on the carrying trade from eastern ports. If one were to use the English experience to illustrate what really counted in the later sixteenth century, one should not look at Francis Drake's various acts of derring-do in the Caribbean or the what-if of the Lost Colony on Roanoke because they in some way point to the Atlantic economy of the future, but rather to the less splashy efforts of English merchants and Elizabeth I's government to cultivate commercial links with the Ottomans. That was where the money was.[34]

In all this, the same strategic considerations that would have made it very difficult for the Turks to occupy Malta in 1565 continued to apply. As the Ottoman fleet became less of a presence in the central and western Mediterranean after the mid 1570s – though there would continue to be several scares – and the rhythms of the cruel sea reverted to the *Kleinkrieg* of predatory raids, the order was able to position itself as an exponent of a counter-*corso* equipped to take on the Barbary corsairs at their own game. To this limited extent its navy was broadly successful up to the first half of the eighteenth century. The order's vessels could make a contribution to the efforts on the part of the authorities in the Christian western Mediterranean to protect their coastlines; and for people living on those vulnerable shores, that might be no small matter. But that was about as far as it went. The rhetoric of Malta as the *propugnaculum*, Christendom's first line of defence, was just that: nine parts self-image and one part, at most, geopolitical and military realism.

The more one looks at the Great Siege dispassionately and avoids the trap of overstating its importance with reference to a 'clash of civilizations' master narrative, the more one is drawn to the experiences of the people who went through it. We shall never know most of their names, nor have more than a general idea of what they may have looked like. But they were the people who lived through the siege or died during it, and they are the reason why the events of 1565 should command our attention. The central fact that these people would have confronted was death. The number of Turkish fatalities is very difficult to establish, in part because of the uncertainty surrounding the size of their forces on Malta as a whole that we considered in an earlier chapter, and partly because Christian authors tended to inflate the figures. Given that the number of enemy casualties ventured by Christian sources ranges between the low tens of thousands and the mid 20,000s, an estimate of between 13,000 and 15,000, of whom about two thirds would have been front-line troops and the remainder auxiliary personnel and galley crews, is probably somewhere near the mark.[35]

If so, that would mean that the 533 named men who are recorded losing their lives in the *Ottoman Campaign Register* would represent only about 3–4 per cent of all the Turkish fatalities; in fact this total amounts to an even smaller proportion of those who died on Malta, because 170 of the names are of those who drowned, most of them almost certainly in the shipwreck off Greece on the outward voyage in which several hundred *sipahis* are known to have perished.[36] For all that the register only captures a fraction of those who died, however, their names may stand for all their nameless colleagues: Osman, whose *timar* was in Biga in north-western Turkey, killed at St Elmo; Ilyas bin Yusuf, a gunner stationed in Rhodes, killed at Senglea; Ferhad, a *tüfenkçi* (arquebusier) from Egypt, killed at Birgu.[37] The Turks were solicitous about the decorous treatment of their dead: Laparelli records that several burial pits were discovered during the building work on Sciberras; and it struck Balbi as noteworthy that it was only towards the very end of the siege, when the Turks' energy and morale were ebbing away, that they abandoned their accustomed efforts to retrieve the bodies of their fallen comrades if at all possible. At the conclusion of the siege, however, there were so many unburied Turkish dead that there was fear of an epidemic; that did not materialize, but there was a plague of flies in Birgu.[38]

We have the most precise data on the casualty rates among the Hospitallers. There were approximately 580 members of the order, about 470 Knights and 110 brother-sergeants and priests, on Malta in May. At the end, about 230 of these Knights were still alive.[39] Some of those who had arrived with the *piccolo soccorso* would also have died, of course. A 50 per cent mortality rate was bad enough, but that tells only part of the story, for many more were grievously injured. It was reckoned that at the end of hostilities only 600 defenders remained in Birgu and Senglea fit enough to bear arms, and one suspects that the order accounted for only a small part of that total.[40] Some of the effects of the fighting could be undone in time: Pietro del Monte had some sort of emotional and physical collapse during the siege and had to be relieved of his command of Senglea, but he went on to become La Valette's successor as Grand Master.[41] Most wounds could not heal, however. To have met a veteran of the siege in the years after 1565 would in a great many instances have been to encounter an invalid.[42]

The death rate among the soldiers fighting alongside the Knights would appear to have been the same, about 50 per cent. The condition of a few of those who survived can be glimpsed in the order's records of letters of accreditation issued to soldiers and adventurers when their period of service in Malta came to an end, sometimes with the grant of a pension. Thus we learn that Antonio de Embun arrived on the island on 7 May, and was wounded in the head by a shot from an arquebus, in addition to suffering many other inconveniences. Diego de Aranda lost his left arm in the fighting at St Michael. Luigi Rocca arrived with the *piccolo soccorso* and was wounded in the right hand – of particular significance to someone who made his living from fighting. Pedro de Escovedo was shot in the throat by an arquebus and almost entirely lost the ability to speak. Sigismund Talhammer from Hallstatt was wounded in both the foot and thigh in the defence of St Elmo, while Benedetto Sanguineo was struck in both legs by a cannonball. Antonio de las Cuencas was injured in the left hand in St Elmo but then served at St Michael and Castile even though the wound had not had time to heal.[43] These records were in the business of noting the physical rather than the psychological effects of the siege. But perhaps we can glimpse what we might now identify as the effects of trauma in the case of an Italian soldier, Pomponio, who had served as a scribe in the order's chancery in addition to fighting at St Michael and Castile. After the siege he sought permission to leave Malta so that he might 'wander around the world, visiting and seeing all sorts of places'.[44] A sense of psychological dislocation, channelled into spiritual yearning, may similarly have informed the intention of a Maltese, Thoma Masi, who had fought in Birgu throughout the siege, to leave the island so that he might fulfil a vow that he had made to go on pilgrimage to Our Lady of Loreto in Italy.[45]

Masi's experience reminds us that most of those who held out in Senglea and Birgu were Maltese. About 5,000 died there, possibly more: even a low estimate would amount to about 20–25 per cent of the population of the island.[46] During the siege, of course, the Maltese would have been subject to the same dangers as the soldiers and Knights. The Grand Master's Maltese tailor, Marco Mastro, for example, was burned to death fighting on 20 August.[47] It is also among the Maltese that we would expect to find the greatest impacts of psychological distress, poverty, malnutrition, disease and mortality in the weeks, months, even years after the Ottomans sailed away. The last casualties of the siege did not die in September 1565. The effects of the siege on the people of Malta also spread beyond those who had been in Senglea and Birgu. There survives a remarkable series of documents, beginning as early as late 1565, and peaking in number in 1566–7, which record the petitions of Maltese peasants for relief from the payment of dues and debts because of the damage done to their farms and the disruption to their livelihoods caused by the Turks. Some documents simply refer elliptically to the 'very great damage' wrought by the *armata turchesca*. But

And in the End

others take us closer to individual experience. Dominico Vella, for example, seems to have come out better than many, conceding in January 1566 that he still had six head of cattle and their harness, but pleading nonetheless that he had lost all his other livestock and had been unable to gather in his harvest. In another petition three men, Benedetto, Antonino and Thomassio Sciberras, probably brothers, were made to declare that they had been so *ruinati* by the Turks' theft of their food and animals that they could no longer endure *la misera vita* to which they had been reduced.[48]

It is to people such as these that one's mind turns when considering the impact and significance of the Great Siege. Yes, the conflict was fuelled in large part by deep hatreds born of the bitter experience of the cruel sea, a kind of ingrained and instinctive reflex that was shared by people from all walks of life. But such visceral animosities could only achieve precise definition and direction when they were co-opted by the ambitions of the powerful. It was powerful men who created the conditions in which the Great Siege could take place and who made it happen. The Maltese, more than any other group of people, were those caught in the middle of a competition pursued by and for others. This is why, in the end, what happened in 1565 is a story that belongs to them.

Postscript

The Great Siege was certainly memorable, and that made it ripe for commemoration. One thinks of the many written accounts that began to appear even before the end of 1565 and which culminated a little more than thirty years later in Bosio's exhaustive and encyclopaedic treatment. One thinks too of Aleccio's famous wall paintings in the Grand Master's Palace in Valletta, now the staple resource if one wishes to re-create something of the visual impression that the siege made on those who were there. But the commemorative impulse could also go in less august, more unorthodox directions. Brantôme notes that when he was in Malta in 1566, he encountered a Spanish captain who suggested that a monument to the siege should be built out of the bones of the Turkish dead.[49] This was not as gratuitously macabre an idea as it might seem, for it must have been intended as a calculated riposte to the notorious tower of Christian, mostly Spanish, skulls that had been erected by the victors on Djerba in 1560 (and which stood until the nineteenth century). The plan came to nothing, but it is an interesting indication that the memory of the siege could be bound up in larger patterns of conflicts and resentments in the Mediterranean, not simply apprehended as a stand-alone epic event.

And so, in word and image, the materials were put in place for the memory of the Great Siege to endure. Voltaire's oft-quoted remark, in his *Annales de l'Empire* published in 1753, that 'nothing is better known than this siege' is not, as it might at first sight appear, an expression of ennui, but rather an authorial sleight-of-hand to allow him to focus on the subject matter of his work, the Holy Roman Empire, without getting unduly drawn into events, however important, in the Mediterranean.[50] The dodge relied for its effect on Voltaire's reasonable assumption that his readers would be perfectly familiar with the story themselves. Nearly two centuries after the fact, the memory of the Great Siege, it appears, was still going strong. In more recent times, that memory came to be reanimated by the fierce assault on Malta by the aerial and naval forces of Italy and Germany between 1940 and 1943.[51] Malta was absolutely pummelled from the air, becoming one of the most bombed places in the world. The Regia Aeronautica and Luftwaffe between them flew about 70,000 sorties over the island, which is to say the same as the number of cannonballs that the Ottomans fired in 1565. Tens of thousands of buildings were destroyed or badly damaged. Meanwhile the Axis attempted to starve the Maltese islands into submission by attacking supply convoys from the air and by submarine. Perhaps the single most evocative image of this 'greater siege' is of the tanker SS *Ohio* limping into Grand Harbour in August 1942 with its precious cargo of the fuel that would sustain the island and its defences for a little longer. So badly damaged that its freeboard was down to a matter of a few feet as it reached Malta, the *Ohio* was one of the few survivors of a convoy, Operation Pedestal, which had been almost completely destroyed.[52] The *Ohio* came to stand for Malta's dogged survival against the odds. Defining moments such as this, and Malta's remarkable resilience over the course of the Second World War, which cannot be overstated, meant that there now seemed to be a pattern of tenacious defiance of strong and fearsome aggressors: 1565 was not a one-off.

The Great Siege had already become a topical and politically charged memory before the Second World War, however. In 1927 a monument to it was erected close to St John's Co-Cathedral on the main thoroughfare in the middle of Valletta, what is now Triq ir-Repubblika. It is a very austere piece of bronze sculpture, hovering somewhere between neoclassical and avant-garde with art deco influences. It comprises three figures: a central male, gaunt and powerful, representing valour or fortitude, who stares unflinchingly out towards the viewer, and two females, representing faith and civilization, who are set behind and to the sides of the male, directing their appreciative gazes towards him. There are distant nods to the sixteenth century, or at least to a premodern past of some sort, in the male figure's helmet and sword, but this was not designed as a period piece. It was, instead, intended as an uncompromisingly contemporary object. This is not surprising, for the installation of the monument was a highly political act at a time when there was substantial support in Malta for an end to British rule and a closer relationship, even federation, with Italy.[53] The sculptor was a Maltese, Antonio Sciortino, who had many contacts with Italian artists, some of whom were connected to Mussolini's regime. The attraction of ties to the Italian state, which had already been losing some of its appeal in the 1930s, disappeared for good as soon as the Regia Aeronautica dropped its first bombs on Malta in June 1940 – this was one of Mussolini's first acts on entering the war. But the monument has lived on, a ceremonial focal point for one of the main Maltese public holidays, Victory Day on 8 September, which combines a Marian feast day, the Nativity of the Blessed Virgin Mary, with a commemoration of both sieges, as well as of Maltese resistance during the brief period of French rule between 1798 and 1800.

There matters stood, the monument part of the architecture, literally and figuratively, of Maltese public memory, until a shocking act of murderous violence meant that the resonances of the Great Siege would be revisited anew. On 16 October 2017 the campaigning journalist Daphne Caruana Galizia was killed by a car bomb near her home in Bidnija. She had long been a thorn in the side of the Maltese political establishment, and had recently been investigating murky and illicit connections between politicians and overseas money. The Maltese people took to the streets of Valletta to protest against the corruption and political malfeasance that they believed, correctly, lay behind Caruana Galizia's assassination. One of the protestors carried a sign that read 'Our country is under siege again. Only this time the enemy is within.' A spontaneous memorial of photographs, candles, flowers and messages of support soon grew up at the foot of the Great Siege monument, a suitably convenient and dignified location because Triq ir-Repubblika was the epicentre of the protests. At first the Maltese authorities routinely sent in road-cleaners, at night, to sweep the memorial away, but the protestors went to court to put a stop to this and won. There are other, more formal monuments to Caruana Galizia's memory, in Sliema where she was from, and in the European Parliament building in Strasbourg. But at the time of writing, in 2024, the Valletta memorial is still going strong. It is in a sense *the* memorial not just because of its organic origins in the wave of popular protests, but also because it plugs into powerful currents within the Maltese historical consciousness by co-opting an earlier memory, an earlier state of siege. There are several pictures of Caruana Galizia placed around the Great Siege monument, but a copy of what has become the canonical image of her takes centre stage. It is propped up against the front face of the plinth supporting Sciortino's sculpture, and visible immediately above it is the plinth's succinct carved inscription, a simple Roman numeral: MDLXV. 1565.

List of Abbreviations

AOM	Archives of the Order of Malta [National Library of Malta]
Balbi (1567)	*Diario del Gran Asedio de Malta 1565*, ed. Q. Aldea Vaquero and L. Zolle (Madrid, 2007) [a rendering with modern orthography of Francesco Balbi da Correggio, *La verdadera relación de todo lo que este añode M.D.LXV. ha sucedido en la Isla de Malta* (Henares, 1567)]
Balbi (1568)	Francesco Balbi da Correggio, *La verdadera relación de todo lo que este año de M.D.LXV. ha sucedido en la Isla de Malta* (Barcelona, 1568)
Besieged	*Besieged: Malta 1565*, ed. M. Camilleri, 2 vols. (Valletta, 2015)
Bosio	Giacomo Bosio, *Dell'istoria della Sacra Religione et Ill.ma Militia di S. Giovanni Gierosolimitano: parte terza* (Rome, 1602)
Brantôme	Pierre de Bourdeille, seigneur de Brantôme, *Oeuvres complètes*, ed. L. Lalanne, 11 vols. (Paris, 1864–82)
Brogini, *1565*	A. Brogini, *1565, Malte dans la tourmente: Le 'Grand Siège' de l'île par les Turcs* (Paris, 2011)
Brogini, *Malte*	A. Brogini, *Malte, frontière de Chrétienté (1530–1670)* (Rome, 2006)
Cambridge History	*The Cambridge History of Turkey*, vol. 2: *The Ottoman Empire as a World Power, 1454–1603*, ed. S. N. Faroqhi and K. Fleet (Cambridge, 2013)
Cirni	Antonfrancesco Cirni, *Comentarii . . . ne quali si descriue la guerra ultima di Francia, la celebratione del Concilio Tridentino, il soccorso d'Orano, l'impresa*

	del Pignone, e l'historia del'assedio di Malta (Rome, 1567)
CODOIN	Colección de documentos inéditos para la historia de España, ed. M. Salvá y Munar et al., 112 vols. (Madrid, 1842–95)
Ottoman Campaign Register	The 1565 Ottoman Malta Campaign Register, ed. A. Cassola et al. (San Ġwann, 1998)
Relazioni	Relazioni degli ambasciatori veneti al Senato, ed. E. Albèri, 15 vols. (Florence, 1839–63) [All references are from ser. III: Relazioni degli stati ottomani]
Setton, *Papacy*	K. M. Setton, *The Papacy and the Levant (1204–1571)*, 4 vols. (Philadelphia, 1976–84)
Spiteri, *Great Siege*	S. C. Spiteri, *The Great Siege: Knights vs Turks MDLXV: Anatomy of a Hospitaller Victory* (Tarxien, 2005)
Vendôme	Pierre Gentil de Vendôme, *Le siège de Malte par les Turcs en 1565*, ed. H. Pernot (Paris, 1910)
Viperano	Giovanni Antonio Viperano, *De bello melitensi historia* (Perugia, 1567)

Bibliography

Primary Sources

Manuscript Sources

Mdina, Cathedral Archives, Curia Episcopalis Melitensis, Acta Originalia
    Ms 46: N 1, N 11, N 17, N 28, N 31, N 37, N 43, N 48, N 52, N 62, N 63
Vatican City, Biblioteca Apostolica
    Ms Vat. lat. 7750
Valletta, National Library of Malta, Archives of the Order of Malta
    Libri Conciliorum 87, 88, 89, 90, 91, 92, 93, 94
    Libri Bullarum 429, 430, 431, 432, 433

Printed Sources

The 1565 Ottoman Malta Campaign Register, ed. A. Cassola et al. (San Ġwann, 1998).
Aleccio, Matteo Perez d', *I veri retratti della guerra e dell'assedio et assalti dati all'isola di Malta dall'armata turchesca l'anno 1565* (Rome, 1582).
Archives ou correspondance inédite de la maison d'Orange-Nassau, vol. I: *1552–1565*, ed. G. Groen van Prinsterer (Leiden, 1835).
'L'Assedio di Malta. Informatione di Malta del "Rangone"', ed. H. P. Scicluna, *Archivum Melitense*, 8 (1929), 35–42.
Autun, Jean Quintin d', *The Earliest Description of Malta (Lyons, 1536)*, ed. and trans. H. C. R. Vella (Sliema, 1980).
Balbi da Correggio, Francesco, *Diario del Gran Asedio de Malta 1565*, ed. Q. Aldea Vaquero and L. Zolle (Madrid, 2007); *La vera relación de todo lo que este año de M.D.LXV. ha sucedido en la Isla de Malta* (Barcelona, 1568).
Barbarigo, Antonio, 'Sommario della relazione', in *Relazioni*, iii, pp. 145–60.

Barbarigo, Daniele, 'Relazione dell'impero ottomano', in *Relazioni*, ii, pp. 1–59.
Belon, Pierre, *Voyage au Levant: Les observations de Pierre Belon du Mans de plusieurs singularités et choses mémorables, trouvées en Grèce, Turquie, Judée, Égypte, Arabie et autres pays étranges (1553)*, ed. A. Merle (Paris, 2001).
Bosio, Giacomo, *Dell'istoria della Sacra Religione et Ill.ma Militia di S. Giovanni Gierosolimitano: parte terza* (Rome, 1602).
Brantôme, Pierre de Bourdeille, seigneur de, *Oeuvres complètes*, ed. L. Lalanne, 11 vols. (Paris, 1864–82).
Busbecq, Ogier Ghiselin de, *Legationis turcicae epistolae quatuor* (Paris, 1595); trans. E. S. Forster, *The Turkish Letters of Ogier Ghiselin de Busbecq*, rev. edn (Baton Rouge, 2005).
Calendar of State Papers, Spain (Simancas), vol. 1: *1558–1567*, ed. M. A. S. Hume (London, 1892).
Catherine de' Medici, *Lettres de Catherine de Médicis*, ed. C. H. de la Ferrière et al., 11 vols. (Paris, 1880–1963).
Castiglione, Sabba da, *Ricordi overo ammaestramenti* (Venice, 1578).
Cavalli, Marino, 'Relazione dell'impero ottomano', in *Relazioni*, i, pp. 273–98.
Cavendish, Thomas, 'A letter of M. Thomas Candish to the right honourable the Lord Hunsdon, Lord Chamberlaine, one of her Majesties most honourable Privy Councell, touching the successe of his voyage about the world', in R. Hakluyt, *The Principal Navigations, Voyages, Traffiques and Discoveries of the English Nations* (Glasgow, 1904), xi, pp. 376–8.
Çelebi, Katib, *The Gift to the Great Ones on Naval Campaigns*, ed. and trans. İ. Bostan (Ankara, 2008).
Cervantes Saavedra, Miguel de, *Don Quijote de La Mancha*, ed. F. Rico et al., 2 vols. (Madrid, 2015); trans. J. Rutherford with an introduction by R. González Ecchevarría, *The Ingenious Hidalgo Don Quixote de La Mancha* (London, 2003).
—— *Información de Argel*, ed. A. J. Sáez (Madrid, 2019).
Chesneau, Jean, *Voyage de Paris en Constantinople*, ed. L. Pochmalicki (Geneva, 2019).
Cirni, Antonfrancesco, *Comentarii . . . ne quali si descriue la guerra ultima di Francia, la celebratione del Concilio Tridentino, il soccorso d'Orano, l'impresa del Pignone, e l'historia del'assedio di Malta* (Rome, 1567).

Contreras, Alonso de, *Vida de este capitán*, ed. A. Pérez-Reverte (Barcelona, 2008); *The Life of Captain Alonso de Contreras, Knight of the Military Order of St. John, Native of Madrid, Written by Himself (1582 to 1633)*, trans. C. A. Phillips (London, 1926).

Copie de plusieurs missives escrites et envoyees de Malte par le Seigneur grand Maistre et autres Chevaliers de sainct Iehan de Hierusalem (Paris, 1565).

Correspondance du Cardinal de Granvelle, 1565–1586, ed. E. Poullet and C. Piot, 12 vols. (Brussels, 1877–96).

Cortes de los antiguos reinos de León y de Castilla, 5 vols. (Madrid, 1861–1903).

Cressino, Antonio, 'Vray discours de la guerre et siege de Malthe par les Turcz', in Nicolas Camusat, *Meslanges historiques, ou recueil des plusieurs actes, traictez, lettres missives et autres memoires* (Troyes, 1619), Part II, fols. 51v–54r.

Crova, Martin, *Brief discours du siege et oppugnation de l'isle de Malte* (Antwerp, 1565); *Compendio della historia di quanto e successo nella impresa di Malta* (np, 1565).

Curione, Celio Secondo, *De Bello Melitensi Historia Nova* (Basel, 1567); *Caelius Secundus Curio, his historie of the warr of Malta*, ed. H. Vella Bonavita (Tempe, AZ, 2007).

Dandalo, Andrea, 'Relazione', in *Relazioni*, iii, pp. 161–72.

Documenta Indica VII (1566–1569), ed. J. Wicki (Rome, 1962).

Donini, Marcantonio, 'Relazione dell'impero ottomano', in *Relazioni*, iii, pp. 173–208.

Foix, Paul de, *Les lettres de Messire Paul de Foix, archevesque de Tolose, et ambassadeur pour le Roy auprés du Pape Gregoire XIII, escrites au Roy Henry III* (Paris, 1628).

Fort Caroline: History and Documents, ed. C. E. Bennett, rev. edn (Tuscaloosa, 2001).

Fourquevaux, Raimond de, *Dépêches de M. de Fourquevaux, ambassadeur du roi Charles IX en Espagne 1565–1572*, ed. C. Douais (Paris, 1896).

Fresne-Canaye, Philippe du, *Le voyage du Levant de Philippe du Fresne-Canaye (1573)*, ed. M. H. Hauser (Paris, 1897).

Galán, Diego, *Cautiverio y trabajos de Diego Galán natural de Consuegra y vecino de Toledo, 1589–1600*, ed. M. Serrano y Sanz (Madrid, 1913).

Geuffroy, Antoine, 'Briefve description de la court du grant Turc', in Jean Chesneau, *Le voyage de Monsieur d'Aramon, ambassadeur pour le roy en Levant*, ed. C. Schefer (Paris, 1887), pp. 227–48.

Histoire du siège de Paris par Henri IV d'après un manuscrit nouvellement découvert, ed. A. Dufour (Paris, 1881).

Hopperus, Joachim, 'Recueil et mémorial des troubles des Pays Bas du roy, 1559–1566', in *Mémoires de Viglius et d'Hopperus*, ed. A. Wauters (Brussels, 1862), pp. 229–374.

In the Sultan's Realm: Two Venetian Ambassadorial Reports of the Early Modern Ottoman Empire, trans. E. R. Dursteler (Toronto, 2018).

The Knights of St John of Jerusalem in Scotland, ed. I. B. Cowan, P. H. R. Mackay and A. Macquarrie (Edinburgh, 1983).

Lanfreducci, F., and G. O. Bosio, 'Costa e discorsi di Barberia', ed. C. Monchicourt, trans. P. Grandchamp, *Revue africaine*, 66 (1925), 419–549.

Laudonnière, René de, 'L'histoire notable de la Floride', in *Les Français en Amérique pendant la deuxième moitié du XVIᵉ siècle*, vol. II: *Les Français en Floride*, ed. S. Lussagnet (Paris, 1958), pp. 50–80; trans. C. E. Bennett in *Three Voyages*, rev. edn (Tuscaloosa, 2001), pp. 17–51.

Le Challeux, Nicolas, 'Discours de l'histoire de la Floride', in *Les Français en Amérique pendant la deuxième moitié du XVIᵉ siècle*, vol. II: *Les Français en Floride*, ed. S. Lussagnet (Paris, 1958), pp. 201–33; trans. in *New American World: A Documentary History of North America to 1612*, ed. D. B. Quinn et al., 5 vols. (New York, 1979), ii, pp. 370–79.

Le Moyne de Morgues, Jacques, *The Work of Jacques Le Moyne de Morgues: A Huguenot Artist in Florida and England*, ed. P. Hulton, 2 vols. (London, 1977).

Léry, Jean de, *Histoire mémorable du Siège de Sancerre (1573)*, ed. G. Nakam (Paris, 1975).

Lettres de Charles IX à M. de Fourquevaux, ambassadeur en Espagne, 1565–1572, ed. C. Douais (Paris, 1897).

Machiavelli, Niccolò, *Il Principe*, ed. M. Martelli and N. Marcelli (Rome, 2006); trans. G. Bull, *The Prince* (London, 2003).

Macuncuzade Mustafa, 'Memoirs of an Ottoman Captive in Malta, 1597–98', trans. H. Anetshofer, in *The Ottoman World: A Cultural History Reader, 1450–1700*, ed. H. T. Karateke (Oakland, CA, 2021), pp. 16–22.

Malta: The Bulwark of Europe. Hieronymus Megiser's Propugnaculum Europae: The First Comprehensive German Description of 16th-Century Malta, ed. and trans. A. Friggieri and T. Freller (Tarxien, 1998).

Marguerite de Valois, *Mémoires et autres écrits 1574–1614*, ed. É. Viennot (Paris, 1999).

Monmouth, Geoffrey of, *The History of the Kings of Britain*, ed. M. D. Reeve, trans. N. Wright (Woodbridge, 2007).

Navagero, Bernardo, 'Relazione dell'impero ottomano', in *Relazioni*, i, pp. 32–110.

Négociations de la France dans le Levant, ed. E. Charrière, 4 vols. (Paris, 1848–60).

Nicolay, Nicolas de, *Dans l'empire de Soliman le Magnifique*, ed. M.-C. Gomez-Géraud and S. Yérasimos (Paris, 1989).

The Philippine Islands 1493–1803, vol. II: *1521–1569*, trans. E. H. Blair and J. A. Robertson (Manila, 1962).

Pigafetta, Filippo, *Relatione dell'assedio di Parigi* (Rome, 1591); trans. A. Dufour, 'Relation du siége de Paris par Henri IV', *Mémoires de la Société de l'Histoire de Paris et de l'Île-de-France*, 2 (1876), 1–105.

Pretty, Francis, 'The prosperous voyage of M. Thomas Candish esquire into the South sea, and so round about the circumference of the whole earth, begun in the yere 1586, and finished 1588', in R. Hakluyt, *The Principal Navigations, Voyages, Traffiques and Discoveries of the English Nations* (Glasgow, 1904), xi, pp. 290–347.

Queen Elizabeth and Her Times, ed. T. Wright, 2 vols. (London, 1838).

Ribault, Jean, *The whole and true discouerye of Terra Florida* (London, 1563), in *New American World: A Documentary History of North America to 1612*, ed. D. B. Quinn et al., 5 vols. (New York, 1979), ii, pp. 285–94.

Ribier, Guillaume, *Lettres et memoires d'estat, des roys, princes, ambassadeurs, et autres ministres, sous les regnes de François premier, Henry II. & François II.*, 2 vols. (Paris, 1666).

The Royal Tour of France by Charles IX and Catherine de' Medici 1564–6, ed. V. E. Graham and W. McAllister Johnson (Toronto, 1979).

Salazar, Pedro de, *Historia de la guerra y presa de África*, ed. M. Federici (Naples, 2015).

Sandys, George, *A relation of a journey begun An. Dom. 1610: foure books containing a description of the Turkish Empire, of Aegypt, of the Holy Land, of the remote parts of Italy and islands adioyning* (London, 1615).

Settlement of Florida, ed. C. E. Bennett (Gainesville, 1968).

The Siege of Malta 1565: Matteo Perez d'Aleccio's Frescoes at the Grand Master's Palace, Valletta, ed. C. Cini (Valletta, 2009).

Solís de Merás, Gonzalo, *Pedro Menéndez de Avilés and the Conquest of Florida: A New Manuscript*, ed. and trans. D. Arbesú (Gainesville, 2017).

Sosa, Antonio de [Diego de Haedo attrib.], *Topografía e historia general de Argel*, ed. I. Bauer y Landauer, 3 vols. (Madrid, 1927–9); part trans. M. A. Garcés and D. de Armas Wilson, *An Early Modern Dialogue with Islam* (Notre Dame, 2011).

Süleymanname: The Illustrated History of Süleyman the Magnificent, ed. E. Atıl (New York, 1986).

The Travels of Reverend Ólafur Egilson: The Story of the Barbary Corsair Raid on Iceland in 1627, trans. K. S. Hreinsson and A. Nichols (Washington, DC, 2016).

Trevisano, Domenico, 'Relazione dell'impero ottomano', in *Relazioni*, i, pp. 111–92.

Vendôme, Pierre Gentil de, *Le siège de Malte par les Turcs en 1565*, ed. H. Pernot (Paris, 1910); *Della historia de Malta et successo della guerra seguita tra quei Religiosissimi Cavalieri et il potentissimo gran Turco Sulthan Solimano, l'anno MDLXV* (Bologna, 1566).

Viglius, 'Discours sur le règne de Philippe II.', in *Mémoires de Viglius et d'Hopperus*, ed. A. Wauters (Brussels, 1862), pp. 7–157.

Villegagnon, Nicolas Durand de, *De bello Melitensi* (Paris, 1553).

Viperano, Giovanni Antonio, *De bello melitensi historia* (Perugia, 1567).

Voisin de la Popellinière, Lancelot de, *Les trois mondes* (Paris, 1582).

Voltaire, *Annales de l'Empire depuis Charlemagne*, ed. G. Laudin and J. Renwick, 3 vols. (Oxford, 2019).

Secondary Works

Abela, J., 'The Great Siege of 1565: Untold Stories of Everyday Life', in *Besieged*, ii, pp. 97–115.

Ágoston, G., *Guns for the Sultan: Military Power and the Weapons Industry in the Ottoman Age* (Cambridge, 2005).

—— 'Information, Ideology, and Limits of Imperial Policy: Ottoman Grand Strategy in the Context of Ottoman–Habsburg Rivalry', in *The Early Modern Ottomans: Remapping the Empire*, ed. V. H. Aksan and D. Goffman (Cambridge, 2007), pp. 75–103.

Airaldi, G., *Andrea Doria* (Rome, 2015).

Aksan, V. H., 'Locating the Ottomans among Early Modern Empires', in her *Ottomans and Europeans: Contacts and Conflicts* (Istanbul, 2004), pp. 81–110.

—— 'Ottoman War and Warfare 1453–1812', in her *Ottomans and Europeans: Contacts and Conflicts* (Istanbul, 2004), pp. 141–72.

Alford, S., *The Watchers: A Secret History of the Reign of Elizabeth I* (New York, 2012).

Allen, B. W., *The Great Siege of Malta: The Epic Battle between the Ottoman Empire and the Knights of St. John* (Lebanon, NH, 2015).

Allen, D. F., 'The Hospitaller Castiglione's Catholic Synthesis of Warfare, Learning and Lay Piety on the Eve of the Council of Trent', in *The Hospitallers, the Mediterranean and Europe: Festschrift for Anthony Luttrell*, ed. K. Borchardt, N. Jaspert and H. J. Nicholson (Aldershot, 2007), pp. 255–68.

Alves, J. S., 'From Istanbul with Love: Rumours, Conspiracies and Commercial Competition in Aceh–Ottoman Relations, 1550s to 1570s', in *From Anatolia to Aceh: Ottomans, Turks and Southeast Asia*, ed. A. C. S. Peacock and A. T. Gallop (Oxford, 2015), pp. 47–62.

Anderson, R. C., *Naval Wars in the Levant: From the Battle of Lepanto to the Introduction of Steam* (Princeton, 1952).

Andrews, K. R., *Trade, Plunder and Settlement: Maritime Enterprise and the Genesis of the British Empire, 1480–1630* (Cambridge, 1984).

Anglo, S., *The Martial Arts of Renaissance Europe* (New Haven, 2000).

Bibliography

Arrighi, D., *Écritures de l'ambassade: Les lettres turques d'Ogier Ghiselin de Busbecq* (Paris, 2011).

Audisio, G., 'Renégats marseillais (1591–1595)', *Renaissance and Reformation*, 16 (1992), 31–58.

Aymard, M., 'Chiourmes et galères dans la seconde moitié du XVIe siècle', in *Il Mediterraneo nella seconda metà del '500 alla luce di Lepanto*, ed. G. Benzoni (Florence, 1974), pp. 71–94.

Babelon, J.-P., *Henri IV* (Paris, 1982).

Bennassar, B., and L. Bennassar, *Les chrétiens d'Allah: L'histoire extraordinaire des renégats, XVIe–XVIIe siècles* (Paris, 1989).

Billacois, F., *Le duel dans la société française des XVIe–XVIIe siècles: Essai de psychosociologie historique* (Paris, 1986).

Blondy, A., *Un prince de la Renaissance à l'aube de la Contre-Réforme: Hugues de Loubens de Verdalle (1531–1582–1595)* (Paris, 2005).

Bonaffini, G., *Un mare di paura: Il Mediterraneo in età moderna* (Caltanissetta, 1997).

Bonello, G., 'Sir Oliver Starkey, Paragon and Victim', in his *Histories of Malta*, 12 vols. (Valletta, 2000–2021), vol. 3: *Versions and Diversions* (2002), pp. 42–53.

—— 'Duelling in Malta', in his *Histories of Malta*, 12 vols. (Valletta, 2000–2021), vol. 3: *Versions and Diversions* (2002), pp. 69–87.

—— 'An Overlooked Eyewitness's Account of the Great Siege', in *Melitensium Amor: Festschrift in Honour of Dun Ġwann Azzopardi*, ed. T. Cortis, T. Freller and L. Bugeja (Malta, 2002), pp. 133–48.

—— 'In and Out of the Knights' Prison: Detentions and Escapes 1530–1600', in his *Histories of Malta*, 12 vols. (Valletta, 2000–2021), vol. 4: *Convictions and Conjectures* (2003), pp. 9–43.

Bono, S., *I corsari barbareschi* (Turin, 1964).

—— *Corsari nel Mediterraneo* (Milan, 1993).

—— 'Naval Exploits and Privateering', in *Hospitaller Malta 1530–1798: Studies on Early Modern Malta and the Order of St John of Jerusalem*, ed. V. Mallia-Milanes (Msida, 1993), pp. 351–97.

Boutier, J., A. Dewerpe and D. Nordman, *Un tour de France royal: Le voyage de Charles IX (1564–1566)* (Paris, 1984).

Bradford, E., *Siege: Malta 1940–1943* (Harmondsworth, 1987).

Bibliography

Brandes, J.-D., *Korsaren Christi: Johanniter und Malteser. Die Herren des Mittelmeers* (Sigmaringen, 1997).

Braudel, F., *The Mediterranean and the Mediterranean World in the Age of Philip II*, trans. S. Reynolds, 1 vol. in 2 (London, 1972–3).

Brogini, A., *Malte, frontière de Chrétienté (1530–1670)* (Rome, 2006).

—— *1565, Malte dans la tourmente: Le "Grand Siège" de l'île par les Turcs* (Paris, 2011).

—— *Une noblesse en Méditerranée: Le couvent des Hospitaliers dans la première modernité* (Aix-en-Provence, 2017).

—— 'La croisade africaine des Hospitaliers de Saint-Jean de Jérusalem (1530–1554)', in *Croisades en Afrique: Les expéditions occidentales à destination du continent africain, XIIIe–XVIe siècle*, ed. B. Weber (Toulouse, 2019), pp. 275–94.

Bull, M. G., 'Francesco Balbi di Correggio's *La verdadera relación*: The Main Eyewitness Account of the Great Siege in Context', in *Besieged*, i, pp. 13–20.

Buttigieg, E., *Nobility, Faith and Masculinity: The Hospitaller Knights of Malta, c.1580–c.1700* (London, 2011).

Calnan, D., *Knights in Durance* (Malta, 1966).

Carmel, C., *Daughters of Eve: Women, Gender Roles, and the Impact of the Council of Trent in Catholic Malta* (Msida, 2002).

Carroll, S., *Blood and Violence in Early Modern France* (Oxford, 2006).

Casale, G., ' "His Majesty's Servant Lufti": The Career of a Previously Unknown Turkish Envoy to Sumatra Based on an Account of His Travels from the Topkapı Palace Archives', *Turcica*, 37 (2005), 43–81.

—— 'The Ottoman Regulation of the Spice Trade in the Sixteenth-Century Red Sea and Persian Gulf', *Journal of the Economic and Social History of the Orient*, 49 (2006), 170–98.

—— 'The Ottoman "Discovery" of the Indian Ocean in the Sixteenth Century', in *Seascapes: Maritime Histories, Littoral Cultures, and Transoceanic Exchanges*, ed. J. H. Bentley, R. Bridenthal and K. Wigen (Honolulu, 2007), pp. 87–104.

—— *The Ottoman Age of Exploration* (New York, 2010).

Cassar, C., *A Concise History of Malta* (Msida, 2000).

Cassar, G., 'The Suffering of the Innocent: Wartime Violence and the Common People – the Case of the Great Siege of Malta, 1565', *History Research*, 3 (2013), 79–89.

Cassar, P., 'The Maltese Corsairs and the Order of St. John of Jerusalem', *Catholic Historical Review*, 46 (1960), 137–56.

Cassola, A., *The Great Siege of Malta (1565) and the Istanbul State Archives* (Valletta, 1995).

Castillo, D., *The Maltese Cross: A Strategic History of Malta* (Westport, CT, 2006).

Champion, P., *Catherine de Médicis présente à Charles IX son royaume (1564–1566)* (Paris, 1937).

Ciappara, F., *Society and the Inquisition in Early Modern Malta* (San Ġwann, 2001).

Çizakça, M., 'The Ottoman Government and Economic Life: Taxation, Public Finance and Trade Controls', in *Cambridge History*, pp. 241–75.

Cocula-Vaillières, A.-M., *Brantôme: Amour et gloire au temps des Valois* (Paris, 1986).

Dale, S. F., *The Muslim Empires of the Ottomans, Safavids, and Mughals* (Cambridge, 2010).

Dalle, I., *Un Européen chez les Turcs: Auger Ghiselin de Busbecq (1521–1591)* (Paris, 2008).

Darby, G., 'Narrative of Events', in *The Origins and Development of the Dutch Revolt*, ed. G. Darby (London, 2001), pp. 8–28.

Dauber, R., *Die Marine des Johanniter-Malteser-Ritter-Ordens. 500 Jahre Seekrieg zur Verteidigung Europas* (Graz, 1989).

Dávid, G., 'Ottoman Armies and Warfare, 1453–1603', in *Cambridge History*, pp. 276–319.

Davis, R. C., *Christian Slaves, Muslim Masters: White Slavery in the Mediterranean, the Barbary Coast and Italy, 1500–1800* (Basingstoke, 2003).

Demir, M., and T. M. P. Duggan, 'Gelibolulu Mustafa Ali's Narrative of the Siege of Malta and His Account of the Death of Turgut Reis Related in His Künhü'l-Ahbar', in *Besieged*, ii, pp. 57–65.

Deswarte-Rosa, S., 'L'expédition de Tunis (1535): Images, interprétations, répercussions culturelles', in *Chrétiens et musulmans à la Renaissance*, ed. B. Bennassar and R. Sauzet (Paris, 1998), pp. 75–132.

Bibliography

DiVanna, I., *Reconstructing the Middle Ages: Gaston Paris and the Development of Nineteenth-Century Medievalism* (Newcastle, 2008).

Drelichman, M., and H.-J. Voth, *Lending to the Borrower from Hell: Debt, Taxes, and Default in the Age of Philip II* (Princeton, 2014).

Dursteler, E. R., *Venetians in Constantinople: Nation, Identity, and Coexistence in the Early Modern Mediterranean* (Baltimore, 2006).

—— *Renegade Women: Gender, Identity, and Boundaries in the Early Modern Mediterranean* (Baltimore, 2011).

Earle, P., *Corsairs of Malta and Barbary* (London, 1970).

Faroqhi, S., *The Ottoman Empire and the World around It* (London, 2004).

—— *Pilgrims and Sultans: The Hajj under the Ottomans*, rev. edn (London, 2014).

Fiorani, F., *The Marvel of Maps: Art, Cartography and Politics in Renaissance Italy* (New Haven, 2005).

Fiorini, S., 'The Resettlement of Gozo after 1551', *Melita Historica*, 9 (1986), 203–41.

Fleet, K., 'The Ottomans, 1453–1603: A Political History Introduction', in *Cambridge History*, pp. 19–43.

Fleischer, C. H., *Bureaucrat and Intellectual in the Ottoman Empire: The Historian Mustafa Âli (1541–1600)* (Princeton, 1986).

Fontenay, M., 'Corsaires de la foi ou rentiers du sol? Les chevaliers de Malte dans le "corso" méditerranéen au XVIIe siècle', *Revue d'histoire moderne et contemporaine*, 35 (1988), 361–84.

—— 'De Rhodes à Malte: L'évolution de la flotte des Hospitaliers au XVIe siècle', in *Navi e navigazione nei secoli XV e XVI: Atti del V convegno internazionale di studi Colombiani, Genova, 26–28 ottobre 1987*, 2 vols. in 1 (Genoa, 1990), i, pp. 107–33.

—— 'Les missions des galères de Malte (1530–1798)', in *Guerre et commerce en Méditerranée, IXe–XXe siècles*, ed. M. Vergé-Franceschi (Paris, 1991), pp. 103–22.

Forey, A. J., 'The Militarisation of the Hospital of St. John', *Studia Monastica*, 26 (1984), 75–89.

Friedman, E. G., *Spanish Captives in North Africa in the Early Modern Age* (Madison, WI, 1983).

La Galleria delle Carte geografiche in Vaticano, ed. L. Gambi and A. Pinelli, 3 vols. (Modena, 1994).

Garcés, M. A., *Cervantes in Algiers: A Captive's Tale* (Nashville, 2002).

Geiss, J., 'The Chia-ching reign, 1522–1566', in *The Cambridge History of China*, vol. 7: *The Ming Dynasty, 1368–1644*, Part 1, ed. F. W. Mote and D. Twitchett (Cambridge, 1988), pp. 440–510.

Gelderen, M. van, *The Political Thought of the Dutch Revolt 1555–1590* (Cambridge, 1992).

Giorgio, R. de, *A City by an Order*, 3rd edn (Valletta, 1998).

Giraldez, A., *The Age of Trade: The Manila Galleon and the Dawn of the Global Economy* (Lanham, MD, 2015).

Glete, J., *Warfare at Sea, 1500–1650: Maritime Conflicts and the Transformation of Europe* (London, 2000).

Goffman, D., *The Ottoman Empire and Early Modern Europe* (Cambridge, 2002).

Goodman, D. C., *Power and Penury: Government, Technology and Science in Philip II's Spain* (Cambridge, 1988).

Graf, T. B., *The Sultan's Renegades: Christian-European Converts to Islam and the Making of the Ottoman Elite, 1575–1610* (Oxford, 2017).

Greene, M., *Catholic Pirates and Greek Merchants: A Maritime History of the Mediterranean* (Princeton, 2010).

Grunebaum-Ballin, P., *Joseph Naci, duc de Naxos* (Paris, 1968).

Guilmartin, J. F., *Gunpowder and Galleys: Changing Technology and Mediterranean Warfare at Sea in the 16th Century*, rev. edn (London, 2003).

Hale, J. R., *War and Society in Renaissance Europe, 1450–1620* (Baltimore, 1985).

Hall, J. W., 'The Muromachi Bakufu', in *The Cambridge History of Japan*, vol. 3: *Medieval Japan*, ed. K. Yamamura (Cambridge, 1990), pp. 175–230.

Hammer, P. E. J., *Elizabeth's Wars: War, Government and Society in Tudor England, 1544–1604* (Basingstoke, 2003).

Haring, C. H., *Trade and Navigation between Spain and the Indies in the Time of the Hapsburgs* (Cambridge, MA, 1918).

Hastings, M., *Operation Pedestal: The Fleet That Battled to Malta, 1942* (London, 2021).

Bibliography

Helgason, Th., *The Corsairs' Longest Voyage: The Turkish Raid in Iceland 1627*, trans. A. Yates and J. A. Pétursdottír (Leiden, 2018).

Hershenzon, D., *The Captive Sea: Slavery, Communication, and Commerce in Early Modern Spain and the Mediterranean* (Philadelphia, 2018).

Hess, A. C., 'The Battle of Lepanto and Its Place in Mediterranean History', *Past and Present*, 57 (1972), 53–73.

—— 'The Ottoman Conquest of Egypt (1517) and the Beginning of the Sixteenth-Century World War', *International Journal of Middle East Studies*, 4 (1973), 55–76.

Höfert, A., *Den Feind beschreiben: "Türkengefahr" und europäisches Wissen über das Osmanische Reich 1450–1600* (Frankfurt, 2003).

Holland, J., *Fortress Malta: An Island under Siege 1940–1943* (London, 2003).

Holt, M. P., *The French Wars of Religion, 1562–1629*, 2nd edn (Cambridge, 2005).

Hoppen, A., *The Fortification of Malta by the Order of St. John 1530–1798*, 2nd edn (Msida, 1999).

Housley, N. J., *The Later Crusades, 1274–1580: From Lyons to Alcazar* (Oxford, 1992).

Hughes, Q., *The Building of Malta 1530–1795*, rev. edn (London, 1967).

—— 'How Fort St. Elmo Survived the Siege for So Long', *Treasures of Malta*, 8 (2002), 109–15.

Imber, C., 'Ideals and Legitimation in Early Ottoman History', in *Süleyman the Magnificent and His Age: The Ottoman Empire in the Early Modern World*, ed. M. Kunt and C. Woodhead (Harlow, 1995), pp. 138–53.

—— 'The Navy of Süleyman the Magnificent', in his *Studies in Ottoman History and Law* (Istanbul, 1996), pp. 1–69.

—— 'The Reconstruction of the Ottoman Fleet after the Battle of Lepanto, 1571–1572', in his *Studies in Ottoman History and Law* (Istanbul, 1996), pp. 85–101.

—— 'Ibrahim Peçevi on War: A Note on the "European Military Revolution"', in *Frontiers of Ottoman Studies: State, Province, and the West*, ed. C. Imber, K. Kiyotaki and R. Murphey, 2 vols. (London, 2005), ii, pp. 7–22.

—— 'Government, Administration and Law', in *Cambridge History*, pp. 205–40.

—— *The Ottoman Empire 1300–1650: The Structure of Power*, 3rd edn (London, 2019).

Inalcık, H., *An Economic and Social History of the Ottoman Empire*, vol. 1: *1300–1600* (Cambridge, 1994).

Isom-Verhaaren, C., *Allies with the Infidel: The Ottoman and French Alliance in the Sixteenth Century* (London, 2011).

Jouanna, A., *Ordre social: Mythes et hierarchies dans la France du XVIᵉ siècle* (Paris, 1977).

Kamen, H., *Spain's Road to Empire: The Making of a World Power, 1492–1793* (London, 2002).

Kedar, B. Z., 'A Twelfth-Century Description of the Jerusalem Hospital', in *The Military Orders*, vol. 2: *Welfare and Warfare*, ed. H. J. Nicholson (Aldershot, 1998), pp. 3–26.

Knecht, R. J., *The French Civil Wars 1562–1598* (Harlow, 2000).

Lalanne, L., *Brantôme, sa vie et ses écrits* (Paris, 1896).

Lane, F. C., 'Wages and Recruitment of Venetian Galeotti, 1470–1580', *Studi veneziani*, n.s. 6 (1982), 15–43.

Lazard, M., *Pierre de Bourdeille, seigneur de Brantôme* (Paris, 1995).

Lesure, M., *Lépante*, rev. edn (Paris, 2013).

Lewis, B., 'Corsairs in Iceland', *Revue des mondes musulmans de la Méditerranée*, 15–16 (1973), 139–44.

Luttrell, A. T., 'Approaches to Medieval Malta', in *Medieval Malta: Studies on Malta before the Knights*, ed. A. T. Luttrell (London, 1975), pp. 1–70.

—— 'Malta and Rhodes: Hospitallers and Islanders', in *Hospitaller Malta 1530–1798: Studies on Early Modern Malta and the Order of St John of Jerusalem*, ed. V. Mallia-Milanes (Msida, 1993), pp. 255–84.

Lyon, E., *The Enterprise of Florida: Pedro Menéndez de Avilés and the Spanish Conquest of 1565–1568* (Gainesville, 1976).

MacCaffrey, W. T., 'The Newhaven Expedition, 1562–1563', *Historical Journal*, 40 (1997), 1–21.

MacMillan, K., 'Exploration, Trade and Empire', in *The Elizabethan World*, ed. S. Doran and N. Jones (Abingdon, 2011), pp. 646–62.

Malcolm, N., *Agents of Empire: Knights, Corsairs, Jesuits and Spies in the Sixteenth-Century Mediterranean World* (New York, 2015).

Mallia-Milanes, V., *Venice and Hospitaller Malta 1530–1798: Aspects of a Relationship* (Malta, 1992).

—— 'Frà Jean de la Valette 1495–1565 – a Reappraisal', in *The Maltese Cross*, ed. T. Cortis (Msida, 1995), pp. 117–29.

Manguin, P.-Y., 'Of Fortresses and Galleys: The 1568 Acehnese Siege of Melaka, after a Contemporary Bird's-eye View', *Modern Asian Studies*, 22 (1988), 607–28.

von Martels, Z. R. W. M., *Augerius Gislenius Busbequius: Leven en werk van de keizerlijke gezant aan het hof van Süleyman de Grote* (Groningen, 1989).

Mas, A., *Les Turcs dans la littérature espagnole du Siècle d'Or*, 2 vols. (Paris, 1967).

Matar, N., 'Two Arabic Accounts of Captivity in Malta: Texts and Contexts', in *Piracy and Captivity in the Mediterranean 1550–1800*, ed. M. Klarer (London, 2019), pp. 258–76.

—— *Mediterranean Captivity through Arab Eyes, 1517–1798* (Leiden, 2021).

McGrath, J. T., *The French in Florida: In the Eye of the Hurricane* (Gainesville, 2000).

Meilak, D., 'David versus Goliath and the Apotheosis of Malta: Romanticizing the Siege of Malta during the Rise of Nationalism (1860–1939)', *Melita Historica*, 17 (2016), 140–72.

Merouche, L., *Recherches sur l'Algérie à l'époque ottomane*, vol. II: *La course, mythes et réalité* (Paris, 2007).

Mikhail, A., *God's Shadow: Sultan Selim, His Ottoman Empire, and the Making of the Modern World* (New York, 2020).

Mitchell, M., *Friar Andrés de Urdaneta, O.S.A.* (London, 1964).

Mitchell, P. D., *Medicine in the Crusades: Warfare, Wounds and the Medieval Surgeon* (Cambridge, 2004).

Montalto, J., *The Nobles of Malta 1530–1800* (Malta, 1979).

Mori Ubaldino, U., *La marina del sovrano militare ordine di San Giovanni di Gerusalemme di Rodi e di Malta* (Rome, 1971).

Murphey, R., *Ottoman Warfare, 1500–1700* (London, 1999).

—— 'A Comparative Look at Ottoman and Habsburg Resources and Readiness for War circa 1520 to circa 1570', in *Guerra y Sociedad en la Monarquía Hispánica: Política, Estrategia y Cultura en la Europa Moderna*

(1500–1700), ed. E. García Hernán and D. Maffi, 2 vols. (Madrid, 2006), i, pp. 75–102.

Necipoğlu, G., *Architecture, Ceremonial, and Power: The Topkapı Palace in the Fifteenth and Sixteenth Centuries* (Cambridge, MA, 1991).

Nicholson, H. J., *Love, War, and the Grail* (Leiden, 2001).

—— *The Knights Hospitaller* (Woodbridge, 2001).

Nierop, H. F. K. van, 'The Nobles and the Revolt', in *The Origins and Development of the Dutch Revolt*, ed. G. Darby (London, 2001), pp. 48–66.

Nordman, D., *Tempête sur Alger: L'expédition de Charles Quint en 1541* (Paris, 2011).

O'Malley, G., *The Knights of the Hospitaller Langue 1460–1565* (Oxford, 2005).

Özbaran, S., 'The Ottoman Turks and the Portuguese in the Persian Gulf, 1534–1581', *Journal of Asian History*, 6 (1972), 45–87.

—— 'Ottoman Naval Policy in the South', in *Süleyman the Magnificent and His Age: The Ottoman Empire in the Early Modern World*, ed. M. Kunt and C. Woodhead (Harlow, 1995), pp. 55–70.

—— *Ottoman Expansion towards the Indian Ocean in the 16th Century* (Istanbul, 2009).

—— 'Ottoman Expansion in the Red Sea', in *Cambridge History*, pp. 173–201.

Palmer, R., 'Slavery, Captivity and Galley Rowing in Early Modern Malta', *Antiquity*, 95 (2021), 1280–97.

Paris, G., 'La *Chanson de Roland* et la nationalité française', in his *La poésie du moyen âge*, 2 vols. (Paris, 1906), i, pp. 87–118.

Parker, G., *The Dutch Revolt*, rev. edn (London, 1985).

—— *The Grand Strategy of Philip II* (New Haven, 1998).

—— *The Army of Flanders and the Spanish Road, 1567–1659*, 2nd edn (Cambridge, 2004).

—— *Imprudent King: A New Life of Philip II* (New Haven, 2014).

Parry, V. J., 'Materials of War in the Ottoman Empire', in *Studies in the Economic History of the Middle East from the Rise of Islam to the Present Day*, ed. M. A. Cook (London, 1970), pp. 219–29.

—— 'La manière de combattre', in *War, Technology and Society in the Middle East*, ed. V. J. Parry and M. E. Yapp (London, 1975), pp. 218–56.

—— 'The Reign of Sulaimān the Magnificent, 1520–66', in *A History of the Ottoman Empire to 1730*, ed. M. A. Cook (Cambridge, 1976), pp. 79–102.

Bibliography

Pearson, M. N., *The Portuguese in India* (Cambridge, 1987).

Peillard, L., *Villegagnon: Vice-amiral de Bretagne, vice-roi du Brésil* (Paris, 1991).

Peirce, L. P., *The Imperial Harem: Women and Sovereignty in the Ottoman Empire* (New York, 1993).

Pepper, S., and N. Adams, *Firearms and Fortifications: Military Architecture and Siege Warfare in Sixteenth-Century Siena* (Chicago, 1986).

Peretti, J., 'Du Vray Discours de la guerre et siege de Malte par les Turcz ou la première relation du Grand Siège publiée en France', *Melita Historica*, 4 (1965), 129–32.

Pérez-Mallaína, P. E., *Spain's Men of the Sea: Daily Life on the Indies Fleet in the Sixteenth Century*, trans. C. R. Phillips (Baltimore, 1998).

Pollak, M., *Cities at War in Early Modern Europe* (Cambridge, 2010).

Poumarède, G., *Pour en finir avec la Croisade: Mythes et réalités de la lutte contre les Turcs au XVIe et XVIIe siècles* (Paris, 2004).

Pryor, J. H., *Geography, Technology, and War: Studies in the Maritime History of the Mediterranean, 649–1571* (Cambridge, 1988).

Reid, A., 'Sixteenth Century Turkish Influence in Western Indonesia', *Journal of Southeast Asian History*, 10 (1969), 395–414.

Remensnyder, A. G., 'Compassion, Fear, Fugitive Slaves, and a Pirates' Shrine: Lampedusa, ca. 1550–ca. 1750', in *Mapping Pre-Modern Sicily: Maritime Violence, Cultural Exchange, and Imagination in the Mediterranean, 800–1700*, ed. E. Sohmer Tai and K. L. Reyerson (Cham, 2022), pp. 149–72.

Riley-Smith, J. S. C., *The Knights Hospitaller in the Levant, c.1070–1309* (Basingstoke, 2012).

Rossi, E., *Storia della marina dell'ordine di San Giovanni di Gerusalemme di Rodi e di Malta* (Rome, 1926).

—— 'L'Assedio di Malta nel 1565 secondo gli storici ottomani', *Malta Letteraria*, 1 (1926), 143–52.

—— 'Documenti turchi inedita dell'Ambrosiana sull'assedio di Malta nel 1565', in *Miscellanea Giovanni Galbiati*, 3 vols. (Milan, 1951), iii, pp. 313–22.

Rostagno, L., *Mi faccio turco: Esperienze ed imagine dell'Islam nell'Italia moderna* (Rome, 1983).

Rothman, T., and P. Brampton Koelle, 'Pedro de Salazar's History of the Great Siege', in *Besieged*, i, pp. 21–8.

Rouillard, C. D., *The Turk in French History, Thought, and Literature (1520–1660)* (Paris, 1940).

Sabba da Castiglione 1480–1554: Dalli corti rinascimentali alla Commenda di Faenza, ed. A. R. Gentilini (Florence, 2004).

Sanminiatelli Zabarella, C., *Lo assedio di Malta 18 maggio–8 settembre 1565* (Turin, 1902).

Santos Alves, J. M. dos, *O domínio do norte de Samatra: A história dos sultanatos de Samudera-Pacém e de Achém e das suas relações com os Portugueses 1500–1580* (Lisbon, 1999).

Scaraffia, L., *Rinnegati: Per una storia dell'identità occidentale* (Rome, 1993).

Schurz, W. L., *The Manila Galleon* (New York, 1959).

Setton, K. M., *The Papacy and the Levant (1204–1571)*, 4 vols. (Phildelphia, 1976–84).

Sire, H. J. A., *The Knights of Malta* (New Haven, 1994).

Skilliter, S. A., 'Catherine de' Medici's Turkish Ladies-in-Waiting: A Dilemma in Franco-Ottoman Diplomatic Relations', *Turcica*, 7 (1975), 188–204.

Smith, P. C., *Pedestal: The Malta Convoy of August, 1942* (London, 1970).

Soler, I., *Miguel de Cervantes: Los años de Argel* (Barcelona, 2016).

Souček, S., 'The Rise of the Barbarossa in North Africa', *Archivum Ottomanicum*, 3 (1971), 238–50.

Spate, O. H. K., *The Spanish Lake* (Minneapolis, 1979).

Spiteri, S. C., *The Great Siege: Knights vs Turks MDLXV: Anatomy of a Hospitaller Victory* (Tarxien, 2005).

—— 'The Maltese Combatants of the Great Siege', in *Besieged*, i, pp. 117–24.

Stein, B., *Vijayanagara: The New Cambridge History of India I:2* (Cambridge, 1989).

Thompson, I. A. A., *War and Government in Habsburg Spain* (London, 1976).

Turbet-Delof, G., *L'Afrique barbaresque dans la littérature française aux XVIe et XVIIe siècles* (Geneva, 1973).

Vargas-Hidalgo, R., *La Batalla de Lepanto* (Santiago, 1998).

Vaucheret, É., *Brantôme mémorialiste et conteur* (Paris, 2010).

Veinstein, G., 'L'hivernage en campagne, talon d'Achille du système militaire ottoman classique: A propos des *sipāhī* de Roumélie en 1559–1560', in his *Etat et société dans l'Empire ottoman, XVIe–XVIIIe siècles: La terre, la guerre, les communautés* (London, 1994), no. V.

Vella, T., 'The 1565 Great Siege Frescos in the Palace, Valletta', in *Celebratio Amicitiae: Essays in Honour of Giovanni Bonello*, ed. M. Camilleri and T. Vella (Valletta, 2006), pp. 193–205.

—— *Splendour and Devotion: The Art Collections of the Order of St John* (San Ġwann, 2023).

Vella Bonavita, H., 'Key to Christendom: The 1565 Siege of Malta, Its Histories, and Their Use in Reformation Polemic', *Sixteenth Century Journal*, 33 (2002), 1021–43.

Vergé-Franceschi, M., 'Andrea Doria (1466–1560), amiral génois de François Ier puis de Charles Quint, ennemi de la Corse', in *Les Doria, la Méditerranée et la Corse*, ed. M. Vergé-Franceschi and A.-M. Graziani (Ajaccio, 2001), pp. 67–88.

Vitkus, D. J., 'Early Modern Orientalism: Representations of Islam in Sixteenth- and Seventeenth-Century Europe', in *Western Views of Islam in Medieval and Early Modern Europe: Perceptions of Other*, ed. D. R. Blanks and M. Frassetto (New York, 1999), pp. 207–30.

Wansbrough, J. E., *Lingua Franca in the Mediterranean* (Richmond, 1996).

Watson, B. A., *Sieges: A Comparative Study* (Westport, CT, 1993).

Wettinger, G., 'The Galley-Convicts and Buonavoglia in Malta during the Rule of the Order', *Journal of the Faculty of Arts*, 3 (1965), 29–37.

—— 'Early Maltese Popular Attitudes to the Government of the Order of St. John', *Melita Historica*, 6 (1974), 255–78.

—— *Slavery in the Islands of Malta and Gozo, ca. 1100–1812* (Malta, 2002).

—— 'Esclaves noirs à Malte', in *Captifs en Méditerranée (XVIe–XVIIIe siècles)*, ed. F. Moureau (Paris, 2008), pp. 155–69.

White, J. M., *Piracy and Law in the Ottoman Mediterranean* (Stanford, 2018).

Williams, P., *Empire and Holy War in the Mediterranean: The Galley and Maritime Conflict between the Habsburgs and the Ottomans* (London, 2014).

Wilson, P. H., 'Summary: Under Siege? Defining Siege Warfare in World History', in *The World of the Siege: Representations of Early Modern Positional Warfare*, ed. A. Fischer-Kattner and J. Ostwald (Leiden, 2019), pp. 288–306.

Wizmayer, J. M., *The Fleet of the Order of St John, 1530–1798* (Valletta, 1997).

Bibliography

Wolfe, M., 'Walled Towns during the French Wars of Religion (1560–1630)', in *City Walls: The Urban Enceinte in Global Perspective*, ed. J. D. Tracy (Cambridge, 2000), pp. 317–48.

Woodhead, C., 'Perspectives on Süleyman', in *Süleyman the Magnificent and His Age: The Ottoman Empire in the Early Modern World*, ed. M. Kunt and C. Woodhead (Harlow, 1995), pp. 164–90.

Yérasimos, S., 'Les relations franco-ottomanes et la prise de Tripoli en 1551', in *Soliman le Magnifique et son temps*, ed. G. Veinstein (Paris, 1992), pp. 529–47.

Zilli, L., 'La frontière de la Chrétienté en 1565. La chronique du siège de Malte par Pierre Gentil de Vendôme', in *Les représentations de l'Autre du Moyen Âge au XVIIe siècle*, ed. E. Barriot-Salvadore (Saint-Étienne, 1995), pp. 53–62.

References

Introduction: Sieges and What They Mean

1 For the tour, see P. Champion, *Catherine de Médicis présente à Charles IX son royaume (1564–1566)* (Paris, 1937); J. Boutier, A. Dewerpe and D. Nordman, *Un tour de France royal: Le voyage de Charles IX (1564–1566)* (Paris, 1984). See also *The Royal Tour of France by Charles IX and Catherine de' Medici 1564–6*, ed. V. E. Graham and W. McAllister Johnson (Toronto, 1979), which includes an edition of the principal eyewitness account by Abel Jouan.
2 Boutier et al., *Un tour de France*, pp. 107–18.
3 *Royal Tour*, ed. Graham and McAllister Johnson, p. 134.
4 R. J. Knecht, *The French Civil Wars 1562–1598* (Harlow, 2000), pp. 85–112; M. P. Holt, *The French Wars of Religion, 1562–1629*, 2nd edn (Cambridge, 2005), pp. 50–59.
5 Knecht, *French Civil Wars*, pp. 80–83.
6 AOM 91, fol. 167r; AOM 430, fol. 246v.
7 *Royal Tour*, ed. Graham and McAllister Johnson, pp. 111, 125.
8 P. Grunebaum-Ballin, *Joseph Naci, duc de Naxos* (Paris, 1968), pp. 111–17. For the impression that the ambassador made on the French, see *Lettres de Catherine de Médicis*, ed. C. H. de la Ferrière et al., 11 vols. (Paris, 1880–1963), v, pp. 278–9; Blaise de Monluc, *Commentaires et lettres*, ed. A. de Ruble, 5 vols. (Paris, 1864–72), v, pp. 37–9.
9 *Négociations de la France dans le Levant*, ed. E. Charrière, 4 vols. (Paris, 1848–60), ii, pp. 781–2, 785, 788.
10 Balbi (1568), fols. 29v, 46r–v.
11 For Brantôme's life and writings, see A.-M. Cocula-Vaillières, *Brantôme: Amour et gloire au temps des Valois* (Paris, 1986); M. Lazard, *Pierre de Bourdeille, seigneur de Brantôme* (Paris, 1995); É. Vaucheret, *Brantôme mémorialiste*

et conteur (Paris, 2010). There is still much of value in L. Lalanne, *Brantôme, sa vie et ses écrits* (Paris, 1896).

12 Marguerite de Valois, *Mémoires et autres écrits 1574–1614*, ed. É. Viennot (Paris, 1999), pp. 23–6, 69–72.

13 Brantôme, v, pp. 215–16. Cf. his summative verdict on La Valette at p. 239.

14 Ibid., pp. 217–18.

15 Ibid., pp. 219–29.

16 CODOIN, xxx, pp. 296–7.

17 E.g. Brantôme, ii, pp. 19, 115; vi, p. 129; vii, pp. 17, 82.

18 Ibid., ii, p. 45; iv, p. 41; v, p. 405; vi, pp. 7, 288; ix, p. 391.

19 Ibid., v, pp. 395–6. Cf. his bitter lament over life's missed opportunities in ix, pp. 374–5.

20 For contemporary notions of social hierarchy and 'race', see A. Jouanna, *Ordre social: mythes et hiérarchies dans la France du XVIe siècle* (Paris, 1977), pp. 15–85.

21 Geoffrey of Monmouth, *The History of the Kings of Britain*, ed. M. D. Reeve, trans. N. Wright (Woodbridge, 2007), pp. 6–31.

22 G. Paris, 'La *Chanson de Roland* et la nationalité française', in his *La poésie du moyen âge*, 2 vols. (Paris, 1906), i, pp. 87–118; I. DiVanna, *Reconstructing the Middle Ages: Gaston Paris and the Development of Nineteenth-Century Medievalism* (Newcastle, 2008), pp. 33–41.

23 B. A. Watson, *Sieges: A Comparative Study* (Westport, CT, 1993), pp. 1–10, 129–64; P. H. Wilson, 'Summary: Under Siege? Defining Siege Warfare in World History', in *The World of the Siege: Representations of Early Modern Positional Warfare*, ed. A. Fischer-Kattner and J. Ostwald (Leiden, 2019), pp. 288–306.

24 Knecht, *French Civil Wars*, pp. 247–53; J.-P. Babelon, *Henri IV* (Paris, 1982), pp. 487–500.

25 Filippo Pigafetta, *Relatione dell'assedio di Parigi* (Rome, 1591), and trans. A. Dufour as 'Relation du siége [sic] de Paris par Henri IV', *Mémoires de la Société de l'Histoire de Paris et de l'Île-de-France*, 2 (1876), 1–105. But cf. the more matter-of-fact account, also from a pro-League perspective, in *Histoire du siège de Paris par Henri IV d'après un manuscrit nouvellement découvert*, ed. A. Dufour (Paris, 1881). See also the thoughtful narrative

of the Catholic siege of Huguenot Sancerre in 1572–3 in Jean de Léry, *Histoire mémorable du Siège de Sancerre (1573)*, ed. G. Nakam (Paris, 1975).

26 E. Rossi, 'L'Assedio di Malta nel 1565 secondo gli storici ottomani', *Malta Letteraria*, 1 (1926), 143–52; Katib Çelebi, *The Gift to the Great Ones on Naval Campaigns*, ed. and trans. İ. Bostan (Ankara, 2008), pp. 103–5; M. Demir and T. M. P. Duggan, 'Gelibolulu Mustafa Ali's Narrative of the Siege of Malta and His Account of the Death of Turgut Reis Related in His Künhü'l-Ahbar', in *Besieged*, ii, pp. 57–65. Cf. E. Rossi, 'Documenti turchi inedita dell'Ambrosiana sull'assedio di Malta nel 1565', in *Miscellanea Giovanni Galbiati*, 3 vols. (Milan, 1951), iii, pp. 313–22. For Ottoman historiographical writing in the sixteenth century in general, see C. H. Fleischer, *Bureaucrat and Intellectual in the Ottoman Empire: The Historian Mustafa Âli (1541–1600)* (Princeton, 1986), pp. 237–52.

27 See the list of significant contemporary works which tell the story of the siege in C. Sanminiatelli Zabarella, *Lo assedio di Malta 18 maggio–8 settembre 1565* (Turin, 1902), pp. 13–16.

28 For Balbi, see *Dizionario biografico degli italiani* (Rome, 1963), v, pp. 363–4; M. G. Bull, 'Francesco Balbi di Correggio's *La verdadera relación*: The Main Eyewitness Account of the Great Siege in Context', in *Besieged*, i, pp. 13–20. For Cirni, see M. Cavanna Ciappina, 'Cirni, Antonio Francesco', *Dizionario biografico degli italiani* (Rome, 1981), xxv, pp. 814–16.

29 Vendôme; *Della historia de Malta et successo della guerra seguita tra quei Religiosissimi Cavalieri et il potentissimo gran Turco Sulthan Solimano, l'anno MDLXV* (Bologna, 1566). See L. Zilli, 'La frontière de la Chrétienté en 1565. La chronique du siège de Malte par Pierre Gentil de Vendôme', in *Les représentations de l'Autre du Moyen Âge au XVIIe siècle*, ed. E. Barriot-Salvadore (Saint-Étienne, 1995), pp. 53–62; H. Vella Bonavita, 'Key to Christendom: The Siege of Malta, Its Histories, and Their Use in Reformation Polemic', *Sixteenth Century Journal*, 33 (2002), 1028–34. For a text that made particularly extensive use of Vendôme's account, see Celio Secondo Curione, *De Bello Melitensi Historia Nova* (Basel, 1567); *Caelius Secundus Curio, his historie of the warr of Malta*, ed. H. Vella Bonavita (Tempe, AZ, 2007) (an edition of the English translation printed in 1579).

30 G. Poumarède, *Pour en finir avec la Croisade: Mythes et réalités de la lutte contre les Turcs aux XVIᵉ et XVIIᵉ siècles* (Paris, 2004), pp. 436–51.
31 S. Faroqhi, *Subjects of the Sultan: Culture and Daily Life in the Ottoman Empire* (London, 2000), pp. 21–40, 43–60.

1. Violence, Vanity and Vocation: The Knights of Malta

1 H. J. Nicholson, *The Knights Hospitaller* (Woodbridge, 2001), pp. 1–4; J. S. C. Riley-Smith, *The Knights Hospitaller in the Levant, c.1070–1309* (Basingstoke, 2012), pp. 16–18.
2 Riley-Smith, *Knights Hospitaller*, pp. 18–22.
3 B. Z. Kedar, 'A Twelfth-Century Description of the Jerusalem Hospital', in *The Military Orders*, vol. 2: *Welfare and Warfare*, ed. H. J. Nicholson (Aldershot, 1998), pp. 3–26; Nicholson, *Knights Hospitaller*, pp. 87–92; Riley-Smith, *Knights Hospitaller*, pp. 22–3, 69–78; P. D. Mitchell, *Medicine in the Crusades: Warfare, Wounds and the Medieval Surgeon* (Cambridge, 2004), pp. 61–85.
4 A. J. Forey, 'The Militarisation of the Hospital of St. John', *Studia Monastica*, 26 (1984), 75–89; Riley-Smith, *Knights Hospitaller*, pp. 27–37.
5 Riley-Smith, *Knights Hospitaller*, pp. 24–6; E. Buttigieg, *Nobility, Faith and Masculinity: The Hospitaller Knights of Malta, c.1580–c.1700* (London, 2011), pp. 91–100.
6 Nicholson, *Knights Hospitaller*, pp. 43–7; Riley-Smith, *Knights Hospitaller*, pp. 223–4.
7 Setton, *Papacy*, iii, pp. 205–15.
8 Brogini, *Malte*, pp. 73–7.
9 Ibid., pp. 58–65. For an excellent survey of the history of Malta before 1530, see A. T. Luttrell, 'Approaches to Medieval Malta', in *Medieval Malta: Studies on Malta before the Knights*, ed. A. T. Luttrell (London, 1975), pp. 1–70.
10 See S. Deswarte-Rosa, 'L'expédition de Tunis (1535): Images, interprétations, répercussions culturelles', in *Chrétiens et musulmans à la Renaissance*, ed. B. Bennassar and R. Sauzet (Paris, 1998), pp. 75–132; D. Nordman, *Tempête sur Alger: L'expédition de Charles Quint en 1541* (Paris, 2011).

References

11 For a thoughtful comparison of the utility of Rhodes and Malta to the Knights and their relationship with the respective populations, see A. T. Luttrell, 'Malta and Rhodes: Hospitallers and Islanders', in *Hospitaller Malta 1530–1798: Studies on Early Modern Malta and the Order of St John of Jerusalem*, ed. V. Mallia-Milanes (Msida, 1993), pp. 255–84.

12 Brogini, *Malte*, pp. 167–8.

13 Nicholson, *Knights Hospitaller*, p. 91; Luttrell, 'Malta and Rhodes', p. 261.

14 N. J. Housley, *The Later Crusades, 1274–1580: From Lyons to Alcazar* (Oxford, 1992), pp. 212–14.

15 For a detailed survey, see H. J. A. Sire, *The Knights of Malta* (New Haven, 1994), pp. 101–206. See also Buttigieg, *Nobility*, pp. 77–83.

16 Brantôme, ii, pp. 51–2.

17 For Starkey's career, see G. Bonello, 'Sir Oliver Starkey, Paragon and Victim', in his *Histories of Malta*, 12 vols. (Valletta, 2000–2021), vol. 3: *Versions and Diversions* (2002), pp. 42–53.

18 *The Knights of St John of Jerusalem in Scotland*, ed. I. B. Cowan, P. H. R. Mackay and A. Macquarrie (Edinburgh, 1983), pp. lii–liv, 201.

19 AOM 91, fol. 120v; A. Brogini, *Une noblesse en Méditerranée: Le couvent des Hospitaliers dans la première modernité* (Aix-en-Provence, 2017), p. 159.

20 Brogini, *Une noblesse*, pp. 64–8.

21 For the order's fleet, see J. M. Wizmayer, *The Fleet of the Order of St John, 1530–1798* (Valletta, 1997), esp. pp. 14–32, 39–41 for life on a Hospitaller galley; R. L. Dauber, *Die Marine des Johanniter-Malteser-Ritter-Ordens: 500 Jahre Seekrieg zur Verteidigung Europas* (Graz, 1989), esp. pp. 75–111, 128–47.

22 Buttigieg, *Nobility*, pp. 19–30; Brogini, *Une noblesse*, pp. 63–105.

23 For the centrality of honour to the Knights' value system, see Buttigieg, *Nobility*, pp. 64–5.

24 H. J. Nicholson, *Love, War, and the Grail* (Leiden, 2001), esp. pp. 187–90, 199–207, 219–21, 234–7.

25 For Sabba da Castiglione and his work, see *Dizionario biografico degli italiani* (Rome, 1979), xxii, pp. 100–106; D. F. Allen, 'The Hospitaller Castiglione's Catholic Synthesis of Warfare, Learning and Lay Piety on the Eve of the Council of Trent', in *The Hospitallers, the Mediterranean and Europe: Festschrift for Anthony Luttrell*, ed. K. Borchardt,

N. Jaspert and H. J. Nicholson (Aldershot, 2007), pp. 255–68; *Sabba da Castiglione 1480–1554: Dalli corti rinascimentali alla Commenda di Faenza*, ed. A. R. Gentilini (Florence, 2004); T. Vella, *Splendour and Devotion: The Art Collections of the Order of St John* (San Ġwann, 2023), pp. 27–35.

26 Sabba da Castiglione, *Ricordi overo ammaestramenti* (Venice, 1578), *Ricordo* no. 121.

27 See e.g. ibid., *Ricordi* nos. 11–14, 19, 21–2, 24, 26–8, 31, 35, 38, 40, 46, 53, 62.

28 Ibid., *Ricordo* no. 120.

29 Ibid., *Ricordo* no. 18. See also no. 106.

30 Allen, 'Hospitaller Castiglione's Catholic Synthesis', p. 268.

31 Castiglione, *Ricordi overo ammaestramenti*, *Ricordo* no. 115.

32 Brogini, *Une noblesse*, pp. 137–9. See also Buttigieg, *Nobility*, pp. 161–85.

33 AOM 429, fol. 189r; *Knights of St John of Jerusalem in Scotland*, ed. Cowan et al., p. 189.

34 For the Knights' various relationships with women, see Buttigieg, *Nobility*, pp. 140–54. For the Order's approach to homosexual activity, ibid., pp. 154–8.

35 Nicolas de Nicolay, *Dans l'empire de Soliman le Magnifique*, ed. M.-C. Gomez-Géraud and S. Yérasimos (Paris, 1989), pp. 76–7 and image at p. 78; George Sandys, *A relation of a journey begun An. Dom. 1610: foure books containing a description of the Turkish Empire, of Aegypt, of the Holy Land, of the remote parts of Italy and islands adioyning* (London, 1615), p. 234. For prostitution in early modern Malta in general, see C. Carmel, *Daughters of Eve: Women, Gender Roles, and the Impact of the Council of Trent in Catholic Malta* (Msida, 2002), pp. 159–77; F. Ciappara, *Society and the Inquisition in Early Modern Malta* (San Ġwann, 2001), pp. 171–4.

36 AOM 87, fol. 110r.

37 Buttigieg, *Nobility*, pp. 150–52.

38 AOM 88, fols. 39r, 40r, 50r, 62r; G. Bonello, 'In and Out of the Knights' Prison: Detentions and Escapes 1530–1600', in his *Histories of Malta*, vol. 4: *Convictions and Conjectures* (2003), p. 13. It is possible that there were two separate rapes, the former in Malta in 1549, the latter in Tripoli in 1550. Brogini, *Une noblesse*, p. 136, plausibly supposes that the victim of the Tripoli rape was a Muslim; if so, she would most

probably have been a member of the Muslim community that lived within the fortifications.

39 AOM 88, fol. 52v.
40 Ibid., fol. 126r.
41 AOM 89, fol. 13r. For a similar incident, see ibid., fol. 49r–v (1555).
42 Ibid., fols. 81r, 112v. Torto was subsequently convicted of murder in 1559 and expelled from the order, but was readmitted in 1560: AOM 90, fols. 50v, 51v, 119v.
43 AOM 90, fol. 50v. Cf. the curious story of three Knights attacking a group of Greek pilgrims in AOM 91, fols. 185v–186r (1567).
44 AOM 89, fol. 65v; AOM 93, fols. 65r, 65v, 74r; Bonello, 'In and Out', p. 22. See also the intervention in 1558 of two French Knights to protect a girl from being beaten by her father, as noted by Brogini, *Une noblesse*, p. 141.
45 AOM 86, fols. 46v–47r; G. O'Malley, *The Knights of the Hospitaller Langue 1460–1565* (Oxford, 2005), pp. 291–2.
46 E.g. AOM 89, fol. 43r (1555); AOM 91, fol. 163v (1566).
47 AOM 89, fol. 31v (1555).
48 AOM 91, fol. 169v.
49 AOM 89, fol. 21r (1554); ibid., fol. 66v (1556); ibid., fol. 80r (1556); ibid., fol. 80v (1556); AOM 90, fol. 101r (1560); AOM 91, fol. 18r (1561); ibid., fols. 21v–22r (1561); ibid., fol. 24r (1561); ibid., fol. 25v (1561); ibid., fol. 92r (1563); ibid., fols. 95v–96r (1563); ibid., fol. 129r (1564); ibid., fol. 141v (1564).
50 AOM 90, fol. 78r.
51 AOM 91, fol. 83v.
52 Ibid., fols. 87v, 95v.
53 Ibid., fol. 109v. See also ibid., fol. 176v (1566).
54 E.g. AOM 88, fol. 146v (1553); AOM 90, fol. 134v (1561); AOM 91, fol. 21v (1561). See Buttigieg, *Nobility*, pp. 165–7; G. Bonello, 'Duelling in Malta', in his *Histories of Malta*, vol. 3: *Versions and Diversions*, pp. 69–87. For the cultural appeal of the duel in this period, see F. Billacois, *Le duel dans la société française des XVIe–XVIIe siècles: Essai de psychosociologie historique* (Paris, 1986); S. Anglo, *The Martial Arts of Renaissance Europe* (New Haven, 2000); S. Carroll, *Blood and Violence in Early Modern France* (Oxford, 2006), pp. 147–59.

References

55 See e.g. AOM 89, fol. 70r (1556); ibid., fol. 113v (1557); AOM 91, fol. 73r (1562).
56 AOM 88, fols. 15v, 19v.
57 E.g. AOM 89 fol. 10v (1554); ibid., fol. 22v (1554); ibid., fol. 112v (1557); AOM 90, fol. 8v (1558); AOM 91, fol. 58v (1562); ibid., fol. 71v (1562); ibid., fol. 83r (1562).
58 E.g. AOM 88, fol. 81v (1551); ibid., fol. 146v (1553); ibid., fol. 161v (1553); AOM 89, fol. 20r (1554); ibid., fol. 49r (1555); ibid., fol. 55r (1555); ibid., fol. 100r (1557); ibid., fol. 112v (1557); AOM 90, fol. 25v (1558); ibid., fol. 44r (1558); ibid., fol. 48v (1559); ibid., fol. 97r (1560); ibid., fol. 115v (1560); ibid., fol. 117v (1560); AOM 91, fols. 30v–31r (1561); ibid., fol. 58v (1562); ibid., fol. 150r (1565); ibid., fol. 168r–v (1566). But for a case of a servant being used by a Knight as 'muscle' in an assault on a Dominican friar, see AOM 88, fol. 120v (1552). And for a Knight falsely accused of wounding a soldier, AOM 91, fol. 45r (1561). See also Brogini, *Une noblesse*, pp. 142–3.
59 AOM 88, fols. 109v, 113r, 120v (1552).
60 See e.g. AOM 89, fol. 3v (1554); ibid., fol. 55r (1555); AOM 91, fol. 25v (1561); ibid., fol. 183r (1567).
61 E.g. AOM 89, fol. 80r (1556); AOM 90, fol. 25v (1558); ibid., fol. 30v (1558); ibid., fol. 101r (1560); AOM 91, fol. 22r (1561); ibid., fol. 64v (1562); ibid., fols. 95v–96r (1563); ibid., fol. 129r (1564); ibid., fols. 179v–180r (1567).
62 AOM 89, fol. 198r; AOM 90, fol. 48r–v; ibid., fol. 115r; AOM 91, fols. 108v–109r; ibid., fol. 132r; ibid., fol. 133v; AOM 429, fol. 189r; *The Knights of St John of Jerusalem in Scotland*, ed. Cowan et al., pp. liii–lv, 184, 185–6, 187–8, 189–90.
63 Bonello, 'In and Out', p. 21.
64 The suggestion of Bonello, 'In and Out', p. 19. For the hearse, see D. Calnan, *Knights in Durance* (Malta, 1966), pp. 18–19.
65 Calnan, *Knights in Durance*, pp. 30–32, where the translation is freer but also more elegant than that here.

2. The Rewards of Relative Efficiency: The Ottomans

1 Z. R. W. M. von Martels, *Augerius Gislenius Busbequius: Leven en werk van de keizerlijke gezant aan het hof van Süleyman de Grote* (Groningen, 1989); I. Dalle, *Un Européen chez les Turcs: Auger Ghiselin de Busbecq (1521–1591)* (Paris, 2008).
2 *Legationis turcicae epistolae quatuor* (Paris, 1595), and trans. E. S. Forster as *The Turkish Letters of Ogier Ghiselin de Busbecq*, rev. edn (Baton Rouge, 2005). See D. Arrighi, *Écritures de l'ambassade: Les lettres turques d'Ogier Ghiselin de Busbecq* (Paris, 2011); C. D. Rouillard, *The Turk in French History, Thought, and Literature (1520–1660)* (Paris, 1940), pp. 220–25.
3 *Legationis turcicae epistolae quatuor*, fol. 34r–v, and *Turkish Letters*, p. 50 (translation revised); Dalle, *Un Européen chez les Turcs*, pp. 166–8.
4 Dalle, *Un Européen chez les Turcs*, pp. 218–21.
5 *Legationis turcicae epistolae quatuor*, fols. 135r–137r, and *Turkish Letters*, pp. 201–5; Dalle, *Un Européen chez les Turcs*, pp. 212–15; von Martels, *Augerius Gislenius Busbequius*, cols. 426–35.
6 'Exclamatio, sive de re militari contra Turcam instituenda consilium', in *Legationis turcicae epistolae quatuor*, fols. 163r–186v; von Martels, *Augerius Gislenius Busbequius*, cols. 457–68.
7 *Legationis turcicae epistolae quatuor*, fol. 8r–v, and *Turkish Letters*, pp. 8–9.
8 *Legationis turcicae epistolae quatuor*, fol. 129r–v, and *Turkish Letters*, p. 190.
9 Quotations at *Legationis turcicae epistolae quatuor*, fol. 12r, and *Turkish Letters*, p. 15.
10 *Legationis turcicae epistolae quatuor*, fol. 72r, and *Turkish Letters*, pp. 111–12.
11 V. J. Parry, 'La manière de combattre', in *War, Technology and Society in the Middle East*, ed. V. J. Parry and M. E. Yapp (London, 1975), pp. 220–21, 223–6. Cf. Andrea Dandalo, 'Relazione', in *Relazioni*, iii, p. 166.
12 G. Dávid, 'Ottoman Armies and Warfare, 1453–1603', in *Cambridge History*, p. 282.
13 R. Murphey, *Ottoman Warfare, 1500–1700* (London, 1999), pp. 36–43; Dávid, 'Ottoman Armies and Warfare', pp. 286–96; C. Imber, *The*

Ottoman Empire 1300–1650: The Structure of Power, 3rd edn (London, 2019), pp. 159–69.

14 M. Çizakça, 'The Ottoman Government and Economic Life: Taxation, Public Finance and Trade Controls', in *Cambridge History*, pp. 258–9.

15 Jean Chesneau, *Voyage de Paris en Constantinople*, ed. L. Pochmalicki (Geneva, 2019), p. 33.

16 Domenico Trevisano, 'Relazione dell'impero ottomano', in *Relazioni*, i, p. 153.

17 Çizakça, 'Ottoman Government and Economic Life', pp. 246–8. See in general Imber, *Ottoman Empire*, pp. 239–59.

18 M. Drelichman and H.-J. Voth, *Lending to the Borrower from Hell: Debt, Taxes, and Default in the Age of Philip II* (Princeton, 2014).

19 Çizakça, 'Ottoman Government and Economic Life', pp. 254–6.

20 R. Murphey, 'A Comparative Look at Ottoman and Habsburg Resources and Readiness for War circa 1520 to circa 1570', in *Guerra y Sociedad en la Monarquía Hispánica: Política, Estrategia y Cultura en la Europa Moderna (1500–1700)*, ed. E. García Hernán and D. Maffi, 2 vols. (Madrid, 2006), i, pp. 75–102. For an assessment of Ottoman military capacity over the long term, see V. H. Aksan, 'Ottoman War and Warfare 1453–1812', in her *Ottomans and Europeans: Contacts and Conflicts* (Istanbul, 2004), pp. 141–72. For a salutary note of caution about the efficiency and insuperability of Ottoman forces, see C. Imber, 'Ibrahim Peçevi on War: A Note on the "European Military Revolution"', in *Frontiers of Ottoman Studies: State, Province, and the West*, ed. C. Imber, K. Kiyotaki and R. Murphey, 2 vols. (London, 2005), ii, pp. 7–22.

21 Niccolò Machiavelli, *Il Principe*, ed. M. Martelli and N. Marcelli (Rome, 2006), pp. 101–5, 266–7; Niccolò Machiavelli, *The Prince*, trans. G. Bull (London, 2003), pp. 16–17, 66.

22 Imber, *Ottoman Empire*, pp. 105–13; D. Goffman, *The Ottoman Empire and Early Modern Europe* (Cambridge, 2002), pp. 164–9; T. B. Graf, *The Sultan's Renegades: Christian-European Converts to Islam and the Making of the Ottoman Elite, 1575–1610* (Oxford, 2017), pp. 41–50.

23 Antonio Barbarigo, 'Sommario della relazione', in *Relazioni*, iii, pp. 149–50; Nicolay, *Dans l'empire de Soliman le Magnifique*, pp. 151–4; Chesneau, *Voyage*, pp. 33–4. See in general Rouillard, *The Turk*, pp. 309–15.

References

24 S. Faroqhi, *The Ottoman Empire and the World around It* (London, 2004), pp. 98–102, 108–10.
25 The literature on western views of the Ottoman world is vast. For a good point of entry, see D. J. Vitkus, 'Early Modern Orientalism: Representations of Islam in Sixteenth- and Seventeenth-Century Europe', in *Western Views of Islam in Medieval and Early Modern Europe: Perceptions of Other*, ed. D. R. Blanks and M. Frassetto (New York, 1999), pp. 207–30. For a detailed study of western Europeans' ideas about the Ottomans, see A. Höfert, *Den Feind beschreiben: "Türkengefahr" und europäisches Wissen über das Osmanische Reich 1450–1600* (Frankfurt, 2003). See also A. Mas, *Les Turcs dans la littérature espagnole du Siècle d'Or*, 2 vols. (Paris, 1967), ii, pp. 153–230.
26 Faroqhi, *Ottoman Empire*, pp. 3–4. Cf. G. Ágoston, 'Information, Ideology, and Limits of Imperial Policy: Ottoman Grand Strategy in the Context of Ottoman–Habsburg Rivalry', in *The Early Modern Ottomans: Remapping the Empire*, ed. V. H. Aksan and D. Goffman (Cambridge, 2007), pp. 75–103.
27 Murphey, *Ottoman Warfare*, pp. 1–11.
28 Trevisano, 'Relazione dell'impero ottomano', pp. 154–6.
29 For a helpful overview of Süleyman's reign and campaigns, see K. Fleet, 'The Ottomans, 1453–1603: A Political History Introduction', in *Cambridge History*, pp. 32–9. See also V. J. Parry, 'The Reign of Sulaimān the Magnificent, 1520–66', in *A History of the Ottoman Empire to 1730*, ed. M. A. Cook (Cambridge, 1976), pp. 79–102. For the Ottoman empire's geopolitical place in the world around this time, see Faroqhi, *Ottoman Empire*, pp. 32–49.
30 E.g. Antonio Barbarigo, 'Sommario della relazione', p. 148; Daniele Barbarigo, 'Relazione dell'impero ottomano', in *Relazioni*, ii, p. 18; Dandalo, 'Relazione', p. 164.
31 Marino Cavalli, 'Relazione dell'impero ottomano', in *Relazioni*, i, pp. 277, 283–8.
32 *Legationis turcicae epistolae quatuor*, fol. 159r, and *Turkish Letters*, pp. 240–41. Cf. G. Veinstein, 'L'hivernage en campagne, talon d'Achille du système militaire ottoman classique: A propos des *sipāhī* de Roumélie en 1559–1560', in his *Etat et société dans l'Empire ottoman, XVIe–XVIIIe*

References

siècles: La terre, la guerre, les communautés (London, 1994), no. V; Fleet, 'Ottomans', p. 36.
33 *Legationis turcicae epistolae quatuor*, fols. 117r–123r and *Turkish Letters*, pp. 169–79.
34 *Royal Tour*, ed. Graham and McAllister, pp. 116–17; Monluc, *Commentaires et lettres*, v, p. 37.
35 *In the Sultan's Realm: Two Venetian Ambassadorial Reports of the Early Modern Ottoman Empire*, trans. E. R. Dursteler (Toronto, 2018), pp. 17–20.
36 *Legationis turcicae epistolae quatuor*, fol. 119r–v, and *Turkish Letters*, pp. 173–4.
37 Antonio Barbarigo, 'Sommario della relazione', p. 148; C. Woodhead, 'Perspectives on Süleyman', in *Süleyman the Magnificent and His Age: The Ottoman Empire in the Early Modern World*, ed. M. Kunt and C. Woodhead (Harlow, 1995), pp. 166–7.
38 Antonio Barbarigo, 'Sommario della relazione', p. 148; Cavalli, 'Relazione dell'impero ottomano', pp. 274–5, 295; Daniele Barbarigo, 'Relazione dell'impero ottomano', p. 17; Dandalo, 'Relazione', p. 164. Busbecq observed the same stern religiosity, but believed that Süleyman's personal frugality dated back to his youth: *Legationis turcicae epistolae quatuor*, fols. 42v–43r, and *Turkish Letters*, pp. 65–6.
39 Woodhead, 'Perspectives', p. 166; Goffman, *Ottoman Empire*, pp. 105–6.
40 Dandalo, 'Relazione', p. 164.
41 For the principal 'stage' on which Ottoman ceremonial governance was played out, see G. Necipoğlu, *Architecture, Ceremonial, and Power: The Topkapı Palace in the Fifteenth and Sixteenth Centuries* (Cambridge, MA, 1991).
42 Trevisano, 'Relazione dell'impero ottomano', pp. 157–9.
43 For the powerful women around Süleyman, see L. P. Peirce, *The Imperial Harem: Women and Sovereignty in the Ottoman Empire* (New York, 1993), pp. 57–90.
44 C. Imber, 'Government, Administration and Law', in *Cambridge History*, pp. 207–9; Imber, *Ottoman Empire*, pp. 74–84.
45 Fleet, 'Ottomans', pp. 38–9.
46 Philippe du Fresne-Canaye, *Le voyage du Levant de Philippe du Fresne-Canaye (1573)*, ed. M. H. Hauser (Paris, 1897), p. 299. See Rouillard, *The Turk*, pp. 218–20.

References

47 Fresne-Canaye, *Le voyage du Levant*, p. 237.
48 Daniele Barbarigo, 'Relazione dell'impero ottomano', p. 33.
49 Chesneau, *Voyage*, p. 35.
50 Busbecq, *Legationis turcicae epistolae quatuor*, fols. 104r–107v, and *Turkish Letters*, pp. 149–56; Chesneau, *Voyage*, pp. 63–5.
51 Fresne-Canaye, *Le voyage du Levant*, pp. 262, 268. For the motif of silent crowds, see Rouillard, *The Turk*, pp. 293–4.
52 Trevisano, 'Relazione dell'impero ottomano', pp. 158–9.
53 *Legationis turcicae epistolae quatuor*, fol. 108v, and *Turkish Letters*, pp. 158–9.
54 Murphey, *Ottoman Warfare*, pp. 25–6; Faroqhi, *Ottoman Empire*, p. 108. For the vulnerability of civilian populations to western armies, see J. R. Hale, *War and Society in Renaissance Europe, 1450–1620* (Baltimore, 1985), pp. 179–208.
55 V. J. Parry, 'Materials of War in the Ottoman Empire', in *Studies in the Economic History of the Middle East from the Rise of Islam to the Present Day*, ed. M. A. Cook (London, 1970), pp. 219–29.
56 G. Ágoston, *Guns for the Sultan: Military Power and the Weapons Industry in the Ottoman Age* (Cambridge, 2005), pp. 61–95. See also Imber, *Ottoman Empire*, pp. 274–8.
57 Ágoston, *Guns for the Sultan*, pp. 96–163.
58 Imber, *Ottoman Empire*, pp. 298–300; C. Imber, 'The Reconstruction of the Ottoman Fleet after the Battle of Lepanto, 1571–1572', in his *Studies in Ottoman History and Law* (Istanbul, 1996), pp. 90–93.
59 Antoine Geuffroy, 'Briefve description de la court du grant Turc', in Jean Chesneau, *Le voyage de Monsieur d'Aramon, ambassadeur pour le roy en Levant*, ed. C. Schefer (Paris, 1887), pp. 244–5; Chesneau, *Voyage*, pp. 28–9; Antonio Barbarigo, 'Sommario della relazione', pp. 151–2; Daniele Barbarigo, 'Relazione dell'impero ottomane', p. 34; Dandalo, 'Relazione', pp. 164–5; Fresne-Canaye, *Le voyage du Levant*, pp. 259–60; Trevisano, 'Relazione dell'impero ottomane', pp. 144–7 (a particularly detailed description).
60 CODOIN, xxix, pp. 39–40, 46–7, 48–50, 87–8, 90–92.
61 Ibid., pp. 35–6; D. C. Goodman, *Power and Penury: Government, Technology and Science in Philip II's Spain* (Cambridge, 1988), pp. 100–101.

62 Murphey, *Ottoman Warfare*, pp. 85–103; Faroqhi, *Ottoman Empire*, pp. 110–11; Dávid, 'Ottoman Armies', pp. 310–12.
63 G. Parker, *The Army of Flanders and the Spanish Road, 1567–1659*, 2nd edn (Cambridge, 2004), pp. 157–76.
64 E.g. Geuffroy, 'Briefve description', pp. 244–5. But for a positive assessment of the quality of Ottoman galleys' construction, see Marcantonio Donini, 'Relazione dell'impero ottomano', in *Relazioni*, iii, pp. 191–2.
65 See S. F. Dale, *The Muslim Empires of the Ottomans, Safavids, and Mughals* (Cambridge, 2010), pp. 10–76. Cf. V. H. Aksan, 'Locating the Ottomans among Early Modern Empires', in her *Ottomans and Europeans*, pp. 81–110.
66 *Süleymanname: The Illustrated History of Süleyman the Magnificent*, ed. E. Atıl (New York, 1986), figures 5, 10, 11, 16, 38, 39, 46, 59, 61. For the *Süleymanname*, see Woodhead, 'Perspectives', pp. 173–5.
67 Imber, *Ottoman Empire*, pp. 92–9; C. Imber, 'Ideals and Legitimation in Early Ottoman History', in *Süleyman the Magnificent*, ed. Kunt and Woodhead, pp. 138–53.
68 Imber, *Ottoman Empire*, pp. 97–8.
69 S. Faroqhi, *Pilgrims and Sultans: The Hajj under the Ottomans*, rev. edn (London, 2014), esp. pp. 54–73, 127–45, 184–6.
70 Imber, *Ottoman Empire*, pp. 93–5.

3. The Cruel Sea

1 See I. A. A. Thompson, *War and Government in Habsburg Spain* (London, 1976), pp. 163–7; M. Vergé-Franceschi, 'Andrea Doria (1466–1560), amiral génois de François Ier puis de Charles Quint, ennemi de la Corse', in *Les Doria, la Méditerranée et la Corse*, ed. M. Vergé-Franceschi and A.-M. Graziani (Ajaccio, 2001), pp. 66–174; G. Airaldi, *Andrea Doria* (Rome, 2015).
2 G. Bonaffini, *Un mare di paura: Il Mediterraneo in età moderna* (Caltanissetta, 1997). See also the author's reference, p. 19, to the Sicilian population's fear of corsair raids as 'la psicosi degli attachi corsari'. Cf. the title of D. Hershenzon's valuable study, *The Captive Sea: Slavery,*

Communication, and Commerce in Early Modern Spain and the Mediterranean (Philadelphia, 2018).

3 For a thoughtful contemporary reflection on the ubiquity of corsairs and the reasons for it, see Pierre Belon du Mans, *Voyage au Levant: Les observations de Pierre Belon du Mans de plusieurs singularités et choses mémorables, trouvées en Grèce, Turquie, Judée, Égypte, Arabie et autres pays étranges (1553)*, ed. A. Merle (Paris, 2001), pp. 249–53.

4 L. Merouche, *Recherches sur l'Algérie à l'époque ottomane*, vol. II: *La course, mythes et réalité* (Paris, 2007), pp. 115–32. For the position of Jews in the flux of Mediterranean identities, see E. R. Dursteler, *Venetians in Constantinople: Nation, Identity, and Coexistence in the Early Modern Mediterranean* (Baltimore, 2006), pp. 105–12.

5 M. Fontenay, 'Les missions des galères de Malte (1530–1798)', in *Guerre et commerce en Méditerranée, IXe–XXe siècles*, ed. M. Vergé-Franceschi (Paris, 1991), pp. 103–22; M. Fontenay, 'De Rhodes à Malte: L'évolution de la flotte des Hospitaliers au XVIe siècle', in *Navi e navigazione nei secoli XV e XVI: Atti del V convegno internazionale di studi Colombiani, Genova, 26–28 ottobre 1987*, 2 vols. in 1 (Genoa, 1990), i, pp. 107–33.

6 Brogini, *Malte*, pp. 40–47.

7 M. Fontenay, 'Corsaires de la foi ou rentiers du sol? Les chevaliers de Malte dans le "corso" méditerranéen au XVIIe siècle', *Revue d'histoire moderne et contemporaine*, 35 (1988), 361–84; Brogini, *Malte*, pp. 118–26; S. Bono, 'Naval Exploits and Privateering', in *Hospitaller Malta 1530–1798*, ed. Mallia-Milanes, pp. 388–97.

8 Brogini, *Malte*, pp. 81–7.

9 P. Williams, *Empire and Holy War in the Mediterranean: The Galley and Maritime Conflict between the Habsburgs and the Ottomans* (London, 2014), pp. 52–3, 182.

10 Brogini, *Malte*, pp. 104–8.

11 AOM 92, fols. 208v–209r, 210v–211r; Bosio, pp. 854–62; Brogini, *Malte*, pp. 105–6.

12 Brantôme, v, p. 235; P. Earle, *Corsairs of Malta and Barbary* (London, 1970), pp. 144–5, 162–7; Brogini, *Malte*, pp. 273–4.

13 P. Cassar, 'The Maltese Corsairs and the Order of St. John of Jerusalem', *Catholic Historical Review*, 46 (1960), 137–56.

14 Earle, *Corsairs*, pp. 107–8; Brogini, *Malte*, pp. 267–71. For the operations of the *Tribunale*, see M. Greene, *Catholic Pirates and Greek Merchants: A Maritime History of the Mediterranean* (Princeton, 2010), pp. 110–22, 167–94.

15 F. Lanfreducci and G. O. Bosio, 'Costa e discorsi di Barberia', ed. C. Monchicourt, trans. P. Grandchamp, *Revue africaine*, 66 (1925), 467–78.

16 'Captain Roger Bodenham to Mr. Anthony Penne: 31 August 1566', in *Queen Elizabeth and Her Times*, ed. T. Wright, 2 vols. (London, 1838), i, pp. 241–2.

17 R. C. Davis, *Christian Slaves, Muslim Masters: White Slavery in the Mediterranean, the Barbary Coast and Italy, 1500–1800* (Basingstoke, 2003), pp. 50–52, 105–6.

18 AOM 430, fols. 255r–256v, 263r.

19 Davis, *Christian Slaves*, pp. 69–102.

20 Williams, *Empire and Holy War*, pp. 75–90. See also M. Aymard, 'Chiourmes et galères dans la seconde moitié du XVIe siècle', in *Il Mediterraneo nella seconda metà del '500 alla luce di Lepanto*, ed. G. Benzoni (Florence, 1974), pp. 71–94.

21 G. Wettinger, 'The Galley-Convicts and Buonavoglia in Malta during the Rule of the Order', *Journal of the Faculty of Arts*, 3 (1965), 29–37.

22 F. C. Lane, 'Wages and Recruitment of Venetian Galeotti, 1470–1580', *Studi veneziani*, n.s. 6 (1982), 15–43; C. Imber, 'The Navy of Süleyman the Magnificent', in his *Studies in Ottoman History and Law*, pp. 51–5; Williams, *Empire and Holy War*, pp. 111–12, 145–6. At the time of the Great Siege, Jean de La Valette believed, incorrectly, that almost all Ottoman oarsmen were volunteers: CODOIN, xxix, p. 366.

23 R. Vargas-Hidalgo, *La Batalla de Lepanto* (Santiago, 1998), p. 278; M. Lesure, *Lépante*, rev. edn (Paris, 2013), p. 190; AOM 430, fols. 273r, 275v, 277r.

24 S. Bono, *I corsari barbareschi* (Turin, 1964), pp. 136–78.

25 Ibid., p. 148; Davis, *Christian Slaves*, pp. 3–26, esp. 6–7.

26 Bono, *I corsari barbareschi*, pp. 193–216. For the equivalent damage caused by Christian raiders to Muslim coastal communities see J. M. White, *Piracy and Law in the Ottoman Mediterranean* (Stanford, 2018), pp. 62–71.

References

27 E. G. Friedman, *Spanish Captives in North Africa in the Early Modern Age* (Madison, WI, 1983), pp. 33–43.
28 *Cortes de los antiguos reinos de León y de Castilla*, 5 vols. (Madrid, 1861–1903), v, p. 543. For petitions made to the authorities in Italy, see Bonaffini, *Un mare di paura*, pp. 16–22.
29 *Cortes de los antiguos reinos*, v, pp. 857–8. Cf. the request in the same *cortes* for improved coastal fortifications: *ibid.*, pp. 858–9.
30 *Queen Elizabeth and Her Times*, ed. Wright, i, pp. 241–2.
31 B. Bennassar and L. Bennassar, *Les chrétiens d'Allah: L'histoire extraordinaire des renégats, XVIe–XVIIe siècles* (Paris, 1989), p. 271.
32 *The Travels of Reverend Ólafur Egilson: The Story of the Barbary Corsair Raid on Iceland in 1627*, trans. K. S. Hreinsson and A. Nichols (Washington, DC, 2016); B. Lewis, 'Corsairs in Iceland', *Revue des mondes musulmans de la Méditerranée*, 15–16 (1973), 139–44; Th. Helgason, *The Corsairs' Longest Voyage: The Turkish Raid in Iceland 1627*, trans. A. Yates and J. A. Pétursdottír (Leiden, 2018).
33 M. A. Garcés, *Cervantes in Algiers: A Captive's Tale* (Nashville, 2002), pp. 26–30.
34 I. Soler, *Miguel de Cervantes: Los años de Argel* (Barcelona, 2016); Garcés, *Cervantes in Algiers*, pp. 38–57; Bono, *I corsari barbareschi*, pp. 378–87.
35 Cervantes' experiences in Algiers are also described in depositions made at his request soon after his return to Spain in order to address slanderous allegations made against him by an opponent, Juan Blanco de Paz: Miguel de Cervantes, *Información de Argel*, ed. A. J. Sáez (Madrid, 2019); Garcés, *Cervantes in Algiers*, pp. 99–106.
36 Miguel de Cervantes, *Don Quijote de La Mancha*, I.39–41, ed. F. Rico et al., 2 vols. (Madrid, 2015), i, pp. 493–539; Miguel de Cervantes, *The Ingenious Hidalgo Don Quixote de La Mancha*, trans. J. Rutherford with an introduction by R. González Ecchevarría (London, 2003), pp. 360–95.
37 Cervantes, *Don Quijote*, i, p. 507; Cervantes, *Don Quixote*, trans. Rutherford, p. 370.
38 Cervantes, *Don Quijote*, i, pp. 507, 515; Cervantes, *Don Quixote*, trans. Rutherford, pp. 370, 375–6.
39 Cervantes, *Don Quijote*, i, pp. 510, 512; Cervantes, *Don Quixote*, trans. Rutherford, pp. 372, 373.

40 Cervantes, *Don Quijote*, i, pp. 516, 518–19, 521; Cervantes, *Don Quixote*, trans. Rutherford, pp. 377, 378–9, 381.
41 Cervantes, *Don Quijote*, i, pp. 518, 519–24; Cervantes, *Don Quixote*, trans. Rutherford, pp. 378, 379–83. For lingua franca, see Antonio de Sosa [Diego de Haedo attrib.], *Topografía e historia general de Argel*, ed. I. Bauer y Landauer, 3 vols. (Madrid, 1927–9), i, pp. 115–16, trans. M. A. Garcés and D. de Armas Wilson as *An Early Modern Dialogue with Islam* (Notre Dame, 2011), p. 185; Davis, *Christian Slaves*, pp. 113–15; J. E. Wansbrough, *Lingua Franca in the Mediterranean* (Richmond, 1996).
42 Cervantes, *Don Quijote*, i, pp. 533–7; Cervantes, *Don Quixote*, trans. Rutherford, pp. 390–93.
43 The *Topografía e historia general de Argel* was not published until after Sosa's death, in 1612. The translation by Garcés and de Armas Wilson, *An Early Modern Dialogue with Islam*, is of the first book (of five), which is the most valuable as a historical and cultural anthropological record. For the tangled history of the text, which led to its being published under another name, see pp. 51–78.
44 Diego Galán, *Cautiverio y trabajos de Diego Galán natural de Consuegra y vecino de Toledo, 1589–1600*, ed. M. Serrano y Sanz (Madrid, 1913).
45 Ibid., pp. 11–12.
46 The figure is that supplied by Sosa, *Topografía e historia general*, p. 46, trans. as *An Early Modern Dialogue*, p. 119. In 1587, Lanfreducci and Bosio gave the number as 20,000: 'Costa e discorsi di Barberia', 473. See generally Davis, *Christian Slaves*, pp. 3–26. The captive communities of Tripoli and Tunis were substantially smaller than in Algiers.
47 Davis, *Christian Slaves*, pp. 82–7, 108–25.
48 Ibid., pp. 128–35. For a more roseate view, see Friedman, *Spanish Captives*, pp. 59–76.
49 Bosio, pp. 105–6; Bono, 'Naval Exploits and Privateering', p. 353.
50 Brogini, *Malte*, pp. 118–26.
51 AOM 88, fol. 39r; AOM 430, fol. 263v.
52 AOM 430, fols. 283v–284r. Many sub-Saharan slaves in the order's hands must have been doubly unfortunate captives who were seized

References

while being shipped from north African coastal entrepôts to the slave markets of Istanbul.

53 AOM 430, fols. 266r–v, 266v–267r.
54 G. Wettinger, *Slavery in the Islands of Malta and Gozo, ca. 1100–1812* (Malta, 2002); G. Wettinger, 'Esclaves noirs à Malte', in *Captifs en Méditerranée (XVI*ᵉ*–XVIII*ᵉ *siècles)*, ed. F. Moureau (Paris, 2008), pp. 155–69; R. Palmer, 'Slavery, Captivity and Galley Rowing in Early Modern Malta', *Antiquity*, 95 (2021), 1280–97.
55 N. Matar, 'Two Arabic Accounts of Captivity in Malta: Texts and Contexts', in *Piracy and Captivity in the Mediterranean 1550–1800*, ed. M. Klarer (London, 2019), pp. 259–63. See also N. Matar, *Mediterranean Captivity through Arab Eyes, 1517–1798* (Leiden, 2021), pp. 44–62.
56 Macuncuzade Mustafa, 'Memoirs of an Ottoman Captive in Malta, 1597–98', trans. H. Anetshofer, in *The Ottoman World: A Cultural History Reader, 1450–1700*, ed. H. T. Karateke (Oakland, CA, 2021), pp. 16–22. See also White, *Piracy and Law*, pp. 60–62, 71–80.
57 Macuncuzade Mustafa, 'Memoirs of an Ottoman Captive', pp. 17–18.
58 Ibid., pp. 18–19.
59 Ibid., pp. 18, 19–22.
60 Ibid., p. 22.
61 Davis, *Christian Slaves*, p. 125.
62 Bennassar and Bennassar, *Les chrétiens d'Allah*, pp. 383–4.
63 See the remarkable story of Gazanfer and his sister Fatima Hatun/Beatrice Michiel told in E. R. Dursteler, *Renegade Women: Gender, Identity, and Boundaries in the Early Modern Mediterranean* (Baltimore, 2011), pp. 1–33; Dursteler, *Venetians in Constantinople*, pp. 119–23, 125–6. For corsairs retaining affectionate family ties across the religious divide, see also Guy Turbet-Delof, *L'Afrique barbaresque dans la littérature française aux XVI*ᵉ *et XVII*ᵉ *siècles* (Geneva, 1973), p. 152; Dursteler, *Venetians in Constantinople*, pp. 126–9. Cf. the tenacious efforts of a Muslim mother not to lose track of her two daughters, who had become Christians in the rarefied atmosphere of Catherine de' Medici's household: S. A. Skilliter, 'Catherine de' Medici's Turkish Ladies-in-Waiting: A Dilemma in Franco-Ottoman Diplomatic Relations', *Turcica*, 7 (1975), 188–204.

64 Bennassar and Bennassar, *Les chrétiens d'Allah*, p. 161. For some of the many others who found themselves in similar circumstances, see ibid., pp. 158–77.
65 Ibid., p. 161.
66 Ibid., p. 259.
67 Ibid., p. 173.
68 G. Audisio, 'Renégats marseillais (1591–1595)', *Renaissance and Reformation*, 16 (1992), 35–8, 53–4.
69 Bennassar and Bennassar, *Les chrétiens d'Allah*, p. 356.
70 Audisio, 'Renégats marseillais', 46–51, 54–5; Bennassar and Bennassar, *Les chrétiens d'Allah*, pp. 349–57; L. Rostagno, *Mi faccio turco: Esperienze ed imagine dell'Islam nell'Italia moderna* (Rome, 1983), pp. 52–9; L. Scaraffia, *Rinnegati: Per una storia dell'identità occidentale* (Rome, 1993), pp. 101–14.
71 Cervantes, *Don Quijote*, i, p. 510; Cervantes, *Don Quixote*, trans. Rutherford, p. 372. See Scaraffia, *Rinnegati*, pp. 115–36. Cf. Galán's scepticism about renegades' *bona fides* in *Cautiverio y trabajos*, pp. 14–15; and Sosa's somewhat more measured emphasis on their cultural and religious liminality in *Topografía e historia general*, pp. 164–5, trans. as *An Early Modern Dialogue*, pp. 228–9.
72 A. G. Remensnyder, 'Compassion, Fear, Fugitive Slaves, and a Pirates' Shrine: Lampedusa, ca. 1550–ca. 1750', in *Mapping Pre-Modern Sicily: Maritime Violence, Cultural Exchange, and Imagination in the Mediterranean, 800–1700*, ed. E. Sohmer Tai and K. L. Reyerson (Cham, 2022), pp. 149–72.
73 Alonso de Contreras, *Vida de este capitán*, ed. A. Pérez-Reverte (Barcelona, 2008), pp. 90–92, trans. C. A. Phillips as *The Life of Captain Alonso de Contreras, Knight of the Military Order of St. John, Native of Madrid, Written by Himself (1582 to 1633)* (London, 1926), pp. 44–6.
74 Sosa, *Topografía e historia general*, pp. 158–9, trans. as *An Early Modern Dialogue*, pp. 223–4. See also Galán, *Cautiverio y trabajos*, p. 38.
75 In the same passage Sosa uses another word, *figura*, of a drawn or painted representation.

4. 1551: *The Precursor of the Great Siege*

1. AOM 411, fols. 202v–203r. The report itself does not survive, but its contents are recorded, in terms probably very close to the original, in Bosio, pp. 29–31. See also Brogini, *Malte*, pp. 62–4.
2. D. Castillo, *The Maltese Cross: A Strategic History of Malta* (Westport, CT, 2006), pp. 2–4.
3. Taxonomies and nomenclature, then and now, vary, especially at the lower end of the scale. I have followed the classification of Williams, *Empire and Holy War*, p. 92. Cf. Earle, *Corsairs*, p. 48n.
4. J. H. Pryor, *Geography, Technology, and War: Studies in the Maritime History of the Mediterranean, 649–1571* (Cambridge, 1988), pp. 12, 21–4, 35–6, 57–86; J. F. Guilmartin, *Gunpowder and Galleys: Changing Technology and Mediterranean Warfare at Sea in the 16th Century*, rev. edn (London, 2003), pp. 73–100, 111–36, 209–34; Williams, *Empire and Holy War*, pp. 43–55, 75–107, 109–21; J. Glete, *Warfare at Sea, 1500–1650: Maritime Conflicts and the Transformation of Europe* (London, 2000), pp. 93–106.
5. Nordman, *Tempête sur Alger*, pp. 153–62.
6. Guilmartin, *Gunpowder and Galleys*, pp. 79–80.
7. Ibid., pp. 78–9; Pryor, *Geography*, pp. 75–86.
8. Imber, *Ottoman Empire*, pp. 292–4; Pryor, *Geography*, pp. 172–92.
9. For the emergence and operations of the Ottoman navy in this period, see Imber, *Ottoman Empire*, pp. 292–318.
10. For the brothers' careers, see S. Souček, 'The Rise of the Barbarossa in North Africa', *Archivum Ottomanicum*, 3 (1971), 238–50; Brogini, *Malte*, pp. 30–32.
11. A. Mikhail, *God's Shadow: Sultan Selim, His Ottoman Empire, and the Making of the Modern World* (New York, 2020), pp. 341–7.
12. Bosio, pp. 191, 236–7, 238, 244, 250–51.
13. Ibid., pp. 257–9.
14. Ibid., p. 282.
15. S. Yérasimos, 'Les relations franco-ottomanes et la prise de Tripoli en 1551', in *Soliman le Magnifique et son temps*, ed. G. Veinstein (Paris, 1992), pp. 529–32.

References

16 Bosio, pp. 279–80.
17 Ibid., pp. 282–4, 286.
18 Ibid., p. 285.
19 Yérasimos, 'Les relations', pp. 538–9.
20 Pedro de Salazar, *Historia de la guerra y presa de África*, ed. M. Federici (Naples, 2015), pp. 301–3, 305–7.
21 Bosio, pp. 296–7.
22 Nicolas Durand de Villegagnon, *De bello Melitensi* (Paris, 1553), fol. Biii v; Bosio, pp. 297, 299.
23 Bosio, p. 298.
24 Ibid., pp. 298–9.
25 Villegagnon, *De bello Melitensi*, fol. Biv v; Bosio, p. 299.
26 Bosio, pp. 299–302.
27 For Villegagnon's role in the crisis, see L. Peillard, *Villegagnon: Vice-amiral de Bretagne, vice-roi du Brésil* (Paris, 1991), pp. 64–80.
28 Bosio, pp. 302–3; Villegagnon, *De bello Melitensi*, fols. Cii v–Ciii v.
29 Bosio, pp. 303–4.
30 Ibid., pp. 304–5; Villegagnon, *De bello Melitensi*, fols. Ciii v–Di v; S. Fiorini, 'The Resettlement of Gozo after 1551', *Melita Historica*, 9 (1986), 203–41, esp. 204–5, 209–10. Bosio's figure for the number of those enslaved is corroborated by a letter sent by the order to Charles V on 12 August 1551: AOM 88, fol. 94r. The Venetians believed the number was only 3,000, however: Setton, *Papacy*, iii, p. 555.
31 Brogini, *Malte*, pp. 171–4; U. Mori Ubaldino, *La marina del sovrano militare ordine di San Giovanni di Gerusalemme di Rodi e di Malta* (Rome, 1971), pp. 174–7. For Tripoli's importance to the order, see A. Brogini, 'La croisade africaine des Hospitaliers de Saint-Jean de Jérusalem (1530–1554)', in *Croisades en Afrique: Les expéditions occidentales à destination du continent africain, XIIIe–XVIe siècle*, ed. B. Weber (Toulouse, 2019), pp. 282–91.
32 Bosio, pp. 289, 293, 294; Villegagnon, *De bello Melitensi*, fols. Aiii v, Bi v–Bii v.
33 Bosio, pp. 306–14; Villegagnon, *De bello Melitensi*, fols. Diii r–Eiv v; AOM 88, fol. 94r–v.
34 Guillaume Ribier, *Lettres et memoires d'estat, des roys, princes, ambassadeurs, et autres ministres, sous les regnes de François premier, Henry II. &*

References

  François II., 2 vols. (Paris, 1666), ii, p. 307; Nicolay, *Dans l'empire de Soliman le Magnifique*, pp. 86–9; Villegagnon, *De bello Melitensi*, fol. Eiv r–v.

35 AOM 88, fols. 94v–95r, 101r–v. Charges were similarly brought against Galatiano de Sese *in absentia*; the case against him was reopened when he was ransomed in 1556 and returned to Malta, but he was cleared, a verdict that dissatisfied several Knights: AOM 88, fol. 95r; Bosio, p. 305.

36 C. Isom-Verhaaren, *Allies with the Infidel: The Ottoman and French Alliance in the Sixteenth Century* (London, 2011), pp. 40–48.

37 See e.g. the verdict of Bernardo Navagero in 1553: 'Relazione dell'impero ottomano', in *Relazione*, i, pp. 81–2.

38 Setton, *Papacy*, iii, pp. 555–6.

39 Yérasimos, 'Les relations', pp. 531–2.

40 Nicolay, *Dans l'empire de Soliman le Magnifique*, pp. 59–64; Yérasimos, 'Les relations', p. 540.

41 Ribier, *Lettres*, ii, pp. 303–4; Villegagnon, *De bello Melitensi*, fols. Di v–Dii r; Nicolay, *Dans l'empire de Soliman le Magnifique*, pp. 74–6; Bosio, pp. 305–6.

42 Ribier, *Lettres*, ii, pp. 304–6; Nicolay, *Dans l'empire de Soliman le Magnifique*, pp. 79–80; Bosio, pp. 308–9; Yérasimos, 'Les relations', pp. 541–2.

43 Ribier, *Lettres*, ii, p. 307; Villegagnon, *De bello Melitensi*, fols. Fi v–Fii r; Nicolay, *Dans l'empire de Soliman le Magnifique*, p. 93; Bosio, pp. 315–16.

44 See e.g. AOM 88, fol. 94r; Bosio, p. 303. For the belief that the armada would return to Malta, see AOM 88, fol. 92v.

45 AOM 88, fols. 92v, 93r–v.

46 The suggestion of d'Aramon in Ribier, *Lettres*, ii, pp. 306–7.

47 Bosio, p. 279; Yérasimos, 'Les relations', pp. 539–40.

48 Villegagnon, *De bello Melitensi*, esp. fols. Aii v–Aiii r, Aiv r, Biii r.

49 Bosio, pp. 290–91, 295–6.

50 *De bello Melitensi*, fol. Cii r; AOM 88, fol. 94r. Cf. Bosio, p. 292.

51 Villegagnon, *De bello Melitensi*, fol. Biii r.

52 Bosio, pp. 280, 288, 291–2.

53 Ibid., pp. 299–300.

54 Villegagnon, *De bello Melitensi*, fols. Civ v–Di r; Nicolay, *Dans l'empire de Soliman le Magnifique*, p. 75; Bosio, pp. 304–5.

5. The Great Siege Begins

1. See S. Alford, *The Watchers: A Secret History of the Reign of Elizabeth I* (New York, 2012), esp. pp. 125–240.
2. G. Parker, *The Grand Strategy of Philip II* (New Haven, 1998), pp. 209–68.
3. H. Kamen, *Spain's Road to Empire: The Making of a World Power, 1492–1793* (London, 2002), pp. 224–7.
4. AOM 88, fols. 92v, 93r.
5. Bosio, pp. 128, 198–9; Q. Hughes, *The Building of Malta during the Period of the Knights of St. John of Jerusalem 1530–1795*, rev. edn (London, 1967), pp. 14–15; Brogini, *Malte*, pp. 156–7.
6. Bosio, p. 353; Hughes, *Building*, pp. 16–17; Brogini, *Malte*, pp. 157–8; A. Hoppen, *The Fortification of Malta by the Order of St. John 1530–1798*, 2nd edn (Msida, 1999), pp. 37–40; Spiteri, *Great Siege*, pp. 124–39 (including very helpful images).
7. Bosio, pp. 198–9; Hughes, *Building*, p. 15; Hoppen, *Fortification*, pp. 33–7, 40–41; Spiteri, *Great Siege*, pp. 108–19.
8. Spiteri, *Great Siege*, p. 306.
9. Brogini, *Malte*, pp. 158–61.
10. Bosio, pp. 327–32; E. Rossi, *Storia della marina dell'ordine di San Giovanni di Gerusalemme di Rodi e di Malta* (Rome, 1926), pp. 42–3; Mori Ubaldino, *La marina*, pp. 179–80.
11. Bosio, pp. 366–7; Mori Ubaldino, *La marina*, pp. 187–90.
12. Sosa, *Topografía e historia general*, p. 196, trans. as *An Early Modern Dialogue*, p. 257.
13. F. Braudel, *The Mediterranean and the Mediterranean World in the Age of Philip II*, trans. S. Reynolds, 1 vol. in 2 (London, 1972–3), ii, pp. 973–87; R. C. Anderson, *Naval Wars in the Levant: From the Battle of Lepanto to the Introduction of Steam* (Princeton, 1952), pp. 8–14; Guilmartin, *Gunpowder and Galleys*, pp. 137–48, esp. 144–6.
14. Braudel, *Mediterranean*, ii, pp. 987–9.
15. See Williams, *Empire and Holy War*, p. 252.
16. Braudel, *Mediterranean*, ii, pp. 1007–12; Thompson, *War and Government*, pp. 16–17, 168, 300–301.

References

17 Williams, *Empire and Holy War*, p. 208.
18 Setton, *Papacy*, iv, pp. 846–7; Housley, *Later Crusades*, pp. 147–8.
19 Braudel, *Mediterranean*, ii, pp. 1012–14.
20 Ibid., pp. 999–1001.
21 *Négociations*, ed. Charrière, ii, pp. 770, 773; Setton, *Papacy*, iv, p. 842.
22 Brantôme, i, p. 50; ii, pp. 83, 88; vi, p. 492; vii, pp. 94–5; Cocula-Vaillières, *Brantôme*, pp. 187–92; Lazard, *Pierre de Bourdeille*, p. 87.
23 Setton, *Papacy*, iv, p. 865. In 1566 the amount of silver arriving at Seville was the most on record up to that point: G. Parker, *Imprudent King: A New Life of Philip II* (New Haven, 2014), pp. 149–50.
24 Balbi (1568), fols. 18r–19r. Cf. the briefer treatment in Balbi (1567), pp. 31–2.
25 Cf. Cirni, fols. 38r–39v (upon which Balbi's second edition probably drew).
26 Brogini, *Malte*, pp. 120–26. Cf. the negative verdict on this policy and its responsibility for the siege, by a noted critic of La Valette and the order, in 'L'Assedio di Malta. Informatione di Malta del "Rangone"', ed. H. P. Scicluna, *Archivum Melitense*, 8 (1929), 35.
27 Bosio, pp. 471–3 (significantly followed by a passage, which was probably inspired in part by Balbi, on the sultan conceiving a mortal hatred for the order). For ransom activity following these seizures, see e.g. AOM 430, fols. 255r–256v.
28 A. Cassola, *The Great Siege of Malta (1565) and the Istanbul State Archives* (Valletta, 1995), pp. 17–19.
29 Ibid., pp. 19–21.
30 Ibid., pp. 14–15, 15–17, 23–4, 24–6, 26–7, 27–9, 29–32.
31 E.g. CODOIN, xxix, pp. 25, 176.
32 For such sentiments informing the narratives of the siege, including exaggerated estimates of the Ottomans' territorial ambitions, see e.g. Balbi (1567), pp. 40–41, 47; Balbi (1568), fols. 22r–v, 26r; Cirni, fol. 63r; Vendôme, p. 23; Viperano, fol. 4v. Cf. the convincing remarks in Williams, *Empire and Holy War*, pp. 62–3, concerning Ottoman designs on Italy.
33 Setton, *Papacy*, iv, pp. 858 and n.107, 859 and n.109. Cf. Cirni, fols. 39v–40r.

34 AOM 431, fols. 255v–256r. See also Bosio, p. 587, repeating the contents of the document.
35 An Ottoman source suggests that he was a *sipahi* named Mehmed bin Davud: *Ottoman Campaign Register*, p. 209. Bosio, p. 587, however, gives his name as Memi Çelebi.
36 Balbi (1567), pp. 121–3; Balbi (1568), fols. 61v–62v. Cf. Bosio, p. 587, which offers up an image of Lascaris living a life of gentlemanly ease in Naples.
37 Cirni, fols. 40v–41r; Vendôme, pp. 6–7.
38 Murphey, *Ottoman Warfare*, pp. 53–9.
39 See Balbi (1568), fol. 24v.
40 For the Ottomans' relationship with the Barbary regimes, see Imber, *Ottoman Empire*, pp. 195–9.
41 See Williams, *Empire and Holy War*, pp. 252–4.
42 Donini, 'Relazione dell'impero ottomano', in *Relazioni*, iii, pp. 188–9.
43 E.g. Balbi (1567), p. 46; Balbi (1568), fols. 25v–26r.
44 Spiteri, *Great Siege*, pp. 29–32.
45 Cassola, *Great Siege*, pp. 15–17, 17–19, 24–6, 26–7, 27–9, 32–3.
46 *Négociations*, ed. Charrière, ii, pp. 774–5.
47 Setton, *Papacy*, iv, pp. 850 and n.77, 852–3.
48 See Brogini, *1565*, pp. 77–8; Spiteri, *Great Siege*, p. 24.
49 A theme that is significantly introduced very early in Cirni, fol. 50v.
50 Balbi (1567), pp. 45–6; Balbi (1568), fol. 25r–v (the sum of his totals for the various types of combatants is actually 28,900).
51 Spiteri, *Great Siege*, pp. 23, 75–87 (Spiteri's overall estimate is somewhat higher than mine); see also Brogini, *1565*, pp. 78–9, favouring a total of approximately 20,000.
52 Balbi (1567), pp. 44–5; Balbi (1568), fol. 24r–v; Cirni, fol. 45r; Vendôme, pp. 8–9; Viperano, fol. 6r.
53 Brogini, *1565*, pp. 80–82, 82–3, 84; Spiteri, *Great Siege*, p. 23.
54 AOM 91, fols. 143v, 144r.
55 AOM 91, fols. 144r, 148r, 150r, 151r, 151v, 152r; Brogini, *Malte*, pp. 179–81.
56 Spiteri, *Great Siege*, p. 28; Brogini, *1565*, p. 80.
57 Balbi (1567), p. 59; Balbi (1568), fols. 31r, 31v–32r.
58 Spiteri, *Great Siege*, pp. 38–40; Brogini, *1565*, pp. 96–7.

References

59 Balbi (1567), pp. 64–5; Balbi (1568), fol. 32r–v; Cirni, fol. 49v; Vendôme, p. 11; Viperano, fols. 6v–7r; Bosio, p. 520.
60 *Ottoman Campaign Register*, p. 271.
61 Balbi (1567), pp. 71–2; Balbi (1568), fol. 34r–v. See also Cirni, fols. 50v–51r.
62 Spiteri, *Great Siege*, pp. 92–9 (a very thorough review of the evidence); Brogini, *1565*, pp. 95–6.
63 Balbi (1567), pp. 83–4; Balbi (1568), fol. 40v; Cirni, fol. 53v; Spiteri, *Great Siege*, pp. 141–3.
64 Q. Hughes, 'How Fort St. Elmo Survived the Siege for So Long', *Treasures of Malta*, 8 (2002), 109–15. But cf. Balbi (1568), fol. 31r–v.
65 Balbi (1567), pp. 85–7; Balbi (1568), fols. 41r–42r; Cirni, fol. 54v; Vendôme, p. 15; Spiteri, *Great Siege*, pp. 155–9.
66 Balbi (1567), pp. 79, 85; Balbi (1568), fols. 38r, 41r; Cirni, fols. 52r, 53r; Vendôme, pp. 12, 13; Viperano, fol. 8r–v; Spiteri, *Great Siege*, pp. 151–2.
67 Balbi (1567), p. 85; Balbi (1568), fol. 41r; Cirni, fol. 53r–v; Viperano, fol. 8v; Bosio, pp. 532–3.
68 See CODOIN, xxix, p. 7, though Setton, *Papacy*, iv, p. 842 n.47 is perhaps correct to characterize this *aviso* from Constantinople, dated 7 December 1564, which states that St Elmo would be the Turks' first target, as 'almost suspiciously prophetic'.
69 Cf. Bosio, p. 525, where two renegades report that the proximity of the navy to the army was the pashas' principal concern. See also the careful analysis in Cirni, fols. 60v–61r.
70 See the letter from La Valette to García de Toledo on 3 June in CODOIN, xxix, pp. 394–6; and the bleak assessment by Rafaele Salvago, the Grand Master's liaison with the authorities in Sicily, on 10 June, in ibid., pp. 396–404. See also Brogini, *1565*, pp. 107–8.
71 Balbi (1568), fol. 43r–v; Cirni, fol. 59r.
72 Balbi (1568), fols. 44v–45v; Cirni, fols. 57v–58r; Bosio, p. 550; Spiteri, *Great Siege*, pp. 190–91.
73 Cirni, fol. 58r–v; Bosio, pp. 551–2; Spiteri, *Great Siege*, pp. 191–4; Brogini, *1565*, pp. 110–12. Vendôme, pp. 28–9, observes that Medina also expressed confidence in the state of the order's defences and the defenders' morale. See also Viperano, fol. 14r.

References

74 Vendôme, p. 27, suggests, however, that plans to evacuate the surviving defenders on twelve or thirteen boats were well advanced.
75 Balbi (1567), pp. 101–2; Balbi (1568), fols. 50r–51r; Spiteri, *Great Siege*, pp. 202–4.
76 Balbi (1567), p. 114; Balbi (1568), fol. 55r; Cirni, fol. 69v; Vendôme, pp. 21, 23, 25; Brogini, *1565*, pp. 117–18.
77 Balbi (1567), p. 109; Balbi (1568), fol. 52v; Cirni, fols. 68r, 71r–v; Vendôme, p. 26. But for a different chronology see Demir and Duggan, 'Gelibolulu Mustafa Ali's Narrative', pp. 57–65.
78 Balbi (1567), pp. 111–13; Balbi (1568), fols. 53v–54r; Cirni, fols. 68v–69r.
79 *Ottoman Campaign Register*, p. 271.
80 Balbi (1567), p. 114; Balbi (1568), fol. 55r; Cirni, fols. 69v–70v; Bosio, p. 573.
81 Balbi (1567), pp. 115–16; Balbi (1568), fol. 58v; Cirni, fols. 70v, 71v; Vendôme, p. 33; Bosio, p. 574.
82 Vendôme, p. 33.
83 Cirni, fol. 69r.
84 For Monserrat as a yes-man, see Vendôme, p. 20.
85 Cirni, fols. 57v, 64r, 66v–67r; Vendôme, pp. 16–17, 18, 32. For La Valette's irritation, see e.g. Balbi (1568), fol. 57r; Vendôme, pp. 35–7; Bosio, p. 543.
86 See La Valette's letter to Philip II on 25 June in Spiteri, *Great Siege*, pp. 223, 605 n.10. See also CODOIN, xxix, pp. 243–4, from La Valette to García de Toledo on the same date; and Cirni, fols. 71v–72r.
87 Balbi (1567), pp. 65, 67, 72–3, 79–80, 100, 109; Balbi (1568), fols. 33r, 35r, 47r, 49r, 52r; Cirni, fols. 51v–52r, 52v, 65r, 68r; Vendôme, pp. 13, 23; Bosio, pp. 521, 524, 525, 530, 539.
88 For an interesting reference to suspicion falling on a Knight believed to have called out to the Turks in Greek, see Viperano, fols. 14v–15r.
89 Bosio, p. 531. See also Balbi (1568), fol. 44r.
90 Balbi (1567), p. 107; Balbi (1568), fol. 51r. The same construction appears in both versions.
91 Cf. Spiteri, *Great Siege*, pp. 218–19; Brogini, *1565*, p. 123.

References

6. The Guns of July and August

1. *Ottoman Campaign Register*, pp. 335–7, 341–3; Cirni, fol. 74r; Vendôme, p. 42.
2. *Ottoman Campaign Register*, pp. 337–9. For the suggestion that Ottoman influence in Tripoli was fragile, see Bosio, p. 612.
3. Brogini, *1565*, pp. 125–7. For the location of the batteries, see Cirni, fols. 78v, 88r; Vendôme, p. 43; Viperano, cols. 19r, 22v; Bosio, pp. 582–3, 592; Spiteri, *Great Siege*, pp. 240, 242–3, 247, 288–9, 314–15.
4. For the development and significance of *trace italienne*, see S. Pepper and N. Adams, *Firearms and Fortifications: Military Architecture and Siege Warfare in Sixteenth-Century Siena* (Chicago, 1986), pp. 3–31; M. Wolfe, 'Walled Towns during the French Wars of Religion (1560–1630)', in *City Walls: The Urban Enceinte in Global Perspective*, ed. J. D. Tracy (Cambridge, 2000), pp. 317–48; M. Pollak, *Cities at War in Early Modern Europe* (Cambridge, 2010).
5. Viperano, fol. 20r–v; Brogini, *1565*, pp. 132–4.
6. Balbi (1567), pp. 119–20; Balbi (1568), fols. 60r–61r; Cirni, fol. 74r–v; Vendôme, p. 34; Bosio, pp. 581–2.
7. Bosio, p. 582, suggests as much. Cf. Balbi's comment that La Valette was disdainful of the Ottomans' use of a captured Christian sailor, Orlando, as a translator when another parley was attempted in late July: Balbi (1567), pp. 155–6; Balbi (1568), fols. 80v–81r.
8. Balbi (1567), pp. 121–3; Balbi (1568), fols. 61v–62v; Cirni, fols. 77v–78r; Vendôme, pp. 34–5 (Vendôme probably met him in Rome). For the defector's name, see *Ottoman Campaign Register*, p. 209; Bosio, p. 587.
9. Balbi (1567), p. 123; Balbi (1568), fol. 62v. Balbi suggests that mysterious smoke signals from Mdina indicating the arrival of the relief, which the Grand Master could not interpret at the time, preceded the defector's arrival, but his two versions give conflicting dates.
10. See Cirni, fol. 86v, a thoughtful analysis of García de Toledo's options.
11. Balbi (1568), fol. 78v; Cirni, fols. 79r–80r, 80v; Vendôme, pp. 43–4; Viperano, fols. 23v–24r; Bosio, p. 596.
12. CODOIN, xxix, pp. 226–30; Brogini, *1565*, p. 136.

References

13 See the comments of the first author to write a detailed description of Malta after the arrival of the Knights: Jean Quintin d'Autun, *The Earliest Description of Malta (Lyons, 1536)*, ed. and trans. H. C. R. Vella (Sliema, 1980), pp. 18–19.
14 Cirni, fol. 81r, suggests that the fear of denuding Naples of troops dampened the viceroy's enthusiasm for relieving Malta.
15 Cirni, fols. 73r–v, 78v–80v, 81r–v, 86r–v, 87v, 88r–89v, 91v–92v.
16 CODOIN, xxix, p. 265. For the composition of the force, see Bosio, pp. 585–6.
17 CODOIN, xxix, p. 424.
18 Balbi (1567), pp. 125–6; Balbi (1568), fol. 64r; Cirni, fols. 75v–76r (a slightly different version of the ruse).
19 Cirni, fols. 75r–77r (which suggests that the governor of Mdina wanted to use part of the relief force to strengthen his own garrison); Vendôme, pp. 38–41 (a rather confused account); Viperano, fols. 18r–19r, 19v–20r (an interesting version of events hinting at disagreement over strategy); Bosio, pp. 584–6, 588–90. García de Toledo's account of the relief operation that he sent to Philip II is in CODOIN, xxix, pp. 252–4.
20 Balbi (1567), p. 129; Balbi (1568), fol. 67r.
21 Balbi (1567), pp. 130, 132; Balbi (1568), fols. 67v, 69r.
22 Balbi (1567), p. 130; Balbi (1568), fols. 67v–68r; Cirni, fol. 78r; Vendôme, pp. 46–7.
23 Balbi (1567), p. 131; Balbi (1568), fol. 68r–v; *Ottoman Campaign Register*, p. 223; Bosio, p. 597; Spiteri, *Great Siege*, pp. 250–51.
24 Balbi (1567), pp. 135–8, 143–7; Balbi (1568), fols. 71v–75v. The other principal narrative sources likewise describe the unfolding drama at some length: see e.g. Cirni, fols. 82r–83v; Vendôme, pp. 45–6, 47; Viperano, fols. 21r–22r. See also Spiteri, *Great Siege*, pp. 251–61.
25 For his arrival, see *Ottoman Campaign Register*, p. 223; CODOIN, xxix, p. 298; Cirni, fol. 82r; Vendôme, p. 45; Bosio, p. 600.
26 For this position, Spiteri, *Great Siege*, pp. 230–35, 246–7.
27 A story retained by Bosio, p. 604.
28 Balbi (1567), p. 134; Balbi (1568), fols. 69v–70r; Cirni, fol. 82r; Viperano, fol. 23r; Bosio, pp. 597–8.

References

29 Balbi (1567), pp. 143–4; Balbi (1568), fols. 72v–73r; Cirni, fols. 82v–83r; Bosio, p. 604.
30 Balbi (1567), p. 143; Balbi (1568), fols. 72v–73r; Cirni, fol. 82r; Viperano, fol. 21r–v.
31 Cirni, fol. 85v; Vendôme, p. 42.
32 Spiteri, *Great Siege*, pp. 288–9.
33 But see Cirni, fol. 74v, for dismissive remarks about the sappers' abilities.
34 Balbi (1567), pp. 149, 161–2; Balbi (1568), fols. 76v, 83v–84v; Cirni, fol. 95r–v; Vendôme, pp. 50, 57, 58; Viperano, fol. 24v; Bosio, pp. 611, 618–19; Spiteri, *Great Siege*, pp. 280–87, 287, 318–20.
35 Balbi (1567), pp. 148–9; Balbi (1568), fols. 75v–76v; Cirni, fol. 84r–v; Vendôme, pp. 49, 50; Bosio, pp. 609–10, 612; Spiteri, *Great Siege*, pp. 278–80.
36 Balbi (1567), p. 154; Balbi (1568), fol. 80r; Bosio, p. 611; Spiteri, *Great Siege*, pp. 358–73. In 1567, when Menga retired after seven years' service to the order, he was granted a generous pension of 300 *scudi*: AOM 431, fol. 258r–v.
37 Balbi (1567), pp. 148, 152; Balbi (1568), fols. 75v, 78r; Cirni, fol. 98r.
38 Balbi (1567), pp. 150, 151–2; Balbi (1568), fols. 77r, 77v, 85r; Cirni, fols. 85v–86r.
39 Balbi (1567), pp. 156–7; Balbi (1568), fol. 81r–v; Cirni, fol. 86r.
40 Balbi (1567), pp. 156–7; Balbi (1568), fol. 81r–v. For the lack of useful intelligence, see Balbi (1567), pp. 164–5; Balbi (1568), fol. 86r–v; Spiteri, *Great Siege*, pp. 321–4.
41 Balbi (1567), pp. 163–4; Balbi (1568), fol. 85r–v; Cirni, fol. 95v; Spiteri, *Great Siege*, pp. 324–5.
42 Cf. Balbi's observations about the compression of the Turkish assaults into narrow spaces in (1568), fol. 81v.
43 Cirni, fols. 96v–98r; Vendôme, pp. 52–3; Spiteri, *Great Siege*, pp. 374–81.
44 For La Valette's inner team, which included a jester, see Balbi (1568), fol. 82r; Cirni, fol. 94v.
45 Balbi (1567), pp. 170–73; Balbi (1568), fols. 90r–91v; Spiteri, *Great Siege*, pp. 374–7.
46 Spiteri, *Great Siege*, pp. 180–87.

47 Balbi (1567), p. 153; Balbi (1568), fol. 79r–v; Cirni, fols. 75r, 81v, 94r; Viperano, fols. 25r–26r.
48 Balbi (1567), p. 118; Balbi (1568), fols. 59v–60r; Spiteri, *Great Siege*, pp. 184–7. But cf. Cirni, fol. 67v; Viperano, fols. 17v–18r; Bosio, pp. 583–4.
49 Balbi (1567), pp. 173–4, 177; Balbi (1568), fols. 91v–92v; Cirni, fol. 97v; Bosio, pp. 629–30; Spiteri, *Great Siege*, pp. 377–81.
50 For Anastagi's account of the siege, see G. Bonello, 'An Overlooked Eyewitness's Account of the Great Siege', in *Melitensium Amor: Festschrift in Honour of Dun Ġwann Azzopardi*, ed. T. Cortis, T. Freller and L. Bugeja (Malta, 2002), pp. 133–48.
51 Balbi (1567), p. 181; Balbi (1568), fol. 95r–v; Cirni, fol. 99r–v; Viperano, fols. 26v–27r, 27v–28r; Bosio, pp. 632–3; Spiteri, *Great Siege*, pp. 382–405.
52 Balbi (1567), p. 171; Balbi (1568), fol. 90r. For the defenders' habituation to the sound of the cannon, see Cirni, fol. 102r.
53 *Ottoman Campaign Register*, pp. 185, 193. For another case of burning, see p. 269.
54 Ibid., pp. 217, 231, 249.
55 Ibid., pp. 225, 227, 241, 259, 275.
56 Balbi (1567), p. 128; Balbi (1568), fol. 66v.
57 Balbi (1567), p. 126; Balbi (1568), fol. 64r; Cirni, fol. 76v; Vendôme, pp. 40–41; Bosio, p. 586; Spiteri, *Great Siege*, pp. 243–4.
58 AOM 430, fol. 277r. For similar cases see also fols. 273r, 275v.
59 *Ottoman Campaign Register*, pp. 213, 263, 285. See Spiteri, *Great Siege*, p. 482. Cf. Cirni, fol. 97v, for a reference to the crew of a 'Sclavonian' ship, that is from the Adriatic, hunting for slaves in open country beyond the Turkish positions.
60 Bosio, p. 627; Vendôme, p. 41. See also Viperano, fol. 26v.
61 Balbi (1567), pp. 166–8, 169; Balbi (1568), fols. 87v–88v, 89r; Cirni, fol. 96r (also mentioning the flight of a convict-oarsman around the same time); Bosio, pp. 626–7.
62 See Viperano, fol. 6v: the Maltese were 'by nature timorous and inexperienced in matters of war'.
63 CODOIN, xxix, pp. 305–6.

References

64 See Bosio, pp. 602, 607, 609. See also the positive comments in Balbi (1567), p. 178; Balbi (1568), fol. 93r–v; Cirni, fols. 85v, 97r; Viperano, fol. 16v.
65 For the suggestion that Maltese were paid for their work, at least some of the time, see Balbi (1567), p. 117; Balbi (1568), fol. 59r. For the Maltese contribution in general, Spiteri, *Great Siege*, pp. 461–6; Spiteri, 'The Maltese Combatants of the Great Siege', in *Besieged*, i, pp. 117–24.
66 Balbi (1567), p. 179; Balbi (1568), fol. 94r; Cirni, fol. 113r; Vendôme, p. 61; Bosio, pp. 674–5; Spiteri, *Great Siege*, p. 381.
67 Viperano, fol. 25r; Bosio, pp. 586, 609, 617; Spiteri, *Great Siege*, p. 464. For Bajada's suspicions, Balbi (1567), p. 167; Balbi (1568), fol. 88r.
68 Cirni, fol. 75r; Viperano, fols. 16v–17r; Bosio, p. 582.
69 Balbi (1567), pp. 133–4; Balbi (1568), fol. 69r–v; Bosio, p. 598.
70 Bosio, p. 615.
71 Cirni, fol. 83v; Viperano, fol. 22r; Bosio, p. 627.
72 AOM 91, fols. 104v, 120r, 135v, 143v; Balbi (1568), fol. 125r; Cirni, fol. 124r; Bonello, 'In and Out', p. 18.
73 AOM 91, fols. 88r, 90r, 129r; Balbi (1568), fols. 110r, 111v.
74 AOM 91, fol. 150r; Cirni, fol. 122r.
75 AOM 91, fols. 88v, 136v; Balbi (1568), fol. 123v.
76 AOM 91, fols. 83r, 106v; Balbi (1567), pp. 146, 152, 178; Balbi (1568), fols. 75r, 78r, 85r, 93r, 125v; Bosio, p. 608.
77 AOM 91, fols. 120r, 141v; Balbi (1567), pp. 137, 138, 178, 189; Balbi (1568), fols. 71v, 72r, 74r, 93r, 124v.

7. Relief

1 Cirni, fol. 101v.
2 Ibid., fols. 113v–114r; Viperano, fols. 34v–35r; Bosio, pp. 680–81.
3 Balbi (1567), pp. 181–2; Balbi (1568), fol. 95v.
4 Balbi (1567), p. 182; Balbi (1568), fols. 95v–96r.
5 Balbi (1567), p. 184; Balbi (1568), fols. 96v–97r.
6 Bosio, pp. 645–6. Cirni, fol. 102r, has the Turks launching preliminary attacks on 17, 18 and 19 August.

References

7 Balbi (1567), pp. 188–9; Balbi (1568), fols. 98v–99v; Cirni, fols. 102r–103v; Vendôme, pp. 60–61 (who insists that the Christian losses were substantial). Cf. Cirni, fol. 101v, for the Ottomans' attempts earlier in August to address their shortage of frontline troops.
8 Balbi (1567), pp. 189–90; Balbi (1568), fol. 100r; Cirni, fols. 102r, 102v, 103v–104r; Vendôme, p. 62; Bosio, pp. 648–9.
9 Balbi (1567), pp. 184, 194, 195; Balbi (1568), fols. 96v, 102v, 103r; Cirni, fols. 101v, 112v–113r; Vendôme, pp. 58, 60, 61; Bosio, pp. 634, 635, 636, 639, 673; Spiteri, *Great Siege*, pp. 429, 440–42. See also the remarks by Vendôme, p. 57, about the Turks' versatility and experimentation.
10 Balbi (1567), p. 190; Balbi (1568), fol. 100v; Spiteri, *Great Siege*, pp. 433–5.
11 Balbi (1568), fol. 100r. See also the skirmish reported in Cirni, fol. 103r.
12 Balbi (1567), pp. 186, 190, 191, 194; Balbi (1568), fols. 97v–98r, 100v, 101v, 102v.
13 Balbi (1567), p. 194; Balbi (1568), 102v; Cirni, fol. 113v; Vendôme, pp. 58, 65; Viperano, fol. 33v.
14 Balbi (1567), p. 187; Balbi (1568), fol. 98r–v; Cirni, fol. 112v; Bosio, pp. 636, 682.
15 Balbi (1567), pp. 187, 194; Balbi (1568), fols. 98r–v, 102v; Viperano, fol. 31v.
16 Balbi (1567), p. 193; Balbi (1568), fol. 102r.
17 Balbi (1567), pp. 191, 195; Balbi (1568), fols. 101r, 103r; Vendôme, pp. 63–4, 66; Viperano, fol. 33r–v; Bosio, pp. 673, 684; Spiteri, *Great Siege*, pp. 435, 486–7.
18 Balbi (1567), p. 190; Balbi (1568), fols. 100v–101r; Viperano, fol. 32v; Bosio, pp. 672–3; Spiteri, *Great Siege*, pp. 484–5.
19 See e.g. Vendôme, pp. 63, 64, 66.
20 Balbi (1567), pp. 191, 192; Balbi (1568), fols. 101r, 101v–102r; Bosio, pp. 672, 679.
21 Balbi (1567), p. 192; Balbi (1568), fol. 101v; Cirni, fol. 114v; Vendôme, p. 66; Viperano, fol. 35r–v; Bosio, p. 682.
22 As noted by Spiteri, *Great Siege*, p. 484.
23 Balbi (1567), p. 197; Balbi (1568), fol. 104r; Vendôme, p. 68; Viperano, fol. 36r; Bosio, p. 693.
24 Viperano, fol. 29r–v. Cf. the stirring speeches placed in his mouth at fols. 29v–30v, 36r–v.
25 Balbi (1567), pp. 212–13; Balbi (1568), fol. 120r.

References

26 Balbi (1568), fols. 106v–109v; Cirni, fols. 105v–108v; Bosio, pp. 650, 661–7. See also Viperano, fol. 29r ('the whole nobility of Christendom seemed to have gathered for this war').
27 Cirni, fol. 105v; Bosio, p. 668. Cf. Cirni, fols. 104r–v, 105r, for García's attempts to restrain enthusiastic Sicilian nobles.
28 CODOIN, xxix, p. 312.
29 Ibid., pp. 263, 266–7, 289; Bosio, p. 652.
30 See e.g. CODOIN, xxix, p. 247, a briefing document addressed to Philip II dated 5 July in which García writes of up to 12,000 'old', i.e. experienced, soldiers. According to Vendôme, p. 55, a spy sent to Malta by García reported back that 10,000 would suffice.
31 Balbi (1567), p. 200; Balbi (1568), fol. 106r–v.
32 Cirni, fols. 92v–93r. See also Bosio, pp. 653–4.
33 Cirni, fols. 92v–93r, 116v; Viperano, fol. 29r; Setton, *Papacy*, iv, p. 871.
34 Balbi (1567), p. 200; Balbi (1568), fol. 105v; Cirni, fol. 110v; Bosio, p. 667.
35 Balbi (1567), p. 200; Balbi (1568), fols. 105v–106r.
36 See García's reference to *los tiempos contrarios* in a letter to Philip II of 25 August: CODOIN, xxix, p. 465.
37 Cirni, fol. 110r–v, suggests that many nobles took offence at being left behind.
38 CODOIN, xxix, p. 469.
39 Balbi (1567), p. 202; Balbi (1568), fol. 112r; Cirni, fols. 110v–111r; Vendôme, p. 64; Bosio, p. 670. Cirni, fols. 104r, 114v, imagines that the Ottomans were anxiously waiting for this ship.
40 CODOIN, xxix, pp. 470, 503–4; Balbi (1568), fol. 112r–v; Cirni, fol. 111r.
41 Balbi (1568), fol. 112r–v; Cirni, fol. 111v; Viperano, fols. 32v–33r; Bosio, p. 677.
42 CODOIN, xxix, p. 477; Balbi (1568), fol. 112v; Bosio, pp. 677, 684.
43 The best source for Doria's movements is his own detailed account of his actions between 23 August and 7 September, addressed to Philip II, in CODOIN, xxix, pp. 494–501. See also Balbi (1568), fols. 113v–114r; Cirni, fols. 105v, 111v–112v, 117r; Bosio, pp. 667, 670–71, 677–8, 683.
44 CODOIN, xxix, pp. 477–8; Cirni, fols. 115v, 116v–117r; Balbi (1568), fol. 113r–v; Bosio, p. 685.
45 Balbi (1568), fol. 114r; Cirni, fols. 117r–118r. See also Bosio, p. 686.

46 CODOIN, xxix, pp. 484–5; Balbi (1568) fols. 114v–115r; Cirni, fol. 118r–v. Vendôme, p. 67, and Bosio, pp. 690–91, believe that by this stage the relief force was down to 8,300 men.
47 His African experience is emphasized by Cirni, fols. 115v–116r.
48 Balbi (1568), fols. 112v–113r; Cirni, fols. 105r, 115v–116v; Viperano, fols. 31v–32r; Bosio, pp. 684–5.
49 Balbi (1567), p. 207; Balbi (1568), fol. 115r–v; Cirni, fols. 118v, 119r–v; Bosio, pp. 667–8, 691.
50 Cirni, fol. 120r; Bosio, pp. 694–5.
51 Balbi (1567), pp. 197–8; Balbi (1568), fols. 104v, 115r; Cirni, fol. 119r; Bosio, p. 693.
52 Balbi (1567), p. 208; Balbi (1568), fol. 116r–v.
53 Balbi (1567), pp. 198–9; Balbi (1568), fols. 104v, 105r–v; Vendôme, p. 69; Bosio, pp. 695, 696; Spiteri, *Great Siege*, pp. 488–90. For indications that the Turks were already dismantling their camp before the 7th, see CODOIN, xxix, pp. 512–13; Balbi (1567), p. 196; Balbi (1568), fols. 101v, 103v; Cirni, fol. 119v; Viperano, fol. 35r.
54 Balbi (1568), fol. 105r.
55 CODOIN, xxix, pp. 513–14; Balbi (1567), pp. 208–9; Balbi (1568), fols. 105r, 117r–v; Cirni, fol. 120v; Viperano, fol. 37r; Bosio, p. 698.
56 Bosio, p. 698.
57 Balbi (1567), p. 208; Balbi (1568), fol. 116v.
58 Balbi (1567), p. 210; Balbi (1568), fols. 118v–119r; Cirni, fol. 121v; Viperano, fol. 37v; Bosio, pp. 699–700.
59 Balbi (1567), p. 210; Balbi (1568), fol. 119r.
60 For a helpful account of events, see Spiteri, *Great Siege*, pp. 508–15. The belief in the very large discrepancy between the respective numbers of casualties became entrenched early on: see e.g. CODOIN, xxix, p. 524 (Álvaro de Sande to Philip II, 14 September 1565).
61 Balbi (1567), pp. 211–13; Balbi (1568), fols. 119r–120r; Cirni, fol. 122r–v; Bosio, pp. 700–701.
62 CODOIN, xxix, pp. 522–4; Balbi (1567), pp. 213–15; Balbi (1568), fols. 120r–121v; Cirni, fols. 123r–124r; Bosio, pp. 701–2.
63 Cirni, fol. 124v; Bosio, pp. 703, 704.

References

64 La Valette was quick off the mark: CODOIN, xxix, pp. 517–19 (to Philip II, 11 and 13 September 1565).

65 Martin Crova, *Compendio della historia di quanto e successo nella impresa di Malta* (np, 1565), fol. 3v. This purports to have been written on Malta on 24 September 1565. A French version, although dated 19 September, is probably a translation of the Italian: *Brief discours du siege et oppugnation de l'isle de Malte* (Antwerp, 1565), equivalent quotation at fol. C2v.

66 Antonio Cressino, 'Vray discours de la guerre et siege de Malthe par les Turcz', in Nicolas Camusat, *Meslanges historiques, ou recueil des plusieurs actes, traictez, lettres missives et autres memoires* (Troyes, 1619), Part II, fols. 52v–53r. Bosio, p. 649, has Cressino leading the procession of thanksgiving after the assault on 21 August.

67 *Copie de plusieurs missives escrites et envoyees de Malte par le Seigneur grand Maistre et autres Chevaliers de sainct Iehan de Hierusalem* (Paris, 1565), fols. 9r, 14r–v. Dated 13 September 1565. For Guevara's heroics, Bosio, p. 642; see also Cirni, fols. 103v, 113r.

68 *Copie de plusieurs missives*, fol. 13r; Cirni, fol. 125r. Vendôme, p. 70, supplies a total of 78,000. Balbi (1567), p. 215, gives 80,000, but this is inflated to an implausible 130,000 in Balbi (1568), fol. 121v.

69 See Spiteri, *Great Siege*, pp. 436–40.

70 Balbi (1567), p. 193; Balbi (1568), fol. 102r; Cirni, fol. 101v; Vendôme, pp. 56, 67; Viperano, fol. 31r–v; Bosio, pp. 636, 637.

71 Spiteri, *Great Siege*, pp. 442–9.

72 AOM 91, fol. 152v; Balbi (1567), p. 110; Balbi (1568), fol. 52v.

73 Spiteri, *Great Siege*, pp. 348–51, 543–4.

74 W. T. MacCaffrey, 'The Newhaven Expedition, 1562–1563', *Historical Journal*, 40 (1997), 17–18; P. E. J. Hammer, *Elizabeth's Wars: War, Government and Society in Tudor England, 1544–1604* (Basingstoke, 2003), pp. 63–6.

8. Meanwhile . . .

1 *Calendar of State Papers, Spain (Simancas)*, vol. 1: *1558–1567*, ed. M. A. S. Hume (London, 1892), pp. 409–10.

2 J. Geiss, 'The Chia-ching reign, 1522–1566', in *The Cambridge History of China*, vol. 7: *The Ming Dynasty, 1368–1644*, Part 1, ed. F. W. Mote and D. Twitchett (Cambridge, 1988), pp. 482–5, 505–7.
3 J. W. Hall, 'The Muromachi Bakufu', in *The Cambridge History of Japan*, vol. 3: *Medieval Japan*, ed. K. Yamamura (Cambridge, 1990), pp. 229–30.
4 B. Stein, *Vijayanagara: The New Cambridge History of India I:2* (Cambridge, 1989), pp. 118–20.
5 G. Parker, *The Dutch Revolt*, rev. edn (London, 1985), p. 69.
6 See H. F. K. van Nierop, 'The Nobles and the Revolt', in *The Origins and Development of the Dutch Revolt*, ed. G. Darby (London, 2001), pp. 48–66. For the role of the grandees in the genesis of the revolt, see M. van Gelderen, *The Political Thought of the Dutch Revolt 1555–1590* (Cambridge, 1992), pp. 30–40.
7 G. Darby, 'Narrative of Events', in *Origins and Development*, ed. Darby, pp. 8–28.
8 Parker, *Imprudent King*, pp. 144–9.
9 Parker, *Dutch Revolt*, pp. 56–7.
10 See G. Parker, *The Army of Flanders and the Spanish Road, 1567–1659*, 2nd edn (Cambridge, 2004).
11 *Archives ou correspondance inédite de la maison d'Orange-Nassau*, vol. I: *1552–1565*, ed. G. Groen van Prinsterer (Leiden, 1835), pp. 368–9; Joachim Hopperus, 'Recueil et mémorial des troubles des Pays Bas du roy, 1559–1566', in *Mémoires de Viglius et d'Hopperus*, ed. A. Wauters (Brussels, 1862), p. 268.
12 Viglius, 'Discours sur le règne de Philippe II.', in *Mémoires de Viglius et d'Hopperus*, ed. Wauters, p. 90.
13 Parker, *Imprudent King*, p. 145.
14 Ibid., p. 147.
15 *The Philippine Islands 1493–1803*, vol. II: *1521–1569*, trans. E. H. Blair and J. A. Robertson (Manila, 1962), pp. 174–82, 188–216.
16 For this expedition, see M. Mitchell, *Friar Andrés de Urdaneta, O.S.A.* (London, 1964), pp. 118–31; O. H. K. Spate, *The Spanish Lake* (Minneapolis, 1979), pp. 100–104; Kamen, *Spain's Road*, pp. 201–3; A. Giraldez, *The Age of Trade: The Manila Galleon and the Dawn of the Global Economy* (Lanham, MD, 2015), pp. 52–6.

References

17 Spate, *Spanish Lake*, pp. 157–62.
18 W. L. Schurz, *The Manila Galleon* (New York, 1959), pp. 219–21; Spate, *Spanish Lake*, pp. 104–5.
19 Kamen, *Spain's Road*, pp. 209–13, 292.
20 Schurz, *Manila Galleon*, pp. 221–31, 246–7; Spate, *Spanish Lake*, pp. 108–9.
21 Schurz, *Malila Galleon*, pp. 253–6, 263–4, 267–70, 275–83. For a sense of scale, cf. the evocative description of the terrible conditions faced by those on the much shorter Atlantic crossings in P. E. Pérez-Mallaína, *Spain's Men of the Sea: Daily Life on the Indies Fleet in the Sixteenth Century*, trans. C. R. Phillips (Baltimore, 1998), pp. 129–89.
22 Schurz, *Manila Galleon*, pp. 209–12; Giraldez, *Age of Trade*, pp. 140–41.
23 Schurz, *Manila Galleon*, pp. 258–9, 265–6.
24 Francis Pretty, 'The prosperous voyage of M. Thomas Candish esquire into the South sea, and so round about the circumference of the whole earth, begun in the yere 1586, and finished 1588', in R. Hakluyt, *The Principal Navigations, Voyages, Traffiques and Discoveries of the English Nations* (Glasgow, 1904), xi, pp. 324–7; Schurz, *Manila Galleon*, pp. 305–13; Kamen, *Spain's Road*, p. 230.
25 'A letter of M. Thomas Candish to the right honourable the Lord Hunsdon, Lord Chamberlaine, one of her Majesties most honourable Privy Councell, touching the successe of his voyage about the world', in Hakluyt, *Principal Navigations*, xi, p. 377.
26 Spate, *Spanish Lake*, pp. 143–5.
27 Kamen, *Spain's Road*, pp. 206–19; Giraldez, *Age of Trade*, pp. 3–4, 34–5, 37.
28 *Documenta Indica VII (1566–1569)*, ed. J. Wicki (Rome, 1962), pp. 33–4, 88–9.
29 G. Casale, ' "His Majesty's Servant Lufti": The Career of a Previously Unknown Turkish Envoy to Sumatra Based on an Account of His Travels from the Topkapı Palace Archives', *Turcica*, 37 (2005), 43–81.
30 See G. Casale, 'The Ottoman "Discovery" of the Indian Ocean in the Sixteenth Century', in *Seascapes: Maritime Histories, Littoral Cultures, and Transoceanic Exchanges*, ed. J. H. Bentley, R. Bridenthal and K. Wigen (Honolulu, 2007), pp. 87–104.

31 S. Özbaran, 'The Ottoman Turks and the Portuguese in the Persian Gulf, 1534–1581', *Journal of Asian History*, 6 (1972), 45–87; H. Inalcık, *An Economic and Social History of the Ottoman Empire*, vol. 1: *1300–1600* (Cambridge, 1994), pp. 335–40.

32 Giraldez, *Age of Trade*, p. 38.

33 Casale, '"His Majesty's Servant"', 52–3. For this incident, see in general G. Casale, *The Ottoman Age of Exploration* (New York, 2010), pp. 124–5, 126–9; and for the broader background, J. M. dos Santos Alves, *O domínio do norte de Samatra: A história dos sultanatos de Samudera-Pacém e de Achém e das suas relações com os Portugueses 1500–1580* (Lisbon, 1999).

34 M. N. Pearson, *The Portuguese in India* (Cambridge, 1987), pp. 5–39; Glete, *Warfare at Sea*, pp. 76–84.

35 For the sending of cannon and gunners to Aceh, see A. Reid, 'Sixteenth Century Turkish Influence in Western Indonesia', *Journal of Southeast Asian History*, 10 (1969), 396–7, 404–5.

36 See the report of the expedition sent to King Manuel I in S. Özbaran, *Ottoman Expansion towards the Indian Ocean in the 16th Century* (Istanbul, 2009), pp. 325–9.

37 Ibid., pp. 332–3; S. Özbaran, 'Ottoman Naval Policy in the South', in *Süleyman the Magnificent*, ed. Kunt and Woodhead, pp. 58–9; Inalcık, *Economic and Social History*, pp. 323–5.

38 S. Özbaran, 'Ottoman Expansion in the Red Sea', in *Cambridge History*, pp. 179–80; Özbaran, *Ottoman Expansion*, pp. 80–84; Inalcık, *Economic and Social History*, pp. 326–7; Casale, *Ottoman Age of Exploration*, pp. 59–63.

39 Özbaran, 'Ottoman Expansion', p. 180; Casale, *Ottoman Age of Exploration*, pp. 69–72.

40 Casale, *Ottoman Age of Exploration*, pp. 75–7.

41 Özbaran, *Ottoman Expansion*, pp. 107–11; Casale, *Ottoman Age of Exploration*, pp. 95–8.

42 Casale, *Ottoman Age of Exploration*, pp. 99–102.

43 Daniele Barbarigo, 'Relazione dell'impero ottomano', pp. 1–15.

44 Inalcık, *Economic and Social History*, pp. 328–9. See also J. S. Alves, 'From Istanbul with Love: Rumours, Conspiracies and Commercial Competition in Aceh–Ottoman Relations, 1550s to 1570s', in *From Anatolia to*

Aceh: Ottomans, Turks and Southeast Asia, ed. A. C. S. Peacock and A. T. Gallop (Oxford, 2015), pp. 47–62. For the text and translation of the letter, see Casale, '"His Majesty's Servant"', 61–80.

45 *Documenta Indica VII*, pp. 514–15; Inalcık, *Economic and Social History*, pp. 329–30; Casale, '"His Majesty's Servant"', 54; Casale, *Ottoman Age of Exploration*, pp. 129–32. See also P.-Y. Manguin, 'Of Fortresses and Galleys: The 1568 Acehnese Siege of Melaka, after a Contemporary Bird's-eye View', *Modern Asian Studies*, 22 (1988), 607–28.

46 Casale, *Ottoman Age of Exploration*, pp. 82–3.

47 Ibid., pp. 93–5, 102–6, 108–14, 125–6.

48 Özbaran, *Ottoman Expansion*, pp. 357–9.

49 Casale, *Ottoman Age of Exploration*, p. 110.

50 G. Casale, 'The Ottoman Regulation of the Spice Trade in the Sixteenth-Century Red Sea and Persian Gulf', *Journal of the Economic and Social History of the Orient*, 49 (2006), 170–98; Özbaran, 'Ottoman Naval Policy', pp. 62–3.

51 Gonzalo Solís de Merás, *Pedro Menéndez de Avilés and the Conquest of Florida: A New Manuscript*, ed. and trans. D. Arbesú (Gainesville, 2017), pp. 47, 221; E. Lyon, *The Enterprise of Florida: Pedro Menéndez de Avilés and the Spanish Conquest of 1565–1568* (Gainesville, 1976), pp. 115–17.

52 For Menéndez's contract for Florida, see Lyon, *Enterprise of Florida*, pp. 43–55.

53 Spate, *Spanish Lake*, pp. 186–8; Kamen, *Spain's Road*, pp. 247–8, 285–7.

54 D. C. Goodman, *Power and Penury: Government, Technology and Science in Philip II's Spain* (Cambridge, 1988), pp. 175–7, 179, 195–200.

55 Spate, *Spanish Lake*, pp. 192–4; Giraldez, *Age of Trade*, pp. 30–32; Goodman, *Power and Penury*, pp. 179–80.

56 Spate, *Spanish Lake*, p. 199; Goodman, *Power and Penury*, pp. 197–8.

57 Giraldez, *Age of Trade*, pp. 33–4; Kamen, *Spain's Road*, p. 290. See also C. H. Haring, *Trade and Navigation between Spain and the Indies in the Time of the Hapsburgs* (Cambridge, MA, 1918), pp. 201–30.

58 Kamen, *Spain's Road*, p. 328.

59 See J. T. McGrath, *The French in Florida: In the Eye of the Hurricane* (Gainesville, 2000), pp. 74–8, with useful map at p. 75.

60 Jean Ribault, *The whole and true discouerye of Terra Florida* (London, 1563), in *New American World: A Documentary History of North America to 1612*, ed. D. B. Quinn et al., 5 vols. (New York, 1979), ii, pp. 285–94 (a contemporary English translation of a report of the expedition that does not survive in the French original); René de Laudonnière, 'L'histoire notable de la Floride', in *Les Français en Amérique pendant la deuxième moitié du VXIe siècle*, vol. II: *Les Français en Floride*, ed. S. Lussagnet (Paris, 1958), pp. 50–80, and trans. C. E. Bennett in *Three Voyages*, rev. edn (Tuscaloosa, 2001), pp. 17–51; McGrath, *French in Florida*, pp. 73–6, 78–81.

61 In addition to Laudonnière, who devotes much of his account of the 1562 expedition to the travails of those left behind, see Lancelot de Voisin de la Popellinière, *Les trois mondes* (Paris, 1582), Part II, fols. 27r–28v, trans. Quinn in *New American World*, pp. 307–8. The very interesting account that Guillaume Rouffin, who stayed behind in 1563, gave to his interrogators when he was discovered by the Spanish is in Quinn, *New American World*, pp. 313–15; and *Fort Caroline: History and Documents*, ed. C. E. Bennett, rev. edn (Tuscaloosa, 2001), pp. 117–22.

62 Lyon, *Enterprise of Florida*, pp. 38–41.

63 Laudonnière, 'L'histoire notable', pp. 81–164, trans. Bennett in *Three Voyages*, pp. 53–147; McGrath, *French in Florida*, pp. 96–109. See also the eyewitness narrative of the artist Jacques Le Moyne de Morgues, which was published by Theodor de Bry in 1591 and is translated in *Settlement of Florida*, ed. C. E. Bennett (Gainesville, FL, 1968), pp. 90–122; for the events up to Ribault's return, see pp. 91–111. For Le Moyne's importance in informing contemporary Europeans' visual sense of the Americas and its inhabitants, see *The Work of Jacques Le Moyne de Morgues: A Huguenot Artist in Florida and England*, ed. P. Hulton, 2 vols. (London, 1977).

64 Lyon, *Enterprise of Florida*, pp. 100–104, 110–14.

65 Ibid., pp. 119–20.

66 For Le Challeux, see his 'Discours de l'histoire de la Floride', in *Les Français en Amérique*, pp. 201–33, trans. Quinn in *New American World*, pp. 370–79.

67 McGrath, *French in Florida*, pp. 116–55; Lyon, *Enterprise of Florida*, pp. 124–9.

References

68 McGrath, *French in Florida*, pp. 156–61.
69 Le Moyne in *Settlement of Florida*, p. 95.
70 Solís de Merás, *Pedro Menéndez de Avilés*, pp. 63–73, 236–46.
71 Ibid., pp. 66–7, 239.
72 *Laudonnière and Fort Caroline*, pp. 128–9, 136.
73 'Discours de l'histoire de la Floride', pp. 206–7, trans. Quinn in *New American World*, p. 371.
74 Quinn, *New American World*, pp. 366–8. Cf. Le Moyne's description of restless and disappointed noblemen in 'splendid outfits': *Settlement of Florida*, p. 95.
75 *Laudonnière and Fort Caroline*, p. 118.
76 *Dépêches de M. de Fourquevaux, ambassadeur du roi Charles IX en Espagne 1565–1572*, ed. C. Douais (Paris, 1896), p. 56. The translation in Quinn, *New American World*, p. 468, is incorrect. Cf. *Négociations*, ed. Charrière, ii, p. 810, for a report of public celebrations of the news from Florida in the streets of Naples.

9. And in the End

1 *La Galleria delle Carte geografiche in Vaticano*, ed. L. Gambi and A. Pinelli, 3 vols. (Modena, 1994); F. Fiorani, *The Marvel of Maps: Art, Cartography and Politics in Renaissance Italy* (New Haven, 2005), pp. 171–207.
2 See *La Galleria delle Carte geografiche*, i, pp. 392–9, 592–5 (reproductions); ii, pp. 377–82 (notes, which contain some misconceptions about the siege).
3 *The Siege of Malta 1565: Matteo Perez d'Aleccio's Frescoes at the Grand Master's Palace, Valletta*, ed. C. Cini (Valletta, 2009), pp. 92–7; *I veri retratti della guerra e dell'assedio et assalti dati all'isola di Malta dall'armata turchesca l'anno 1565* (Rome, 1582), plate XIV.
4 Cervantes, *Don Quijote*, i, p. 497; Cervantes, *Don Quixote*, pp. 362–3.
5 A. C. Hess, 'The Battle of Lepanto and Its Place in Mediterranean History', *Past and Present*, 57 (1972), 53–73; Braudel, *Mediterranean*, ii, pp. 1103–6; Housley, *Later Crusades*, pp. 142–3.
6 Bosio, p. 709.

References

7 For the building of Valletta, see Hughes, *Building*, pp. 20–29; Hoppen, *Fortification*, pp. 49–71; R. de Giorgio, *A City by an Order*, 3rd edn (Valletta, 1998), pp. 46–79; Brogini, *Malte*, pp. 205–23. See also Pollak, *Cities at War*, pp. 157–62.

8 Bosio, pp. 720, 722, 723, 726–7.

9 *Lettres de Charles IX à M. de Fourquevaux, ambassadeur en Espagne, 1565–1572*, ed. C. Douais (Paris, 1897), p. 67.

10 For the view that La Valette's reputation, at first enhanced by the siege, had subsequently been diminished by the suggestion that Malta would be abandoned, with the result that popular enthusiasm for donating money to the Knights' cause waned, see *Correspondance du Cardinal de Granvelle, 1565–1586*, ed. E. Poullet and C. Piot, 12 vols. (Brussels, 1877–96), i, p. 322.

11 CODOIN, xxx, pp. 121–4, 125–6, 131–2, 134–5, 205–8; Bosio, pp. 739, 741.

12 AOM 91, fols. 163v, 164r; 93, fols. 6v–7r; Bosio, pp. 744–5, 871–2.

13 See e.g. *Malta: The Bulwark of Europe. Hieronymus Megiser's Propugnaculum Europae: The First Comprehensive German Description of 16th-Century Malta*, ed. and trans. A. Friggieri and T. Freller (Tarxien, 1998).

14 AOM 91, fol. 152r–v; Bosio, pp. 730, 732, 785, 842; Bonello, 'In and Out', p. 32. The investigation into his case was instituted less than a week before the Turks' arrival.

15 AOM 91, fols. 156r, 163r–v, 165r, 166r.

16 Ibid., fols. 184v, 186r; 92, fol. 23r; 34v; Bonello, 'In and Out', pp. 17–18.

17 Brantôme, v, 233, 408. Cf. ii, p. 45, for an argument which flared up around the Grand Master's dinner table between one of Brantôme's French companions and Gianandrea Doria.

18 Vatican City, Biblioteca Apostolica, Ms Vat. lat. 7750, fol. 53r–v; AOM 430, fols. 247v, 278v–280r; Bosio, pp. 723–4, 766–7.

19 AOM 92, fol. 55r; Bosio, pp. 660, 698, 705, 715–16.

20 Brogini, *Une noblesse*, pp. 245–61; Buttigieg, *Nobility*, pp. 83–7.

21 The national rivalries at stake are a recurrent theme in one of the principal sources for the crisis, the correspondence of the French ambassador in Rome, Paul de Foix, to King Henri III: *Les lettres de Messire Paul de Foix, archevesque de Tolose, et ambassadeur pour le Roy auprés*

du Pape Gregoire XIII, escrites au Roy Henry III (Paris, 1628), pp. 85–91, 132–6, 163–72, 181–5, 241–3, 247–9, 255–6, 260–69.

22 A. Blondy, *Un prince de la Renaissance à l'aube de la Contre-Réforme: Hugues de Loubens de Verdalle (1531–1582–1595)* (Paris, 2005), pp. 37–60.

23 AOM 92, fols. 208v–209r, 210v–211r, 213r; Bosio, pp. 854–62; Rossi, *Storia della marina*, pp. 48–9; Mori Ubaldino, *La marina*, pp. 258–62.

24 Sosa, *Topografía e historia general*, i, pp. 158–9, trans. as *An Early Modern Dialogue*, pp. 223–4; Bosio, p. 860.

25 Balbi (1567), pp. 154–6; Balbi (1568), fols. 80v–81r; Bosio, p. 861; Spiteri, *Great Siege*, pp. 464–5.

26 Spiteri, *Great Siege*, p. 519; *Négociations*, ed. Charrière, ii, pp. 805–6.

27 Setton, *Papacy*, iv, pp. 893–906.

28 Vella Bonavita, 'Key to Christendom', 1021–43; Bull, 'Francesco Balbi di Correggio's *La verdadera relación*', pp. 13–20; T. Rothman and P. Brampton Koelle, 'Pedro de Salazar's History of the Great Siege', in *Besieged*, i, pp. 21–8.

29 Brantôme, v, pp. 215–17, 229–33, 239.

30 For a thoughtful discussion of La Valette's life and reputation, see V. Mallia-Milanes, 'Frà Jean de la Valette 1495–1565 – a Reappraisal', in *The Maltese Cross*, ed. T. Cortis (Msida, 1995), pp. 117–29. See also Brogini, *Noblesse*, pp. 120–22.

31 Imber, 'Reconstruction of the Ottoman Fleet', pp. 85–101.

32 See Braudel, *Mediterranean*, ii, pp. 1007–12; Thompson, *War and Government*, pp. 14, 16–17, 67–8, 167–75; Housley, *Later Crusades*, p. 145.

33 Cf. Williams, *Empire and Holy War*, pp. 227–46.

34 K. R. Andrews, *Trade, Plunder and Settlement: Maritime Enterprise and the Genesis of the British Empire, 1480–1630* (Cambridge, 1984), pp. 87–100; K. MacMillan, 'Exploration, Trade and Empire', in *The Elizabethan World*, ed. S. Doran and N. Jones (Abingdon, 2011), pp. 646–62.

35 Brogini, *1565*, p. 186.

36 *Ottoman Campaign Register*, pp. 122–3, 359–63, 372–82 and *passim*. For those who were injured, pp. 364–5.

37 Ibid., pp. 195, 231, 283.

38 Spiteri, *Great Siege*, p. 271; Balbi (1568), fol. 116r. See also Bosio, p. 710. Cf. Cirni, fol. 125r, for the smell of death and disease.

39 Brogini, *1565*, pp. 186–7. See also Brogini, *Malte*, pp. 192–3; Spiteri, *Great Siege*, p. 519.
40 Cirni, fol. 125v.
41 Balbi (1568), fol. 84v.
42 Cf. Bosio, p. 710, for the demands made on the Infirmary, and on private houses in and around Birgu, for months after the siege simply by those who had been part of the *gran soccorso*.
43 AOM 430, fols. 270r–v, 272r, 272v, 273v, 276v, 285v.
44 Ibid., fol. 277v.
45 Ibid., fols. 271v–272r. For another pilgrimage of thanks, by an escapee, see Bosio, p. 710.
46 Cf. Brogini, *1565*, pp. 187–8, whose figures seem a little too high. See Balbi (1568), fol. 127v; Bosio, p. 711; Brogini, *Malte*, pp. 200–201.
47 Balbi (1567), p. 189; Balbi (1568), fol. 99v.
48 Mdina, Cathedral Archives, Curia Episcopalis Melitensis, Acta Originalia, Ms 46: N 48, N 62. See also N 11, N 17, N 31, N 43, N 52, N 63. Cf. J. Abela, 'The Great Siege of 1565: Untold Stories of Everyday Life', in *Besieged*, ii, pp. 97–115. See also G. Cassar, 'The Suffering of the Innocent: Wartime Violence and the Common People – the Case of the Great Siege of Malta, 1565', *History Research*, 3 (2013), 79–89.
49 Brantôme, ii, pp. 124–5.
50 Voltaire, *Annales de l'Empire depuis Charlemagne*, ed. G. Laudin and J. Renwick, 3 vols. (Oxford, 2019), iii, p. 210.
51 E. Bradford, *Siege: Malta 1940–1943* (Harmondsworth, 1987); J. Holland, *Fortress Malta: An Island under Siege 1940–1943* (London, 2003).
52 P. C. Smith, *Pedestal: The Malta Convoy of August, 1942* (London, 1970); M. Hastings, *Operation Pedestal: The Fleet That Battled to Malta, 1942* (London, 2021).
53 C. Cassar, *A Concise History of Malta* (Msida, 2000), pp. 194–7, 204–7, 211–12, 213–14; D. Meilak, 'David versus Goliath and the Apotheosis of Malta: Romanticizing the Siege of Malta during the Rise of Nationalism (1860–1939)', *Melita Historica*, 17 (2016), 160–62.

Index

Abbasid caliphate 64
Abdullah, slave 83
Acapulco 200, 201
Aceh 203, 205, 206, 208, 209, 210
Achilles 11
Acre 25
adelantado 210
Adorno, Giorgio, Knight 103, 111
Adorno, Gregorio de, Knight 171
adventurers 8, 120, 151, 178–9, 180–1
Aegean 71, 121, 126–7
Aeneas 11, 12
Agatha, St 103
Aguilar, Francisco de 166–7, 169
Ala'ad-din Ri'ayat Syah, sultan of Aceh 203, 204
Alamo 12, 16
alapa 41
Alba, Álvarez de Toledo y Pimentel, duke of 196–7, 198, 227
Albert, Captain 215
Alcántara, order of 77
Alcaudete, Martín Alonso Fernández, count of 118
Aleccio, Matteo Perez d' 223–4, 239
Alexander the Great 56
Alexandria 26, 52, 72, 94, 98, 121–2, 207
Algiers 69, 72, 73, 77, 79–81, 82–3, 88, 91, 98, 106–7, 118, 122, 123, 128, 136, 153, 231
  Charles V's campaign against (1541) 27–8, 95, 99
Ali, Anatolian 164

Ali, timariot 164
Ali bin Hüseyin 164
Ali Pasha 45
Almadén 82, 212
Almería 77
Amalfi 21
Amboise 3
Anastagi, Vincenzo, Knight 163
Anatolia 26, 63, 64
Anne of Cleves 194–5
Antwerp, sack of (1576) 63
Aragon, post of 146
Aramon, Gabriel de Luetz d' 100, 105–8, 110
Aranda, Diego de 237
Arellano, Alonso de 200
aristocracy, male culture of 5, 6, 10, 27–8, 32–6, 43, 111, 112, 113–14, 168–9, 178–9, 234
Armada, Spanish 15, 113–14, 202
arquebus 7
artillery, *see* cannon
askeri 47
Asuard, Claude, Knight 38
Atlantic Ocean 69, 72, 82–3, 95, 199, 202, 204, 213–14
Attard 102
auberges 37, 40–1
Augusta 76, 101
Augustus, emperor 12, 44
Auvergne, post of 146
Avalos, Fernando Francesco d', marquess of Pescara 8

Index

Avilés, Pedro Menéndez de 210–11, 213, 214, 216–17, 219, 221
azabs 102, 131
Azores 213, 214

Baghdad 53, 64
Bahamas 214, 220
baili 48, 52, 53, 54, 55–6, 57, 60, 106, 208
Bairan, Gian Battista 88
Bajada, Toni 168–9
Balbi, Francesco 4, 18, 121–2, 124, 126, 131, 133, 134–5, 142, 147–8, 148–9, 152, 153, 154–5, 156, 158, 159, 160, 162, 163, 164, 166–7, 169, 170, 171, 173, 174, 175, 178, 180, 184, 185, 186, 236–7
Balearics 99
baños 82
Barbarigo, Antonio di Gabriele 56
Barbarigo, Daniele 60, 208
Barbarossa (Hayreddin) 98–9, 106, 129
Barbary coast 68, 69, 71, 72, 73, 74–5, 76, 79–81, 82–3, 87–9, 90–1, 117, 118, 119–20, 122, 123, 128–9, 130, 132, 153, 165, 181, 186, 235
Barcelona 62
Barré, Nicolas 215
Bartolomeo, great-nephew of Sabba da Castiglione 35
Basra 53, 204, 206
Bayezid, son of Süleyman I 56, 59
Bayonne 1, 4, 196–7
beeldenstorm 196
Behram, son of Abdullah 164–5
Belgrade 52
Bellavanti, Nicolò 115
Belsius, Johannes 44–5
bezistan 81, 88
Bidnija 242
Birgu 16–17, 30, 37, 42, 102, 116, 127, 134, 141–2, 144, 146, 152, 154, 160, 168, 170, 173, 176, 184, 190, 226, 227–8, 236, 237, 238
Birkirkara 102
biscuit 62, 95, 143, 181, 183
Bizerte 89
Blois 3
Bodenham, Roger 73–4, 78
Bodrum 26
Bône 107
Bordeaux 1
Borja, Francisco de 203, 204
Bormla 144, 145, 146, 147, 167, 184
Bosio, Giacomo, Knight 19, 35, 101, 102, 104, 110, 111, 117, 123, 137–8, 142, 169, 170, 171, 178, 187, 230, 232, 239
Bosio, Giovanni Ottone, Knight 72
El Bosque de Segovia 196, 197
Bourbon, Jacques le Bâtard de 7
Bracamonte, Hernando de, Knight 83–4
Bracamonte, Maria, slave 83–4
Bracamonte, Ynes de, slave 83
Brantôme, Pierre de Bourdeille, abbé de 5–10, 21, 31 70, 71, 120, 178, 229, 234, 239–40
Brederode, Henry of 194, 195
Breughel, Peter the Elder 192
brigantine 94
Brogini, Anne 36
Brunefay-Quincy, Esprit de, Knight 151
Brussels 197, 198
Brutus 12
Buda 45, 53
buonovoglia 75
Busbecq, Ogier Ghiselin de 44–6, 53–4, 55, 60, 61, 118, 183

Cabo de Santa Maria 73
Cabo de São Vicente 78
Cabrera, Bernardo de, Knight 171, 175

Index

Cádiz 73, 88
Calatrava, order of 77
Cali, Michalis 162
caliphate 64
Calli, Isabella 39
Calli, Michele 231
Canaries 214
Canassa, Jean 88
cannon 4, 7, 16, 39, 61, 92, 103, 104, 105, 131, 132, 134, 135, 139, 143, 144, 145, 147, 152, 155–6, 158, 159, 160, 165, 172, 175, 184, 187, 216, 223, 224, 240
Cape Passero 133, 181, 182
Cape Verde Islands 214
Capitana, galley 40, 231
captivity 71, 73–7, 78, 79–89, 90, 91, 99, 104, 118, 121–2, 164, 165, 166
caravan 37, 39–40
Cardinale, Antonia 39
Cardona, Juan de 151
Caribbean 211, 213, 214, 215, 216, 219, 220
Cartagena 77
Cartagena de Indias 213
Caruana Galizia, Daphne 242
Cassar, Girolamo 157
Cassière, Jean de La, Grand Master 230–1
Castello (Gozo) 92, 103–5
Castello a mare 116
Castile, *cortes* of 77–8
   post of 146, 156, 160, 162–3, 172, 173–4, 191, 234, 238
Castiglione, Baldassare 34–5
Castiglione, Sabba da, Knight 34–6, 43, 169
Castriota, Costantino, Knight 138–9, 141
Catarinetta, galley 99
Cateau-Cambrésis, Treaty of (1559) 119, 150

Catherine de' Medici 1, 2–3, 5, 6, 130
Catholic League 14
Cavalli, Marino 53
Cavendish, Thomas 201–2
çavuş 146–7, 148
Cebu 198, 199
Cerda, Juan de 137, 141
Ceresole, battle of 223
Cervantes Saavedra, Miguel de 79–81, 82, 86, 87, 90, 225
Ceylon 205
Chanson de Roland 13
Charles V, emperor 8, 26–8, 44, 49, 64, 77, 95, 98, 99, 100, 101, 105–6, 110, 115, 198, 205
Charles IX, king of France 1, 2–3, 4, 6, 59, 215, 221
Charlesfort 215, 220
Chenonceaux 3
Chesneau, Jean 48, 60
China 114, 193, 199, 202–3
Chios 233
Chu Hou-ts'ung, Chinese emperor 193
Cirni, Antonfrancesco 18–19, 147, 150–1, 169, 170, 172, 178, 180, 181, 182
cisterns 190
ciurme 75, 94, 95, 115, 117, 131–2, 165, 180, 181, 186, 236
Clement VII, pope 29
Clermont-Ferrand 3
Coligny, Gaspard de 214–15, 218
Collège de France 13
Colonna, Marc Antonio 230
Constant, Claude, Knight 38
Constantinople, *see* Istanbul
Content, ship 201–2
Contreras, Alonso de 90–1
Cook, James 201
Corfu 222
Corgna, Ascanio della 178, 183, 185, 227

313

Index

Corradino 144
Corregio, Francesco Balbi da, *see* Balbi
corsairs 26, 31, 68–79, 81, 82–3, 84, 87–9, 90–1, 92, 96, 97, 98, 99, 100, 101, 102, 107, 117, 123, 125, 128–9, 131, 132, 136, 140, 153–4, 186, 189, 208–9, 235
Corsica 18–19, 87, 126, 227
corso 68–9, 70
Cortés, Hernán 204, 211
Cottonera Lines 127
Cressing Temple 30
Cressino, Antonio, prior 187
Crete 26, 52, 81
Crimea 45, 123
crossbows 175, 180, 189–90
Crova, Martin 186–7
Cruzada 119
Cuba 213, 216
Cuencas, Antonio de las 238
Cyprus 25, 26, 52, 84
  conquest of (1570–1) 17, 234

Dandalo, Andrea 56
Danti, Egnazio 222, 224
dating systems 192
Deccan sultanates 194
Dernschwan, Hans 44–5
Desire, ship 201–2
devşirme 50
Diane de Poitiers 3
Dieppe 218
Diu 207–8, 209
divan 57
Djerba 54, 55, 98, 101, 118, 119, 129, 143, 164, 165, 177, 181, 183, 232, 240
Dockyard Creek 116
  bridge across 145, 154
  chain across 116, 148, 152–3, 155
Don Quixote 79–81, 82, 225

Doria family 68
  Andrea 98, 100–1, 103, 106, 108
  Gianandrea 118, 129, 151, 181–2, 231
Dormer, Jane 178
Drake, Francis 211, 235
duels 5, 40, 230
Dutch Revolt 62–3, 194–8, 220–1, 235

Edinburgh 192–3
Edirne 48
Egmont, Lamoral, count of 194, 195, 196, 197
Eguaras, Melchior d', Knight 139
Egypt 236
  Ottoman conquest of (1516–17) 26, 52, 64, 71, 97–8, 123, 128, 204
Elizabeth I, queen of England 69, 113, 178, 193, 202, 235
Embun, Antonio de 237
England 31
  post of 146
  'enterprises' 113–14
Eraso, Antonio de 168
Escovedo, Pedro de 237

falcon 27–8
Famagusta, siege of 17
Faroqhi, Suraiya 51
Favignana 181
felucca 94
Ferdinand I, emperor 44
Ferhad 236
Ferlito, Giovanni Fabricio 87
fermans 123–4, 130
Ferramolino, Antonio, 115, 116
Flanders 114
Fliegu 134, 182
Florence 180
Floriana Lines 127
Florida 210–11, 214, 215–21

314

flota, see silver fleet
Fort Caroline 215–17, 221
Fourquevaux, Raimond de Beccarie de Pavie, baron de 221
France 1–3
   alliance with Ottomans 4, 10, 53, 54, 97, 99, 100, 105–8, 110
   post of 146
   settlements in Florida 214–21
   Wars of Religion 1–3, 14, 59, 215, 218
François I, king of France 8, 26, 105
François II, king of France 2, 5
Frangiscu 153
French Creek 116, 152–3, 168, 223
Fresne-Canaye, Philippe du 59, 60
frigate 94
Fuggers bank 130, 212
fusta 94

Gálan, Diego 81, 82
galeones 213
Gallèria delle Carte Geografiche 222–4, 234
galleys 25, 30, 31, 39–40, 61–2, 63, 68, 69–70, 71, 72, 73, 75–6, 77, 78, 79, 83, 84, 88, 89, 91, 94–6, 99, 101–2, 115, 117, 118, 119–20, 130, 131–2, 151, 152, 153–4, 166, 171, 175–6, 180, 181–2, 190, 209, 222, 225, 228, 231–2
galliot 94, 130
Gallows Point 144
Genga, Bartolomeo 226
Genoa 26, 62, 68, 83, 89, 98, 126, 142, 180
Geoffrey of Monmouth 12
Georgia 65, 127
Gerard, Blessed 22
Germany 31
   post of 146
Gesualdo, Francesco, Knight 38

Għar il-Kbir 162
ghazis 65–6
Gianni tal-Pont 153
Giansever 121
Gibraltar 77, 93, 94, 99
gileffo 82
Giou, Pierre de, Knight 122
Goa 203
gold 201–2, 211
La Goletta, 126, 132–3, 179
Gonzalo, Bartolomé 157
Gonzalo Pérez 197
Gothic language 45
Gozo 76, 92, 99, 100, 103, 134, 136, 167, 170, 182, 230, 231
   attack of 1551 on 76, 103–4, 107, 109, 111–12, 114
gran soccorso 15–16, 20, 161–2, 170, 176–86, 188, 189, 194, 210, 224, 226, 230
Granada 76, 77
Grand Harbour 16–17, 30, 38, 71, 92, 93, 102, 115–17, 127, 134, 140, 141, 143, 144, 150, 152, 161, 184, 185, 223, 225–6, 232
   amphibious assault on 152–6, 189, 223
Grand Master's Palace, Valletta 223–4, 239
Great Siege, *see* Malta, Great Siege of
Greece 71, 81, 83, 99, 121, 132, 133, 149, 166, 236
Greenwich 202
Gregory XIII, pope 176, 222, 230
Guevara, Francesco, Knight 187
Guilmartin, John Francis 118
Guiral, Francisco de, Knight 155–6, 167
Guise, François II, duc de 2, 70
Guise, François de, brother of François II, Knight 70
Gulf Stream 214

Index

gunpowder 61, 103, 140, 143, 174–5, 175–6, 189–90
guva 42–3

Hadım Süleyman Pasha 208
Hadrian VI, pope 8
Hafsids 99, 100
Hajji Murad 4, 59
Hasan Pasha 106–7, 118, 122, 123, 153–4, 186
Hasim el-Hasimi 85
Havana 213, 214
Hawaii 201
Hawkins, Jack 216, 219
Hector 11
Henri II, king of France 2, 3, 105, 106, 107, 109
Henri IV, king of France 14
Henri I, prince de Condé 59
Henry VIII, king of England 26, 194–5
Henry Stuart, Lord Darnley 192–3
Heredia, Fernando de, Knight 40
heresy 195–6, 197
Heyn, Piet 213
Hijaz 64, 98, 122
Holy League 68, 222
Homedes, Juan de, Grand Master 33–4, 107, 108, 110, 111, 115, 117
Homer 11
Hormuz 206, 208
Hospitallers, *see* St John, Order of
Hsü Chieh 193
Huancavelica 212
Huatulco 201
Hungary 45, 46, 52–3, 128, 233
The Hunters in the Snow, 192, 196
Hürrem (Roxelana) 57, 58–9, 122, 124

Ibrahim Pasha 52, 53
Iceland 78
Îles d'Hyères 227
Ilyas bin Yusuf 236
India 63, 65, 194, 205, 207–8, 209
Indian Ocean 203–10
Inquisition 73, 84, 86–90
Inter gravissimas 176
Iran 53, 59, 63, 64, 65, 235
Iraq 204
Is Salvatur 156
Istanbul 26, 44, 48, 52, 54, 55, 60, 62, 64, 81, 86, 97, 98, 100, 106, 108, 118, 119, 120, 122, 124, 128, 132, 133, 136, 143, 183, 197, 208
Istemad (Yunus) 166
Italy 32, 68, 76–7, 78, 79, 99, 106, 125, 150–1, 177–8, 179, 183, 222, 240, 241
post of 146, 153, 156–7

James, St 158
James VI & I, king of Scotland and England 192–3
Janissaries 7, 45, 49, 50, 60, 61, 62, 69, 89, 102, 128, 131, 153, 164, 173, 188–9
Japan 56–7, 193–4, 199
Jeddah 207
Jericho 10–11
Jerusalem 21–3, 25, 64
Jesuit order 203
Jülich-Cleves-Berg, William of 194–5

Kalkara 144, 146, 158, 176
Kapi Aga 122
Kleinkrieg 26, 76, 235
Knights of Malta, *see* St John, Order of
Kyoto 194

La Herradura 119
La Rochelle 4, 81
Labrador Current 214
Lafréry, Antoine 223

316

Index

Lajos II, king of Hungary 52–3
Lambres, Claude de Tarsac de, Knight 170
Lampedusa 90–1, 182
Lanci, Baldassare 226
Lanfreducci, Francesco, Knight 72
langues 146
Laparelli, Francesco 226, 227, 236
Lascaris, Filippo de 126, 128, 148–9, 152, 153, 165
Laudonnière, René de 216, 217, 218, 220
Le Challeux, Nicolas 217, 219
Le Havre 190
Le Moyne, Jacques 217
Legazpi, Miguel López de 198–9, 199–200, 205
Leo X, pope 8
Lepanto, battle of 68, 70, 75–6, 79, 88, 222, 223, 224–5, 234
Lesbos 98
L'Hôpital, Michel de 2, 6, 10, 28
Libelli diffamatori 229
Licata 231
Lija 102
lingua franca 80
Linosa 181, 182
Lisbon 88
L'Isle-Adam, Philippe de Villiers de, Grand Master 6
Livy 12
Lombardy 177, 179
London 12, 190
Loreto, Our Lady of 238
Lost Colony 220, 235
Loubès, Pierre de, Knight 170–1
Louis IX, king of France 59
Lufti 203–4, 208
Luftwaffe 240
Lugny, Adrien de, Knight 38
Lugny, Jean de, Knight 162, 163

Machiavelli, Niccolò 49
Macuncuzade Mustafa 84–6
Magro, Orlando 232
Mahdia 100–1, 102, 106, 107, 109, 110
Malacca 203, 204, 208
Málaga 119
Maldonado, Antonio, Knight 229–30
Mallet, Gaspard, Knight 39
Malta 27, 68, 69, 72, 84–6, 92–4, 96–7, 98, 99, 100, 101, 110–11, 150, 181, 197, 198, 204, 208, 221, 222–3
  attack of 1551 on 99–104, 107, 108, 110–12, 114–15, 133, 161, 163
  corsairing traditions in 71, 74, 83
  defences of 8, 28, 29–30, 31, 85, 92, 93, 102–3, 104, 109, 115–17, 127, 133, 135–6, 144–6, 147, 156, 157–8, 159–60, 161, 167, 172, 225–7, 228, 233
  French expedition of 1566 to 8–9, 21, 71, 229
  in Second World War 94, 240–1
Malta, Great Siege of
  as site of memory 28–9, 111–12, 186–7, 222–5, 230, 233–4, 239–42
  casualties in 134–5, 142, 173, 174, 185, 187, 188–9, 236–9
  effects of 3–4, 36–7, 228–33, 236–9
  monument to 241–2, 243
  nature of 7–8, 15–20
  reactions to 17, 18–19
  relative to other sieges 6–8
  sources for 17–20
  terminology for 14–15
Maltese 30, 38–9, 231, 232
  as militia 103, 111, 112, 135, 144, 146, 161, 168
  role in Great Siege 15, 20, 30, 38–9, 110–11, 133, 134, 135, 140, 142, 151, 153, 162, 167–9, 190–1, 232, 238–9
Mamluks 25, 52, 64, 97, 207

317

Mandra 145
Manila 199
  Galleons 200–3, 221
marabout 91
Marcelo, Bartulo 87–8
Margaret of Parma 195, 197, 198
Marguerite de Valois 5
Marsa 134, 135, 146, 152, 153, 156, 162, 185
Marsala 87
Marsamxett 93, 102, 115, 116, 136, 143, 152, 156, 162, 176, 185, 223, 224, 225
Marsaxlokk 99, 133, 134, 136, 143, 165
Marseille 99, 106
Marso, Louis de, Knight 39
Martin, St 3
Martin, Maltese swimmer 153
Mary, Queen of Scots 5, 31–2, 192–3
Mary Tudor, queen of England 31, 178
Mas, Colonel (Pierre de Massuez-Vercoirin, Knight) 139
Masi, Thoma 238
Massingberd, Oswald, Knight 38
Masso, Michele, Knight 39
Mastro, Marco 238
Mdina 15, 102–3, 104, 109, 111, 136, 144, 149, 151–2, 161–2, 163, 165, 169, 172, 183, 184, 185, 194
Mecca 22, 64, 121, 206–7
Medici, Cosimo de' 180
Medina 64, 122, 206–7
Medina, Ruiz de, Knight 138–9
Medina Sidonia, Alonso Pérez de Guzmán, duke of 114
Mediterranean 25–6, 27, 32–3, 59, 67–91, 93–100, 119–20, 126, 197–8, 208–9, 210, 221, 224–5, 232, 234–5, 240
Medrano, Gonzalo de 137
Mehmed II, sultan 56, 97
Mehmed III, sultan 58, 86
Mehmed bin Davud 148

Mehmed bin Mustafa 134, 140
Mehmed, son of Hüsrev 164
Mehmet, slave 84
Melleghini, Giacomo, Knight 38
Mellieħa Bay 182, 184
Memi Çelebi 148
Menga, Evangelista 157
Merás, Gonzalo Solís de 218–19
Mercedarian order 86
mercury 82, 211–12
Mesquita, Pedro de, Knight 161–2, 163, 165, 169, 172, 183
Mesquita, Vendo de, Knight 134
Messina 180, 228
Methoni 59, 83
Mexico, *see* New Spain
Mġarr (Gozo) 103
Mġarr (Malta) 134
Michault, Nicholas 44
Mihrimah 57
Milan 8
mines 156–7, 174, 175–6
Miranda, Juan de 137, 141
Mohács, battle of 52–3
Moluccas 199, 205
Monastir 100
Monemvasia 121
Monserrat, Melchior de, Knight 139, 141
Mont-de-Marsan 4
Monte, Pietro del, Grand Master 237
Montmorency, Anne de 6–7, 10
Montmorency, Philippe de, count of Hornes 194, 197
Montpellier, Jean de 41
Monumentum Ancyranum 44
Morgues la Motte, Guy de, Knight 171
Mosta 102
Mostaganem 118, 177
Moulins 3

Index

Moulins, Martin des, Knight 40
Mughals 63, 65
Muñatones, Andreas de 157, 159
Murad Agha 109–10
Murcia 80
Mussolini, Benito 241
Mustafa Pasha 123, 129–30, 136–7, 140, 147, 163, 166, 167, 172, 173, 176, 186, 189, 233
Mustafa bin Abdullah 164
Mustafa, son of Mehmed Reis 164
Mustafa, son of Süleyman I 56, 58–9
Myers, Christopher, Knight 39

Naples 27, 29, 30, 75, 76, 79, 88, 126, 149, 150, 171, 177, 179, 180
Navarino 133
Navidad 199, 200
Naxxar 102
Nelson, Horatio 96
Netherlands 62–3, 117–18, 194–8, 235
New Spain 120, 198–9, 200–1, 202, 204, 205, 211–12, 213
Nicolay, Nicolas de 38
Noailles, François de 60
Nobunaga, Oda 194
North Atlantic Drift 214
North Equatorial Current 214

oficiales 118
Ōgimachi, Japanese emperor 194
SS Ohio 240–1
Oliventia, Juan Martinez de 182
Olivier, Hieronyma 39
Olivier, Léon de 88–9
Oran 81, 118
Orange, William of Nassau, prince of 194, 195, 197
Oruç Reis 98
Osman 236

Otranto 97
Ottoman Campaign Register 17–18, 134, 153, 164–5, 236
Ottoman state
governance of 4, 26, 44, 45, 47–9, 55, 56–8, 60–1, 69, 126–7
ideology of 55, 58, 63–6
interests in the Indian Ocean 203–10
military capacity of 17, 45–51, 53–5, 60, 61, 62–3, 67, 126–8, 130–2
naval strength of 48, 54, 61–2, 63, 68, 75–6, 96, 97–9, 101–2, 107, 109–10, 118, 126–7, 129, 130–2, 136–7, 149–50, 184, 188, 204, 207–10, 222, 224–5, 234, 235
overall strategy of 29, 51–2, 53, 54, 96–7, 109–10, 119, 120–1, 124–9
reaction to Great Siege 232–4
resources of 45–6, 47–8, 49, 50–1, 55, 61–3
strategy towards Malta of 20, 52, 54, 64, 72, 96–7, 109, 110, 120, 121–9, 136–7, 147–8
subjects of 20, 51, 55, 60, 61, 65

Pacific Ocean 199, 200–3, 213
Pagano, Giovanni Battista, Knight 170
Panama 213
Pantelleria 107
Paris 3, 13, 14
Paris, Gaston 13
Parma, Alessandro Farnese, duke of 114
Parris Island 215
Paul, St 94, 223
Pedestal, Operation 240–1
Penny, Anthony 73
Peñón de Vélez de la Gomera 119–20, 122, 178

pepper 203, 204, 205
Peres, Lourenço 203, 204, 205
Perpignan 77
Persian Gulf 53, 204, 206, 207, 210
Peru 120, 202, 205, 211, 212, 213
Petremol, Antoine de 120, 130, 232
Petrucci, Giovanni Maria 1
Philip II, king of Spain 1, 8, 15, 49, 57, 62, 113–14, 117–18, 119, 121, 124, 126, 132–3, 149, 150, 158, 168, 177, 178, 179, 186, 194, 195, 196–8, 198–9, 199–200, 205, 211, 212, 213, 214, 219, 229–30, 233
Philippines 114, 198–9, 200, 202–3
piccolo soccorso 20, 149–52, 161, 165, 237
Pie postulatio voluntatis 22–3
Pietra Negra 151
Pietru Bola 153
pilgrimage 21–2, 23, 30, 64, 71, 89, 98, 121, 122, 123–4, 206–7, 208, 209, 238
Pir Mehmed 164
Piri Reis 208
Piri, *sipahi* 164
Pius IV, pope 125, 130, 151, 178, 186, 227
Pius V, pope 126, 149, 231
Piyale Pasha 118, 126, 129–30, 132, 136–7, 155, 163, 186, 233
Pizarro, Francisco 211
placards 195
plague 190
Plessis-lèz-Tours 1, 2, 3, 6–7, 8, 10, 26, 28, 138, 187
Pomponio 238
porcelain 199
Port Royal 215
Port Said 94
Portugal 73, 77, 78
Portuguese, in Asia 199–200, 203–4, 205–6, 207–8, 209–10, 220–1
Potosí 211, 212

Prato, Pietro 115
presidios 27, 81, 118, 119–20, 126, 128, 132
Preveza 99
prostitutes 38, 39, 230
Provence, post of 146, 232

Qormi 102

Rabat 102–3, 185
Ragusa 181, 188
Rama Raja 194
ransoming 73–4, 79, 82, 83, 85–6
reaya 47, 48, 49
Récicourt, Georges de Hautoy de, Knight 170
Red Sea 98, 204, 206–7, 208–9, 210
Reggio 101, 109
Regia Aeronautica 240, 241
reliefs, *see gran soccorso, piccolo soccorso*
Remensnyder, Amy 90
renegades 69, 79, 80, 86–90, 142, 165–7, 169, 175, 176, 184
responsions 31
retrenchments 157–8, 173
Rhodes 25–6, 28–9, 30, 71, 83, 92, 96, 97, 126, 236
  siege of (1480) 6, 7, 26, 97
  siege of (1522) 6, 7–8, 10, 26, 28–9, 52, 117, 124, 148, 187
Ribault, Jacques 217
Ribault, Jean 214–17, 218
Rinella 152, 176
Rivière, Adrien de La, Knight 134, 140
rixae 40–1
Roanoke 220, 235
Robles, Melchior de 151, 152, 153, 156–7, 159, 167
Rocca, Luigi 237
Roche, Antoine de Flotte de La, Knight 3–5, 6, 7, 28, 137–8

Index

Rome 11–12, 63, 89
Romegas (Mathurin d'Aux de Lescout), Knight 117, 121–2, 141, 230
Rouffin, Guillaume 220
Ruffo, Carlo, Knight 159
Rüstem Pasha 48–9, 56, 59, 61, 99

Sacra Infermeria 23, 29–30, 85, 190
Safavids 53, 59, 63, 64, 65
St Angelo, fortress 42–3, 102, 103, 116–17, 135, 137, 138, 139, 144, 152, 155, 168, 176, 189, 190–1, 226
St Augustine, Rule of 24–5
St Augustine, settlement 211, 216, 217
St Benedict, Rule of 24–5
St Elmo, fortress 4, 16, 102, 115–16, 126, 143, 146, 151, 157, 164, 165, 166, 168, 170, 171, 172, 176, 225, 226
    assault on 135–42, 174, 187, 189, 223, 224, 228–9, 236
St John, order of
    aristocratic ethos of 27–8, 32–6, 41, 43, 112, 137–8, 168–71, 178–9, 230, 234
    as corsairs 26, 40, 70–1, 72, 74, 76, 78, 83, 84, 121–4
    as slave owners 42, 74–5, 83–4, 85, 122, 135
    attitudes towards Malta and the Maltese 27–9, 30, 92–3, 94, 96–7, 108, 110–11, 112, 115, 161, 167–9, 190–1, 227, 228
    attitudes towards women 35, 37–9, 230
    effects of Great Siege upon 228–31
    hospitaller role of 21–3, 24, 29–30, 85
    nature of 19–20, 22–5, 29
    origins of 21–5
    recruitment to 9, 10, 24–5, 32, 33–4
    resources of 10, 24, 30–1, 32, 69, 115, 133
    national tensions within 40, 100, 107, 108, 110, 229–30
    naval operations of 25–6, 30, 32–3, 37, 39–40, 69–71, 75, 77, 78, 83, 84, 91, 93, 117, 118, 121–2, 148, 175, 222, 231, 235
    violence and criminality within 36–43, 169–71
St Johns River 215, 217
St Julian's Bay 102
St Michael, fortress 116–17, 145, 153, 157, 173, 175, 237, 238
St Paul's Bay 102, 103, 185, 186
St Stephen, order of 180
Saint-Clément, François de, Knight 70, 231–2
Saint-Jean-d'Angély 4
Saladin 25
Salah Reis 99
Salazar, Pedro de 101
Salcedo, Felipe de 200
Salcedo, Luis de, Knight 228
Salerno 23
Salgues, Jacques de Fanes de, chaplain 41
Salih bin Mahmud 153
Salvago, Rafaele, Knight 228
Samuel ben Iomtov 84
San Antonio, ship 201
San Claudio, galley 70
San Filipo, galley 40
San Giovanni, galley 91, 231
San José, ship 201
San Lucas, ship 200
San Pablo, ship 200
San Paulo, galley 91
San Pelayo, ship 216
sancak 47

Sande, Álvaro de 183
Sandilands, James, Knight 31–2, 37, 42
Sandilands, John James, Knight 37, 41–3
Sandys, George 38
Sanguineo, Benedetto 238
Sanoguera, Francisco de, Knight 154, 155
Santa Ana, ship 201–2
Santa Anna, galley 231
Santa Margarita, ship 201
Santa Margherita 145
    Lines 127
Santa Maria della Vittoria, galley 231
Santiago, order of 77, 151, 158
Sardinia 27, 68, 177, 179
Sarrac Ali 164, 165
Savorgnano, Mario 46
Savoy 180
Schwendi, Lazarus von 46–7
Sciberras family 239
Sciberras peninsula 102, 115, 116, 126, 127, 135, 142, 144, 148, 152, 162, 165, 184, 225–6, 233, 236
Sciortino, Antonio 241, 242
Scotland 31–2
Sebastian I, king of Portugal 209
Sefer Reis 208–9
Selim I, sultan 52, 64, 98
Selim II, sultan 233
Seljuks 64
Selman Reis 207
Sengle, Claude de La, Grand Master 116
Senglea 16–17, 115, 126, 127, 141–2, 144, 145, 148, 152, 153–5, 159, 160, 163, 164, 168, 171, 172, 184, 190, 236, 237, 238
Serbelloni, Gabrio, Knight 227
serdar 130
Sese, Galatiano de, Knight 104

Seville 77, 120, 213
shipbuilding 61–2, 63, 74, 93, 215
Sicily 27, 75, 76, 81, 83, 87–8, 92–3, 94, 101, 112, 115, 119, 125, 133, 137, 141, 150–1, 156, 178, 180–1, 182, 184, 188, 227, 228, 230, 231, 232
Sidra, Gulf of 93
siege engines 157, 175
sieges
    cultural and political resonances of 6–14, 16–17, 20, 239–42
    definition of 12–14
Siġġiewi 101
silk 199
Silva, Diego Guzmán de 193
Silva, Ruy Breo de, Knight 170
silver 120–1, 129, 202–3, 205, 211–13, 219
    silver fleet 72, 120–1, 212–13, 219–20, 221
    silver mines 211–12
Sinan Pasha 99–100, 101, 102, 104, 107, 108, 109
sipahis 47–8, 126, 131, 132, 148, 164, 173, 188–9
Sliema 242
Sosa, Antonio de 81, 82, 86, 91, 118
Spain 76–8, 125, 158
    as imperial power 27–8, 57, 67–8, 96, 118, 129, 198–203, 210, 211–12, 217–19, 221
    naval resources of 62, 67–9, 119–21, 122, 129, 177, 180, 183–4, 234–5
Spanish Road 196
Sparke, John 219–20
spices 199, 203, 205–6
Spilioti, Giovanni 170
Spiteri, Stephen 131
Stagno, Filippo, Knight 42
Stalingrad, battle of 14
Starkey, Oliver, Knight 31, 42

Stephano di Castra 165–6
Strasbourg 242
Strozzi, Filippo di Piero 9, 21, 70
Strozzi, Leone, Knight 101, 115, 117
Sublime Porte, *see* Ottoman state
Suez 207
Suez Canal 94
Süleyman I, sultan 3, 26, 44, 52, 53–4, 55–6, 57, 58–9, 64, 65, 100, 105, 121, 122, 123–4, 126–7, 129, 130, 209, 233
Süleymanname 63
Sultana, ship 123
Syracuse 180, 181
Szigetvár 233

Tabriz 53
Tahmasp, shah 59
Tajoura 110
Talhammer, Sigismund 237–8
Tempesta, Antonio 224
Templars 24, 29, 30
Tenochtitlan 211
tercios 149, 177, 178, 179
terreplein 158
Tétouan 81
Tierra Firme 213
timars 47–8, 164
Timucuans 216, 218
Tlemcen 98
Todoro 166
Toledo, García Álvarez de 62, 114, 119, 125, 141, 144, 149–50, 151, 158, 168, 176–7, 179, 180, 181, 182, 183–4, 233
Toledo, Marcos de 178
Tordesillas, Treaty of (1494) 199, 200, 217
Torphichen 32, 42
Torto, Torquato, Knight 38–9
Toulon 96, 99, 106, 227
Toulouse 1

Tour, Gerard de La, Knight 38, 39
Tours 1, 2, 3
trace italienne 145
Trapani 181
Trent, Council of 32
Trevisano, Domenico 48, 52, 57, 60
Tribunale degli Armamenti 71
Trieste 93
Trinitarian order 86
Tripoli 27, 28, 83, 92, 93, 96–7, 98, 102, 104–5, 107–8, 109–10, 115, 117, 122, 123, 128, 136, 143, 227
Triq ir-Repubblika 241, 242
Troy 11–12
Tunis 87–8, 99, 100, 118, 128, 132, 179
  Charles V's conquest of (1535) 27, 87, 205
  Ottoman conquest of (1574) 54, 188
Turgut Reis 98, 99–103, 118, 122, 136–7, 139–40, 143, 161, 209
'Turk', meanings of 20, 63, 73
Tuscany 180

Uluç Ali 91, 136, 143, 186, 231
Upton, Nicholas, Knight 102
Urdaneta, Andrés de 199, 200, 205

Vagnon, Alexandre, Knight 39
Valette, Henri de La, Knight 157
Valette, Jean de La, Grand Master, 3, 4, 6, 19, 28, 29, 83, 105, 107, 108, 110, 117, 125, 126, 130, 133, 134–5, 137, 138–9, 140, 141, 142, 143, 147–8, 148–9, 150, 151, 152, 158–9, 160, 167, 168, 169–70, 173, 174, 180, 190–1, 226–7, 228–9, 233–4, 237
Valletta 30, 75, 116, 127, 144, 157, 223, 225–8, 230, 234, 239, 241, 242
Vallier de Chambert, Gaspard de, Knight 105, 108

Index

Vaz, Gomes 203
Vega, Juan de 101, 115
Velasco, Luis de 198–9
Vella, Dominico 239
Vendôme, Pierre Gentil de 19
Venice 26, 46, 52, 53, 55–6, 68, 69, 75, 97, 99, 116, 122, 123, 150, 207
Ventura, Vincenzo, Knight 163
Venturina, Constantia 38
Verdalle, Hugues de Loubens de, Grand Master 231
Verdun, battle of 14
Vianen 194–5, 196
Vienna 53
Vijayanagara 194
Villavicencio, Lorenzo de 198
Villegagnon, Nicolas Durand de, Knight 103, 107, 110, 111
Virgil 11–12

vizierate 50, 57
Voltaire 240

Walsingham, Francis 113
Wassy, massacre of 2
Whitehall Palace 193
women, *see* St John, Order of

Yemen 206, 209
Yen Shih-fan 193
Yen Sung 193
Yoshiteru, Ashikaga 194

Zacatecas 211
Zamora, Francisco de 89
Żejtun 99
Zoraida 79, 80–1, 82
Żurrieq 170
Zuwara 117